In this book James N. Rosenau explores the enormous changes which are transforming world affairs. He argues that the dynamics of economic globalization, new technologies, and evolving global norms are clashing with equally powerful localizing dynamics. The resulting encounters between diverse interests and actors are rendering the boundaries between domestic and foreign affairs ever more porous and creating a political space, designated as the "Frontier," wherein the quest for control in world politics is joined. The author contends that it is along the Frontier, and not in the international arena, that issues are contested and the course of events configured. The book examines a number of contexts and agents through which local, national, and international affairs are woven together. Rosenau's recurring theme is the challenge of achieving governance along the turbulent domestic–foreign Frontier.

Along the domestic–foreign Frontier

CAMBRIDGE STUDIES IN INTERNATIONAL RELATIONS

Series list continues after index

Along the domestic–foreign Frontier

Exploring governance in a turbulent world

James N. Rosenau

The George Washington University

CAMBRIDGE
UNIVERSITY PRESS

PUBLISHED BY THE PRESS SYNDICATE OF THE UNIVERSITY OF CAMBRIDGE
The Pitt Building, Trumpington Street, Cambridge CB2 1RP, United Kingdom

CAMBRIDGE UNIVERSITY PRESS
The Edinburgh Building, Cambridge, CB2 2RU, United Kingdom
40 West 20th Street, New York, NY 10011-4211, USA
10 Stamford Road, Oakleigh, Melbourne 3166, Australia

First published 1997

Typeset in 10/12.5 Palatino

A catalogue record for this book is available from the British Library

Library of Congress Cataloguing in Publication data

Rosenau, James N.
    Along the domestic–foreign Frontier: exploring governance in a
turbulent world / James N. Rosenau.
        p.   cm. – (Cambridge Studies in International Relations: 53)
    ISBN 0 521 58283 0 (hb) – ISBN 0 521 58764 6 (pb)
    1. International relations – Political aspects.   2. Political
science.   3. World politics.   I. Title.   II. Series.
JX1395.R5698   1997
327.1'09'045 – dc20   96-35842   CIP

ISBN 0 521 58283 0 hardback
ISBN 0 521 58764 6 paperback

Transferred to digital printing 2001

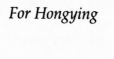

For Hongying

Contents

Contents

Figures and tables

Preface

This book cuts a wide and lengthy swathe across the political landscape for two essential reasons. One is the subject matter, that elusive realm where the necessities of global governance and the deepening complexity of global life intersect. With boundaries eroding, identities shifting, and some political structures cohering while others are fragmenting, the dangers of oversimplification far outweigh those of excessive elaboration. If domestic and foreign affairs are increasingly part and parcel of each other, the analyst has little choice but to probe both the internal and external dynamics of societal life and the intricate connections between them. Hence, while I would rather have written a short, concise and incisive volume, I have opted for addressing multiple causes, coping with subtle nuances, and tracing contradictions that cannot readily be ignored.

And even as one acknowledges that this strategy has resulted in an extensive manuscript, so is one aware of all the questions that still cry out for examination and all the gaps that still need to be filled. From the perspective of these limitations, what follows is truly a set of explorations rather than a definitive work.

A second reason for the wide-ranging scope of the ensuing chapters derives from the heuristic power of the model that I developed nearly a decade ago and subsequently presented in *Turbulence in World Politics: A Theory of Change and Continuity* (Princeton University Press, 1990). While the model is open to question along a number of lines, it nonetheless proved generative in the sense that it intensified an impulse to dig deeper and explore more fully along the rapidly expanding overlap of domestic and foreign affairs. Accordingly, imbued with the essential premises of the model (summarized here in chapter 4), I was led to apply it to a variety of diverse dimensions of the changing global scene.

These applications stimulated the idea for this book, but it soon became clear that it would not be sufficient simply to reproduce them as a collection of separate essays, and that they could be integrated and aggregated into a project much larger than the sum of its parts, a task that resulted in much rewriting and, indeed, the crafting of entirely new chapters. More than that, it led to a whole new formulation in which the political space opened up by the erosion of the boundaries between domestic and foreign affairs emerged as the frontier where most of the action on the global stage unfolds.

At the risk of inadvertently overlooking some of the many colleagues who contributed to the framing and development of this volume, I wish to express heartfelt thanks to those who provided encouragement and feedback for one or another of the chapters: Hugh De Santis, Mary Durfee, Michael W. Fagen, Yale Ferguson, Martha Finnemore, Matthew Joel Hoffmann, David Johnson, Joseph Lepgold, Richard Mansbach, James H. Mittelman, Ervin Rokke, Steve Smith, and Paul Wapner; and to two anonymous reviewers for the publisher. I am also very grateful to John Haslam of the Cambridge University Press for his continued support and patience.

Finally, let me acknowledge the contribution of Hongying Wang. Her reactions to early drafts and her continuing support made a big difference, the former in the sense that she did not flinch from highlighting weaknesses and the latter in the sense that she invariably discerned ways in which the weaknesses could be overcome.

While the help of others enriched the quality of what follows, none should be blamed for any discrepancies, far-fetched ideas, or misinterpretations that remain. For these I alone am responsible.

Acknowledgments

Although they have been rewritten a number of times, some sections of various chapters originated in previously published works. I am grateful to the following publishers for permission to draw upon parts of the indicated materials in revised form: Cambridge University Press, for permission to include in chapter 2 several paragraphs from my chapter in Steve Smith, Ken Booth and Marisa Zalewski (eds.), *International Theory: Positivism and Beyond* (Cambridge, 1996), pp. 309–17; Sage Publications, for permission to include in chapter 2 excerpts from my article, "Signals, Signposts, and Symptoms: Interpreting Change and Anomalies in World Politics," *European Journal of International Relations*, vol. 1 (March 1995), pp. 113–22; Cambridge University Press, for permission to include in chapter 3 several paragraphs from my chapter in Stephen Gill and James H. Mittelman (eds.), *Innovation and Transformation in International Studies* (Cambridge, 1997), pp. 220–35; the International Peace Academy, for permission to include in chapter 4 materials from my book, *The United Nations in a Turbulent World* (Boulder, CO: Lynne Rienner, 1992); Sage Publications, for permission to include in chapter 5 parts of my article, "The Dynamics of Globalization: Toward an Operational Formulation," *Security Dialogue*, vol. 27 (September 1996), pp. 27–38, and a table from Gwyn Prins, "Notes Toward the Definition of Global Security," *American Behavioral Scientist*, vol. 38 (May 1995), pp. 820–1; Sage Publications, for permission to include in chapter 6 excerpts from my article, "New Dimensions of Security: The Interaction of Globalizing and Localizing Dynamics," *Security Dialogue*, vol. 25 (September 1994), pp. 255–81; Macmillan Press Ltd., for permission to include in chapter 7 materials from my chapter in Robert W. Cox (ed.), *The New Realism: Perspectives on Multilateralism and World Order* (Houndmills, UK, 1997, pp. 57–80); Lynne Rienner

Acknowledgments

Publishers, for permission to include in chapters 8 and 23 sections from my article, "Governance in the 21st Century," *Global Governance*, vol. 1. (Winter 1995), pp. 13–44; the Carnegie Council on Ethics and International Affairs, for permission to include in chapter 9 paragraphs from my article, "Normative Challenges in a Turbulent World," *Ethics and International Affairs*, vol. 6 (1992), pp. 1–19; the State University of New York Press, for permission to include in chapter 10 parts of my chapter in Sheldon Kamieniecki (ed.), *Environmental Politics in the International Arena: Movements, Parties, Organizations, and Policy* (Albany, 1993), pp. 257–74; the Columbia University Press, for permission to include in chapter 10 sections of my chapter in Ronnie D. Lipschutz and Ken Conca (eds.), *State and Social Power in Global Environmental Politics* (New York, 1993), pp. 71–93; Kluwer Academic Publishers, for permission to include in chapter 10 excerpts from my chapter in Mats Rolin, Helen Sjoberg, and Uno Svedi (eds.), *Environmental Governance: A Global Challenge* (Dordrecht, The Netherlands, forthcoming); the Johns Hopkins University Press, for permission to include in chapter 11 parts of my chapter in Gene M. Lyons and Michael Mastanduno (eds.), *Beyond Westphalia? State Sovereignty and International Intervention* (Baltimore, 1995), pp. 191–227; the American Academy of Arts and Sciences, for permission to include in chapter 13 excerpts from my co-authored (with Michael Fagen) chapter in Carl Kaysen, Robert A. Pastor, and Laura W. Reed (eds.), *Collective Responses to Regional Problems; The Case of Latin America and the Caribbean* (Cambridge, 1994), pp. 29–68; Zed Books, for permission to include in chapter 14 parts of my chapter in Björn Hettne (ed.), *International Political Economy: Understanding Global Disorder* (London, 1995), pp. 46–64; Kluwer Law International, for permission to include in chapter 14 parts of my paper in *Issues in Global Governance: Papers Written for the Commission on Global Governance* (London, 1995), pp. 1–58; Macmillan Press Ltd., for permission to include in chapter 14 excerpts from my chapter in Michel Girard (ed.), *Individualism and World Politics* (Houndmills, UK, forthcoming); Sage Publications, for permission to include in chapter 14 paragraphs from my chapter in T. K. Oommen (ed.), *Citizenship and National Identity: Between Colonialism and Globalism* (New Delhi, 1997), pp. 227–59; the Editors of *Comparative Politics*, for permission to include in chapter 15 parts of my article, "The Relocation of Authority in a Shrinking World," *Comparative Politics*, vol. 24 (April 1992), pp. 253–72; Sage Publications, for permission to include in chapter 16 excerpts from my article, "Notes on the Servicing of Triumphant Subgroupism," *International Sociology*, vol. 8 (March 1993), pp. 77–90; Kluwer Law International, for permission to include in chapters 17 and 18 parts of my papers in *Issues in Global Governance: Papers Written for the Commission on Global Governance* (London, 1995), pp. 371–403 and 265–94, respectively; Westview Press, for permission to include in chapter 19 excerpts from my chapter in James Burk (ed.), *The Military in New Times: Adapting Armed Forces to a Turbulent World* (Boulder, CO, 1993), pp. 25–60; Macmillan Press Ltd., for permission to include in chapter 20 excerpts from my chapter in Chris Reus-Smit, Anthony Jarvis, Albert Paolini, and Joseph Camilleri (eds.), *The United Nations: Between Sovereignty and Global Governance* (Houndmills, UK, forthcoming); Polity Press, for permission to include in chapter 21 sections of my chapter in Daniele Archibugi, David Held, and Martin Köhler (eds.), *Citizenship, Sovereignty and Cosmopolitanism: Studies in Cosmopolitan Democracy* (Cambridge, forthcoming); Addison-Wesley Educational Publishers Inc., for permission to include in chapter 22 parts of my chapter in Charles W. Kegley, Jr. (ed.) *The Long Postwar Peace: Contending Explanations and Projections* (Glenview, IL, 1991), pp. 302–28. Finally, I am grateful to Harcourt Brace & Company, for permission to include in the Epilogue the poem "Psalm" by Wislawa Szymborska, from her *View With a Grain of Sand: Selected Poems* (New York, 1995), pp. 99–100.

Part I
Intellectual contexts

1   Frontiers

> For years, with considerable care
> I traced a boundary that wasn't there
> It wasn't there every day
> Gee, I wanted it to go away
>
> At last, I am ready to declare
> That the boundary was never there
> And no matter what you say
> It wasn't there again today
>
> And so now it seems clear
> We must let the boundary disappear
> Let it yield pride of place
> To a new and wide political space
>
> A space that is so manifestly near
> As to be a broad and porous frontier
> Where new and old actors vie
> Seeking to shape pieces of the pie

This adaptation of a well-known nursery rhyme is not simply autobiographical. More than a few observers have come to recognize that in a rapidly changing, interdependent world the separation of national and international affairs is problematic.[1] The rhyme gives voice to a desire

---

[1] See, for example, John Agnew and Stuart Corbridge, *Mastering Space: Hegemony, Territory and International Political Economy* (New York: Routledge, 1995); Hugh De Santis, *Beyond Progress: An Interpretive Odyssey to the Future* (Chicago: University of Chicago Press, 1996); Yale Ferguson and Richard W. Mansbach, *Polities: Authority, Identities, and Change* (Columbia: University of South Carolina Press, 1996); and Ronnie D. Lipschutz, with Judith Mayer, *Global Civil Society and Global Environmental Governance: The Politics of Nature from Place to Planet* (Albany: State University of New York Press, 1996).

for stability, to a longing for certitude as to what organizes and governs the course of events, to a sense that logically boundaries should divide domestic and foreign affairs. But it also acknowledges that such boundaries may continually elude our grasp because the phenomena, problems, and processes of greatest interest are not confined by them. To probe the domestic as aspects of "comparative politics" and examine the foreign as dimensions of "international politics" is more than arbitrary: it is downright erroneous. Domestic and foreign affairs have always formed a seamless web and the need to treat them as such is urgent in this time of enormous transformation. In effect, the rhyme suggests that we can no longer allow the domestic-foreign boundary to confound our understanding of world affairs, that it is best problematized by those who seek a deeper grasp of why events unfold as they do. Border guards may check passports and customs officials may impose duties, but to conceive of the foreign-domestic distinction in this simple way is to mislead, to mistake surface appearances for underlying patterns.

Replacing "a boundary that isn't there" with "a new and wide political space" – here called the Frontier, with a capital "F" to stress its centrality – highlights the perspective of this book. The chapters that follow converge on a problem with which not only this author has wrestled; rather it is one that seems to plague all those who probe for the essential nature of governance in a turbulent world. The problem involves sorting out multiple contradictions: The international system is less commanding, but it is still powerful. States are changing, but they are not disappearing. State sovereignty has been eroded, but it is still vigorously asserted. Governments are weaker, but they can still throw their weight around. At certain times publics are more demanding, but at other times they are more pliable. Borders still keep out intruders, but they are also more porous. Landscapes are giving way to ethnoscapes, mediascapes, ideoscapes, technoscapes, and financscapes, but territoriality is still a central preoccupation for many people.[2]

Sorting out contradictions such as these poses a number of difficult

---

[2] For a discussion of the nature of these diverse "scapes," see Arjun Appadurai, "Disjuncture and Difference in the Global Cultural Economy," *Public Culture*, vol. 2 (1990), pp. 1–23. One observer characterizes a financscape as a "space without rules" wherein a "several trillion-dollar pool . . . sloshes around in what is effectively a supranational cyberspace." Jessica Mathews, "We Live in a Dangerous Neighborhood," *Washington Post*, April 24, 1995, p. A19.

4

questions: How do we assess a world in which the Frontier is continuously shifting, widening and narrowing, simultaneously undergoing erosion with respect to many issues and reinforcement with respect to others? How do we reconceptualize political space so that it connotes identities and affiliations (say, religious, ethnic, and professional) as well as territorialities? How do those active along the Frontier manage to absorb, circumvent, or otherwise cope with shifting and porous boundaries? How long can an ever more interdependent and transnational world organize its affairs in terms of elusive boundaries? And to the extent people still cling to the idea of a domestic-foreign boundary even as they recognize its continual erosion, what determines whether a problem is located along the Frontier or defined as either a domestic or foreign issue? Under what circumstances does authority along the Frontier accrue to like-minded states, to global regimes, to transnational organizations, to subnational entities, or to coalitions of diverse types of actors?

A variety of responses to such questions is possible. One, the most rigid, is to treat the indicators of change as superficial and to assert that the fundamentals of international life are no different today from what they were in the past. A second is to perceive the changes as real and powerful, but to assert that they have not altered the basic parameters of world affairs. From this perspective, the problem is one of understanding how the nation-state system has absorbed and adapted to the changes and thereby maintained its long-standing structures intact. A third is to regard the changes as newly recognized rather than as new phenomena. A fourth response, and the one that guides the analysis in ensuing chapters, is that of treating the Frontier as becoming ever more rugged and, thus, as a widening field of action, as the space in which world affairs unfold, as the arena in which domestic and foreign issues converge, intermesh, or otherwise become indistinguishable within a seamless web – what might be called the politics of the Frontier or, alternatively, "transversal" politics since it encompasses conflicts that "transverse all boundaries" and are also *about those boundaries.*[3] In effect, it is along the Frontier and not through the nation-state system

[3] David Campbell, "Political Prosaics, Transversal Politics, and the Anarchical World," in Michael J. Shapiro and Hayward R. Alker (eds.), *Challenging Boundaries: Global Flows, Territorial Identities* (Minneapolis: University of Minnesota Press, 1996), p. 23 (italics in the original).

that people sort and play out the many contradictions presently at work on the global scene.[4]

More questions follow: What transpires in the widening political space represented by the Frontier? What sort of individuals and collectivities are impelled by what motives to engage in what kinds of activities in and across the space? What issues sustain the politics of the Frontier? Have structures evolved that differentiate the Frontier from the political spaces on which it is encroaching as it widens? Or is it differentiated by a pervasive incoherence and a lack of mechanisms through which authority is exercised?

Such questions are not easily addressed. We are so accustomed to thinking of domestic and international politics as separate playing-fields that it is difficult to conceptualize any structures and processes that may be superseding them as a new field of play. The Frontier is in some respects an underorganized domain with fragile sources of legitimacy,[5] while in other respects nascent structures of authority can be discerned. Put differently, the Frontier is a *terra incognita* that sometimes takes the form of a market, sometimes appears as a civil society, sometimes resembles a legislative chamber, periodically is a crowded town square, occasionally is a battlefield, increasingly is traversed by an information highway, and usually looks like a several-ring circus in which all these – and many other – activities are unfolding simultaneously. Given this diversity, it is not so much a single frontier as a host of diverse frontiers (even though here it is referred to generically in the singular) in which background often becomes foreground, time becomes disjointed, nonlinear patterns predominate, organizations bifurcate, societies implode, regions unify, markets overlap, and politics swirl about issues of identity, territoriality, and the interface between

---

[4] For a similar formulation that focuses on some of the processes considered here to be central to the Frontier, see Mathias Albert and Luthar Brock, *Debordering the World of States: New Spaces in International Relations* (Frankfurt: World Society Research Group, Working Paper No. 2, 1995). Another formulation that downplays the domestic-foreign boundary – calling it a "nonplace" (p. 260) – is developed in Richard K. Ashley, "Living on Border Lines: Man, Poststructuralism, and War," in James Der Derian and Michael J. Shapiro (eds.), *International/Intertextual Relations* (Lexington, MA: Lexington Books, 1989), pp. 259–321.

[5] See, for example, Cynthia Hardy, "Underorganized Interorganizational Domains: The Case of Refugee Systems," *Journal of Applied Behavioral Science*, vol. 30 (September 1994), pp. 278–96, and James L. Gibson and Gregory A. Caldeira, "The Legitimacy of Transnational Institutions: Compliance, Support, and the European Court of Justice," *American Journal of Political Science*, vol. 39 (May 1995), pp. 459–89.

long-established patterns and emergent orientations. As different issues widen or narrow the Frontier, moreover, so do corresponding shifts occur in the distinction between "us" and "them" or – to use a less combative distinction – between self and other.

In short, the Frontier points to an epochal transformation, a new worldview as to the essential nature of human affairs, a new way of thinking about how global politics unfold. At the center of the emergent worldview lies an understanding that the order which sustains families, communities, countries, and the world through time rests on contradictions, ambiguities, and uncertainties. Where earlier epochs had their central tendencies and orderly patterns, the present epoch derives its order from contrary trends and episodic patterns. The long-standing inclination to think in either/or terms has given way to framing challenges as both/and problems. People now understand, emotionally as well as intellectually, that unexpected events are commonplace, that anomalies are normal occurrences, that minor incidents can mushroom into major outcomes, that fundamental processes trigger opposing forces even as they expand their scope, that what was once transitional may now be enduring, and that the complexities of modern life are so deeply rooted as to infuse ordinariness into the surprising development and the anxieties that attach to it.

Being complex, the new conditions that have widened the Frontier cannot be explained by a single source.[6] The information revolution and other technological dynamics are major stimulants, but so is the breakdown of trust, the shrinking of distances, the globalization of economies, the explosive proliferation of organizations, the fragmentation of groups and the integration of regions, the surge of democratic practices and the spread of fundamentalism, the cessation of intense enmities and the revival of historic animosities – all of which in turn provoke further reactions that add to the complexity. In chapter 3 an attempt is made to organize these diverse sources into a coherent whole

---

[6] Since repercussions of the end of the Cold War were clearly evident at all levels of organization, it is tempting to treat this development as an epochal turning-point. Such an interpretation, however, is misleading; it exaggerates the impact of a single historical moment and does not allow for the possibility that the end of the Cold War was the culmination of underlying and long-standing processes of change which, as stressed here, ushered in a common sense of dynamics and structures that amounted to a new epoch. For an analysis in which the Cold War is seen as having "left so light an impact on the living memory of states and societies that it is already en route to oblivion," see Ian Gambles, "Lost Time – The Forgetting of the Cold War," *National Interest*, vol. 41 (Fall 1995), p. 35.

– if not into a broad theory, then into a set of causal priorities that differentiate first- from second-order effects. Anticipating the formulation, the Frontier is conceived as being traversed by three main paths, the first being that of the first-order effects in which enlarging emotional and analytic skills of individuals at the micro level interact with authority structures at the macro level in such a way as to nudge politics along either integrative or fragmenting paths (see figure 3.1).

The question arises as to whether the Frontier will continue to widen and the contradictions on which its worldview rests continue to persist, or whether eventually new institutions and boundaries will evolve and settle into place as the basis of still another epochal transformation wherein the politics of the Frontier become the politics of normalcy? Recognizing that the elusiveness of the Frontier may or may not be short-lived, the answer offered here leans toward the latter explanation. As will be seen throughout the ensuing chapters, there are reasons to anticipate that as the Frontier widens, so will it manifest recurrent patterns that could well settle into presently unfamiliar political institutions and political arrangements. The new patterns may continue to be rooted in contradiction as groups, organizations, and societies both integrate and fragment, but humankind is presumed to be profoundly adaptable and thus capable of managing conditions rife with discrepancies.

In other words, much is new and much is old, and it is difficult to maintain a perspective that focuses on the balance between the two, with the result that all too often we yield to the temptation to regard one or the other as predominant. Yet, it is precisely the new dynamics that focus attention on governance along the Frontier as a prime mechanism for maintaining a modicum of order in a complex, highly interdependent world. In effect, among the central tasks of governance at all levels of community is that of achieving order over and across shifting, elusive, and often unrecognizable boundaries.

So what follows may seem audacious. It amounts to nothing less than the task of assessing how the changes and continuities that mark our time have melded and, in so doing, have rendered governance both recognizable and unfamiliar. The ensuing pages are marked by audacity because they ask the reader not only to view the Frontier as withering and widening even as it remains intact, but also to proceed from the presumption that its shifting characteristics should be the object of political analysis. They call for a tolerance of ambiguity that enables one to perceive governance along the Frontier as the central political challenge of those who seek control over the course of events. They ask for suspension of established conceptual premises and a readiness to think afresh. They require accepting the possibility that the core of political units has shrunk as effective authority has shifted toward and beyond their peripheries. And, not least, they demand appreciating that both the dynamics of global change *and* the resistances to them are part and parcel of the human condition as one millennium ends and another begins.

Overview

In order to set aside long-standing analytic habits, the chapters that follow are short on assessments of realism, neorealism, liberalism, and other long-established approaches to international relations (IR).[7] And they are also lacking in quarrels with such well-entrenched concepts as power, hierarchy, and anarchy. Neither the approaches nor the concepts are dismissed as inappropriate; rather, they are treated as problematic and relied upon sparingly. To do otherwise, to treat the established frameworks as the baseline from which the balance between change and continuity should be assessed, amounts to a procedure that seems bound to hinder thinking afresh. Put differently, if explorations of governance along the Frontier are to yield new and valuable insights into world affairs, it seems preferable to frame a new perspective – one based on a new worldview from which alternative ontologies, paradigms, and theories are derived – that frees the analysis of the burdens of past approaches and concepts.

The organization of the volume follows from this reasoning. The three chapters of part I briefly set forth the procedures and premises that are necessary to reconfiguring our grasp of governance along the domestic-foreign Frontier. Those of part II focus on the global contexts wherein the dynamics of change are unfolding and offer conceptual foundations on which to build an understanding of the Frontier, the processes that are widening it, and the new spheres of authority that are emerging as sources of governance. Part III probes the ways in which historic societal institutions are affected by the challenges of governance along the Frontier. Part IV consists of seven chapters in which both individual and

[7] For contrasts and summaries of these approaches, see James N. Rosenau, "International Relations," in J. Krieger (ed.), *The Oxford Companion to Politics of the World* (New York: Oxford University Press, 1993), pp. 455–60.

collective actors central to world affairs are examined with a view to evaluating how they participate in the processes of governance that constitute their global and societal contexts. Part V offers three sets of conclusions. One chapter focuses on the prospects for democratic institutions evolving along the Frontier, while another sets forth an interpretation of how governance along the Frontier is likely to impact on the prospects for war and peace in the decades ahead. The last chapter provides conclusions as to the future of governance in a turbulent world racked by change and wedded to continuity.

Implicit in this overview is a premise on which all the chapters rest – namely, that while the pervasiveness of the Frontier necessitates probing governance on a global scale, this does not require an exclusive focus on the agents and structures that are global in scope. On the contrary, the organizing perspective is that of governance *in* the world rather than governance *of* the world. The latter implies a central authority that is doing the governing, an implication that clearly has no basis in fact. The former suggests patterns of governance wherever they may be unfolding in the world as a consequence of wherever authority may be located – in communities, societies, nongovernmental organizations, international relationships, and along the Frontier. To assess global governance, in other words, is to trace the various ways in which the processes of governance are aggregated. The cumulation encompasses individuals, their skills and orientations, no less than private and public collectivities at the local, provincial, national, transnational, international, and global levels. As one observer put it, "political governance in modern societies can no longer be conceived in terms of external governmental control of society but emerges from a plurality of governing actors."[8]

Do the diverse processes and locales of governance cumulate to a coherent pattern of global governance? No, probably they do not, or at least they have yet to do so. A map of the world that highlights the Frontier would depict a wide, contested domain in which governance is highly disaggregated even as many of its spheres are overlapping. Global governance is not so much a label for a high degree of integration and order as it is a summary term for highly complex and widely

---

[8] Quoted from B. Marin and R. Mayntz, *Policy Networks*, in Jan Kooiman, "Findings, Speculations and Recommendations," in J. Kooiman (ed.), *Modern Governance: New Government–Society Interactions* (London: Sage Publications, 1993), p. 258 (italics in the original).

disparate activities that culminate in a modicum of worldwide coherence. The sum of the disparate and often conflicting activities can be regarded as an emergent world order, but it is an orderliness only in the sense that it depicts the way things currently work in the political arena. Assessed from the perspective of an integrated and harmonized set of arrangements, the emergent world is marked by a high degree of disorder and turbulence.

The disorder is partially a consequence of the fact that the spheres of authority which sustain governance along the Frontier are still very much in the process of emergence, of developing new patterns that are consistent with the changing conditions of economic, social, and political life. Most of the new arrangements are still fluid and pervaded with uncertainty because many of the patterns that prevailed in communities throughout the world for the previous five decades underwent slow, unrecognized decay before coming to a clear-cut and abrupt end. As a result, the habits, relationships, and structures through which an emergent order becomes an enduring one have yet to evolve as bases for managing the course of events at every level of community. Yet, as previously noted, the incoherence of the prevailing disorder is not without patterns and may eventually undergo an epochal transformation to greater degrees of coherence.

In sum, if one is ready to suspend conventional ways of grasping world affairs and to trace the Frontier as the basis for understanding present-day governance, then one is obliged to roam widely over a broad range of phenomena that sustain both the dynamics of change and the sources of constancy. The task is far from simple; but the rewards are worth the effort inasmuch as they offer the prospect of breaking with long-standing analytic habits in all the realms where the consequences of governance are experienced.

2   Change

> We playwrights, who have to cram a whole human life or an entire historical era into a two-hour play, can scarcely understand this rapidity [of change] ourselves. And if it gives us trouble, think of the trouble it must give political scientists, who have less experience with the realm of the improbable.
>
> Vaclav Havel[1]

To break with conventional approaches to any subject demands considerable effort. One must be continuously alert to the danger of slipping back into old analytic habits and, even more, of doing so unknowingly. Even if they are no longer functional, the old habits are comfortable. They worked earlier, one tends to reason, so why abandon them when thinking afresh can as readily lead to dead-ends as down paths to greater understanding. Happily, several intellectual mechanisms are available for countering temptations to cling to the familiar, and they are briefly noted here as much to keep the author on track as to acquaint the reader with the core procedures that underlie much of what follows.

Puzzles

As the foregoing epigraph implies, and as the initial stanza of the nursery rhyme set forth at the outset of the previous chapter makes explicit, present-day world politics is bewildering and, more particularly, it is far from clear as to why the domestic-foreign Frontier is so porous even as it also seems so salient. And, indeed, this quandary per-

---

[1] From an address to the United States Congress, as reported by the *Los Angeles Times*, February 22, 1990, p. A8.

vades the ensuing analysis. Not only does it serve to sustain the inclination to think afresh and break out of long-standing conceptual jails, but it can even be said that a concern for perplexing phenomena is a prime methodological impulse guiding the analysis. The impulse is not in itself a methodology, but it is a necessary attribute of any inquiry into phenomena as unruly as those that presently constitute world affairs. To be sure, there are good and sound reasons to observe the highest standards of research and to insure thereby that data are processed systematically, that alternative interpretations are pondered, and that conclusions are drawn cautiously and their limits carefully delineated. But the pace of change is too great to justify avoidance of those phenomena that cannot be easily classified or that turn out to negate conventional wisdom.[2]

Retaining a sense of puzzlement, however, can be intensely challenging. It requires a continuing appreciation that the dynamics of change persist even as one senses progress toward comprehending their sources and consequences. It asks one to remain in awe of the complexities of human affairs and the sheer craziness involved in trying to tease a semblance of order out of them. The response of analysts to the end of the Cold War offers a good illustration of the difficulties of clinging to puzzlement and awe. One would think, given the stunning collapse of the superpower rivalry and the Soviet Union, that humility and a sense of awe might have reached new heights among students of world affairs. So much is new and unfamiliar, how can one not pause and wonder what it all means? So much is surprising and unprecedented, how is it possible not to consider the possibility that one's approach to the subject is in need of repair, if not replacement? So much no longer seems relevant, how can one not return to the theoretical drawing-board and give free rein to a combination of one's humility and creativity in order to explore new ways of describing and explaining what is transpiring on the world stage?

For all three questions, the answer would appear to be, "easily!" Many analysts appear to have had no hesitation in acknowledging their

---

[2] For an extensive elaboration of my understanding of scientific methods and the standards of research to which systematic inquiry ought to adhere, see James N. Rosenau, *The Scientific Study of Foreign Policy*, rev. edn. (London: Frances Pinter 1980). A discussion of how the dynamics of change may necessitate some relaxation of these standards and an examination of phenomena that are not readily classified can be found in James N. Rosenau, *Turbulence in World Politics: A Theory of Change and Continuity* (Princeton: Princeton University Press, 1990), chap. 2.

surprise over the turn of events in recent years, but their surprise has not turned to humility and puzzlement. Rather, collectively we seem to have picked up where we left off, as if on second thought the old formulas seem to fit, allowing us to stay the course and proceed as we always have. We are a bit chastened perhaps, but not to the point of yielding to puzzlement as to whether there may be new underlying forces at work in the world.

To the extent this is so, to the extent analysts have not yielded to awe over the gap between the dynamics of world affairs and their tools for explaining what has happened and anticipating what may lie ahead, why have they remained so immune to rethinking the foundations of their undertaking? A number of reasons can be offered – ranging from the felt professional need to protect one's standing in the field to a conviction that this is a time for discipline rather than awe – but I suggest the primary reason is that the virtues of puzzlement over the continuing and complex changes have never been extolled and championed. So reiteration is in order: there is much to be said for remaining in awe of the enormity – the utter absurdity – of the task we face in trying to trace and comprehend governance along the domestic-foreign Frontier in a turbulent world.

It should be made clear, however, that puzzlement does not simply mean a relentless capacity to ask questions. Nor does puzzlement consist merely of awe over the complexity of the global system. As conceived here, puzzlement is more disciplined than sheer curiosity and bewilderment. The discipline derives from two criteria: first, one needs to be puzzled by observable outcomes (or, in the language of science, by dependent variables) for which existing explanations seem insufficient or erroneous; second, one needs to be puzzled by huge outcomes, by events or patterns that encompass most of humankind and that appear to spring from somewhere in the core of human affairs. If these two criteria are met when posing a problem, one has what I call a genuine puzzle, the kind that is not easily answered but that is sufficiently engaging to linger, agitate, or otherwise sustain motivation in the face of continuous frustrations over the elusiveness of the answer.[3] To probe puzzles persistently, in other words, is neither a license to investigate trivial questions, the answers to which are relevant only to a narrowly defined set of phenomena, nor is it latitude to ask endlessly open-ended

---

[3] James N. Rosenau, "Puzzlement in Foreign Policy," *Jerusalem Journal of International Relations*, vol. 1 (Summer 1976), pp. 1–10.

questions that cannot be fully and satisfactorily resolved because they allow for a multitude of diverse answers.

As already implied, the Frontier subsumes a number of genuine puzzles. Not only are there many puzzling outcomes relating to the erosion of long-standing boundaries, but taken together these are huge in scope because they pose questions of how and where spheres of authority (SOAs) have been relocated in human affairs, and of who and what presides over the loci of action along the Frontier? In effect, SOAs are the dependent variables with which this inquiry is primarily concerned.

Anomalies

Another mechanism for sustaining the commitment to think afresh is that of being ever alert to the presence and meaning of anomalies, of recognizing that some exceptions to prevailing patterns may portend future shifts in the patterns. Few anomalies, of course, will prove to be significant. Most occur for unexplored reasons and their consequences are of no great moment. During times of pervasive transformation, however, anomalies can be indicative of underlying dynamics that eventually form the bases of new patterns and, in effect, become the established procedures. A readiness to acknowledge that exceptional events signify future change is not easily sustained. Observers tend to see what they want to see and thus treat the course of events as confirming their long-held understanding of why and how events unfold as they do. Clinging to such an understanding leads readily to the dismissal of anomalies as momentary and irrelevant. Yet, if one is prepared to think afresh, this tendency needs to be contested. Anomalous events need to be assessed as possible instances of underlying change before they are dismissed.[4]

Again the abrupt end of the Cold War is illustrative. Presumably indicators of this sudden and surprising development were manifest well before the Berlin Wall came down and the Soviet empire collapsed. Yet, most analysts failed to anticipate these swift and peaceful outcomes. Why? Why did events of this magnitude take so many well-informed observers by surprise? Why did the existing conceptual equipment and

---

[4] For an elaboration of the relevance of anomalies, see James N. Rosenau, "Signals, Signposts, and Symptoms: Interpreting Change and Anomalies in World Politics," *European Journal of International Relations*, vol. 1 (March 1995), pp. 113–22.

theoretical perspectives not pick up early indicators that huge changes lay ahead? In retrospect, the answer seems obvious. Analysts were prisoners of their theories and were thus insensitive to incidents that could be interpreted as possible shifts in underlying forces. Rather than pausing to ask whether the incidents were early indicators of change, they were inclined to overlook them as merely anomalous occurrences that had no real significance.[5]

To a large degree, of course, anomalies have much in common with puzzles. Indeed, they would not stand out as deviations from established central tendencies if they did not trigger at least momentary bewilderment. But while all anomalies are in some sense puzzling, not all puzzles involve anomalous behavior. The difference is that anomalies are exceptions to a known pattern, whereas puzzles derive from known patterns in which the dynamics that sustain them are perplexing. Anomalies are often provocative precisely because it is far from clear whether they are expressive of emergent patterns or whether they are simply idiosyncratic events along the unique historical path traversed by actors or systems. In addition, anomalies and puzzles are distinguished by the fact that the former may not involve outcomes of huge significance, an attribute which above is posited as a defining characteristic of the latter. In the case of the Cold War's end, for example, the huge outcome had not occurred even though anomalies indicative of tendencies toward a culmination were presumably crying out for interpretation.

If we are open to perceiving changes that may prove to be so stunning as (retrospectively) to qualify as historical breakpoints – those moments in time, like the end of the Cold War, when past precedents are abandoned and people and communities move in new directions – it follows that we need to be continuously on the alert for anomalies that signal change, that may suggest a cumulation of tendencies toward change, and that may indicate increasingly wide support for the new directions in which change is taking world affairs. Discerning anomalies, in other

---

[5] For a cogent analysis that explores the failure of observers to anticipate the momentous events of 1989–91, see John Lewis Gaddis, "International Relations Theory and the End of the Cold War," *International Security*, vol. 17 (Winter 1992–3), pp. 3–58. See also Michael Cox, "Rethinking the End of the Cold War," *Review of International Studies*, vol. 20 (1994), pp. 187–200; Timur Kuran, "The Inevitability of Future Revolutionary Surprises," *American Journal of Sociology*, vol. 100 (May 1995), pp. 1528–51; and Richard Ned Lebow and Thomas Risse-Kappen (eds.), *International Relations Theory and the End of the Cold War* (New York: Columbia University Press, 1995).

words, is in some respects a prime task that students of the political scene must assume. Wherever else our inquiries may lead us, and whatever the more specific substantive and analytic perspectives on which they may be founded, we are obliged to allow for transformative dynamics. If we are not inclined to be startled by indicators of possible change, if all anomalies are considered too improbable to be taken seriously, it could be said that we are violating any trust we may enjoy as social scientists.

This is not to argue for locating crystal balls next to our computers and data bases. Nor is it to contend that generating forecasts and predictions should be a prime preoccupation. Anticipating specific events at a precise time in a particular place is not our task. We look ahead in probabilistic terms and any claim to knowing exactly what will happen is sheer pretense. Our milieu is the central tendency, our commitment the recurrent pattern, our mode the range of possible outcomes. If we can trace central tendencies, recurrent patterns, and alternative outcomes, we can rightly be proud.

In short, to take anomalies seriously is not to engage in forecasting. Nor need the analysis of symptoms evolve into predictions. Rather, to be sensitive to indicators of possible change is to make room for the unexpected, to allow for new interpretations, and to be open to thinking afresh even as one remains bound by the empirical materials at hand.

Our collective failure not to anticipate the end of the Cold War is thus far more serious than it may seem. It was neither a forecasting failure nor a predictive embarrassment. It was rather a collective failure to allow for the possibility that the arrangements which dominated some forty-five consecutive years of global politics in the twentieth century would end abruptly, turning history in sharply new directions.

Recognizing change

Among the steps that can be taken to sustain puzzlement and heighten sensitivity to anomalies, perhaps the most important involves the concept of change. The dynamics of turbulence penetrate to the very core of the human experience. They pose challenges to conventional conceptions that delineate territoriality, community, productivity, commitment, work, religion, loyalty, and a host of other factors that have long been taken for granted. To grasp fully these challenges, however, one has to be ready to acknowledge that such basic features of the human condition are subject to profound transformation. Such an

17

acknowledgment does not come easily. Analytic habits die hard. Reared and trained in an era when the domestic-foreign distinction referred to a meaningful and all-powerful boundary differentiating cultures and separating "us" from "them," when states and their system served as the basic political form of organization, and when national economies were presumed to be the logical context within which supplies and demands converge to create markets, many analysts are reluctant to entertain the idea that the world is undergoing fundamental transformation. Yes, they admit, national economies have had to adjust to a global system of exchange and, yes, political communities both larger and smaller than the nation-state have become salient in world politics, but such changes are not viewed as so profound as to require the adoption of new analytic frameworks.[6]

In other words, while we may pay lip service to the centrality of change dynamics, all too many of us fail to wrestle with the concept and specify how we know change when we see it. Rather, there is a pervasive tendency to use the concept loosely, as a result of which it becomes possible to discern change in some situations when it suits our analysis and to dismiss its presence in other circumstances when it undermines our line of inquiry.[7] Such a procedure, of course, also has the consequence of precluding any chance of responding creatively to anomalies. Perhaps even worse are analyses which assert the presence of change and then quickly undo the assertion by introducing the criterion of "fundamental" change and arguing that the initial assessment was in error because it did not involve a fundamental transformation. Lines of reasoning such as these are, in some deep sense, evasive and deceptive. It is almost as if to declare the presence of basic change is to risk abandoning one's organizing paradigm. It is reasoning that acknowledges change in the guise of denying it; or, perhaps more accurately, it denies change in the guise of acknowledging it. In so doing no guidelines are offered as to when prior patterns of behavior take on new

[6] Much the same has been said about military strategy: in an increasingly complex, non-linear environment, strategic communities cling to relatively simple and linear plans for future military operations. Cf. Steven R. Mann, "Chaos Theory and Strategic Thought," *Parameters* (Autumn 1992), pp. 54–68.

[7] Indeed, reasoning about change can be so loose that, "As a grand cliche about modernity, the claim that we live in an era of rapid transformations has even become a form of continuity among diverse currents of contemporary social and political thought." R.B.J. Walker, *Inside/Outside: International Relations as Political Theory* (Cambridge: Cambridge University Press, 1993), p. 3.

forms, as if the similarity of behavior at some high level of abstraction renders irrelevant any shifts that may occur in the patterns.

An insight into this ambiguous, even ambivalent, reaction to a sense that underlying transformations are at work is evident in an inquiry by Eugene B. Skolnikoff. The title of his book – *The Elusive Transformation* – directly and succinctly expresses uncertainty as to whether basic changes really do result in fundamental transformations. Consider, for example, the following paragraph:

> There is no doubt that international politics is quite different, in almost all dimensions, than it has been, or than it will be. It is evolving under the influence of technological advance perhaps faster than ever before. The more telling observation, however, is the persistence and adaptability of traditional concepts in the face of rapid evolution. Technology-related changes may be modifying the dimensions of national autonomy but not the assumptions of autonomy in national policies, changing the substance of dependency relationships but not the fact of dependency, altering the nature of weapons but not denying a role for power in international affairs, modifying the distribution of power and capabilities but not the significance of those attributes of states, creating new patterns of economic interaction among societies but leaving the management of the economic system largely in national hands, altering the relationships between government and nongovernment actors but not the basic authority of governments, raising wholly new issues and altering traditional issues that must be dealt with internationally – but thereby making foreign policy more complex, not fundamentally different.[8]

It is a beguiling paragraph. In each of the seven assertions set forth in the last sentence Skolnikoff admits to the presence of change but quickly negates the admission by claiming the change is not so thoroughgoing as to prevent the attachment of well-worn descriptors. More significantly, these assertions are demonstrably erroneous if one presumes that huge changes in substance can lead to alterations in kind even though form remains the same. Considering each of the assertions, for example, it can readily be shown that while officials still pay lip service to their autonomy as national decision-makers, in fact this autonomy has been greatly reduced by the globalization of national economies; that even as developing countries remain dependent on resources in the industrial world, their dependency relationships have in many

---

[8] Eugene B. Skolnikoff, *The Elusive Transformation: Science, Technology, and the Evolution of International Politics* (Princeton: Princeton University Press, 1993), p. 7.

instances been so lessened by the transfer of capital to their cheap labor markets as to raise the question of exactly who is dependent on whom; that the advent of nuclear weapons has so fully transformed the readiness of political leaders of major countries to advocate, much less use, military force that the role of power in interstate relations has largely become an instrument of economic rather than military statecraft; that although states do indeed possess attributes of power, its distribution among them has been so decentralized as to diminish – and in some instances eliminate – the hierarchical structures of world politics; that not only have new patterns of economic interaction among societies evolved, but for all practical purposes these are no longer managed by national states; that not only have relationships between the public and private sectors of most societies been altered, but in fact the "basic authority" of governments has been so depleted in many parts of the world as to result in stalemated and paralyzed political systems; and that while foreign policy still designates the efforts of societies to maintain a modicum of control over their external environments, new global interdependence issues such as pollution, currency crises, AIDS, and the drug trade have so profoundly changed the tasks and goals of foreign policy officials as to make for differences in kind rather than degree.

In short, in the absence of criteria of what he regards as change and continuity, Skolnikoff cannot lose. He agrees with both those who argue that profound transformations are at work and those who say they are not really significant. As he puts it in summary, "the fundamentals of the nation-state system . . . will not be materially altered in the foreseeable future, though much on the international scene will change . . . [T]here are some specific and important changes in these fundamentals, but not enough, in my view, to invalidate the overall conclusion."[9]

---

[9] Skolnikoff, *Elusive Transformation*, p. 7. For similar ambivalent expressions in which states are conceived to have undergone profound changes that nevertheless have not altered their role and competence, see Robert Gilpin, *War and Change in World Politics* (New York: Cambridge University Press, 1981), p. 7; Alan James and Robert H. Jackson, "The Character of Independent Statehood," in A. James and R.H. Jackson (eds.), *States in a Changing World: A Contemporary Analysis* (Oxford: Clarendon Press, 1993), pp. 5–8; Stephen D. Krasner, "Sovereignty: An Institutional Perspective," in James A. Caporaso (ed.), *The Elusive State: International and Comparative Perspectives* (Newbury Park, CA: Sage Publications, 1989), chap. 4; and Kenneth N. Waltz, *Theory of International Politics* (Reading, MA: Addison-Wesley, 1979), p. 94. For a somewhat more cautious argument that posits the state system as "becoming more firmly entrenched rather than declining" but that allows for its possible transformation, see Hendrik Spruyt, *The Sovereign State and its Competition* (Princeton: Princeton University Press, 1994), p. 192.

This critique is not to suggest that meaningful, consistent, and applicable criteria of change can easily be developed. The key variables of world politics do not lend themselves readily to measurement and thus I do not want to imply that Skolnikoff has failed to solve a major problem for which I have a solution.[10] It may well be that he is correct in concluding that "ultimately" proof relative to system transformation "can only be a matter of definition or post hoc evaluation."[11] Still, the degree to which one can grasp the significance of the widening Frontier and the challenges it poses to governance will, in my judgment, depend greatly on whether one errs on the side of perceiving change or continuity. Those who treat continuity as ancillary to the dynamics of change are more likely to perceive relevant anomalies than are those who are predisposed to discern the similarity between present and past events.

The tendency to highlight continuities stems from excessive caution and a lack of clarity as to the nature of anomalies. One can never be sure whether an unexpected event signals the beginning of a new pattern or merely an anomalous blip in a recurring pattern. Given this uncertainty, there is a tendency to go for the blip interpretation inasmuch as it does not require us to consider rethinking our theoretical premises. Much as there is to be said for analytic caution in this regard, what harm can follow from pursuing the possibility that the anomaly is an enduring deviation and thus the start of something new? If an anomaly is truly surprising and unexpected, if it takes the variation of our variables further than we had ever imagined they could vary, why not treat it seriously? If in 1980 note was taken of a Polish labor leader in Gdansk pulling off a successful strike against an unrelenting authoritarian regime, was that not a signal of change because it involved an unimagined variation of a key variable? The last question is, admittedly, loaded, and it is surely the beneficiary of hindsight; but that is the point: we need to refine our concept of change so that it is operational rather than ambiguous and allows for anomalies that may reflect variations susceptible to evolving into future trend-lines.

Differences in degree and in kind

In the absence of criteria for delineating basic change, a widely employed technique for reinforcing inclinations to be cautious about

[10] For an elaborate effort to delineate the nature of change in world politics that identifies (rather than solves) the measurement problem, see Rosenau, *Turbulence in World Politics*, chap. 4.   [11] Skolnikoff, *Elusive Transformation*, p. 7.

transformative dynamics is that of claiming the current era is not unique, of arguing that for every example of change cited one can find a historical equivalent, thereby demonstrating that no event or pattern represents change and is essentially new, and of then concluding that therefore historical comparisons are bound to involve differences in degree and can never yield differences in kind. Thus it can be claimed that the present era is not the only moment in history when disaggregation has marked the loci of governance. In earlier eras, for example, considerable authority was exercised by members of the Hanseatic League and the Medici and Rothschild families. Indeed, it is not difficult to find numerous historical circumstances that parallel any of those that appear central to the dynamics of boundary erosion and change today. Just as AIDS moves quickly across national boundaries today, so did the plague in the sixteenth century; just as the Internet, fax machine and global television render boundaries ever more porous today, so did the advent of the printing press, the wireless, and the telephone spread ideas irrespective of national borders in earlier eras; and much the same can be said for all the channels whereby the processes of globalization and localization are presently expanding and contracting horizons.

Yet, there are at least three major dimensions of the present era that have led to differences in kind and not just in degree when compared with earlier times. One concerns the structures that sustain the politics of the Frontier, another involves the structures of the globalized world economy, and the third focuses on the time frame within which events and trends unfold. The first of these differences has been well summarized by David Held:

> [T]here is a fundamental difference between, on the one hand, the development of particular trade routes, and the global reach of nineteenth-century empires, and, on the other hand, an international order involving the conjuncture of a global system of production and exchange which is beyond the control of any single nation-state (even of the most powerful); extensive networks of transnational interaction and communication which transcend national societies and evade most forms of national regulation; the power and activities of a vast array of international regimes and organizations, many of which reduce the scope for action of even leading states; and the internationalization of security structures which limit the scope for the independent use of military force by states. While in the eighteenth and nineteenth centuries trade routes and empires linked distant populations together through quite simple networks of interaction, the contemporary global order is defined by multiple systems of transaction

and coordination which link people, communities and societies in highly complex ways and which, given the nature of modern communications, virtually annihilate territorial boundaries as barriers to socio-economic activity and relations, and create new political uncertainties.[12]

As for the structure of the global economy, the differences have been argued in terms of whether it consists of an "extension of the modern international economy into somewhat unfamiliar territory or a systemic transformation which entails both changes in quantity (breadth and depth) and quality, defining new structures and new modes of financing." Having identified this basis for addressing the kind-or-degree question, Kobrin has no difficulty answering it:

> [W]e are in the midst of a qualitative transformation of the international world economy. Our argument is based on three related propositions. First, dramatic increases in the scale of technology in many industries – in its cost, risk and complexity – have rendered even the largest national markets too small to be meaningful economic units; they are no longer the "principal entities" of the world economy. National markets are fused transnationally rather than linked across borders. Second, the recent explosion of transnational strategic alliances is a manifestation of a fundamental change in the mode of organization of international economic transactions from markets and/or hierarchies (i.e., trade and MNEs) to *post-modern* global networks. Last, and related to the second point, the emerging global economy is integrated through information systems and information technology rather than hierarchical organizational structures.[13]

Thirdly, the elapse of time in the current period is distinguished by processes of aggregation and disaggregation that are occurring and interacting so rapidly – more often than not instantaneously to the point of being simultaneous – that this difference can readily be viewed as one of kind rather than of degree. One need only compare the dynamics of organizational decision-making, societal mobilization, and inter-societal relationships in the present and previous eras to appreciate that the differences are not trivial, that they are so substantial as to be far more

[12] David Held, "Democracy and the New International Order," in Daniele Archibugi and David Held (eds.), *Cosmopolitan Democracy: An Agenda for a New World Order* (Cambridge: Polity Press, 1995), p. 101.

[13] Stephen J. Kobrin, "The Architecture of Globalization: State Sovereignty in a Networked Global Economy," in John H. Dunning (ed.), *Globalization, Governments and Competition* (Oxford: Oxford University Press, 1996), pp. 3–4 [in xerox version] (italics in the original).

than merely updated repetitions of earlier patterns. Or, to use a more specific example, a comparison of the collapse of the Roman empire across centuries and of the British empire across decades with that of the Soviet empire across weeks and months will highlight how modern technologies have fostered differences in kind rather than degree.[14] In addition, with the pace of politics at all levels of community having accelerated to the extent that reactions to events occur roughly at the same time as the events themselves, actors are perpetually in a mode of seeking to catch up with the decisions to which they are also parties. It is for this reason that the emergent worldview points to a new understanding of the temporal dimension of politics.

In sum, while there often appears to be nothing new in history, the speed, simultaneity, and scope of events infuse new meanings and structures into seemingly familiar patterns. Accordingly, one can be misled by the past if in the present context one fails to allow for the dynamics of transformation. Perhaps the most efficacious way of accounting for these dynamics is to employ the distinctions drawn among three forms of change by the French historian, Fernand Braudel (1) immediate events, which consist of the short time-spans that constitute daily life; (2) conjunctural trends, which span decades and cumulate slowly and only become manifest when they culminate in unfamiliar events; and (3) the *longue durée*, which consist of durable structures that stretch across centuries.[15] The epochal transformations that form the central foci of this inquiry are conceived as expressive of all three of these forms of change, albeit it might be argued that the time frames for the three types have been diminished by the impact of modern technologies. If Braudel were to reformulate his three periods today, he might well differentiate immediate events in terms of days and weeks, conjunctural trends in terms of months and years, and the *longue durée* in terms of decades.

---

[14] For an amusing fantasy that captures these differences by imagining King George III in 1776 tuned into CNN and possessing fiber optic phone lines, a pocket beeper, and access to the World Wide Web as he copes with a rebellious colony in America – with the result that "had the communications miracle been granted us earlier, there would be no Washington, DC, for our politicians to blame for everything that annoys their constituents" – see Russell Baker, "Beep Beep King," *New York Times*, July 2, 1996, p. A15.

[15] An insightful discussion of this formulation is developed in Eric Heilleiner, "Fernand Braudel and International Political Economy," *International Studies Notes*, vol. 15 (Fall 1990), pp. 73–8.

3   Worldviews

Even a realist like former Secretary of State Henry A. Kissinger is at a loss to describe the world in a comprehensive way. He told a conference in Washington recently: "It's probably not possible to have some overarching concept."

news item[1]

[The passing of the Keynesian welfare state] represents much more than a series of strategic responses to a changing international political economy. It signals a paradigm shift in governing practices – a historic alteration in state form which enacts simultaneous changes in cultural assumptions, political identities and the very terrain of political struggle. Restructuring represents a prolonged and conflict-ridden political process during which old assumptions and shared understandings are put under stress and eventually rejected while social forces struggle to achieve a new consensus – a new vision of the future to fill the vacuum created by the erosion of the old.

Janine Brodie[2]

The sense of disarray that underlies these epigraphs exemplifies a widely shared concern over where the world is today and where it is headed tomorrow. Yet, the concern need not be paralyzing, albeit more is required – much more – than puzzlement, anomalies, and a sensitivity to change to comprehend governance along the Frontier in a turbulent world. Sure, thinking afresh requires us to acknowledge our

---

[1] Elaine Sciolino, "Call It Aid or a Bribe, It's the Price of Peace," *New York Times*, March 26, 1995, sect. 4, p. 3.

[2] Janine Brodie, "New State Forms, New Political Spaces," in Robert Boyer and Daniel Drache (eds.), *States Against Markets: The Limits of Globalization* (London: Routledge, 1996), p. 386.

puzzles, be open to recognizing anomalies, and be ever ready to discern transformative dynamics; but such orientations occur in a context and as analysts we need to be continuously aware of that context – namely, the ontology, paradigms, and theories that, taken together, might be called the "worldview" on which any observer relies to describe events, to draw causal inferences, to evaluate policy implications, or otherwise to infuse order into whatever he or she observes. Analysts can be puzzled by patterns and intrigued by anomalous developments, but in so doing they neither suspend nor reject their worldview. Such intellectual gymnastics are not possible. To know anything, one has to treat some phenomena as significant and dismiss others as trivial. It cannot be otherwise. There can be no descriptions or interpretations that are not anchored in some larger context, vague and contradictory as that context may be. And it is this context that serves as the basis of the worldview that guides us through the welter of detail that forms global affairs.[3]

To be sure, given enough puzzles and anomalies that persist and cumulate, it is possible to modify one's worldview, or even to exchange the seemingly insufficient worldview for a new, seemingly more appropriate one. However, at high levels of abstraction – at, say, the level where one seeks to comprehend the structures that sustain world affairs – such shifts rarely occur. Why? Because at such levels worldviews are so general that their basic premises enable observers to account for and explain any developments that may unfold. Indeed, for this reason the broad formulation tends to entrap its users: they cannot break out of it because its breadth is such as to include presumptions as to the meaning of seemingly contrary events or patterns. No matter how puzzling and anomalous developments may be, rare is the observer who can escape his or her most fundamental premises long enough to see the world through new lenses.[4] As one observer puts it, "Absorbed by the transitory, we ignore the epochal."[5]

---

[3] For an extensive elaboration of the point that observers and practitioners inevitably bring a larger context to bear, since the only way they can impose order on events is by selecting some as important and dismissing others as trivial, see James N. Rosenau and Mary Durfee, *Thinking Theory Thoroughly: Coherent Approaches to an Incoherent World* (Boulder, CO: Westview Press, 1995), chaps. 1 and 8.

[4] For an insightful examination of the problems associated with modifying or replacing worldviews, see Andrew C. Janos, *Politics and Paradigms: Changing Theories of Change in Social Science* (Stanford: Stanford University Press, 1986).

[5] Steven R. Mann, "Chaos Theory and Strategic Thought," *Parameters* (Autumn 1992), p. 54.

Thus it is important that as observers we explicate our fundamental assumptions about the nature of world affairs. The more we are explicit, the more can we infuse our interpretations with meaningful contexts, and the more we will be able to articulate our puzzlement and ponder the anomalies we discern. In addition, the more explicit our worldviews are, the more incisive will be our observations and the fewer will be our misunderstandings when we communicate with each other.

But the need for worldviews is not confined to public affairs analysts. Everyone – governmental officials and private citizens as well as specialists – needs a worldview. None is exempt from the inability to grasp reality in its entirety and the need to select some features of the ongoing scene as important and dismiss the rest as trivial. So as to make sense out of the welter of phenomena they select as important, people need to link the various phenomena to each other coherently; that is, they need to intrude a modicum of order on the world so that they can understand and adapt to it. The way in which the important features are arranged in relation to each other form the bases of the ontologies, paradigms, and theories through which the course of events is understood and interpreted. The end result for collectivities is an intersubjective – and not an objective – understanding. As Cox puts it, "Reality is made by the collective responses of people to the conditions of their existence. Intersubjectively shared experience reproduces reality in the form of continuing institutions and practices."[6] In short, to the extent that ontologies, paradigms, and theories are shared, they "tell us what is significant in the particular world we delve into – what are the basic entities and key relationships."[7]

Larger contexts

For a variety of reasons, our worldviews today seem antiquated, perhaps even counterproductive. As indicated in the previous chapter, in an era marked by shifting boundaries, emergent authorities, weakened states, and proliferating nongovernmental organizations (NGOs) at local, provincial, national, transnational, international, and global levels of community, the time has come to confront the insufficiency of our worldviews. Just as the business world has begun to appreciate that

[6] Robert W. Cox, "Critical Political Economy," in Bjorn Hettne (ed.), *International Political Economy: Understanding Global Disorder* (London: Zed Books, 1995), p. 35.

[7] Cox, "Critical Political Economy," p. 34.

27

"the labels 'international' and 'domestic' which adequately described our business structure in the past, no longer apply,"[8] thereby creating "a company without a country,"[9] so must those in the political world begin to think in terms of authority without territoriality. Unless we confront our ways of thinking, talking, and writing about governance, our analysis will suffer from a reliance on artifacts of the very past beyond which it seeks to move. It will remain plagued by a lack of conceptual tools appropriate to the task of sorting out the underpinnings of political processes sustained by the altered borders, redirected legitimacy sentiments, impaired or paralyzed governments, and new identities that underlie the emergence of new SOAs along the Frontier.

A depleted tool-shed suggests that understanding is no longer served by clinging to the notion that the Frontier is firmly fixed and in place, that boundaries do indeed bind. We have become so accustomed to treating states and national governments as the foundations of politics that we fall back on them when contemplating the prospects for governance on a global scale, thereby relegating the shifting boundaries, relocated authorities, and proliferating NGOs to the status of new but secondary dimensions of the processes through which communities allocate values and frame policies. To be sure, few observers would dismiss the impact of these dimensions as peripheral. Nonetheless, the predominant tendency is to cling to old ways of thought that accord primacy to states and national governments. Even an otherwise praiseworthy attempt to clarify and define the nature of global governance proved unable to break free of this conventional conception: while acknowledging the enormous changes at work in the world, in the end this definitional undertaking falls back on old ways of thought and specifies that global governance involves "doing internationally what governments do at home."[10] Such a formulation amply demonstrates the large extent to which we remain imprisoned by the idea that the line

---

[8] Robert C. Goizeta, CEO of the Coca-Cola Company, in announcing the restructuring of his company, adding it is a global company that "just happens to be" headquartered in the United States. Quoted in Glenn Collins, "Coke Drops 'Domestic' and Goes One World," *New York Times,* January 13, 1996, p. 35.

[9] A description of the Ford Motor Company when it announced a corporate restructuring in which centralized management controls were largely eliminated and replaced by "executive authority . . . distributed around the globe." Warren Brown and Frank Swoboda, "Ford's Brave New World," *Washington Post,* October 16, 1994, p. H1.

[10] Lawrence S. Finkelstein, "What Is Global Governance?" *Global Governance,* vol. 1 (Sept.-Dec. 1995), pp. 367–72 (the quote is from p.369).

dividing domestic and foreign affairs still serves as the cutting edge of analysis.[11]

How, then, to update our worldview so that it can more fully and accurately account for a global scene in which the dynamics of governance are undergoing profound transformations? How to render political inquiry more incisive, more able to treat seemingly anomalous developments as part and parcel of modern-day governance? How to enable us to see problems as struggles for identity and equality as well as conflicts within or among states? How to equip ourselves so that we are not surprised by a Soviet Union that peacefully collapses overnight, by a Canada that borders on fragmentation, by a Yugoslavia that seeks membership in the European Union even as it comes apart, by a currency crisis that surfaces simultaneously around the world, by a South Africa that manages to bridge a long-standing and huge racial divide, or by international institutions that intrude deeply into the domestic affairs of states (to mention only a few of the surprising developments of recent years)?

The answers to these questions lie in the need to develop a new worldview – and the ontology, paradigm, and theory on which it rests – for understanding the deepest foundations of governance along the Frontier. Such a worldview should recast the relevance of territoriality, highlight the porosity of boundaries, treat the temporal dimensions of governance as no less significant than the spatial dimensions, recognize that networking organizations have become as important as hierarchical ones, and posit shifts of authority to subnational, transnational, and nongovernmental levels as normal.

---

[11] Similarly, an otherwise commendable effort to assess where and how the boundary between domestic and foreign affairs is transgressed missed a chance to move beyond the conventional conception by framing the problem in terms of the choices made by states as they seek to balance the demands they face from home and abroad. Indeed, this formulation perpetuates the idea of a rigid boundary between the two domains by focusing on its transgression as a "two-level game" played by states while treating transnational alliances between domestic constituencies as secondary dynamics that only become relevant under the unlikely condition of "private groups [being] opposed by their own state." Peter B. Evans, Harold K. Jacobson, and Robert D. Putnam (eds.), *Double-Edged Diplomacy: International Bargaining and Domestic Politics* (Berkeley: University of California Press, 1993); the quote is from p. 32. For a more theoretical inquiry into another kind of cross-boundary linkage, see Robert O. Keohane and Elinor Ostrom (eds.), *Local Commons and Global Interdependence: Heterogeneity and Cooperation in Two Domains* (Thousand Oaks, CA: Sage Publications, 1995).

Without delving into the various definitional distinctions analysts draw among worldviews, ontologies, paradigms, and theories, here all these concepts are viewed as central to the nature of knowledge and are treated as layered, with worldviews incorporating the last three.[12] Of the latter, ontologies are conceived to be the most encompassing, followed by paradigms and then theories. The three are highly interdependent: one's theories depend on the paradigm one employs which, in turn, depends on the ontology with which one is comfortable. Put briefly in the present context, ontologies involve our most basic understanding of the nature of global politics, whereas paradigms specify the parameters or boundary conditions within which political activities occur, and theories specify how the relationships among individual or collective actors vary within any given set of parameters. Viewed from the perspective in which people perceive and talk about political reality, of course, ontologies, paradigms, and theories overlap and cannot be clearly delineated from each other.[13] Here we separate them only for analytical purposes (combined together they constitute what is often referred to as the "social construction of reality"), so that when any or all of them shift it involves "a change in the world under our feet, in the whole context in which our knowledge and awareness are rooted."[14]

Table 3.1 outlines the layered links among the ontologies, paradigms, and theories that compose the worldviews of the waning epoch (rows A and B) and the one that is conceived to mark the emergent epoch (row C). Here it can be seen that the realist and liberal worldviews are founded on ontologies that share a conception of unit boundaries and primary units but differ over the central issues on the global agenda. The emergent worldview (here tentatively labeled "fragmegration"), on the other hand, consists of a very different understanding of the unit boundaries, units, and issues regarded as primary. Likewise, while the parameters that comprise the realist and liberal paradigms specify the kinds of gains sought by the actors and the basic systemic structure in

[12] A similar conception in which worldviews are regarded as "simple devices" that encompass "more demanding" theories is developed in Jürg Martin Gabriel, *Worldviews and Theories of International Relations* (New York: St. Martin's Press, 1994), pp. 2–3.

[13] For evidence that the philosophical literature is not marked by clear-cut distinctions among ontologies, paradigms, and theories, see Margaret Masterman, "The Nature of a Paradigm," in I. Lakatos and A. Musgrave (eds.), *Criticism and Growth of Knowledge* (Cambridge: Cambridge University Press, 1970), pp. 59–89, where twenty-one different versions of the paradigm concept are identified.

[14] Michael Heim, *The Metaphysics of Virtual Reality* (New York: Oxford University Press, 1993), p. xiii.

Table 3.1. *Two waning worldviews and an emergent worldview*

Worldviews	Ontologies			Paradigms	Theories
	Unit boundaries	Main units	Main issues	Parameters	Key variables
(A) Realism	Firm	States	Security	Actors seek relative gains in confrontational anarchic structures	Relative power
(B) Liberalism	Firm	States	Economic	Actors seek absolute gains in cooperative anarchic structures	Overlapping unit-level preferences
(C) Fragmegration	Porous	Diverse actors	Diverse issues	Citizen skills Authority relations Structural bifurcation	Turbulence

which these goals are pursued, those of the emergent paradigm focus, respectively, on the skills of citizens, the authority relationships between them and their collectivities, and the overall structure of the global system. Each paradigm subsumes various theories, but table 3.1 lists only the essential theoretical perspective that each generates: relative power in the realist worldview, overlapping unit-level preferences in the liberal worldview, and the dynamics of turbulence in the emergent worldview.[15]

Ontologies

The concept of an ontology originated in the field of philosophy and refers to the broad assumptions that are made about the nature of reality. Here the concept is adapted through two sets of broad assumptions about global affairs that people embed in their worldviews: the first-order assumption concerns whether domestic and foreign affairs are separate or convergent or, more precisely, whether any boundaries that differentiate them are firm or porous; the second-order assumption focuses on the nature of the primary actors and issues that sustain governance along the Frontier. As such, an ontology is foundational in that it highlights what basic elements are regarded as comprising the existing order. But compared to paradigms and theories, ontologies are static: while they identify the essential parts of the whole they constitute, they are too all-encompassing to include elaboration of the way in which the parts interact with each other.

As understandings that extend intersubjectively across publics, "Ontologies are not arbitrary constructions; they are the specification of the common sense of an epoch."[16] Consequently, as indicated in table 3.1, it has come to be widely understood in our emergent era that the boundaries separating domestic and foreign affairs are no longer firm and have, instead, been eroded and become porous, being transgressed by a variety of diverse types of actors and issues. This essential difference between the common sense of the new epoch and the realist and liberal ontologies that predominate in the waning epoch can be grasped by comparing the graphic summaries presented in tables 3.2 and 3.3.

[15] Since the concern here is that of probing what is considered to be the emergent worldview, no effort is made to elaborate on the various versions of the two waning worldviews summarized in table 3.1. For extensive accounts and assessments of the latter, see all twelve of the essays in David A. Baldwin (ed.), *Neorealism and Neoliberalism: The Contemporary Debate* (New York: Columbia University Press, 1993).

[16] Cox, "Critical Political Economy," p. 34.

The columns of the former call attention to the firmness of the bound-aries that differentiate the various types of territorial communities, ranging from the least to the most encompassing. Each column repre-sents a governance entity that has responsibility for the issues and qual-ities of life within its jurisdiction. Likewise, the rows in table 3-2 depict some of the diverse issues encompassed by any community in one of the two waning ontologies. Each row represents an issue area and the concerns that set apart the groups active within it.

Framed against the background of the same rows and columns, table 3.3 summarizes the emergent ontology in which the political issues and territorial units, though still part of the global scene, are no longer con-strained by firm boundaries. Instead, the table's diagonal spaces high-light some of the nonterritorial actors or networks which contribute to the processes of governance that comprise the Frontier and inter-dependently link the issues and units. To be sure, in various parts of the world the long-established boundaries remain fully intact, and it may also be the case that the ontology implied in table 3.3 has yet to surface fully as the common sense of the epoch; but here the analysis proceeds from the presumption that, indeed, the diagonal spaces represent common threads sufficiently woven into the fabric of global life to form the foundations of a new, widely shared ontology in the decades ahead. The essential argument is that the overlaps among communities depicted by the diagonal spaces have become increasingly salient pre-cisely because they subsume numerous problems that cannot be accounted for, much less managed, by established collectivities. The enormous complexities and interdependencies that have been fostered by a multiplicity of postindustrial dynamics are simply too extensive for the diverse problems of territorial communities not to meld into a larger set of challenges which, in turn, foster the evolution of new arrange-ments for sustaining governance in a turbulent world. Among the new arrangements, perhaps none is more crucial than the advent of net-works as organizational forms no less central to the conduct of world affairs than are hierarchical structures.[17] It follows that if the interactions

---

[17] Cf. Francis Fukuyama, "Social Networks and Digital Networks," unpublished paper, Rand Corporation, Washington, DC (1996); Dee W. Hock, "Institutions in the Age of Mindcrafting" (paper presented at the Bionomics Annual Conference, San Francisco 1994); David Ronfeldt, "Tribes, Institutions, Markets, Networks: A Framework About Societal Evolution" unpublished paper, Rand Corporation, Santa Monica (1996). For a succinct discussion of the challenges analysts face in studying networks, see Mustafa Emirbayer and Jeff Goodwin, "Network Analysis, Culture, and the Problem of Agency," *American Journal of Sociology*, vol. 99 (May 1994), pp. 1411–54.

Table 3.2. *Governance sustained by territorial units and issue areas*

Levels of political organization

Issue areas	Towns	Cities	Provinces	Nation-states	International agencies
Science and technology					
Commerce and trade					
Conservation vs development					
Labor					
Agriculture					
Immigration					
Education					
Human rights					
Religion					
Environment					
Health and welfare					
Housing					
Employment					
Constitutional issues					
Elections					
etc.					

Table 3.3. *Governance along the domestic–foreign Frontier*

Levels of political organization

Issue areas	Towns	Cities	Provinces	Nation-states	International agencies
Science and technology					
Commerce and trade					
Conservation vs development					
Labor					
Agriculture					
Immigration					
Education					
Human rights					
Religion					
Environment					
Health and welfare					
Housing					
Employment					
Constitutional issues					
Elections					
etc.					

Diagonal entries: arms trade, the Internet, international regimes, market forces, subnational governments, transnational organizations, multinational corporations, ethnic minorities, social movements, professional societies, humanitarian associations, church groups, terrorist organizations, coalitions of the willing, miscellaneous NGOs, political parties, crime networks, drug trade, labor unions, epistemic communities, etc.

of sovereign states in an anarchical world constitute the theoretical core of the waning ontologies, the theoretical center of the emergent one consists of interactions among a diversity of globalizing and localizing forces, of tendencies toward integration and fragmentation that are so simultaneous and interactive as to collapse into erratic – but discernible – processes.

This is not to imply that the realist and liberal worldviews fail to recognize that the Frontier is porous or that actors other than states are active on the global stage. Quite to the contrary, most subscribers to both worldviews appreciate the enormous complexities of world affairs. For both, however, such complexities are not considered so powerful as to yield understandings that justify not presuming the paramount relevance of the goals and actions of states. Here it is argued, on the other hand, that the analytic clarity achieved by focusing on states is misleading, that the attention paid by the emergent ontology to the porosity of the Frontier, the diversity of actors, and the salience of networks has an analytic potential that is likely to yield more powerful and fruitful insights. At the same time, in stressing the complexity and pervasiveness of governance along the Frontier, the emergent ontology poses a terminological dilemma. Since worldviews are so thoroughgoing, so capable of highlighting the structural features that are perceived relevant to the maintenance of the political world, that people can summarize their understanding of complex phenomena by reference to a few organizing principles, is it possible to capture the extensive complexities of the emergent worldview in a summarizing label? In the past the common sense of the epoch was captured by phrases describing the essential structural features of the international system. Prior to World War II, for example, the "balance of power" served to express the common sense of that epoch, whereas thinking about the world in the subsequent period was summarized by referring to the "Cold War" and its superpower rivalry. But what structural label can be used today to capture the mosaic of global interactions suggested by table 3.3? It is not sufficient to characterize the complexities of present-day interdependencies as simply the "emergent worldview." Clearly, a new, more descriptive label is needed to differentiate the common sense of the emergent epoch from its predecessors and to facilitate clarity as to the ways in which it breaks with the past.

But the present offers no dominant relationship such as the superpower competition that underlay the labeling of the Cold War. Nor is the present distribution of power so self-evident as to warrant recourse to hegemonic or balance-of-power labels. On the other hand, while many of the labels that have been offered as alternatives – such as "polyarchy,"[18] "triadization,"[19] "panarchy,"[20] "geopolinomic,"[21] "plurilateralism,"[22] "geogovernance,"[23] and "collibration"[24] – highlight the degree to which the world has undergone decentralization since the end of the Cold War, they seem unsuitable in that they imply static structural hierarchies and fail to indicate the tensions between the fragmenting consequences of conflict and the integrative effects of cooperation. Perhaps even less suitable is a terminology which characterizes the present period as "the post-Cold War order." Such a label merely highlights that the earlier period has ended and conveys no image of what the core dynamics of the new epoch involve. Consequently, it is "tentative, vague; it lacks authority."[25] It is also insufficient because even as it concedes the presence of patterns yet to form, it may also mislead us into overlooking or downplaying the

---

[18] Seyom Brown, *New Forces, Old Forces, and the Future of World Politics*, Post-Cold War Edn, (New York: HarperCollins, 1995), chap. 8.

[19] "By 'triadization' is meant the fact that the process of technological, economic, and socio-cultural integration among the three most developed regions of the world (Japan plus the NICs from South-East Asia, Western Europe and North America) is more diffused, intensive and significant than 'integration' between these three regions and the less-developed countries, or between the less-developed themselves." Riccardo Petrella, "Globalization and Internationalization: The Dynamics of the Emerging World Order," in Robert Boyer and Daniel Drache (eds.), *States Against Markets: The Limits of Globalization* (London: Routledge, 1996), p. 77.

[20] James P. Sewell and Mark B. Salter, "Panarchy and Other Norms for Global Governance," *Global Governance*, vol. 1 (Sept.–Dec. 1995), pp. 373–82.

[21] George J. Demko and William B. Wood, "International Relations Through the Prism of Geography," in G. J. Demko and W. B. Wood (eds.), *Reordering the World: Geopolitical Perspectives on the 21st Century* (Boulder, CO: Westview Press, 1994), pp. 10–11.

[22] P. G. Cerny, "Plurilateralism: Structural Differentiation and Functional Conflict in the Post-Cold War World Order," *Millennium: Journal of International Studies*, vol. 22 (Spring 1993), pp. 27–51.

[23] Richard Falk, *On Humane Governance: Toward a New Global Politics* (University Park: Pennsylvania State University Press, 1995), pp. 9–14.

[24] Andrew Dunsire, "Modes of Governance," in J. Kooiman (ed.), *Modern Governance: New Government–Society Interactions* (London: Sage Publications, 1993), p. 31.

[25] James Atlas, "Name That Era: Pinpointing a Moment on the Map of History," *New York Times* (March 19, 1995), sect. 4, p. 1.

emergence of processes that systematically link integrating and fragmenting dynamics.[26]

What is needed, in short, is a terminology that suggests neither a relationship nor a pecking order but, rather, calls attention to the basic processes on which the emergent worldview is founded and enables interested citizens as well as those charged with the tasks of governance to remain sensitive to its underlying dynamics. For want of a better term, the label used in table 3.1 to summarize the essential perspective of the emergent worldview will be used in subsequent chapters. The synthesized word "fragmegration" serves to suggest the simultaneity and interaction of the fragmenting and integrating dynamics that are giving rise to new spheres of authority and transforming the old spheres.[27] It is also a label that suggests the absence of clear-cut distinctions between domestic and foreign affairs, that local problems can become transnational in scope even as global challenges can have repercussions for neighborhoods.[28] In effect, the label tends to highlight the large extent to which the global system is so disaggregated that it lacks overall patterns and, instead, is marked by various structures of systemic cooperation and subsystemic conflict in different regions, countries, and issue areas.[29]

[26] Much the same can be said about the label, "postinternationalism," I used in *Turbulence in World Politics: A Theory of Change and Continuity* (Princeton: Princeton University Press, 1990). At that time (1989) so much about the course of events was murky that the processes linking integrating and fragmenting dynamics were not readily discernible. One knew that enormous changes were under way, but their central tendencies were far from evident. Thus it seemed necessary to recognize the transformations without estimating their direction. For that purpose the postinternational label seemed appropriate, as it did subsequently when Durfee and I compared the turbulence and realist models in *Thinking Theory Thoroughly*.

[27] This concept was first developed in James N. Rosenau, "'Fragmegrative' Challenges to National Security," in Terry Heyns (ed.), *Understanding U.S. Strategy: A Reader* (Washington, DC: National Defense University, 1983), pp. 65–82.

[28] Other terms suggestive of the contradictory tensions that pull systems toward coherence and collapse are "chaord," a label that juxtaposes the dynamics of chaos and order, and "glocalization," which points to the simultaneity of globalizing and localizing dynamics. The former designation is proposed in Dee W. Hock, "Institutions in the Age of Mindcrafting," pp. 1–2, while the latter term is elaborately developed in Roland Robertson, "Glocalization: Time–Space and Homogeneity–Heterogeneity," in Mike Featherstone, Scott Lash and Roland Robertson (eds.), *Global Modernities* (Thousand Oaks, CA: Sage Publications, 1995), pp. 25–44. I prefer the term "fragmegration" because it does not imply a territorial scale and broadens the focus to include tensions at work in organizations as well as those that pervade communities.

[29] See chapter 6 for a full discussion of the dynamics of fragmegration. For book-length treatments concerned with these dynamics, see Benjamin Barber, *Jihad vs. McWorld*

Admittedly, the fragmegration label may prove too grating and too technical to generate broad usage. Until a simpler and more compelling terminology evolves, however, this label – being at once descriptively expressive and disconcertedly awkward – serves as a reminder of the essential dynamic wherein the emergent epoch is marked by continual tensions and interactions between the forces propelling the fragmentation of communities and those conducing to their integration. Whatever label may eventually be adopted, it is likely to point incisively to these key arrangements that distinguish the present epoch from its predecessors.

An appropriate label for the ontology will not fully solve the terminological problems it poses. There is also the need for a concept that facilitates analysis of the relocation of authority inherent in a fragmegrated world. Most notably, with states treated as only one of many sources of authority, a term is needed that allows for the moving centers of power that roam around the Frontier and depict the units of governance implied by the diagonals that traverse table 3.3. As previously indicated, an appropriate term can be derived from the fragmegration ontology's premise that the world is not so much a system dominated by states and national governments as a congeries of spheres of authority (SOAs) that are subject to considerable flux and not necessarily coterminous with the division of territorial space. SOAs are, in effect, the analytic units of the new ontology. They are distinguished by the presence of actors who can evoke compliance when exercising authority as they engage in the activities that delineate the sphere. The sphere may or may not correspond to a bounded territory: those who comply may be spread around the world and have no legal relationship to each other, or they may be located in the same geographic space and have the same organizational affiliations. If the sphere involves the allocation of values through certifying the reliability of bond issuers, for example, then its actors will include Moody's, Standard and Poor's, and a number of other credit-rating agencies whose evaluations determine which firms, governments, and NGOs in various parts of the world can raise money at favorable rates and which cannot.[30] In contrast to these nonterritorial SOAs, on the other hand, are those in which the allocation of values remains linked to geographic space, thus enabling local, provincial, and

(New York: Times Books, 1995), and Betty Jean Craige, *American Patriotism in a Global Society* (Albany: State University of New York Press, 1996).

[30] Timothy J. Sinclair, "Investment, Knowledge and Governance: Credit-Rating Processes and the Global Political Economy" Ph.D. dissertation, York University, Toronto, 1995.

national governments to achieve compliance when they exercise authority over taxes, parklands, police activities, and whatever other domains wherein they have not experienced a shift and contraction of their jurisdictions.

The advent of nonterritorial actors and relocated authorities helps to explain the recent tendency to focus on processes of governance rather than on governments as the instruments through which authority is exercised. While governments are concrete actors accorded formal jurisdiction over specified territorial domains, governance is a broader concept which highlights SOAs that may not be territorial in scope and that may employ only informal authority to achieve compliance on the part of those within the sphere. Governance, in other words, refers to mechanisms for steering social systems toward their goals,[31] a conception which is far more amenable to understanding a world in which old boundaries are becoming obscure, in which new identities are becoming commonplace, and in which the scale of political thought has become global in scope.

Another sign of the emergent ontology can be discerned in the variety of new terms that have evolved to designate units of governance which are not instruments of states and governments. At least ten such SOAs have achieved acceptance in (and in some cases pervade) the literature on world politics: NGOs, nonstate actors, sovereignty-free actors, issue networks, policy networks, social movements, global civil society, transnational coalitions, transnational lobbies, and epistemic communities.[32] While an intersubjective consensus has yet to shake this terminology down into a shared vocabulary, the proliferation of such terms represents a restlessness over the prevailing ontological preoccupation with states and governments. More importantly, the terms express processes of social construction wherein new agents of action are conceived as acquiring authority sufficient to frame and implement policies that shape the course of events.

In a disaggregated, decentralized world, what might the fragmegration ontology specify as common sense with respect to the pervasiveness of hierarchy? Again it may be difficult to move on to new ways of thinking. Hierarchy involves power and the relative capability of actors, and we are so accustomed to positing pecking orders in these terms that it will not be easy to come to grips with a disaggregated array of actors

---

[31] See chapter 8 for an elaboration of this conception.
[32] I am indebted to Ken Conca for this listing.

whose power is limited to a particular expertise or set of issues, thus rendering them essentially autonomous and not dependent on where they stand in a pecking order. For example, some credit-rating agencies may be more influential than others, but there is no basis for presuming either that the most high-status credit agency can achieve compliance from actors outside its SOA or that its compliance can be achieved by actors in other spheres. "Wait a minute," those wedded to the waning ontologies might exclaim, "what about the state's sovereignty? Surely that enables it to curb or override any credit agency operating within its borders!" "Not at all," respond those who have adopted the emergent ontology; authority inheres in a sphere and if a state or national government succeeds in curbing or overruling the actions of a credit agency, such an outcome will be a consequence of the circumstances of the SOA in which the two actors compete rather than of the state having sovereign authority which the credit agency lacks.

Put differently, what enables one actor to obtain compliance from another actor in a disaggregated world is an interdependent convergence of needs and not a constitutional specification that assigns the highest authority exclusively to states and national governments. In addition, the hierarchy that derives from the military power over which states have a monopoly and through which they exercise their sovereignty in the last resort can no longer, given the disaggregation of SOAs, be translated into leverage over credit agencies or, for that matter, a host of SOAs operating throughout the world.

And whose needs delineate the size and scope of SOAs? The answer is obvious: the needs of the individuals and groups encompassed by its jurisdiction as these are defined by its politically effective leaders – by those whose resources, followership, knowledge, or legal status provides them with the capacity to speak and act on behalf of the individuals and groups affected by the issues out of which the SOA's legitimacy is constructed.

Paradigms

Like ontologies, paradigms derive from worldviews as systems of understandings about how the world is organized, but they are not so all-encompassing. Here they are conceived to narrow the world down to the parameters within which activities occur and vary. Parameters are the boundary conditions of any political entity, those rules, habits, institutions, and patterns beyond which its individuals and groups normally do not stray. In effect, therefore, paradigms serve as the sources of constancy and historical continuity that people impose on the world in order to grasp how political entities move through time intact.

As implied in table 3.1, the ontological assumptions that realists and liberals make about the centrality of the state leads them both to paradigmatic premises in which the prime structure of world affairs is that of anarchy – the absence of a central authority – and thus to the necessity of states having to rely on their own conduct to advance and protect their interests. For realists, such a structure results in parameters that define their interests in terms of security and the need to pursue goals that maintain their relative position in the anarchic structure through confrontational behavior. On the other hand, since those who subscribe to the liberal worldview treat states as primarily concerned with economic issues as the prime vehicle for advancing their interests, they employ parameters in which states are seen as seeking absolute gains irrespective of the goals sought by other states and, as a result, the anarchic interstate system is conceived to be more cooperative than confrontational. In contrast, founded on an ontology that emphasizes the porosity of the Frontier and the diversity of the main actors and issues that sustain global affairs, the paradigm derived from the emergent worldview is conceived to consist of three parameters, one that involves the skills of individuals, another that focuses on the authority that links them to their collectivities, and still another that sustains global structures through coalitions of actors that sometimes conflict and sometimes cooperate.

Theories

Whereas ontologies focus on the nature of politics, and paradigms on the parameters within which political action unfolds, theories and models – the terms are used interchangeably here – focus on the action itself. Some theories consist of specific hypotheses about patterns of behavior tightly linked into a framework such that a failure or affirmation of any hypothesis has anticipated consequences for all the others. Other theories are less rigorous and offer broad hypotheses that are loosely tied together and point only in a general way to expected outcomes. However, the hypotheses of all theories, whatever their degree of specificity, are marked by a concern with anticipating varying outcomes (called dependent variables in the language of science) as consequences of variations in the presumed sources of the outcomes (the independent variables). In the case of complex models that encompass the interactions of variables across time, some activities are posited as independent variables at the outset of a causal sequence and as dependent variables at later stages of the sequence.

Given the numerous actors, institutions, and processes that make up the political world, a vast number of theories can be developed within the context of any worldview. As indicated in table 3.1, the ontological and paradigmatic presumptions of the realist worldview generate theories about state competition for relative power and how the configuration of power among states leads to different forms and degrees of balance among them. In the case of the liberal worldview, the theoretical enterprise consists of hypotheses anticipating varying degrees of overlapping preferences that result in interest harmonization when states pursue absolute gains in the global economy. As for the emergent worldview, its theories focus on the SOAs formed by the responses of diverse actors in diverse issue areas to the fragmegrative dynamics stimulated by the skill revolution, authority crises and a bifurcated global structure. In the chapters that follow, these relationships anticipated by the emergent worldview do not amount to a tightly knit theoretical formulation, but a variety of hypotheses are offered relevant to governance along the Frontier and clustered together in a model of turbulence that treats three of the prime parameters of the long-standing world of states as having been transformed into powerful variables. This model is outlined in chapter 4 and in the subsequent three chapters the transformations are treated as dependent variables driven by the dynamics of globalization, localization, and fragmegration.

Briefly anticipating these theoretical themes, the three prime parameters-turned-variables of the turbulence model point to broad hypotheses in which a skill revolution is posited at the micro level of individuals, a spread of authority crises is postulated at the intermediate level that links individuals at the micro level with collectivities at the macro level, and a bifurcation of the collectivities at the macro level in which a multi-centric world of diverse SOAs is hypothesized as having emerged to compete, cooperate, or otherwise interact with the state-centric world of national governments. These transformations are conceived to be driven by the technological innovations of the microelectronic revolution and other powerful sources of globalization as well as by heightened sensitivities to ethnic identity and other powerful sources of localization.

In short, we live in and study a fragmegrative world that often cascades events through, over, and around the long-established boundaries of states and, on some occasions, relocates authority outwards to transnational and supranational organizations, sidewards to social movements and NGOs, and inwards to subnational groups. It is a world in which the logic of governance does not necessarily follow hierarchical lines, in which what is distant is also proximate, and in which the spatial and temporal dimensions of politics are so confounded by fragmegrative dynamics as to rid event sequences of any linearity they may once have had.

It follows, given the widening porosity of conventional political boundaries, the shifting loci of authority, and the emergence of a nonterritorial, nonlinear politics, that fragmegrative dynamics are no less relevant to societal systems as they are to international systems. SOAs are as likely in societal processes as in global ones to span the Frontier and cascade directives across space and time in an erratic fashion, flowing first in one direction, then in another, followed by still a third redirection, even a reversal to the point of origin, with the result that compliance cumulates, gets modified, or is terminated in nonlinear sequences.

Thus it bears repeating that today's chains of causation follow crazy-quilt patterns that cannot be adequately discerned if one clings to an ontology that presumes the primacy of states and national governments. As will be seen throughout the rest of the book, the fragmegration worldview does not dismiss states as irrelevant, but it does highlight those points at which the erosion of state authority and the proliferation of SOAs have resulted in a disaggregation of the loci of governance. Notwithstanding the overriding power of globalizing forces in the economic, communications, and cultural realms, and despite the signs of expanding integration to be found in Europe and other regions today, fragmegration has been accompanied by a dispersion of the sites at which authority can be exercised and compliance generated. The weakening of states has not been followed by authority vacuums (although there may be situations where this is the case) so much as it has resulted in a vast growth in the number of spheres into which authority has moved. Fragmegration points to a redistribution of authority and not to its deterioration.

Fragmegration as a synthesizing worldview

Having suggested earlier that it was possible to specify a set of causal priorities among the diverse sources of fragmegration, and having claimed above that the fragmegrative worldview is likely to yield more fruitful insights into the dynamics of present-day global politics than either the realist or liberal worldviews, at least brief note needs to be taken of the causal priorities and how they have the potential for incisive understanding. Not to do so is to allow for the conclusion that the fragmegration worldview does not yield viable theory, that it posits such a high degree of complexity that everything is consequential, and that thus it cannot anticipate outcomes because all causes are also treated as effects and all effects are also treated as causes. Clearly, such a conclusion does not obtain with respect to the realist and liberal worldviews, both of which specify which actors matter and how they matter, and this outcome-oriented dimension accounts for why both are compelling theoretical perspectives. How then, to synthesize the diverse dynamics that sustain fragmegrative processes such that alternative outcomes can be envisioned?

The answer to this question is suggested in figure 3.1, which employs a flow diagram to trace the causal links among the first- and second-order effects of key fragmegrative dynamics. Here it can be seen that while the fragmegration worldview does not achieve the parsimonious elegance of the other two, it is not lacking in theoretical foundations. Rather, the virtue of a fragmegration concept is that it offers branching alternatives (or, from a policy perspective, choice-points) which enable the theorist to anticipate the paths actions and systems will follow as a consequence of prior developments (or decisions). Instead of attributing common goals to actors, in other words, such a perspective uses the tensions between fragmentation and integration as a basis for narrowing likely outcomes and excluding a wide range of other outcomes, depending on which set of tensions prevail when globalizing and localizing dynamics interact. Admittedly, a branching perspective is not as theoretically powerful as one which ascribes common motives and goals to relevant actors; in a complex world of convoluted time and space, however, fragmegration does offer a means for anticipating how diverse actors and issues may acquire patterns and thus provide meaningful insights into the course of events. If theories are supposed to specify which actors are relevant and how their actions matter – as the realist and liberal worldviews do – figure 3.1 indicates that fragmegration accomplishes this task in the limited sense of pointing to how alternative sets of actors and issues matter under varying conditions.

More specifically, figure 3.1 highlights the presumption that technological innovation underlies the dynamics of transformation. These dynamics are posited as flowing along three causal streams. One,

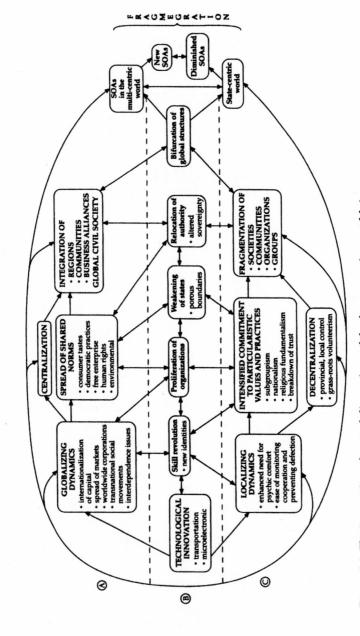

Figure 3.1 The interaction of central dimensions of the fragmegration worldview.

the top stream (A), depicts the flow of globalizing or centralizing dynamics facilitated by innovative technologies, whereas the bottom stream (C) indicates the causal flow that unfolds when technologies introduce dynamism into localizing or decentralizing processes. The center stream (B) depicts dynamics that are essentially neutral in the sense that, depending on situational determinants, they contribute to and enhance the flow of both the other two. In effect, stream B is the turbulence model and the two-way arrows that connect its components to streams A and C suggest its causal consequences. The arrows that encircle around all three streams are indicative of the feedback processes that sustain fragmegration. They signify that none of the streams flows independently of the other two and that the interactions of all three are marked by rapidity and simultaneity. The horizontal lines that separate the streams are purposely broken into segments in order to suggest the shifting porosity of the Frontier's political spaces.

While the ensuing chapters, which elaborate on the entries in each of the streams, make clear how a variety of technological innovations have facilitated the causal flows, it is important to emphasize that the connections illustrated in figure 3.1 ought not be considered a form of technological determinism. The key word here is "facilitated." Figure 3.1 facilitates identification of the alternatives and choices through which people respond to new technologies. Without new transportation and communications technologies, the dynamics of change presently at work would not be unfolding; but this is not a form of determinism because the new technologies do not carry humankind in a single direction. They facilitate several causal streams, and it is the dynamics of individuals and communities that determine which stream will be followed in particular situations or regions. Where the groups of a community share a wide set of values, for example, they are more likely to follow the globalizing stream than those who are deeply divided along class, ethnic, religious, or linguistic lines and who thus may be inclined to traverse the localizing path.

Juxtaposing the three worldviews

Another way of distinguishing among the three worldviews is to focus on the centrality of the motives and identity of actors in the realist and liberal ontologies as a basis for comparison. The premises involving actor identity yield a distinction between those circumstances under which national governments are central to the realist and liberal world-

Table 3.4. *Juxtaposing three worldviews in terms of the actors and behavior deemed central*

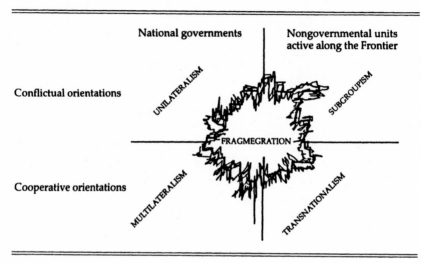

	National governments	Nongovernmental units active along the Frontier
Conflictual orientations	UNILATERALISM	SUBGROUPISM
	FRAGMEGRATION	
Cooperative orientations	MULTILATERALISM	TRANSNATIONALISM

views and those situations where states are seen as following the lead of, or sharing power with, the diverse nongovernmental actors considered active along the Frontier from a fragmegrative perspective. The premises relevant to actor behavior distinguish between situations in which conflictual orientations are viewed as predominant and those in which cooperation is treated as the primary wellspring of action. By juxtaposing these two sets of premises in table 3.4, both the logic and the lacunae of the worldviews that people impose on global affairs can be discerned.

The logic of the realist worldview is represented by the upper-left cell of table 3.4, which suggests that *unilateral* behavior on the part of states can be anticipated when they are regarded as predominant and as compelled by the anarchical structure of the interstate system to preserve their independence and well-being through self-help and the maximization of their power relative to other states. They may cooperate with other states through alliances and intergovernmental organizations if it is in their immediate interest, but they are seen as being ready at all times to break any commitments they have made to more encompassing international systems if unilateral and conflictual actions are seen as better enabling them to realize their subsystemic goals in a distrustful and hostile world. In short, by treating the world as an anarchic system that fosters conflict in the absence of enduring authorities with which states must comply, realists impose unilateralism as the basis for order in global affairs.[33]

The logic of those who subscribe to the liberal worldview is evident in the lower-left cell of the table. Here it can be seen that while they assume the predominance of states to be unchallenged, their sensitivity to the world's mounting interdependence orients them toward seeking absolute goals through participation in the global economy. Thus states are seen as inclined to cooperate in the institutions and regimes of the global system, inclinations that lead them to engage predominantly in *multilateral* behavior. In this imposed order the world's anarchic structure is perceived to be a system of balanced constraints that allow for cooperation and inhibit states from clinging to narrow self-interests.[34]

The right-hand cells of table 3.4 depict lacunae which result from the realist and liberal worldviews according only peripheral status to non-governmental actors. But space for two additional types of pervasive behavior is opened up by the presumption of the fragmegration worldview that global structures have undergone bifurcation and accorded central roles to subnational and transnational collectivities that act either independently of, or interactively with, governments in the state-centric world along the Frontier. One lacuna is represented by the upper right-hand cell and is founded on a perspective that treats the forces of fragmentation as proliferating, the centers of authority as fraying, and the world stage as so dense with actors that all of them have little choice

---

[33] For succinct statements of the unilateral form of imposed order, see Robert H. Jackson and Alan James (eds.), *States in a Changing World: A Contemporary Analysis* (Oxford: Clarendon Press, 1993) Alan James, *Sovereign Statehood: The Basis of International Society* (London: Allen & Unwin, 1986); and John J. Mearsheimer, "The False Promise of International Institutions," *International Security*, vol. 19 (Winter 1994–5), pp. 5–49.

[34] Compelling illustrations of the multilateral form of imposed order can be found in Emanuel Adler and Beverly Crawford (eds.), *Progress in Postwar International Relations* (New York: Columbia University Press, 1991); James L. Richardson, "Asia-Pacific: The Case for Geopolitical Optimism," *The National Interest*, no. 38 (Winter 1994–5), pp. 28–39; Volker Rittberger (ed.), *Regime Theory and International Relations* (Oxford: Clarendon Press, 1993); and John Gerard Ruggie (ed.), *Multilateralism Matters: The Theory and Praxis of an Institutional Form* (New York: Columbia University Press, 1993). For a cogent articulation of the multilateral form of imposed order in which it is argued that the long-term history of international organizations has been more successful in facilitating progress and stability than is appreciated, see Craig Murphy, *International Organization and Industrial Change: Global Governance since 1850* (New York: Oxford University Press, 1994).

but to enhance their own narrow self-interests. Like states, in other words, numerous actors along the Frontier are presumed to distrust cooperative arrangements and to be inclined toward narrow, self-serving courses of action. In effect, they place their subsystemic interests well ahead of larger systemic needs and aspirations. In so doing they seek out like-minded others in their close-at-hand environment for support and psychic comfort, a behavioral pattern that is perhaps best designated as *subgroupism*. This term is conceived to be more generic than the term "nationalism" since there are many other groups besides nations that have cohered more fully around common identities and sought thereby to advance shared goals.[35] It is not mere coincidence, for example, that in addition to secessionist movements in Europe and Russia, such diverse collectivities as the Mafia, youth gangs, the Palestinians, the Zapatistas, and the residents of Staten Island, have simultaneously experienced rampant subgroupism. Nor does the relocation of authority inherent in this powerful tendency toward subsystems and away from whole systems necessarily reach an end point. It is the nature of the process that subgroupism begets subgroupism (as Quebec presses for autonomy within Canada, for example, so do the Mohawks press for autonomy within Quebec), with the result that tendencies toward conflict tend to sustain the dynamics of subgroupism.[36]

The lacunae indicated by the lower right-hand cell of the matrix also spring from the premise that greater interdependence has eroded the authority of states, intensified the relevance and salience of other types of actors and thus brought into being bifurcated structures; but in this case these tendencies are viewed as having heightened the necessity of cooperation and as rendering less salient those that foster conflict. The result is a world stage posited as crowded with NGOs, multinational corporations, social movements, professional societies, epistemic communities, and other transnational entities concerned with environmental, humanitarian, and developmental goals that incline them

---

[35] Rosenau, *Turbulence in World Politics* pp. 132–35.

[36] While the processes of subgroupism are normally conflictual, it should be noted that some fragmentation is motivated by attempts to achieve better services through decentralization without harm to other groups. Subgroupism occurred in New York City, for example, when numerous municipal services were privatized and were "filling in for government" through business improvement districts, otherwise known as BIDs. See Thomas J. Lueck, "Business Districts Grow at Price of Accountability," *New York Times*, November 20, 1994, p. 1. More than 1,000 BIDs are presently functioning in the United States Cf. Judith Evans, "D.C. Wants to Join The Boom for BIDs," *Washington Post*, January 13, 1996, p. E1.

toward cooperative solutions as they participate in governance along the Frontier. For those who impose this form of order, *transnational* behavior is conceived as derived from a multiplicity of institutionalized and *ad hoc* arrangements through which governments and nongovernmental collectivities accommodate to each other and, in so doing, come to share responsibility for the course of events.[37]

But is it possible for these dissimilar and contradictory tendencies to be encompassed by a single worldview? The answer is simple: yes, by conceiving of each of them as subject to the dynamics and simultaneity of integration and fragmentation, both the logic and the lacunae of the realist and liberal perspectives are brought together under the same ontological roof. Thus the fragmegrative worldview is located at the center of table 3.4 and derives from the presumption that, indeed, world affairs are pervaded by contradiction, that powerful tendencies toward systemic cooperation and subsystemic conflict are both likely to endure, and that thus all four forms of behavior reflect some part of the true state of affairs. In effect, unilateral, multilateral, subgroup, and transnational activities are all conceived to be operative in SOAs along the Frontier, sometimes reinforcing each other, sometimes negating each other, but at all times at work in one part of the world or another. In effect, fragmegration is seen as sustaining deep-seated processes that foster both conflict and cooperation. Moreover, as indicated by the ragged edges of the space in the center of table 3.4, and as will be seen in chapter 6, the variability of the different forms of behavior is regarded as extensive enough to justify also labeling the worldview as one of *uneven fragmegration*, a term that further captures the diversity of the underlying order.

Given its many contradictions, does fragmegration have staying power or, like its predecessors, will it soon be replaced by a common sense of the epoch that is more stable and uniform? If both cooperative and conflictual processes are unfolding throughout the world, if disquieting tendencies are at work among domestic publics even as multilateral institutions become stronger, will the world eventually work itself out of these contradictory patterns and evolve a measure of order in the years ahead? Or does the deterioration of societal cohesion every-

---

[37] For affirmations of the transnational form of order, see Kenichi Ohmae, *The Borderless World: Power and Strategy in the Interlinked Economy* (New York: HarperBusiness, 1990), and Thomas Risse-Kappen (ed.), *Bringing Transnational Relations Back In: Non-State Actors, Domestic Structures and International Institutions* (Cambridge: Cambridge University Press, 1995).

where suggest the world is headed for more and more fragmentation – and in some instances for the breakdown of civility into outright warfare – even as shared norms about human rights and environmental improvement become increasingly widespread and valued?

The fragmegration worldview takes no position on such questions. As will be seen in chapter 6, it allows for the possibility that globalizing dynamics are more powerful than the localizing reactions they provoke, but it does not anticipate that either the cooperative or the conflictual tendencies are headed for ascendancy. Rather, unilateralism, multilateralism, transnationalism, and subgroupism are seen as existing side-by-side precisely because that is the complexity of our time. Such contradictory trends need to be viewed for what they are: reflections of the underlying structures of world affairs, few (if any) of which are temporary and most (if not all) of which are likely to become ever more deeply embedded in the course of events.

In other words, a fragmegrative perspective presumes that governance along the Frontier is more an emergent, chaotic pattern than a fixed arrangement. If order is slowly developing out of the ruins of the Cold War, it is not doing so with linearity or with clear-cut dimensions. Globalizing and localizing dynamics are not necessarily conflictual, but they unfold simultaneously and when they clash, they do so in different ways at different times in different parts of the world, with the result that fragmegration is profoundly nonlinear, uneven in its evolution, uneven in its intensity, uneven in its scope, and uneven in its direction.

Having identified the ontology, paradigm, and theory that form the core of the ensuing analysis, the chapters of part II undertake to elaborate these formulations as dimensions of the global contexts that shape governance along the Frontier. The goal of the elaboration is not so much the specification of hypotheses as it is that of indicating how the turbulence model, globalization, and fragmegration are linked to each other and to the dynamics of present-day governance.

Part II

Global contexts

4   Turbulence

> [World leaders today] are playing on a chessboard where international and domestic transactions form a seamless web, where the number of public and private players are barely countable let alone controllable, where the rules are yet to be defined, where the true nature of threats remains shrouded by their very multiplicity and complexity and where it is hard to judge what constitutes winning and losing.
>
> Leslie H. Gelb[1]

Notwithstanding differences among observers over how fundamental and pervasive the transformations at work in the world may be, few are prepared to argue against the description of the world summarized in this epigraph. Even those who view history as incessantly repeating itself acknowledge that some dimensions of the current scene are unfamiliar and not easily accommodated by comparisons with the past. As already noted, however, while some analysts judge the transformations to be important but not so crucial as to undermine or alter the underlying structures of the interstate system, others view the changes as giving rise to a new worldview and transforming long-standing parameters into dynamic variables. Since the latter perspective is the focus of this book, the objective of this chapter is to integrate these transformed variables into a theory – the turbulence model – that can facilitate analysis of governance along the Frontier.

This goal may seem to spring from a profound oxymoron. If the world is presently going through a period of considerable turbulence, one might well ask, how can it possibly be susceptible to governance? Does not turbulence signify the absence of the minimal degree of order required for the evolution of new SOAs or the alteration of old ones?

---

[1] Leslie H.Gelb, "Smog of Peace," *New York Times*, May 9, 1993, sect. 4, p. 15.

The answer offered here is twofold. First, governance along the Frontier does not necessarily imply success in maintaining control over its emergent dynamics; it refers only to the efforts through which SOAs are established and maintained. Thus governance can occur in the midst of upheaval and conflict, which is what we are witnessing as the twentieth century draws to a close. The subtitle of this book is perhaps best viewed as an accurate summary rather than a misleading oxymoron.

Second, the turbulence model takes no position on the degree to which the world is orderly. It is rather a theory designed to identify the dynamics that are both driving change and sustaining continuity, and my reliance on the model stems from satisfaction with its prior use as a means of probing closer to the dynamics of change[2] and its apparent advantages over the worldview, realism, which presently enjoys intellectual primacy among observers of world politics.[3]

A main advantage of the turbulence model is that it focuses less on outcomes and more on underpinnings, on the underlying patterns that lead to change and new configurations through which authority is exercised and new forms of governance created. As will be seen, such underpinnings include the viability of the sovereignty principle, the emergence of new types of actors and the capacity of states to manage them, the basic orientations which publics and governments have toward the nature of legitimacy, and the skills through which citizens and officials exercise their responsibilities and participate in world affairs. If such dynamics undergo transformation, then new forms of governance along the Frontier can be expected to have moved into place.

The distinction between underpinnings and outcomes is important because the former are not readily observable. The origins and sustenance of a widely shared worldview are to be found in minds and hearts – in ideas, orientations, predispositions, habits, and belief systems – and their existence thus has to be inferred from behavior rather than being the behavior itself. If these mental-emotional dynamics take a long time to mature, however, the outcomes that are observed in world politics

---

[2] A lengthy presentation of the turbulence model can be found in James N. Rosenau, *Turbulence in World Politics: A Theory of Change and Continuity* (Princeton: Princeton University Press, 1990).

[3] Realist theory and the turbulence model are elaborately contrasted in James N. Rosenau and Mary Durfee, *Thinking Theory Thoroughly: Coherent Approaches to an Incoherent World* (Boulder, CO: Westview Press, 1995).

can, for a long time, continue to seem like the same old way of conducting business. Manifest behavior, in other words, can reflect long-standing habits that still get acted upon even as they are steadily being undermined by the transformation of the deeper underpinnings from which the habits originally sprung. Thus a time lag exists between the time when underpinnings change and the reflection of those changes in the outcomes that comprise the daily routines and crises of global affairs.

Viewed in this way, the worldview on which the Cold War rested did not collapse suddenly in 1989. Rather, it began its long downhill slide well before the Berlin Wall came down and the people of Eastern Europe threw off the yoke of their communist regimes. These latter developments were only the last stage in a complex process whereby the foundations of the post-World War II order underwent transformation. While pundits, politicians, academics, and people everywhere were surprised when governments throughout Eastern European capitals were, suddenly, replaced, the pervasiveness of the surprise is not so much a measure of the rapidity with which history changed course as it is a measure of how fully people tend to focus on outcomes rather than underpinnings when they respond to the course of events. Had they been sensitive to underpinnings, to the deeper sources of the events that caught their eyes, they would have appreciated well before 1989 that the theories, paradigms, and ontology necessary to shape a new worldview were in the process of evolving.

The turbulence model

At the theoretical heart of the shift to a fragmegration worldview is the simultaneous transformation of three primary parameters. If only one or two had undergone change, it is unlikely that this worldview would have emerged. But with the complexity and dynamism of all three having greatly increased, the world entered into a period of turbulence that continues until this day and, for reasons that will become clear, that will probably endure for decades. Indeed, the turbulence model presumes that not since the period which culminated in the Treaty of Westphalia in 1648 have these basic parameters undergone extensive and rapid alteration. Yes, there have been world wars, massive revolutions, prolonged depressions, and other world-shaking developments, but in all such cases the basic parameters of world affairs either remained intact or returned to their prior state once the upheaval had subsided. In the present period, however, all three parameters have undergone the transformations described below, transformations that continue to roil world politics and infuse the prevailing global scene with an aura of pervasive uncertainty.[4]

The three parameters involve the overall structure of global politics (a macro parameter), the authority structures that link macro collectivities to citizens (a macro-micro parameter), and the skills of citizens (a micro parameter).[5] The transformation of each of these parameters is judged to have begun in the 1950s and the continuing simultaneity of the transformations is considered a major reason why signs of a new worldview – of deep underpinnings fostering unexpected outcomes and a new common sense of the epoch – took politicians, journalists, academics, and others so utterly by surprise when the collapse of communism rendered them unmistakably manifest late in 1989. Table 4.1 summarizes the changes that have infused high degrees of complexity and variability into the three parameters.

Incisive insights into the fragmegration worldview are crucially dependent on appreciating the profoundly interactive nature of the three parameters – on recognizing that even as individuals shape the actions and orientations of the collectivities to which they belong, so do the goals, policies, and laws of the latter shape the actions and orientations of individuals. Much of the rapidity of the transformations at work in world politics can be traced to the ways in which the changes in each parameter stimulate and reinforce the changes in the other two.

The micro parameter: a skill revolution

The transformation of the micro parameter is to be found in the shifting capabilities of citizens everywhere. Individuals have undergone what can properly be termed a skill revolution. For a variety of reasons ranging from the advance of communications technology to the greater

---

[4] For the analysis which concludes that the system's parameters are undergoing their first profound transformation since 1648, see Rosenau, *Turbulence in World Politics*, chaps. 4–5.

[5] Rosenau, *Turbulence in World Politics*, pp. 10–11. For a formulation that identifies six parameters, see Mark W. Zacher, "The Decaying Pillars of the Westphalian Temple: Implications for International Order and Governance," in James N. Rosenau and Ernst-Otto Czempiel (eds.), *Governance Without Government: Order and Change in World Politics* (Cambridge: Cambridge University Press, 1992), chap. 3.

Table 4.1. *The transformation of three global parameters*

	From	To
micro parameter	individuals less analytically skillful and emotionally competent	individuals more analytically skillful and emotionally competent
macro-micro parameter	authority structures in place as people rely on traditional and/or constitutional sources of legitimacy to comply with directives emanating from appropriate macro institutions	authority structures in crisis as people evolve performance criteria for legitimacy and compliance with the directives issued by macro officials
macro parameter	anarchic system of nation-states	bifurcation of anarchic system into state- and multi-centric subsystems

intricacies of life in an ever more interdependent world, people have become increasingly more competent in assessing where they fit in international affairs and how their behavior can be aggregated into significant collective outcomes. Included among these newly refined skills, moreover, is an expanded capacity to focus emotion as well as to analyze the causal sequences that sustain the course of events.[6]

Put differently, it is a grievous error to assume that citizenries are a constant in politics, that the world has rapidly changed and complexity greatly increased without consequences for the individuals who comprise the collectivities that interact on the global stage. As long as people were uninvolved in and apathetic about world affairs, it made sense to

[6] For extensive surveys of findings that highlight the importance of emotional skills, see Daniel Goleman, *Emotional Intelligence* (New York: Bantam Books, 1995), and Shinobu Kitayama and Hazel Rose Markus (eds.), *Emotion and Culture: Empirical Studies of Mutual Influence* (Washington, DC: American Psychological Association, 1994). The case for focusing conceptual and empirical attention on these skills is cogently made in Jonathan Mercer, "Approaching Emotion in International Politics," paper presented at the Annual Meeting of the International Studies Association, San Diego (April 1996).

treat them as a constant parameter and to look to variabilities at the macro level for explanations of what transpires in global affairs. Today, however, the skill revolution has expanded the learning capacity of individuals, enriched their cognitive maps, and elaborated the scenarios with which they anticipate the future. It is no accident that the squares of the world's cities have lately been filled with large crowds demanding change.

It is tempting to affirm the impact of the skill revolution by pointing to the many restless publics that have protested authoritarian rule and clamored for more democratic forms of governance. While the worldwide thrust toward an expansion of political liberties and a diminution in the central control of economies is certainly linked to citizens and publics having greater appreciation of their circumstances, there is nothing inherent in the skill revolution that leads people in more democratic directions. The change in the micro parameter is not so much one of new orientations as it is an evolution of new capacities for cogent analysis. The world's peoples are not so much converging around the same values as sharing a greater ability to recognize and articulate their values. Thus this parametric change is global in scope because it has enabled Islamic fundamentalists, Asian peasants, and Western sophisticates alike to serve better their respective orientations. And thus, too, the commotion in public squares has not been confined to cities in any particular region of the world. From Seoul to Prague, from Soweto to Beijing, from Paris to the West Bank, from Belgrade to Rangoon – to mention only a few of the places where collective demands have lately been voiced – the transformation of the micro parameter has been unmistakably evident.

Equally important, evidence of the skill revolution can be readily discerned in trend data for education, television viewing, computer usage, travel, and a host of other situations in which people are able to extend their analytic and emotional skills. And hardly less relevant, a number of local circumstances – from traffic jams to water shortages, from budget crises to racial conflicts, from flows of refugees to threats of terrorism – relentlessly confront people with social, economic, and political complexities that impel them to forego their rudimentary premises and replace them with more elaborate conceptions of how to respond to the challenges of daily life.

This is not say that people everywhere are now equal in the skills they bring to bear upon world politics. Obviously, the analytically rich continue to be more skillful than the analytically poor.[7] But while the gap between the two ends of the skill continuum may be no narrower than in the past, the advance in the competencies of those at every point on the continuum is sufficient to contribute to a major transformation in the conduct of world affairs. In effect, the turbulence model posits a world of individuals who cannot be easily deceived and who can be readily mobilized on behalf of goals they comprehend and means they approve. This worldview is thus more inclusive than its predecessors. Elites are conceived to retain control over resources, communications, and policy-making processes, but they are also viewed as increasingly constrained by publics who follow their activities, who are more skilled at knowing when to engage in collective action, and who are ever ready to demand appropriate performances in exchange for support.

The macro-micro parameter: a relocation of authority

This parameter-turned-variable consists of the recurrent orientations, practices, and patterns through which citizens at the micro level are linked to their collectivities at the macro level. In effect, it encompasses SOAs wherein large aggregations, private organizations as well as public agencies, achieve and sustain the cooperation and compliance of their memberships. Historically, SOAs were founded on traditional criteria of legitimacy derived from constitutional and legal sources. Under these circumstances individuals were habituated to compliance with the directives issued by higher authorities. They did what they were told to do because . . . well, because that is what one did. As a consequence, authority structures remained in place for decades, even centuries, as people unquestioningly yielded to the dictates of governments or the leadership of any other organizations with which they were affiliated. For a variety of reasons, including the expanded analytic skills of citizens as well as a number of other factors noted below, the foundations of this parameter have also undergone erosion. Throughout the world today, in both public and private settings, the sources of authority have shifted from traditional to performance criteria of legitimacy. Where SOAs were once in place, in other words, now they are in crisis,

---

[7] For systematic data on the greater skills of elites across sixty years, see James N. Rosenau and W. Michael Fagen, "Increasingly Skillful Citizens: A New Dynamism in World Politics?," paper presented at the Joint Conference of the Japan Association of International Relations and the International Studies Association, Makuhari, Japan (September 20–22, 1996).

with the readiness of individuals to comply with governing directives being very much a function of their assessment of the performances of the authorities.[8] The more the performance record is considered appropriate – in terms of satisfying needs, moving toward goals, and providing stability – the more they are likely to cooperate and comply. The less they approve the performance record, the more they are likely to withhold their compliance or otherwise complicate the efforts of macro authorities.

As a consequence of the pervasive authority crises, states and governments have become less effective in confronting challenges and implementing policies. They can still maintain public order through their police powers, but their ability to address substantive issues and solve substantive problems is declining as people find fault with their performances and thus question their authority, redefine the bases of their legitimacy, and withhold their cooperation. Such a transformation is being played out dramatically today in the former Soviet Union, as it was earlier within the countries of Eastern Europe. But authority crises are equally evident in every other part of the world, albeit the crises take different forms in different countries and different types of private organizations. In Canada the authority crisis is rooted in linguistic, cultural, and constitutional issues as Quebec seeks to secede or otherwise redefine its relationship to the central government. In France the devolution of authority was legally sanctioned through legislation that privatized several governmental activities and relocated authority away from Paris and toward greater jurisdiction for the provinces. In China the provinces enjoy a wider jurisdiction by, in effect, ignoring or defying Beijing. In Yugoslavia the crisis led to violence and civil war. In some crisis-ridden countries of Latin America the challenge to traditional authority originates with insurgent movements or the drug trade. In the United States the government was forced to shut down twice in late 1995. In Israel, India, Bangladesh, and many other countries, uneasy stalemates prevail in the policy-making process as governments have proven incapable of bridging societal divisions sufficiently to undertake the decisive actions necessary to address and resolve intractable problems.

---

[8] For recent formulations of the nature of authority and the kinds of crisis into which it can evolve, see Nicholas N. Kittrie, *The War Against Authority: From the Crisis of Legitimacy to a New Social Contract* (Baltimore: Johns Hopkins University Press, 1995), and Bruce Lincoln, *Authority: Construction and Corrosion* (Chicago: University of Chicago Press, 1994).

Nor is the global authority crisis confined to states and governments. It is also manifest in subnational jurisdictions, international organizations, and transnational entities. Indeed, in some cases the crises unfold simultaneously at different levels: just as Moldavia rejected Moscow's authority, for example, so did several ethnic groups within Moldavia seek to establish their own autonomy by rejecting Moldavia's authority. Similarly, to cite conspicuous examples of crises in international and transnational organizations, UNESCO and the Catholic Church have experienced decentralizing dynamics that are at least partly rooted in the replacement of traditional with performance criteria of legitimacy.

The relocating of authority precipitated by the structural crises of states and governments at the national level occurs in several directions, depending in good part on the scope of the enterprises people perceive as more receptive to their concerns and thus more capable of meeting their increased preoccupation with the adequacy of performances. In many instances this has involved "inward" relocation toward subnational groups – toward ethnic minorities, local governments, single-issue organizations, religious and linguistic groupings, political factions, trade unions, and the like. In some instances the relocating process has moved in the opposite direction, across the domestic-foreign Frontier, toward more encompassing collectivities that transcend national boundaries. The beneficiaries of this "outward" reallocation of authority range from supranational organizations like the European Union to intergovernmental organizations like the International Labor Organization, from nongovernmental organizations like Greenpeace to professional groups such as the Médecins Sans Frontières, from multinational corporations to inchoate social movements that join together environmentalists or women in different countries, from informal international regimes like those active in different industries to formal associations of political parties like those that share conservative or socialist ideologies – to mention but a few types of larger-than-national entities that have become the focus of legitimacy sentiments.

Needless to say, these multiple directions in which authority is being relocated serve to widen the Frontier and reinforce the tensions between the centralizing and decentralizing dynamics that underlie the turbulence presently at work in world affairs. As will be seen in chapter 11, they also undermine the principle of national sovereignty.

It follows that governance along the Frontier rests on an increasingly fluid pecking order. Although still hierarchical in a number of respects, the weakening of states and the pervasiveness of authority crises has rendered the pecking order more vulnerable to challenges and more susceptible to changes. Put differently, with states weakened by paralysis and stalemate, the power equation underlying the pecking order has been substantially altered. Where raw elements of power – armies, nuclear weapons, oil deposits, etc. – were once the major terms of the equation, now their values have declined relative to such complex terms as societal cohesion, the capacity to draft soldiers, decisiveness in policy-making, and the many other components of a country's ability to surmount authority crises and avoid paralyzing political stalemates. Put in journalistic terms, "In the post-Cold War era, a better measure of a country's power than the number of its nuclear missiles is the number of votes it controls in the International Monetary Fund."[9]

The macro parameter: a bifurcation of global structures

For more than three centuries the overall structure of world politics has been founded on an anarchic system of sovereign nation-states that did not have to answer to any higher authority and that managed their conflicts through accommodation or war. States were not the only actors on the world stage, but traditionally they were the dominant collectivities which set the rules by which the others had to live. The resulting state-centric world evolved its own hierarchy based on the way in which military, economic, and political power was distributed. Depending on how many states had the greatest concentration of power, at different historical moments the overall system was varyingly marked by hegemonic, bipolar, or multipolar structures.

Today, however, the state-centric world is no longer predominant. Due to the skill revolution, the worldwide spread of authority crises, and several other sources of turbulence (noted below), it has undergone bifurcation. A complex multi-centric world of diverse, relatively autonomous actors has emerged, replete with structures, processes, and decision rules of its own. The sovereignty-free actors of the multi-centric world consist of multinational corporations, ethnic minorities, subnational governments and bureaucracies, professional societies, social movements, political parties, transnational organizations, and the like. Individually, and sometimes jointly, they compete, conflict, cooperate, or otherwise interact with the sovereignty-bound actors of the state-

---

[9] Michael Dobbs, "Christopher Pursues Political Objectives by Economic Means," *Washington Post*, February 12, 1996, p. A14.

centric world.[10] Table 4.2 delineates the main differences between the multi-centric and state-centric worlds.

While the bifurcation of world politics has not pushed states to the edge of the global stage, they are no longer the only key actors. Now they are faced with the new task of coping with disparate rivals from another world as well as the challenges posed by counterparts in their own world. A major outcome of this transformation of macro structures is, obviously, a further confounding of the arrangements through which governance across the Frontier is sustained. Not only have authority crises within states rendered the international pecking order more fluid, but the advent of bifurcation and the autonomy of actors in the multi-centric world have so swollen the population of entities that occupy significant roles on the world stage that their hierarchical differences were scrambled well before the end of the Cold War intensified the struggle for global status. Or at least there are only a few issue areas – such as nuclear proliferation – where the outlines of hierarchy are unequivocal.

Good insights into the sometimes-conflict-sometimes-cooperate interactions of the state-centric and multi-centric worlds are readily available when the United Nations convenes summit meetings on one or another issue high on the global agenda and the multi-centric world organizes simultaneous deliberations on the same issues in or around the same city. A Rio de Janeiro meeting on the environment in 1992, a Vienna meeting on human rights in 1993, and a Beijing meeting on the rights of women in 1995 are illustrative in this regard. Indeed, such parallel conferences have become institutionalized and serve as main channels through which the two worlds interact in both formal and informal settings.

Sources of global turbulence

Thus far, however, the discussion has been more descriptive than explanatory. To depict a world with the new parametric values represented by the skill revolution, the relocation of authority, and the bifurcation of global structures is not to account for the dynamics that underlie the parametric transformations. What drives the turbulence? The factors relevant to this question were suggested earlier in figure 3.1,

---

[10] For an explanation of why the terms "sovereignty-free" and "sovereignty-bound" seem appropriate to differentiate between state and nonstate actors, see Rosenau, *Turbulence in World Politics*, p. 36.

Table 4.2. *Structure and process in the two worlds of world politics*

	State-centric world	Multi-centric world
Number of essential actors	Fewer than 200	Hundreds of thousands
Prime dilemma of actors	Security	Autonomy
Principal goals of actors	Preservation of territorial integrity and physical security	Increase in world market shares; maintenance of integration of subsystems
Ultimate resort for realizing goals	Armed force	Withholding of cooperation or compliance
Normative priorities	Processes, especially those that preserve sovereignty and the rule of law	Outcomes, especially those that expand human rights, justice, and wealth
Modes of collaboration	Formal alliances whenever possible	Temporary coalitions
Scope of agenda	Limited	Unlimited
Rules governing interactions among actors	Diplomatic practices	*Ad hoc*, situational
Distribution of power among actors	Hierarchical by amount of power	Relative equality as far as initiating action is concerned
Interaction patterns among actors	Symmetrical	Asymmetrical
Locus of leadership	Great powers	Innovative actors with extensive resources
Institutionalization	Well-established	Emergent
Susceptibility to change	Relatively low	Relatively high
Control over outcomes	Concentrated	Diffused
Bases of decisional structures	Formal authority; law	Various types of authority; effective leadership

Source: Reproduced from James N. Rosenau, *Turbulence in World Politics: A Theory of Change and Continuity* (Princeton: Princeton University Press, 1990), p. 250.

but these need to be amplified, at least briefly, if we are to assess the institutions and processes of governance along the Frontier.

Proliferation of actors

Perhaps few facts about world politics are better known than those which describe the huge increase in the human population since the end of World War II. Where the world's population was in excess of 2.5 billion in 1950, by 1990 the figure had passed 5 billion and it continues to grow at a rapid rate. This demographic explosion lies at the heart of many of the world's problems and is also a continual source of the complexity and dynamism that has overwhelmed the parameters of the global system. Ever greater numbers of people have exerted pressure for technological innovations. They have meant larger, more articulate, and increasingly unwieldy publics. They have contributed to the unmanageability of public affairs that has weakened states, stimulated the search for more responsive collectivities, and hastened the advent of paralyzing authority crises. And through the sheer weight of their numbers they have created new and intractable public issues, of which famines and threats to the environment are only the more conspicuous examples.

But the proliferation of relevant actors is not confined to the huge growth in the number of individual citizens. No less important for present purposes is the vast increase in the number and type of collective actors whose leaders can clamber onto the global stage and act on behalf of their memberships. Indeed, this deepening density of the global system may be due less to the unorganized complexity fostered by the population explosion and more to the organized complexity consisting of millions of factions, associations, parties, organizations, movements, interest groups, and a host of other kinds of collectivities that share an aspiration to advance their welfare and a sensitivity to the ways in which a rapidly changing world may require them to network with each other.

The dizzying increase in the density of actors that sustain world politics stems from a variety of sources. In part it is a product of the trend toward ever greater specialization that is the hallmark of industrial and postindustrial economies and the greater interdependence that they foster. In part, too, it is a consequence of widespread dissatisfaction with large-scale collectivities and the performance of existing authorities, a discontent that underlies the turn to less encompassing organizations that are more fully expressive of close-at-hand needs and wants.

Relevant here also are the expanded analytic skills of citizens which enable them to appreciate how they can join in collective actions that serve as avenues for expressing their aspirations. Whatever the reasons for the proliferation of collective actors, however, their sheer number has been a prime stimulus to the evolution of the multi-centric world and to the authority crises that have wracked the state-centric world.

The state-centric world has also undergone substantial enlargement, although on a lesser scale, with the number of member states of the UN having more than tripled since its inception in 1945. Indeed, this growth has contributed to the huge increase of actors in the multi-centric world, since each new state carved out of the former colonial empires has spawned its own array of nongovernmental actors who have then contributed to the formation of new transnational networks. The organized complexity and deepening density of the global system, in other words, has derived from formal state-making dynamics as well as the multiplication of organizations within societies.

Impact of dynamic technologies

The technological explosion since World War II is no less impressive than its demographic counterpart. In a wide number of fields, from agriculture to transportation, from communications to medicine, from biogenetics to artificial intelligence, substantial advances have been made in humankind's ability to cope with the laws of nature. As a result, geographic distances have been shortened, social distances have been narrowed, and economic barriers have been circumvented. The world gets smaller and smaller as its peoples become more and more interdependent, processes that have had enormous consequences for the skills of individuals, their relations with higher authorities, and the macro structures through which their affairs are (or are not) managed. It is highly doubtful, in short, whether world affairs would have been overtaken by turbulence had major technologies not exploded in the last forty years.

Two of these explosions, the nuclear and communications revolutions, stand out as especially relevant to the complexity and dynamism that have inundated the three prime parameters. The extraordinary advances in military weaponry subsequent to World War II, marked by nuclear warheads and the rocketry to deliver them, imposed a context on the conduct of world affairs that, in effect, increasingly inhibited recourse to military action and reduced the probability of a major global war. The nuclear revolution thus had the ironic consequence of depriving states of one of their prime instruments for pursuing and defending their interests. To be sure, arms races, the Cuban missile crisis, the stand-off with North Korea, and other such events infused this context with a high degree of volatility that often made it seem very fragile indeed. Even as it emphasized the extraordinary capacities several states had acquired, however, so did the nuclear context point up the limits of state action and thereby opened the door for challenges to the authority of states. It is no accident that a series of transnational, large-scale, and powerful social movements – in the realms of peace, ecology, and women's rights – acquired momentum during the same period as states added substantially to their nuclear arsenals.

The communications revolution is hardly less central as a source of global turbulence. The rapidity and clarity with which ideas and information now circulate through television broadcasting, VCRs, the Internet, fax machines, satellite hook-ups, fiber-optic telephone circuits, and many other microelectronic devices have rendered national bound-aries ever more porous and world affairs ever more vulnerable to cas-cading demands. Events that once took weeks and months to unfold now develop within days and hours. Financial transactions that once were mired in long delays can now be consummated in seconds. Diplomats, adversaries, military commanders, and publics who once had to wait long periods before reaching conclusions are now able to act decisively. Today the whole world, its leaders and its citizenries, crowds the information highway and instantaneously shares the same pictures and descriptions, albeit not necessarily the same understandings, of what is transpiring in any situation.

Examples of the cascading effects of the communications revolution abound. Most conspicuous perhaps is the impact of the Cable News Network (CNN), which is said to be on and continuously watched in every embassy and every foreign office of every country in the world and which during the Gulf War served as the basis for diplomatic and military action on both sides of the conflict.[11] Hardly less telling is the example of the French journal *Actuel* that was so upset by the crack-down in Tiananmen Square that, having compiled a mock edition of the *People's Daily* that contained numerous accounts the Chinese leadership did not want their people to read, sent it to every fax machine in China

---

[11] On the first night of the Gulf War CNN's prime-time viewership went from its normal 560,000 to 11,400,000. Cf. Thomas B. Rosenstiel, "CNN: The Channel to the World," *Los Angeles Times*, January 23, 1991, p. A12.

in the fall of 1989.[12] Or consider the explosive implications of the fact that 5 percent of Brazil's households had television receiving sets when its 1960 presidential election was held and that this figure had swollen to 72 percent at the time of the next presidential contest in 1989.

Given the magnitude of these communications dynamics, it is hardly surprising that people everywhere have become more analytically skill-ful, more ready to challenge authority, and more capable of engaging in collective actions that press their demands. Their information may be skewed and their understanding of the stakes at risk in situations may be loaded with bias, but the stimuli to action are now ever present. Today individuals can literally see the aggregation of demands – i.e., the coming together of publics and the acquiescence of governments – and how the participation of their counterparts elsewhere can have mean-ingful consequences. Likewise, the availability of high-tech communications equipment has enabled leaders in the public and private sectors to turn quickly to their memberships and mobilize them in support of their immediate goals in the multi- and state-centric worlds.[13]

Globalization of national economies

If the communications revolution has been a prime stimulus of the ten-dencies toward decentralization through the empowering of citizens and subnational groups, the dynamics at work in the economics realm are equally powerful as sources of the centralizing tendencies. The power of these globalizing economic processes is elaborated in several of the ensuing chapters, but suffice it to note that they started in the technologically most advanced sectors of the global economy where, following the economic crisis of 1973-4, a new kind of production organization geared to limited orders for a variety of specialized markets began to replace the large plants that produced standardized goods. Consequently, with the products of numerous semi-skilled workers brought together in big plants no longer competitive with the outputs of a large number of small units that could be tailored to shift-ing demands, business became concerned about restructuring capital so as to be more effective in world markets. And as capital became increas-

---

[12] An account of *Actuel's* efforts can be found in *Europe: Magazine of the European Community* (April 1990), pp. 40–1.

[13] For an extensive elaboration of the diverse ways in which the microelectronic revolu-tion has impacted on the conduct of public affairs, see Rosenau, *Turbulence in World Politics*, chap. 13.

ingly internationalized, so did groups of producers and plants in different territorial jurisdictions become linked in order to supply markets in many countries, all of which fostered and sustained a financial system global in scope and centered in major cities such as New York, Tokyo, and London. In short, "geographic space is losing meaning as a basis for the organization of markets."[14]

Stated differently, capital, production, labor, and markets have all been globalized to the point where financiers, entrepreneurs, workers, and consumers are now deeply enmeshed in networks of the world economy that have superseded the traditional political jurisdictions of national scope. Such a transformation was bound to impact upon the established parameters of world politics. Among other things, it served to loosen the ties of producers and workers to their states, to expand the horizons within which citizens pondered their self-interests, and to foster the formation of transnational organizations that could operate on a global scale to advance the interests of their members. The rapid growth and maturation of the multi-centric world can in good part be traced to the extraordinary dynamism and expansion of the global economy. And so can the weakening of the state, which is no longer the manager of the national economy and has become, instead, an instrument for adjusting the national economy to the exigencies of an expanding world economy. As one observer put it, "In effect, governments are acting as the midwives of globalization."[15]

Advent of interdependence issues

But the evolution of the world economy is not the only source of centralizing tendencies at work in global life. There are also a number of new, transnational problems that are crowding high on the world's agenda and forcing the globalization of certain kinds of issues. Where political agendas used to consist of issues that governments could cope with on their own or through interstate bargaining, now these conventional

---

[14] Stephen J. Kobrin, "The Architecture of Globalization: State Sovereignty in a Networked Global Economy," in John H. Dunning (ed.), *Globalization, Governments and Competition* (Oxford: Oxford University Press, 1996), p. 4 [in typescript version].

[15] Janine Brodie, "New State Forms, New Political Spaces," in Robert Boyer and Daniel Drache (eds.), *States Against Markets: The Limits of Globalization* (London: Routledge, 1996), p. 386. For a formulation in which states are posited as being "whipsawed" by economic globalization, see Philip G. Cerny, "The Dynamics of Financial Globalization: Technology, Market Structure, and Policy Response," *Policy Sciences*, vol. 27 (1994), pp. 319–42.

issues are being joined by challenges that by their very nature do not fall exclusively within the jurisdiction of states and have rendered the Frontier increasingly porous. Six current challenges are illustrative: environmental pollution, currency crises, crime and the drug trade, terrorism, AIDS, and the flow of refugees. Each of these issues embrace processes that involve participation by large numbers of citizens and that inherently and inescapably transgress national boundaries – the winds at Chernobyl, for example, carried the pollution into many countries and intruded upon many lives – and thus make it impossible for governments to treat them as domestic problems or to address them through conventional diplomatic channels.

Since these challenges are fueled by shrinking social and geographic distances, such problems can appropriately be called "interdependence" issues. And, given their origins and scope, they can also be regarded as important centralizing dynamics in the sense that they impel cooperation on a transnational scale. Each of the six issues, for instance, is the focus of either transnational social movements or *ad hoc* international institutions forged to ameliorate, if not to resolve, the boundary-crossing problems it has created. To be sure, many of the issues may originate in local settings that are addressed by local or state authorities, but the fact that their consequences are global in scope means that transnational authorities have to address them as well.

The advent of interdependence issues has contributed to the present era of turbulence in world politics in several ways. First, as in the case of the economic changes, such issues have given citizens pause about their states as the ultimate problem-solver and, in the case of those who join social movements, they have reoriented people to ponder a restructuring of their loyalties. In so doing, interdependence issues have also fostered the notion that transnational cooperation can be as central to world politics as interstate conflict. Equally important, given their diffuse, boundary-crossing structure, these types of issues are spawning a whole range of transnational associations that are furthering the density of the multi-centric world and, as a result, are likely to serve as additional challenges to the authority of states.

The weakening of states

As stressed in chapter 18, while it seems clear that states have suffered a loss in their authority, they have not become peripheral to global affairs. On the contrary, states continue to maintain their world and its international system, and in so doing they continue to infuse it with vitality and a capacity for adapting to change. After all, it was the state-centric and not the multi-centric world that created multilateral organizations such as the United Nations, that developed the arrangements through which the nuclear revolution has been contained, that responded to the demands for decolonization in such a way as to produce the hierarchical arrangements that have enabled the industrial countries to dominate those in the Third World, and that framed the debate over the distribution of the world's resources – to mention only a few of the more obvious ways in which states have shaped and still shape the ongoing realities of world politics. To discern a decline in the capacity of states, therefore, is not in any way to imply that they are no longer relevant actors on the world stage.

Indeed, some analysts see states as increasingly robust and explicitly reject the patterns highlighted here. This reasoning posits the state as so deeply ensconced in the routines and institutions of politics, both domestic and international, that the erosion of its capabilities and influence is unimaginable. The state has proven itself, the argument goes, by performing vital functions that serve the needs of people, which is why it has been around more than three hundred years. In its longevity, moreover, the state has overcome all kinds of challenges, many of which are far more severe than the globalization of national economies and the emergence of new types of collectivities. Indeed, the argument concludes, there are all kinds of ways in which states may actually be accumulating greater capabilities[16] and their interstate system may be increasingly competent in managing global affairs.[17]

Chapter 18 undertakes to amplify a refutation of this perspective. Here it is sufficient to note that it seems just as erroneous to treat states as constants as it is to view the skills of citizens as invulnerable to change. States are not eternal verities; they are as susceptible to variability as any other social system, and this includes the possibility of a decline in their sovereignty as well as an erosion of their ability to address problems, much less to come up with satisfactory solutions to

---

[16] For cogent arguments along these lines, see Robert H. Jackson and Alan James, "The Character of Independent Statehood," in R.H. Jackson and A. James (eds.), *States in a Changing World: A Contemporary Analysis* (Oxford: Clarendon Press, 1993), chap. 1, and Arie Kacowics, "Reinventing the Wheel: The Attacks on the State and Its Resilience," paper presented at the Annual Meeting of the International Studies Association, Chicago (February 22–25, 1995).

[17] Cf. G. John Ikenberry, "The Myth of Post-Cold War Chaos," *Foreign Affairs*, vol. 75 (May/June 1996), pp. 79–91.

them. Indeed, viewed from the perspective of the growing density of populations, the expanding complexity of the organized segments of society, the globalization of national economies, the relentless pressures of technological innovation, the challenge of subgroups intent upon achieving greater autonomy, and the endless array of intractable problems which forms the modern political agenda, it seems evident that world affairs have cumulated to a severity of circumstances that are likely to continue to lessen the capacity of states to be decisive and effective. And added to these difficulties is the fact that citizenries, through the micro-electronic revolution, are continuously exposed to the scenes of authority crises elsewhere in the world, scenes which are bound to give rise to doubts and demands in even the most stable of polities and thus to foment a greater readiness to question the legitimacy of governmental policies.[18]

Accordingly, while states may not be about to exit from the political stage, they do seem likely to become increasingly vulnerable. And as such, as less effective managers of their own affairs, they also serve as stimuli to turbulence in world politics – as sources of autonomy in the multi-centric world, of internal challenges to established authority, and of more analytically skillful citizens demanding more effective performances from their leaders.

Subgroupism

Since there is a widespread inclination to refer loosely to "nationalism" as a source of the turbulent state of world politics, it is perhaps useful to be more precise about the collective nature of those decentralizing tendencies wherein individuals and groups feel readier to challenge authority and reorient their loyalties. As previously noted, the authority crises that result from such challenges can be either of an "outward" or an "inward" kind, depending on whether the aspiration is to relocate authority in more or less encompassing jurisdictions than those that operate at the national level. In a number of instances of both kinds of relocation, the motivation that sustains them is not so deeply emotional as to qualify as an "ism." The creation of subnational administrative divisions, for example, can stem from detached efforts to rationalize the

---

[18] There is evidence, for example, that the collapse of authority in East Germany in the fall of 1989 was stimulated by the televised scenes of authority being challenged in Tiananmen Square several months earlier. See Tara Sonenshine, "The Revolution Has Been Televised," *Washington Post National Weekly Edition*, October 8–14, 1990, p. 29.

work of a governmental agency or private organization, and the process of implementing the decentralized arrangements can occur in the context of reasoned dialogue and calm decision-making. Often, however, intense concerns and powerful attachments can accompany the press for new arrangements, feelings and commitments strong enough to justify regarding the outward relocations as evoking "transnationalism," "supranationalism," or "internationalism." The inward relocations marked by comparable intensities are perhaps best labeled by the generic term "subgroupism."

As previously indicated, subgroupism refers to those deep affinities which people develop toward the close-at-hand associations, organizations, and subcultures with which they have been historically, professionally, economically, socially, or politically linked and to which they attach their highest priorities. Subgroupism values the in-group over the out-group, sometimes treating the two as adversaries but sometimes positing them as susceptible to extensive cooperation. Subgroupism can derive from and be sustained by a variety of sources, not the least being disappointment in – and alienation from – the performances of the whole system in which the subgroup is located. Most of all perhaps, its intensities are the product of long-standing historical roots that span generations and that get reinforced by an accumulated lore surrounding past events in which the subgroup survived trying circumstances.

That subgroupism can be deeply implanted in the consciousness of peoples is manifestly apparent in the resurfacing of strong ethnic identities throughout Eastern Europe and the former Soviet Union when, after decades, the authoritarian domination of communist parties came to an end. In those cases, the subgroups were historic nations and the accompanying feelings can thus be readily regarded as expressions of nationalism. Not all, or even a preponderance, of these decentralizing tendencies attach to nations, however. Governmental subdivisions, political parties, labor unions, professional societies, and a host of other types of subgroups can also evoke intense attachments, and it would grossly understate the relevance of the decentralizing tendencies at work in world affairs to ignore these other forms of close-at-hand ties. Indeed, in some respects these tendencies resemble the decentralized arrangements of the medieval era[19] and its highly decentralized, con-

---

[19] The possibility of a neomedieval order is set forth in Hedley Bull, *The Anarchical Society: The Study of Order in World Politics* (New York: Columbia University Press, 1977), pp. 254–5.

flictual, and disparate structures.[20] Accordingly, it seems preferable to regard the emotional dimensions of the generic decentralizing tendencies as those of subgroupism and to reserve the concept of nationalism for those subgroup expressions that revolve around nations and feelings of ethnicity.[21]

The spread of poverty and the developing world

Underlying the bifurcation of world politics into state- and multi-centric worlds has been another split – between industrially developed and underdeveloped countries – that has also contributed substantially to the onset of turbulence. This regional split between the North and the South – known during the Cold War as the First and Third Worlds – is a gulf that seems destined to widen and sustain, even extend, the processes of turbulence. The terrible problems and thwarted aspirations of peoples in the South are not going to be ameliorated in the foreseeable future and will thus continue to roil global waters. Among other things, the diverse and numerous countries of the South have added to the complexity and dynamism of global structures, sharpened performance criteria of legitimacy, enriched the analytic skills of the underprivileged, hastened the transnationalization of economies, corporations, and social movements, limited the authority of Northern states over their production facilities, intensified the flow of people from South to North, lengthened the list of interdependence issues, and strengthened the tendencies toward subgroupism.

Even as the developing countries have become resentful over their dependence on the industrialized world for trade, technology, and many of the other prerequisites necessary to fulfill their desire for industrial development, so have they added to the decentralizing tendencies in the multi-centric world. Composed of tribes and ethnic groups artificially brought together under state banners by decolonization, besieged by multinational corporations seeking to extend their operations and

---

[20] A disquieting exploration of the structures of subgroupism is available in Robert D. Kaplan, "The Coming Anarchy: How Scarcity, Crime, Overpopulation, Tribalism, and Disease Are Destroying the Social Fabric of Our Planet," *The Atlantic Monthly*, February 1994, pp. 44–76.

[21] For more elaborate inquiries into the problems that attach to the various concepts associated with nationalism, see Michael Billig, *Banal Nationalism* (London: Sage Publications, 1995); Ernst B. Haas, "What Is Nationalism and Why Should We Study It?" *International Organization*, vol. 40 (Summer 1986), pp. 707–44; and Arthur N. Waldron, "Theories of Nationalism and Historical Explanation," *World Politics*, vol. 37 (April 1985), pp. 416–33.

markets, and plagued with internal divisions and massive socio-economic problems, developing countries have added greatly to the breadth and depth of the multi-centric world. Their negative-sovereignty keeps them active in the state system,[22] but the multi-centric world has been hospitable to their fragmenting dynamics and thereby has contributed to the process wherein subgroup networks are proliferating.

If the foregoing sources of the parametric transformations that are driving and sustaining turbulence on a global scale are taken as a whole and seen as interactively reinforcing processes of globalization and localization, the result is a vast array of fragmegrative dynamics. The variety and complexity of these dynamics serve as the foci of the next three chapters.

---

[22] In *Quasi-states: Sovereignty, International Relations and the Third World* (Cambridge: Cambridge University Press, 1990), pp. 26–31, Robert H. Jackson treats their sovereignty as "negative" in the sense that it protects them against outside interference but does not empower them to address their problems successfully.

5   Globalization

Everyone feels their life is determined by someone outside, and everyone wants to know who is this person? Who is this force? We thought
that we were on the path to the first world and suddenly something
went wrong. One minute the World Bank and IMF were saying Mexico
was the best example. Now we are the worst example. What did we
do? We are losing control. If we don't find another type of development, we are finished. We surrender.

Enrique del Val Blanco[1]

In the 19th century people thought the machine was going to destroy
their lives as they knew it, and today many people think that globalization is going to destroy their life as they know it. We have gotten
accustomed to the idea that globalization will inevitably succeed. But
I am not so sure anymore. Those of us who believe in globalization
need to be more pro-active.

Klaus Schwab[2]

As indicated by the enumeration of the dynamics driving turbulence on
a global scale, it has become commonplace to stress the large degree to
which powerful communications and transportation technologies are
rendering the world ever more interdependent and the boundaries that
divide local, national, and international communities ever more porous.
Today a development in any part of the world can have consequences
for every other part. What is distant is also proximate, paradoxical as

---

[1] An official of Mexico's Human Services Ministry commenting on his country's 1995
currency crisis, quoted in Thomas L. Friedman, "New Mexico," *New York Times*, March
15, 1995, p. A25.
[2] Managing Director of the Davos Forum, as quoted in Thomas L. Friedman, "Revolt of
the Wannabes," *New York Times*, February 7, 1996, p. A19.

that may seem. Chaos theorists who describe how a butterfly flapping its wings over Brazil can affect the weather over Chicago nicely capture this paradox inherent in the globalization that is transforming world affairs late in the twentieth century.[3]

But the very proximity of distant developments is fostering pressures for localization as well as globalization, pressures that together appear no less powerful as contextual factors fostering the formation of SOAs and impinging on the conduct of governance along the Frontier than the parametric transformations which fostered the onset of turbulence in the first instance. The tensions fostered by the clash of global and local horizons often result in increments of the former fostering comparable increments in the salience of the latter, and vice versa. One analyst captures the dynamism of this causal web by referring to "globalization and its corollary, domestic fragmentation."[4] Another suggests that not only do the frictions between integrating and fragmenting forces "drive each other," but that, indeed, they result in a "meta-stability."[5] Still another observer puts it more bluntly by noting that as a consequence of "the deprovincialization of the world, . . . we're going to be in each other's faces more,"[6] Indeed, as indicated in the above epigraphs, such confrontations can be very threatening.

Globalization and localization

Given the rapidity and the complexities of the changes unfolding on a global scale, it is essential to clarify what is meant here by globalization, localization, and the fragmegrative processes that sustain the linkages between them. So many new phenomena – or, in some instances, new extensions of past practices – now mark the course of events that a large lexicon of terms, many imprecise, some overlapping, a few contradictory, has evolved for differentiating actors, processes, and struc-

[3] James Gliek, *Chaos: Making a New Science* (New York: Viking, 1987), p. 8.

[4] Joseph A. Camilleri, "Rethinking Sovereignty in a Shrinking, Fragmented World," in R.B.J. Walker and Saul H. Mendlovitz (eds.), *Contending Sovereignties: Redefining Political Community* (Boulder, CO: Lynne Rienner 1990), p. 29. For cogent assessments of the tensions between global and local concerns, see the various essays in Antoni Kuklinski (ed.), *Globality versus Locality* (Warsaw: University of Warsaw, 1990).

[5] Ole Waever, "Identity, Integration and Security: Solving the Sovereignty Puzzle in E.U. Studies," *Journal of International Affairs*, vol. 48 (Winter 1995), p. 414.

[6] Clifford Geertz, quoted in David Berreby, "Unabsolute Truths," *New York Times Magazine*, April 9, 1995, p. 44.

tures.[7] All the terms, moreover, are loaded with value connotations. Are globalizing dynamics to be welcomed or regretted? Are they preferable to those that move communities in localizing directions? By clarifying the conceptual underpinnings of our terminology, we will be better situated to respond to these questions as well as to engage in more incisive analysis.[8]

Although related to the many other concepts associated with what one observer has called "the coming together of the world as a world"[9] – such as interdependence, world society, centralizing tendencies, world system, globalism, universalism, internationalization, globality – the notion of globalization developed here is narrower in scope and more specific in content. It refers neither to values nor to structures, but to processes, to sequences that unfold either in the mind or in behavior, to interactions that evolve as people and organizations go about their daily tasks and seek to realize their particular goals.

What distinguishes globalizing processes is that they are not hindered or prevented by territorial or jurisdictional barriers. They can spread readily across national boundaries and are capable of reaching into any community everywhere in the world. They can be initiated from above by transnational elites or from below by ecologically oriented or other civic-minded local groups.[10] Whatever their origins,

[7] For a warning against collapsing too many phenomena under the globalization rubric and thus building "a community of usage when there needs to be strict differentiation of meanings," see Paul Hirst and Grahame Thompson, *Globalization in Question* (Oxford: Blackwell Publishers, 1996), p. 4. Whatever the dangers that attach to overuse of the concept, however, its popularity stems from more, much more, than convergence around a buzz word to denote perplexing changes. As one observer puts it, "The acceptance of globalization by an increasing number of people is not due to fashion alone. It expresses the need for understanding processes that have lost meaning in terms of the more traditional concepts." Riccardo Petrella, "Globalization and Internationalization: The Dynamics of the Emerging World Order," in Robert Boyer and Daniel Drache (eds.), *States Against Markets: The Limits of Globalization* (London: Routledge, 1996), p. 64.

[8] For other recent efforts to probe phenomena associated with globalization, see Mike Featherstone (ed.), *Global Culture: Nationalism, Globalization and Modernity* (Newbury Park, CA: Sage Publications, 1990); Hans-Henrik Holm and Georg Sorensen (eds.), *Whose World Order? Uneven Globalization and the End of the Cold War* (Boulder, CO: Westview Press, 1995); and James H. Mittelman (ed.), *Globalization: Critical Reflections* (Boulder, CO: Lynne Rienner, 1996);

[9] Peter Sloterdijk, "Nationality – A View From Above and Within," *Bard College Bulletin* (Spring 1991), p. 3.

[10] Richard Falk, "The Making of Global Citizenship," in Jeremy Brecher, John Brown Childs, and Jill Cutler (eds.), *Global Visions: Beyond the New World Order* (Boston: South End Press, 1993), pp. 39–50.

however, they consist of all those forces that impel individuals, groups, societies, governments, institutions, and transnational organizations toward engaging in similar forms of behavior or participating in more encompassing and coherent processes, organizations, or systems.[11] Contrariwise, localization derives from all those pressures that lead people, groups, societies, governments, institutions, and transnational organizations to narrow their horizons and withdraw to less encompassing processes, organizations, or systems. In other words, any technological, psychological, social, economic, or political developments that foster the expansion of interests and practices beyond established boundaries are both sources and expressions of the processes of globalization, just as any developments in these realms that limit or reduce interests are both sources and expressions of localizing processes.

Note that the processes of globalization are conceived as only *capable* of being worldwide in scale. In fact, "complete planetary penetration"[12] has not been achieved by any company, group, government, or civilization and few cascading sequences actually encircle and encompass the entire globe. Televised events such as famines in Africa or successful protests against government policies in Eastern Europe may sustain a spread that is worldwide in scope. But such a scope is not viewed as a prerequisite of globalizing dynamics. As long as it has the potential of an unlimited spread that can readily transgress national jurisdictions, any interaction sequence is considered to reflect the operation of globalization.

As will be seen at greater length in chapter 7, the differences between globalizing and localizing forces also give rise to contrary conceptions of territoriality. Globalization is rendering boundaries and identity with the land less salient while localization, being driven by pressures to narrow and withdraw, is highlighting borders and intensifying the deep attachments to land that can dominate emotion and reasoning. Today outcomes and functions can serve as prime foci irrespective of their spatial location for some people, just as for others they are meaningful only as they fall within the boundaries of cherished land.

In short, globalization is boundary-eroding and localization is boundary-strengthening. The former allows people, goods, information,

---

11 For an interesting sevenfold formulation of these dynamics, see Petrella, "Globalization and Internationalization," p. 66.

12 Derek Leebaert, "Innovations and Private Initiatives," *Washington Quarterly*, vol. 15 (Spring 1992), p. 114.

norms, practices, and institutions to move about oblivious to or despite boundaries.[13] On the other hand, the boundary-strengthening processes of localization are designed, for reasons noted below, to inhibit, control, or (in some instances) prevent the movement of people, goods, information, norms, practices, and institutions. Efforts along this line, however, can be only partially successful. Community or state boundaries can be strengthened to a considerable extent, but they cannot be rendered impervious. Authoritarian societies try to seal them tight, but such policies are bound to be undermined in a shrinking world with increasingly interdependent economies and communications technologies that cannot be monitored at checkpoints. Thus it is hardly surprising that some of the world's most durable tensions flow from the fact that no geographic borders can be made so impervious as to prevent the infiltration of ideas and goods. Stated more emphatically, some globalizing dynamics are bound, at least in the long run, to prevail. We return below to this conclusion that globalization is the dominant of the two basic processes.

The boundary-eroding dynamics of globalization have become highly salient precisely because recent decades have witnessed, for a variety of reasons, a mushrooming of the facilities, interests, and markets through which a potential for worldwide spread can be realized. Likewise, the boundary-strengthening dynamics of localization have become increasingly significant, not the least because some people and cultures feel threatened by the incursions of globalization. Their jobs, their icons, their belief systems, and the lives of their communities seem at risk as the boundaries that have sealed them off from the outside world in the past no longer assure protection. And there is, of course, a basis of truth in these fears. Globalization does intrude; its processes do shift jobs elsewhere; its norms do undermine traditional mores.[14] The responses to these threats can vary considerably. At one extreme are adaptations which accept the boundary-eroding processes and make the best of them by integrating them into local customs and practices. At the other extreme are responses intended to ward off the globalizing processes by resort to ideological purities, closed borders,

---

[13] A measure of the extent of globalizing dynamics is suggested by the 150 percent increase in foreign visitors traveling for pleasure in the United States between 1985 and 1992. See US Department of Commerce, *Statistical Abstract of the United States* (Washington, DC: Government Printing Office, 1994), table 422.

[14] For an elaboration of these dynamics, see Ethan B. Kapstein, "Workers and the World Economy," *Foreign Affairs*, vol. 75 (May/June 1996), pp. 16–37.

and economic isolation, to mention only the main ways in which boundaries are strengthened.

As previously implied, neither globalization nor localization consists of a single dynamic. Both are a cluster of forces which, in different ways and through different channels, contribute to more encompassing processes in the case of globalization and to less encompassing processes in the case of the localizing cluster. Both sets of dynamics, moreover, are conceived to operate in all realms of human activity, from the cultural and social through the economic and political. In the political realm globalizing dynamics underlie any developments that facilitate the expansion of authority, policies, and interests beyond the existing socially constructed, territorial boundaries, whereas the politics of localization involve any trends in which the scope of authority and policies undergoes contraction and reverts to concerns, issues, groups and/or institutions that are less extensive than the prevailing socially constructed, territorial boundaries. In the economic realm globalization encompasses the expansion of production, trade, and investments beyond their prior locales, while localizing dynamics are at work when the activities of producers and consumers are constricted to narrower boundaries. In the social and cultural realms globalization operates to extend ideas, norms, and practices beyond the settings in which they originated, and localization is operative whenever the original settings are highlighted or compressed and the inroad of new ideas, norms, and practices thereby inhibited.

It must be stressed that in all these realms both sets of dynamics are long-term processes. Both express fundamental human needs and thus both span all of human history. The expansion processes of globalizing dynamics derive from peoples' need to enlarge the scope of their self-created order so as to increase the goods, services, and ideas available for their well-being. The agricultural revolution, and the subsequent industrial and postindustrial transformations, are among the major sources that have sustained globalization. Even as these expansion-driven forces have been operating, however, so have contrary tendencies toward contraction been continuously at work. Localizing dynamics derive from peoples' need for the psychic comforts of close-at-hand, reliable support – for the family and neighborhood, for local cultural practices, for a sense of "us" that is distinguished from "them." Put differently, globalizing dynamics have long fostered large-scale order, whereas the history of localizing dynamics as sources of pressure for small-scale order has been no less lengthy.

While globalizing dynamics suggest tendencies toward "centralization," "coherence," and "integration," and while localization points to "decentralization," "fragmentation," and "disintegration," such synonyms need to be used cautiously lest they be seen as implying that globalization is judged favorably while localizing trends are seen as regrettable. To offset such implications it needs to be recalled that the globalizing synonyms refer to tendencies toward similarity and uniformity across people, groups, and social systems, whereas those reflective of localization denote tendencies toward differences within and among people, groups, and social systems. Given many occasions to celebrate uniformities and many others when differences can be championed, it is clear that the analysis of globalizing and localizing dynamics need not be founded on a premise that one of these sets of dynamics is to be preferred over the other.

Likewise, although the powerful impact of the industrial and postindustrial revolutions suggests that globalization might foster a degree of civility and order to be preferred over the xenophobic impulses seemingly built into localizing dynamics, such a presumption is unwarranted. History records more than a few large-scale orders that denigrated individuals and violated their rights (Nazi Germany comes immediately to mind), just as there have been numerous instances of small-scale patterns that have been free of xenophobic tendencies and have been conducive to the deepening of community ties.[15] On the other hand, since "the idea of locality assumes a new political importance" as "global problems become overwhelming,"[16] globalizing dynamics do have the potential of generating xenophobic reactions, a possibility that leads one observer to call for "the restoration of national sovereignty . . . before globalization drags the world into a dark age of chaotic instability and conflict."[17] More than that, from this state-centric perspective

> Globalization is essentially a negative phenomenon, destroying the sovereignty and cohesion of nation-states, and thereby depriving markets of the social and political guidance without which they cannot function effectively. Since those vital management and intermediation functions cannot be performed at a global level, it will prove impossi-

[15] Pam Belluck, "In Era of Shrinking Budgets, Community Groups Blossom," *New York Times*, February 25, 1996, p. 1.
[16] "The Talk of the Town," *New Yorker*, October 9, 1989, p. 37.
[17] Manfred Bienefeld, "Is a Strong National Economy a Utopian Goal at the End of the Twentieth Century?" in Boyer and Drache (eds.), *States Against Markets*, p. 434.

ble to contain the centrifugal forces generated by unconstrained competitive markets. Such markets will not serve social or political objectives because it will prove impossible to prevent the competitive struggle for survival from transgressing all social, ethical, and legal limits. The result will be socially divisive, politically destructive, ethically abhorrent and even economically inefficient.[18]

Clearly, neither globalizing nor localizing dynamics are innately desirable or noxious. Considered normatively, there is a good deal to be said for and against both of them, depending on the nature of the arrangements which they foster and the perspective from which they are assessed.

Moreover, both sets of dynamics involve processes which promote and culminate in change. Neither is static. As previously noted, globalization is not the equivalent of everything that happens on a global scale and localization does not refer to all the activities that occur at local levels. Rather, both concepts specify a dynamism in which movement occurs: as it unfolds, globalization fosters more globalization, thus expanding the scope of the global activities, just as localization is conducive of more localization as it ensues, thereby contracting the space within which local activities transpire. The evolution of similar institutions in locales separated by great distances, the extension of markets, the proliferation of satellite dishes that widen television audiences, the spread of social movements, the growth of tourism, the westward or northward flow of people seeking work or asylum, an increase in the frequency of domestic elections monitored by international organizations, the continued institutionalization of the European Union – all these exemplify globalizing tendencies; whereas the maintenance of unique institutions, constant levels of international trade, television viewing, movement membership, tourism, migration, election monitoring, and routinized administration within the EU are illustrative of practices on a global scale that simply repeat prior activities and, as such, are static. Similarly, the reinforcement of institutional differences, the restructuring of organizations that transfer functions from headquarters to field offices, the advent of breakaway provinces, unions, or factions, the growth of cottage industries, and the resurgence of native cultures are all trends which exemplify localizing tendencies. To analyze globalizing and localizing processes, in short, is to observe a world in motion, an expanding and contracting blur of changing

[18] *Ibid.*, pp. 434–5.

orientations, organizations, institutions, and patterns that transform the ways in which people conduct their affairs.

Considered in a short time perspective, both the globalizing and localizing dynamics can be viewed as deriving in part from independent sources. At any moment in time the growth of similar institutions, the expansion of markets, the onset of pervasive environmental problems, the spread of new technologies for the electronic transfer of money, ideas and pictures, and a host of other factors sustain the processes of globalization irrespective of the historical precedents designed to maintain local and national controls over the pace and direction of change. Likewise, at that same moment in time, the psychic comfort derived from close-at-hand activities and loyalties, the habits inherent in long-standing cultures, and the unique features of the immediate neighborhood are among the many factors propelling the processes of localization.

On the other hand, neither set of dynamics is fully independent. In recent years ever more frequent occasions have arisen when the dynamics have interacted directly and, in effect, operated as causal sources of each other. And as the pace of interaction increases, as new increments of globalization foster new increments of localization, and vice versa, enormous social and political power is unleashed. Indeed, moving as they do in opposite directions, the fragmegrative dynamics foster many of the conflicts that crowd the global agenda and underlie attempts at governance along the Frontier – the tensions between those who would conserve and those who would develop natural resources, between transnational social movements and national governments, between domestic unions and migratory labor, between the norms of historic cultures and those of global television, between domestic and imported products, and so on across all the realms of human endeavor. These fragmegrative dynamics and their causal power are considered so relevant to the processes of governance that they are further elaborated in table 5.1 and separately analyzed in the next two chapters.

Processes of globalization

Thus far globalization and localization have been equated with spreads beyond and contractions within national or community boundaries; but such a formulation is too spare. Greater specificity is needed. Does globalization mean the spread of knowledge that diverse peoples have about each other; or does it refer to the weakening of boundaries and a more unified world; or is it a process wherein peoples, communities, societies and their institutions are becoming more alike? The subtleties of globalizing dynamics are suggested by the fact that all these processes are at work. Knowledge is spreading, boundaries are weakening, and institutions are becoming increasingly similar. Yet, while the three processes are interactive and reinforcing in a number of ways, there may be important exceptions to their overlap and convergence. For example, if the growing similarities of some societies includes a tendency toward more intense and widespread patriotism on the part of their members, the emergence of patriotic institutions would clearly be contradictory to those dynamics that are weakening the boundaries that divide societies from each other.

Additional subtleties derive from an appreciation that all three processes can evolve in both positive and negative directions. More knowledge about distant places can foster either parochial or cosmopolitan orientations, but it can also lead to neutral perspectives. Likewise, weakened boundaries may benefit some groups (say, businesses) but may be detrimental to others (say, peasants or workers). And in some cases greater similarity may involve an expansion of human rights, while in others it can encompass tendencies toward racial prejudice.

To recognize the multiple meanings and implications of globalization, however, is not sufficient to resolve the need for greater specificity. A number of other issues remain. What is it that spreads when individuals, groups, societies, governments, institutions, and transnational organizations move in globalizing directions? What is it that contracts when they revert to localizing processes? What forces impel the spreads and sustain the contractions? Answers to these questions take the analysis further into the subtleties of governance along the Frontier. Let us start with those pertaining to globalization.

The objects and activities that spread across boundaries can usefully be identified in terms of six categories – goods and services, people, ideas and information, money, normative orientations, and behavioral patterns and practices. The most tangible of these is probably goods and services, virtually all of which can be theoretically observed, checked, and turned back as they cross borders, but not all of which get carefully checked because the volume of trade is so great. In an era of free enterprise economies, moreover, the inclination to turn back goods and services is minimal. Indeed, the flow of goods and services is continuous and expands all the time, with few impediments to hinder the evolution of vast global markets.

Table 5.1. *On the knife-edge: agents of globalization that cut both ways*

Agent	Globalizing	Fragmenting
Technology		
(Type 1) Automobile, airplane, and other military-derived technology	Shrinking distance intranationally and then internationally	Social emulsification, increased loneliness, social differentiation between those with and the majority without access: facilitating Hobbesian tendencies; facilitating terror and civil war
(Type 2) Telecommunication: phone and fax	Extending size and complexity of individual's moral community; breaching authoritarian rule	Social emulsification, increased loneliness, social differentiation between those with and the majority without access; increased fear from surveillance; facilitating narrow and shifting patterns of relationships; automanipulative personalities
Television	Informing; facilitates simultaneous shared images	Desensitizing, homogenizing, stimulus overload fosters superficiality, encouraging passivity and intellectual laziness; alienating, reason-destroying
(Type 3) IT; computers, "Nintendo"	Facilitating new institutional agents; convenience; abolishing distance; cyberspace and information highways	Huge increase in surveillance potentials: alienating, reason-destroying games; desensitizing, homogenizing; excessive power of processing information triggers feedback crises, especially in global electronic financial markets
Values		
Human rights, property	Enlarging the scope for extended responsibilities in current institutions; builds from familiarity	Human rights honored in the breach: war crimes, especially in civil and undeclared wars; gun law. Exclusive property rights are archetypic fragmenters, but less pervasive than one might think

Faith in science and other fundamentalism	The main fiber in world-binding ideology	Promotes exclusive religions; intolerance; stereotyping, especially when coupled to new technologies
Effects		
Global trade	Antiwar prophylactic	Stimulus to resource conflict over raw and scarce materials and, increasingly, over disposal capacities
Environmental stress and threat	Galvanizes awareness of shared vulnerability	Galvanizes self-protective denial and inaction
Institutions (Type 1) English	As universal functional control system; as key to individuals' liberation	As key to globalizing technologies and their fragmenting consequences; as reactor for introspective linguistic nationalism
(Type 2) Functional institutions: e.g., air traffic control; organized crime	Policing and steering world systems; providing state and trade substitute in gray zones	"There is no such thing as society": terror. Antisocial political ideologies of the culture of contentment: both are corrosive of structure and culture of welfare, strengthening stereotyping and racism
Multinational corporations; global electronic finance; insurance	Defining the boundaries and rules of the world economy and actuating it within those limits	Local powerlessness; regional protectionism leads to bloc confrontation; collapse of imperial ideologies; proliferation of unquantifiable risks
(Type 3) Nongovernmental organizations	Using new technologies to exert political leverage for new values	Using new technologies to undermine local opposition to global political economy

Source: Reproduced from Gwyn Prins, "Notes Toward the Definition of Global Security," *American Behavioral Scientist*, vol. 38 (May 1995), pp. 820–1.

The flow of people, either as tourists, professionals, refugees, or migrants, is hardly less continuous and tangible, and again almost all of them can be subjected to observation, checking, and rejection at border crossings. The rate of rejection will vary depending on the reasons why people present themselves at borders, with tourists and professionals routinely getting through the checkpoints while refugees and migrants, because of their numbers, often have their movement controlled by immigration authorities.

The flow of ideas and information is also profuse, perhaps more so than any other source of spread, as the channels of communication throughout the world widen and deepen in response to ever more dynamic technologies.[19] The volume for those that are circulated by the electronic media is so stupendous as to be beyond full control (though jamming broadcasts and prohibiting satellite dishes are policies still in use in selected parts of the world), but the flow for those conveyed by the printed media is no trivial amount either and requires extensive censoring operations for even a modicum of control to be exercised.

Much the same can be said about the flow of legal and laundered monetary exchanges through electronic media. Not only are the speed and amounts involved in such transactions staggering, but their volume and complexity have also become so great as to render exceedingly difficult the task of monitoring them.

Finally, the categories that are least tangible and controllable are the two that encompass the spread of normative orientations – those values that shape how people relate to each other and feel about their health, apparel, jobs, churches, schools, countries, and the many other foci of their concerns that can be subtly, even unknowingly, imported from other cultures – and the behavioral patterns through which the norms find expression in the practices that enable people to get through their daily routines. Ironically, some of these subtle boundary-eroding norms and practices are difficult to trace and control precisely because they are too obvious and familiar; they stare us in the face all the time and there is a tendency to overlook that they became part of our way of life because globalizing processes brought them to us. All kinds of consumption patterns – from dress to food to toys – can have their origins abroad and are illustrative of how globalization can occur unbeknownst to those that experience it.

---

[19] See, for example, Mark Landler, "The Next Thing to Go Global Will be Toll-Free Numbers," *New York Times*, June 17, 1996, p. D5.

And how does globalization occur? In what ways or through what channels do goods and services, people, ideas and information, money, norms and attitudes, and behavioral patterns spread across boundaries and thereby create distant proximities? Put most succinctly, the processes of spread occur in four interconnected and overlapping ways: (1) through two-way interactions, (2) through one-way telecommunications, (3) through emulation, and (4) through institutional isomorphism.

The first of these is straightforward and easy to grasp. Two-way interaction occurs either directly in face-to-face contacts or indirectly via correspondence, telephone, fax, or e-mail. Such interactions are globalizing whenever they result in the transmission of information that enables, say, corporation executives to be in touch with the work of their far-flung organizations or citizens to stay abreast of famines in distant places and oscillations in distant crises; whenever the spread of goods and services renders the well-being and jobs of individuals, communities, and societies dependent on distant markets and production facilities; whenever the movement of people – be they merchants, academics, tourists, or troops – establishes links and attitudes that transcend local or national boundaries; and whenever the exchange of messages leads to the furtherance of connections abroad among businesses, professionals, nonvoluntary organizations, and a variety of other groups. For better or worse, to put it more simply, two-way interactions broaden horizons. Being interactive and tangible, they have immediate consequences in the short run and enhance sensitivities in the long run.

The other three means of global spread, however, are more complex and circuitous. Consider the spread sustained by one-way telecommunications. It circulates (in writing and in pictures) facts, ideas, concepts, and descriptions that, as they get received and repeated in distant places, become part of the working knowledge of those who receive them. Involved here is information about both immediate situations and general circumstances. Television and other media of communications not only provide first-hand information and short-term learning that keeps people and organizations up to date with the matters of concern to them, but through repetitive exposures they also contribute to the formation and sustenance of long-term working knowledge – that set of premises and understandings that enable individuals and organizations to categorize and evaluate any immediate situation that arises. Working knowledge is not so much factual as conceptual. It is information that takes the form of broad cognitive images and that serves to facilitate interpretation. Put differently, it is information that provides familiarity with the way the world works. The following observation is illustrative:

> As adults we may feel more or less at home more or less everywhere. This is not just a question of habit . . . [I]t's rare that we find ourselves in places that are truly incomprehensible. This is not just because buildings fall into recognizable types . . . but also because television and movies have brought us in contact with so many places we would never ordinarily visit: prisons, morgues, missile silos. Last summer I toured a World War II submarine moored alongside San Francisco's Fisherman's Wharf; it was the first time I had ever been on board such a vessel, but thanks to Lloyd Bridge's Sea Hunt and many submarine movies, the confined, mechanical interior felt, if not exactly familiar, at least not unfamiliar. Similarly, when I was obliged to go to a hospital, a place I had not been in for thirty years but seen innumerable times on television, the layout of the long corridors flanked by dreary wards, and the curious hospital atmosphere that combines boredom and urgency, personal attention and impersonal neglect, felt quite normal, and I think I would have been surprised had it been otherwise.[20]

If one extrapolates from the submarine and hospital to the Iraqi desert, the Rwandan refugee camps, the chambers of the UN Security Council, and the many other locales where information about world affairs has become commonplace, one begins to appreciate the vast ways in which modern media of communications have shrunk the world and enlarged the working knowledge with which people respond to the course of events.

The spread that occurs through emulation also involves subtle and long-term processes. People see – through movies, luxury goods, television, and other means – the actions, practices, and artifacts of other communities and countries that they regard as worthwhile and begin, knowingly or otherwise, to imitate them. The emulation may not be a perfect reproduction. Allowance needs to be made for cultural precepts and the maintenance of local variations and innovations, but the broad outlines of the imitated behaviors and institutions evolve in such a way as eventually to be readily recognizable. McDonald's fast-food restaurants, for example, are replicated throughout the world, but there are numerous variations in their menus to account for local tastes. It is noteworthy, moreover, that emulative processes do not necessarily derive from approval of that which is imitated. Throughout the world many people wear bluejeans, sing rock songs, or otherwise emulate American

---

[20] Witold Rybezynski, "Mysteries of the Mall," *The New York Review*, July 14, 1994, p. 31

practices even as they may deeply distrust the country. More relevant to issues of governance, groups may emulate the protests or other collective actions of counterparts abroad without necessarily valuing the goals that are sought or the means that are used by the emulated group.

While two-way interactions, one-way telecommunications, and emulation are all integral parts of the fourth means through which globalizing dynamics spread, the processes of institutional isomorphism are also sufficiently distinctive and complex to warrant treatment as a separate category. For isomorphism – the tendency to become alike – can evolve out of a variety of additional sources. Greater similarity does result from interaction, communications, and emulation, but it can also stem from the functional necessities inherent in the pressures for globalization. If the leaders and publics of a society are unwilling to contest these pressures, then they are likely to respond in similar ways to the minimal economic, social, and political requirements that allow for the operation of globalizing dynamics. Such responses follow from calculations as to the best way to adapt to the changes unfolding abroad. The rapid spread of free-enterprise economies in recent decades offers a quintessential illustration of this form of isomorphism. Not only did officials in developing and former communist countries want to emulate the developmental successes of Western economies, but they also felt that they might fall further behind if they did not evolve comparable institutions that could compete with their rivals abroad and add to the efficiency and success of productivity and management at home. Or if this reasoning was widely shared throughout their societies, the isomorphism was stimulated as much by adaptation from below as by imposition from above.[21] Likewise, publics in different parts of the world can initiate similar responses when they experience common consequences of economic globalization. It seems highly probable, for example, that "families are changing in similar ways, even in very different cultures," because of transformations in "the economic status of women and changes in the gender-based division of labor."[22]

Put differently, the evolution of isomorphic institutional practices

---

[21] For a cogent analysis of isomorphism in the realm of national economies, see Thomas J. Biersteker, "The 'Triumph' of Neoclassical Economics in the Developing World: Policy Convergence and Bases of Governance in the International Economic Order," in James N. Rosenau and Ernst-Otto Czempiel (eds.), *Governance without Government* (Cambridge: Cambridge University Press, 1992), pp. 102–31.

[22] Frank Furstenberg, a specialist in family demographics, quoted in Tamara Lewis, "Family Decay Global, Study Says," *New York Times*, May 30, 1995, p. A5.

need not be driven by policies or collective actions. The similarities can develop independently of conscious coordination. Airports are not everywhere alike because each time one was built an effort was made to copy the parking, check-in, security, and baggage-claim procedures of other airports. Rather their construction stemmed from situational needs as well as information about other airports. In some important sense, in other words, the worldwide similarity of airports just happened. It is the result of diverse factors that, taken together, amount to globalization. Much the same line of explanation can be offered for why it is that schools, bureaucracies, tax procedures, militaries, healthcare facilities, and a host of other institutions are similar around the world. Indeed, especially relevant to the concerns of this book is the isomorphism that has resulted from the aspiration to statehood on the part of former Soviet and Yugoslav republics – and perhaps ethnic, religious, and linguistic minorities everywhere – not to mention the similarity of human rights concerns in diverse parts of the world.

A vivid illustration of the rapidity and breadth of isomorphic processes is provided by the aftermath of the Gulf War when "more than 120 countries [were] reported to be developing 'information warfare techniques.'"[23] While the rush to develop these techniques in so many countries may have derived partly from observing – and then seeking to emulate – the US success in that war, perhaps even more relevant was the advent of the communications revolution and the functional need on the part of governments to equip their military establishments with a capacity to cope with the information requirements necessary to the waging of modern warfare. That more than 120 countries should turn in this direction within a short time frame offers a cogent insight into the significance of institutional isomorphism as a central dynamic of globalization. As will be seen throughout the ensuing chapters, isomorphic tendencies can also be detected in the mechanisms through which governance is undertaken and achieved in widely separated communities.[24]

The logic of history

Fascinating questions follow from a recognition of the enormous social and political power that results when globalization and localization are

---

[23] Philip Shenon, "Report Warns of Security Threats Posed by Computer Hackers," *New York Times*, May 23, 1996, p. A22.

[24] A useful discussion of isomorphism and how it operates to induce similarities in organizations can be found in W. Richard Scott, *Organizations: Rational, Natural, and Open Systems*, 3rd edn. (Englewood Cliffs: Prentice Hall, 1992), pp. 183–8 and 209–13.

linked together in fragmegrative processes:[25] Do the links merely establish a continuous process of dynamic interaction that, depending on unique circumstances, move history along any one of numerous paths? Or are they founded on underlying tendencies that infuse direction into the course of events? That is, are the links between them driven by dialectical processes that evolve along a single path that adheres to a historical logic?

A full response to such questions requires a close study of the transformations that mark long stretches of history and of the ways in which the dialectics of fragmegration might underlie the transformations.[26] Such an undertaking lies beyond the scope of the present inquiry, but there are good reasons to anticipate that such an inquiry would yield a clear-cut pattern in which the dialectical processes evolve along a single, if erratic, historical path. This conclusion derives from the premise that the more the time frame is broadened, the clearer it will become that in the interaction between globalizing and localizing dynamics it is the former that tends to drive the latter. Such an attribution of causal power is based on a number of factors. Most notably, recorded human experience is a history of expanding horizons – of individuals, families, tribes, and societies driven by their own growth as well as by technology and industrialization to build ever more encompassing forms of social, economic, and political organization. To be sure, no less historically conspicuous than the movement along these lines have been the resistances to globalizing dynamics, counter-reactions driven by the need for identity and the psychic comforts of shared territory and culture to retreat into narrower forms of social, economic, and political organization, all of which can be seen as localizing processes that infuse further fragmentation into the course of events. Still, when the globalizing and localizing dynamics collide and interact, the latter seem unlikely to offset the consequences of technological innovation, the skill revolution, and the global scale on which economic processes are now conducted.

It follows that fragmegration's historical paths are likely to waver as

---

[25] The enormity of this power was perhaps initially recognized by Polanyi, who described "a double movement" in which the thrust of global market forces gave rise to demands for self-protection within societies. This seminal idea is developed in Karl Polanyi, *The Great Transformation: The Political and Economic Origins of Our Time* (Boston: Beacon Press, 1957).

[26] For an initial effort to chart a strategy for investigating these questions, see James N. Rosenau, "Distant Proximities: The Dynamics and Dialectics of Globalization," in Bjorn Hettne (ed.), *International Political Economy: Understanding Global Disorder* (London: Zed Books, 1995), pp. 46–64.

globalizing and localizing dynamics fluctuate in response to varying conditions. Indeed, fragmegration unfolds so unevenly that it is difficult to anticipate the breadth and speed with which globalizing processes will outpace those fostering localization. Furthermore, since localizing dynamics partially derive from independent sources associated with the psychic need for comfort through close-at-hand affiliations, it seems doubtful that globalization will be so predominant as to overwhelm localizing processes and reduce local communities to mere appendages of global institutions. The local entity, in short, is likely to mark the human landscape as far as one can see into the future even as it will also be continuously assaulted by the requirements of a global economy and the intrusions of communications technologies.

Not all analysts accept this uneven conception of fragmegration. Some posit the globalization of national economies through the diffusion of technology, consumer products, the rapid transfer of financial resources, and the efforts of transnational companies to extend their market shares as so forceful and durable as to withstand and (sooner or later) surmount any and all pressures toward fragmentation. Sure, this line of reasoning acknowledges, these globalizing dynamics have not in the past effectively suppressed the tendencies toward localization, but in the present era a level of economic development has been achieved that makes it possible for innovations occurring in any country or any sector of its economy to be readily transferred to and adopted in any other country or sector. As a consequence,

> When this process of diffusion collides with cultural or political protectionism, it is culture and protectionism that wind up in the shop for repairs. Innovation accelerates. Productivity increases. Standards of living improve. There are setbacks, of course. The newspaper headlines are full of them. But we believe that the time required to override these setbacks has shortened dramatically in the developed world. Indeed, recent experience suggests that, in most cases, economic factors prevail in less than a generation, probably within one or two political cycles (five to ten years). Thus understood, globalization – the spread of economic innovations around the world and the political and cultural adjustments that accompany this diffusion – cannot be stopped.[27]

While it is surely the case that robust economic incentives sustain and quicken the processes of globalization, this line of reasoning neverthe-

---

[27] William W. Lewis and Marvin Harris, "Why Globalization Must Prevail," *McKinsey Quarterly*, 1992, no. 2, p. 115.

less suffers from not allowing for its own negation. As summarized, it offers no alternative interpretations as to how the interaction of economic, political, and social dynamics will play out. One cannot demonstrate the falsity – if falsity it is – of such reasoning because any contrary evidence is seen merely as "setbacks," as expectable deviations from the predicted course that are presumed to be temporary. The day may come, of course, when events so perfectly conform to the predicted patterns of globalization that one is inclined to conclude that the thesis has been affirmed. But in the absence of alternative scenarios, it provides no guidance as to how to interpret intervening events, especially those that highlight the tendencies toward fragmentation. Viewed in this way, it is less a line of reasoning and more an article of faith to which one can cling without concern about the consequences of localizing patterns.

Globalization is not unidirectional

Although many of the ideas, goods, and norms associated with globalization originated in the industrial countries of the West, it would be a grave mistake to equate globalization with Westernization. The technologies that underlie the spread of globalizing dynamics enable the flow of ideas, goods, and norms to spring from any culture and move in a variety of directions. So it is, for example, that some of the premises of Chinese medicine and the practices of Zen Buddhism have spread westward, just as the products of the West have moved eastward. It might be exaggerated to contend that for every McDonald's fast-food restaurant in the Far East, a comparable Asian facility is available in the United States, but fast-food Chinese, Korean, Japanese, Thai, and Vietnamese restaurants are spreading to more and more American cities. Or consider how,

> Long a tradition in the Far East, the millennia-old craft of feng shui (pronounced FUNG-shway) has begun to exert a subtle influence on the hard-edged world of real estate in America. Feng shui, which means "wind" and "water" in Chinese, is a blend of astrology, design and Eastern philosophy aimed at harmonizing the placement of man-made structures in nature. Driven by the influx of investors from Hong Kong, Singapore, Taiwan and China, the use of feng shui has surfaced in the design and marketing of projects from mini-malls in Los Angeles to skyscrapers in Manhattan.[28]

[28] Ashley Dunn, "Ancient Chinese Craft Reshaping Building Design and Sales in U.S.," *New York Times*, September 22, 1994, p. 1.

Localization as globalization

Much the same can be said about localization. It too can spread in diverse directions. All four of the aforementioned processes of spread can be operative with respect to localizing dynamics. Two-way and one-way communications, emulation, and institutional isomorphism can serve as channels through which boundaries are contracted whenever people and communities seek guidance on how to construct more effective barriers between themselves and the distant proximities that seem threatening. The classic example of localization as a globalizing process involves trade barriers: when one country raises them in response to comparable actions by trading partners, the globalization of heightened boundaries is initiated and may well continue to spread. Similar illustrations of this process are evident when subgroups are motivated by messages and examples from abroad to seek autonomy from the more encompassing systems in which they are located or when xenophobic leaders imitate counterparts in other countries enjoying political success by ratcheting up their appeals. Paradoxically, in other words, the more people and communities react against the dynamics of globalization, or the more they seek to take advantage of globalizing forces through new volunteer organizations, the more are their localizing responses likely to accelerate system-wide uniformities.

In sum, the dynamics of both globalization and localization are powerful enough to move in any and all directions as the world shrinks. As will be seen in the next chapter, this power is further multiplied when the two sets of dynamics interact and shape each other.

6   Fragmegration

> We care about being Lombards first and Europeans second. Italy means nothing to us.
>
> Paul Friggerio[1]

To speak of an uneven fragmegrative worldview is to conjure up processes and arrangements undergoing continual fluctuations in every country and region between globalizing and localizing tendencies, between expanding coherence and contracting solidarity. It suggests the tensions fostered by the compelling lure of both distant and immediate horizons that are succinctly captured in the above comment of a leader of an Italian regional party, the Northern League, at the time of its first electoral triumph. As the common sense of an epoch, it summarizes all the distant proximities that are leading individuals, groups, and societies to intensify their search for meaning in a world that has lost its familiar signposts.

Since globalization and localization can have both positive and negative consequences, the tensions generated by uneven fragmegration greatly complicate the task of governance along the Frontier. As will be seen in chapter 8, it highlights a mismatch between the rapid extension of boundary-crossing activities and the authority necessary to give direction to them.[2] On the other hand, globalizing and localizing tendencies can co-exist, and when they do, it can be expected that the more

[1] Quoted in Frank Viviano, "Separatist Party on the Rise in Italy," *San Francisco Chronicle*, March 3, 1993, p. 1.

[2] This mismatch is cogently discussed in Michael Zurn, "What Has Changed in Europe? The Challenge of Globalization and Individualization," in Hans-Henrik Holm and Georg Sorensen (eds.), *Whose World Order? Uneven Globalization and the End of the Cold War* (Boulder, CO: Westview Press, 1995), pp. 137–64.

pervasive globalizing tendencies become, the more will localizing reactions accommodate to them.[3] This expectation derives from the probability that in such situations people will become increasingly accustomed to resolving the tensions that pull them into the Frontier and those that contract their perceptual space.

For globalizing and localizing tendencies to accommodate to each other, individuals have to come to appreciate that they can achieve psychic comfort in collectivities through multiple memberships and multiple loyalties, that they can advance both local and global values without one detracting from the other. A growing appreciation along these lines can be anticipated because, as stressed in chapter 14, the contrary premise that psychic comfort can only be realized by having a highest loyalty seems likely to become increasingly antiquated. To be sure, people have long been accustomed to presuming that, in order to derive the psychic comfort they need through collective identities, they have to have a hierarchy of loyalties and that, consequently, they have to have a highest loyalty which can only be attached to a single collectivity. Such reasoning, however, is a legacy of the state system, of centuries wherein crises encouraged people to feel compelled to place nation-state loyalties above all others. Indeed, it is a logic that long served to reinforce the predominance of the state as the "natural" unit of political organization and that probably reached new heights during the intense years of the Cold War. But if it is the case, as chapters 7 and 18 seek to demonstrate, that conceptions of territoriality are in flux and that the failure of states to solve pressing problems has led to a decline in their capabilities and a loss of their performance legitimacy, it follows that the notion that people must have a "highest loyalty" will also decline and give way to the development of multiple loyalties and an understanding that local, national, and transnational affiliations need not be mutually exclusive. For the reality is that human affairs are organized at a variety of levels for good reasons, that people have some needs that can only be filled by close-at-hand organizations and other needs that are best served by distant collectivities at the national or transnational levels.

Of course, there are bound to be moments when people are required to act on behalf of one of their affiliations and, in so doing, to act counter

---

[3] For a provocative discussion of the ways in which globalizing and localizing dynamics can be mutually reinforcing as well as "polar opposites," see Roland Robertson, "Glocalization: Time–Space and Homogeneity–Heterogeneity," in Mike Featherstone, Scott Lash and Roland Robertson (eds.), *Global Modernities* (Thousand Oaks, CA: Sage Publications, 1995), pp. 25–44.

to the goals of another organization with which they are associated. But there is no necessary reason why such choices have to be consistent. Circumstances vary, values change, people learn, and as a result opting for one collectivity at one moment in time does not preclude acting contrary to its interests at another moment. In other words,

> human beings today identify themselves in a variety of ways with relevance to politics. As a result, they are enmeshed in a multitude of authoritative networks, have loyalties to a variety of authorities, and distribute the resources they control (including their own labor) depending upon the relative importance of these networks to them. Each of these networks has the potential to mobilize its adherents to action in the context of issues which touch their interests and/or excite their passions.[4]

In sum, the mismatch between the extension of transnational activities and a lag in governing capacity of states is here conceived to be moderated by the increasing ability of individuals and local entities to see their interests as served by further globalization. As the global economy expands and people become increasingly aware of the extent to which their well-being is dependent on events and trends elsewhere in the world, so are the tendencies toward multiple loyalties and memberships likely to grow. At the same time, the distant economic processes serving their interests are impersonal and hardly capable of advancing the need to share with others in a collective affiliation. This need was long served by the nation-state, but with globalizing and localizing dynamics having undermined the national level as a source of psychic comfort and with transnational entities seeming too distant to provide the psychic benefits of affiliation, the virtues of the satisfactions to be gained through more close-at-hand affiliations are likely to be increasingly salient and the state is less likely to be viewed as the optimal collectivity for coping with the challenges that beset humankind.

But, it might be argued, there is a substantial basis for presuming that people are unable to handle the coexistence of attitudes that value their homeland and those that look beyond territorial horizons. Certainly there is no evidence of an eroding sense of territoriality in the former Soviet Union, Yugoslavia, and Czechoslovakia; these situations – and

---

[4] Yale H. Ferguson and Richard W. Mansbach, "The Past as Prelude to the Future: Changing Loyalties in Global Politics,"paper presented to the Annual Meeting of the International Studies Association, Acapulco (March 23–27, 1993), p. 4.

many others that could be cited – all point to a withdrawal to subgroup identities and thus to an ever greater value being attached to cultural homelands. How, then, can it be hypothesized that localizing tendencies are becoming less resistant to globalizing tendencies? Easily, if it is recalled that such processes are conceived not to operate evenly across the continents. Although the intensity of localization can persist and deepen, such is likely to be the case only in societies segmented by deepseated and competing ethnic, linguistic, or religious commitments that continue to exercise a powerful hold on people. But, as noted, such situations are only pockets of antagonism between globalizing and localizing tendencies in a larger setting marked by the skill revolution that underlies a redrawing of the balance between the two sets of tendencies. Indeed, the larger setting includes a number of situations where ethnic ties have been retained even as the concept of territoriality has changed:

> Almost none of the attempts to intensify ethnic identification in Europe, for example, can be interpreted as antithetical to globalization. Most are not movements that seek to turn society inward in order to contemplate its ethnic soul. Nor, with a few exceptions, are they efforts to impose their hegemony over other peoples. On the contrary, their primary mission, beyond the preservation of languages and traditions, is to participate in the global economy on a more favorable basis than the status quo allows.[5]

The variability of fragmegrative processes

Until recently, the importance of fragmegrative processes could not be readily grasped in a short time frame. Such a perspective tends to highlight globalization and localization as separate and unrelated dynamics. Only as the time frame was lengthened to allow for a full array of the impacts and consequences of each dynamic could the interactions between them be discerned. And even then it was difficult to draw the connections. Their consequences for each other were obscured in the twentieth century by world wars and the Cold War (which focused attention on national concerns), and in earlier times (when it took weeks and months for ideas, people, and goods to move around the world) the occurrence of integrative developments such as the formation of states, the industrialization of societies, the evolution of empires, or the

---

[5] William W. Lewis and Marvin Harris, "Why Globalization Must Prevail," *McKinsey Quarterly*, 1992, no. 2, pp. 130–1.

opening of new trade routes was not readily apparent as a source of fragmenting consequences. Nor did the onset of fragmenting processes such as civil wars or class conflicts lend themselves easily to tracing their integrative consequences. Doubtless both sets of causal links did exist and could be discerned in retrospect if a decadal context was used. But only as technologies fostered extensive overlaps among local, national, and international systems did the simultaneity and interaction of fragmegrative dynamics became so readily evident, so widely pervasive, and so fully operative as immediate stimuli to tensions that career back and forth through systems at all levels of economic, social, and political organization. Indeed, there has been a continual flow of materials which, in one way or another, explore the tensions and posit them as central to the course of events.[6]

In order to probe how individuals and diverse collectivities respond to these dislocations of an ever more interdependent world, the ensuing analysis focuses on the interactions that link globalizing dynamics and their fragmenting corollaries in the economic, social, and political realms. As will be seen in chapter 7, a major consequence of these interactions involves the impact of fragmegrative dynamics on the identities and boundaries that differentiate people and collectivities. But here the task is that of anticipating these consequences by suggesting the variability of fragmegrative processes in different areas of activity and how they can contribute both to different orientations toward the role of individuals and to different capacities possessed by their collectivities.

Economic sources of fragmegration

Perhaps the economic realm offers the most easily discernible processes through which fragmegration is shifting long-established boundaries and assaulting the principles of territoriality. The shifts might be said to have begun in the 1970s when financial deregulation opened up national boundaries to the flow of money and new kinds of production organization fostered the rapid spread of workers, plants, and goods across borders that once constrained their movement. Nor do these structural changes fostered by the globalization of national economies derive only from the activities of the large, privately owned transna-

[6] See, for example, Joseph A. Camilleri and Jim Falk, *The End of Sovereignty? The Politics of a Shrinking and Fragmenting World* (Aldershot, England: Edward Elgar, 1992); Antoni Kuklinski (ed.), *Globality versus Locality* (Warsaw: University of Warsaw, 1990); and Zdravko Mlinar (ed.), *Globalization and Territorial Identities* (Aldershot, England: Avebury, 1992).

tional corporations of the industrial world. The imperatives embedded in the need to seek additional markets abroad in order to gain the profits necessary to amortize investments have also motivated smaller private companies, state-owned enterprises, and firms based in developing countries to become integrated into the global economy. "Thus it is not the phenomenon of the transnational corporation that is new, but the changed balance between firms working only for a local or domestic market, and those working for a global market and in part producing in countries other than their original home base."[7]

It follows that the globalization of national economies – which involves, among its many dimensions, "the spatial reorganization of production, the interpenetration of industries across borders, the spread of financial markets, the diffusion of identical consumer goods to distant countries, and massive transfers of population within the South as well as from the South and the East to the West"[8] – has lessened ties to the national state and encouraged activities and orientations that revolve around both narrower and wider organizational units. These fragmegrative dynamics foster narrower horizons through both the influx of large numbers of immigrants who cling to their subcultural networks and the conflicts engendered by their presence in the established communities of formerly tight-knit neighborhoods.[9] And they promote wider horizons through the dramatic increases in capital mobility. As businesses shift their capital and production facilities to new locations abroad, and as global financial markets become increasingly integrated, national authorities are less capable of steering their economies toward such desired outcomes as stable growth, low inflation, and lowered unemployment. The days when states had the capacity to conduct autonomous economic and social policies for the protection of their populations are over, encouraging people to reorient themselves to ward those authorities who may be more able to provide protection. Moreover, governments not only lose at least a modicum of control and sovereignty with respect to their domestic autonomy, but also have to cope with severe social cleavages generated by the relocation of production organizations.

---

[7] Susan Strange, "States, Firms, and Diplomacy," *International Affairs*, Vol. 68 (1992), p. 3.
[8] James H. Mittelman, "The Dynamics of Globalization," in J.H. Mittelman (ed.), *Globalization: Critical Reflections* (Boulder, CO: Lynne Rienner, 1996), p. 2.
[9] James H. Mittelman. "The Global Restructuring of Production and Migration," in Yoshikazu Sakamoto (ed.), *Global Transformation: Challenges to the State System* (Tokyo: United Nations University Press, 1994), pp. 276–98.

For all practical purposes, in short, the boundaries of states with respect to economic matters have begun to yield to those of international markets. One observer even contends that

> The nation state has become an unnatural, even dysfunctional, unit for organizing human activity and managing economic endeavor in a borderless world. It represents no genuine, shared community of economic interests; it defines no meaningful flows of economic activity. In fact, it overlooks the true linkages and synergies that exist among often disparate populations by combining important measures of human activity at the wrong level of analysis . . . the lines that now matter are those defining what may be called "region states." The boundaries of the region state are not imposed by political fiat. They are drawn by the deft but invisible hand of the global market for goods and services . . . Region states are natural economic zones.[10]

That the leaders of traditional political territories have begun to yield to the requirements of a global economy has also become manifest in their changing relationships with transnational corporations (TNCs). Where the pre-1980s pattern of TNC–state relations was one of continuous confrontation and expropriation by state agencies in countries where TNCs sought to do business, today nationalization is no longer a recurring phenomenon. Instead there has been a surge of cooperation between national governments and TNCs. The reasons for this change are numerous, but taken together they reveal a need on the part of both states and TNCs to accommodate to each other.[11]

Of course, these emergent relationships are not free of tension. There are continuing frictions generated by the attempts of states to raise the foreign investment necessary to compete in a globalized economy without yielding their national sovereignty over investment, regulation, taxation, labor and environmental laws, and a host of other issues. Indeed, a "spill-over" of TNC–state conflict into state–state confrontations can be discerned. These more subtle, norm-bounded conflicts were evident in international negotiations over NAFTA and the pressures of US firms to get China to respect intellectual property rights.

That fragmegrative dynamics interactively pull in opposite directions

---

[10] Kenichi Ohmae, "The Rise of the Region State," *Foreign Affairs*, vol. 72 (Spring 1993), pp. 78–9. For an elaboration of Ohmae's perspective, see his *The Borderless World: Power and Strategy in the Interlinked Economy* (New York: HarperCollins, 1990), and *The End of the Nation State: The Rise of Regional Economies* (New York: Free Press, 1995).

[11] An extended analysis leading to this conclusion is provided by Charles R. Kennedy, Jr., "Relations Between Transnational Corporations and Governments of Host Countries: A Look to the Future," *Transnational Corporations*, vol. 1 (February 1992), pp. 67–92.

is also evident in the internal development of TNCs. Owing in large part to the intensified competition that has accompanied the quickening pace of globalization, but also as a consequence of wanting to minimize their conflicts with the nationalist sentiments and policies of host governments, more than a few TNCs are finding reasons to alter their structures, policies, and conduct. Contrary to expectations, falling trade barriers, spreading computer technologies, and the growing efficiency of capital markets are narrowing economies of scale in manufacturing and distribution, thereby lessening the advantage very large firms have over those that are medium-sized or small. Indeed, there are increasing signs that the gigantic firms are losing out in the competition and finding it necessary to restructure their modes of operation. Instead of benefiting from globalization, the corporate giants are beset with challenges they may not be able to meet without major overhauls. "Their presumption of invincibility," *The Economist* has noted, "is now in shreds . . . An age of broader, fiercer global competition, with all its risks and uncertainties has begun."[12]

The response of TNCs to the liabilities of large size and nationalist sentiments has been both to decentralize and to federate – a seemingly contradictory pattern that is in fact highly consistent with the dynamics of fragmegration. Instead of purchasing other firms, many large TNCs are forming alliances with competitors and allowing their subunits greater autonomy to take advantage of local conditions. In effect, they are developing federal rather than hierarchical structures in order to compete better with their smaller rivals. One label given to these newly emergent business structures is that of the "relationship-enterprise," which is described as

> a network of strategic alliances among big firms, spanning different industries and countries, but held together by common goals which encourage them to act almost as a single firm . . . A multi-national alliance of independently owned firms can draw on lots of money; they can dodge antitrust barriers; and with home bases in all the main markets they have the political advantage of being a local firm almost everywhere.[13]

In short, whether emphasis is given to the fact that relationship-enterprises will be even larger than the present corporate giants – one estimate is that they will have total revenues approaching $1 trillion by the

---

[12] "The Fall of Big Business," *The Economist*, April 17, 1993, p. 13.
[13] "The Global Firm: R.I.P.," *The Economist*, February 6, 1993, p. 69.

beginning of the twenty-first century[14] – or to the fact that they are nonetheless comprised of local firms that chose to ally and thus take on all the instabilities that inhere in alliance structures, TNCs are undergoing a redrawing of long-time boundaries. Plainly they are experiencing the fragmegrative dynamics wherein jurisdictions are being revised in both more and less encompassing directions.

The contribution of individuals to such global economic outcomes derives from an inclination to downplay the protection of national boundaries and, instead, to favor full participation in the world economy. Where people holding such attitudes predominate on a society-wide scale, the support for a free and open trading system is likely to be converted into lower tariff barriers, the formation of common markets, the transnational transfer of currencies, and a variety of other policies which facilitate the global flow of goods and services. On the other hand, strong reactions against the internationalization of production are discernible. Some groups feel their livelihood is threatened by freer trade and a wider distribution of production facilities, with the result that fragmegrative dynamics, from strikes to protest rallies reflecting protectionist sentiments and economic nationalism, may surface whenever sharp turns occur in the global economy.[15] It is doubtful, however, that the localizing tendencies inherent in economic nationalism will replace the globalizing tendencies associated with free-trade orientations. As previously noted, the internationalization of production has become so pervasive that too many people hold jobs linked into the world economy for economic nationalism to spread far and wide at the micro level. There is no dearth of politicians espousing protectionist ideas, but their capacity to mobilize support for their policies seems limited. Thus, while there are surely interaction effects between an expanding world economy and its fragmenting corollary, the correlation is not likely to be very high. Some protection-minded politicians may get elected to high offices and some trade wars may well develop as the world moves increasingly beyond Cold War preoccupations with military security, but the globalization of national economies makes it unlikely that such politicians will be able to expand their power bases or that future trade wars will ever achieve the intensity of such conflicts in earlier eras.

[14] *Ibid.*

[15] For a case study of this fragmegrative dynamic, see June Nash and Christine Kovic, "The Reconstitution of Hegemony: The Free Trade Act and the Transformation of Rural Mexico," in Mittelman (ed.), *Globalization*, pp. 165–85.

In other words, while the economic realm can sustain globalizing and localizing tendencies that are corollaries of each other, the connections may be weak and subject to much variation. Indeed, conceivably, the consequences of an expanding world economy will stimulate economic transnationalism in individuals – an orientation that acknowledges no territorial boundaries and focuses on the ways in which the internationalization of production and services can be exploited on behalf of narrow, self-serving interests.

The self-serving interests induced by globalizing processes are further extended by a continuing refinement of consumer tastes. As the internationalization of production yields goods increasingly tailored to specialized markets, as people thus become increasingly accustomed to acquiring goods made abroad, and/or as they are increasingly exposed to the existence and appeal of foreign-made products through television and other media of the microelectronic revolution, the boundaries of their countries will decreasingly seem coterminous with the markets relevant to their tastes and well-being. Neither localizing processes nor economic nationalism, in other words, will offer much of a match for the dynamics of the world economy insofar as consumers are concerned.

Social sources of fragmegration

Institutions in the social realm – such as the family, school, workplace, and healthcare – are profoundly affected by the obfuscation of borders in the economic and political realms. Indeed, one is hard put to conceive of any issue or aspect of the social and cultural life of communities at all levels not being modified by the dynamics of fragmegration. Only a few of these repercussions are noted here, but they can be viewed as illustrative of a pervasive set of influences presently at work on a global scale.

One of the most notable repercussions has been the various ways in which ethnic groups, professional societies, subnational governments, social movements, and a host of other noneconomic actors have, for a variety of reasons, found it expedient to enlarge their contacts and interactions abroad. On the other hand, the social realm differs markedly from the economic realm in the kinds of people most immediately affected by globalization. While the latter tends to encourage micro transnational orientations that are essentially private and self-serving, the social realm embraces people who think and feel in aggregate terms, who see themselves in association with counterparts abroad working on shared problems and evolving or sustaining institutions that can enhance their goals. Thus have national jurisdictions been transgressed by individuals belonging to diasporas, professional societies, subnational governments, social movements, and a host of other noneconomic and nonpolitical organizations. And thus too have a variety of ideas, cultural norms, aesthetic criteria, religious alternatives, and humanistic values spread across continents and regions, thereby infusing some concrete substance into the concept of a world society.[16] The notion of globally shared perspectives that move individuals to engage in new forms of behavior may still be largely confined to activists concerned about human rights and environmental issues, but wider traces of universalizing tendencies are not difficult to find. There is persuasive evidence, for example, that in advanced industrial societies the younger generations are less and less likely to subscribe to material values, preferring instead a wide range of post-materialist values.[17]

It would be a mistake to locate the roots of these emergent tendencies exclusively in the transnational roles that are the product of mounting interdependence. The activities of a jet-setting elite are surely a critical element of the globalizing dynamics, but the predispositions of individuals centered on distant shores derive from a variety of sources in addition to role requirements. Fear, curiosity, civic values, social conscience, empathy for the underprivileged, concern about the environment – all such preoccupations have been heightened by the increasing irrelevance of territoriality and a lessening reliance on the state.

The mushrooming of social movements in recent years offers still another instance of fragmegrative dynamics. Generated by the advent of interdependence issues, social movements provide people with meaningful opportunities to engage in collective action. The ominous threat of nuclear war energized the peace movement, just as indicators of potential environmental disasters served to stimulate an active ecological movement, and just as growing concerns about individual well-being fostered a surge on the part of the human rights and feminist movements. As one observer put it, "The point about these antisystemic

---

[16] For cogent efforts to elaborate on the world society concept, see Hedley Bull, *The Anarchical Society: A Study of World Order in Politics* (New York: Columbia University Press, 1977); Hedley Bull and Adam Watson (eds.), *The Expansion of International Society* (Oxford: Oxford University Press, 1985); John W. Burton, *World Society* (Cambridge: Cambridge University Press, 1972); and Alex Inkeles, "The Emerging Social Structure of the World," *World Politics*, vol. 27 (July 1975), pp. 467–95.

[17] Ronald Inglehart, *Culture Shift in Advanced Industrial Society* (Princeton: Princeton University Press, 1990).

movements is that they often elude the traditional categories of nation, state, and class. They articulate new ways of experiencing life, a new attitude to time and space, a new sense of history and identity."[18]

Much the same can be said about tourism – which is the world's largest industry and perhaps the most personalized example of fragmegrative dynamics – religious pilgrimages, migrations, professional meetings, and cultural exchanges. All these activities are part and parcel of the process whereby ideas and individuals transgress national boundaries and fashion networks of interaction that ignore or otherwise spread well beyond the principles of territoriality even as they may also heighten peoples' sense of attachment to their local community. In the case of tourism, for example, it not only continuously expands – "few industries can hope to attain growth rates of between 4 and 5 per cent per annum during the next decade" – but it is also a means by which upwards of a half-billion people cross boundaries into different cultures every year and return home either with reinforced ties to their own community or with loosened territorial bonds and a restless readiness to venture abroad again.[19]

Another insightful illustration of the extent to which fragmegration has occurred in the social realm is provided by the changing practices through which families adjust to overseas assignments. Rather than children being left "home" to go to school, today the family joins the bread-winner on his or her foreign assignment. In effect, for such people the meaning of "home" has changed. It is anywhere the occupation of parents takes them, while the meaningful, long-term "home" to which deep emotional ties are attached remains only "a second away in communications and a day away in reality."[20]

Yet, the social consequences of fragmegration are not without their downside. Some observers stress that by yielding to the transnational corporations and the "natural" economic requirements of region-states,

---

[18] Joseph A. Camilleri, "Rethinking Sovereignty in a Shrinking, Fragmented World," in R.B.J. Walker and Saul H. Mendlovitz (eds.), *Contending Sovereignties: Redefining Political Community* (Boulder: Lynne Rienner, 1990), p. 35.

[19] Marie-Françoise Lanfant, "International Tourism, Internationalization and the Challenge to Identity," in Marie-Françoise Lanfant, John B. Allcock, and Edward M. Bruner (eds.), *International Tourism: Identity and Change* (London: Sage Publications, 1995), p. 27.

[20] Derek Leebaert, "Innovations and Private Initiatives," *Washington Quarterly*, vol. 15 (Spring 1992), p. 115. For reasons to be concerned about the consequences of fragmegration for the family, see Robert N. Bellah, *et al.*, *The Good Society* (New York: Alfred A. Knopf, 1991), pp. 91–3.

national governments "are also accomplices in a global development strategy that excludes most of the world's population."[21] This line of reasoning posits region-states as facilitating the sale of new products designed for new customers in new markets without concern for the innumerable consumers who cannot afford to buy the products, thus insuring the persistence of large pockets of poverty, ill-health, illiteracy, and squalor around the world. Such a process is conceived to necessitate a redrawing of "the world map: On one side we would see a dynamic, tightly linked, fast-developing archipelago of technopoles comprising less than one-eighth of the world's population; on the other would be a vast, disconnected and disintegrating wasteland which is home to seven out of every eight inhabitants of the earth."[22]

Furthermore, hostility on the part of local groups whose jobs or cultures seem at risk often greets the arrival of the products of transnational corporations. When Kentucky Fried Chicken opened restaurants in India, for example, farm organizations promoted riots against them on the grounds their food was unhealthy.[23] On the other hand, the McDonald's Corporation has, for better or worse, contributed to a global spread of values and tastes through more than 18,000 restaurants in 91 countries. Indeed, confronted with

> stiff competition in the United States, [the company] is looking overseas for growth. The fast-food giant said today that it would speed up expansion, opening about eight restaurants a day, or 6,400 over the next two years. About two-thirds of the estimated 3,200 restaurants to be opened each year would be outside the United States.[24]

At the same time it is a measure of the dynamics of fragmegration that McDonald's menu is not uniform on a global scale. The requirements of business success has compelled an expansion of its cuisine to include local tastes in various parts of the world.

Hardly less conspicuous are the fragmegrative dynamics reshaping social and cultural processes that have their roots in the impact of communications technologies. On the one hand, as a consequence of the continuing development and diminishing costs of fiber optic cable, satellite dishes, fax machines, electronic mail, computer hook-ups, global television, and many other mechanisms for circulating ideas,

---

[21] Ricardo Petrella, "Techno-Racism: The City-States of the Global Market Will Create a `New Apartheid,'" *The Toronto Star*, May 9, 1992.   [22] Petrella, "Techno-Racism."
[23] "Irate Farmers Ruffle KFC's Feathers in India," *New York Times*, January 31, 1996, p. A3.
[24] *New York Times*, January 18, 1996, p. D20.

information, pictures, and news, these technologies are drawing peoples ever closer together. With Africa as a notable exception, most of the world is now wired on a global scale, thereby creating "information highways" that link every community to every other and make it theoretically possible to send a signal from any sending station to any point anywhere on the earth. While it may be premature to assert that these new highways have fostered the evolution of a world society – much depends on how the concept is defined – it surely is the case that they have contributed to the obsolescence of traditional social, economic, and political boundaries and furthered the growth of new transnational systems. The enormous system-encouraging potential of these highways is vividly suggested in the basic dimensions of one of them: the Internet, a web of thousands of networks that include military, government, academic and corporate computer systems throughout the world, is used by rapidly growing numbers of people. At the same time it should be noted that the new channels of communication may not always be used by people to expand the scope of their activities. They can also serve to sustain existing patterns of behavior. As one analyst put it with respect to a particular practice, "People talk about the pursuit of European union when it already exists with everybody watching everybody else's softcore pornography channels."[25]

On the other hand, the very same globalizing technologies are also encouraging a retreat to more local communities. As people and organizations experience the losses of autonomy and authority that accompany globalization, so do they seek to protect their interests and achieve psychic comfort by reverting to the more close-at-hand groups with which they are affiliated. A surge of regional languages, a deepening of the ties that bind ethnic minorities and diasporas,[26] repeated acts of terrorism against the United States as the agent of globalization,[27] and a rising tide of religious fundamentalism are but the more conspicuous of the localizing dimensions of fragmegration.[28] Put differently, as the microelectronic revolution and a number of other factors have led to the aforementioned parametric transformation of the analytic and emo-

---

[25] Martin Mayer, as quoted in Leebaert, "Innovations and Private Initiatives," p. 113.

[26] The deepening of these ties is cogently analyzed in Timur Kuran, "Ethnic Dissimilation and Its Global Transmission," paper presented at a conference of the Institute on Global Conflict and Cooperation, Davis CA (March 1995).

[27] Ronald Steel, "When Worlds Collide," *New York Times*, July 21, 1996, sect. 4, p. 15.

[28] See, for example, Mustapha Kamal Pasha and Ahmed I. Smatar, "The Resurgence of Islam," in Mittelman (ed.), *Globalization*, pp. 187–201.

tional skills of people everywhere, and as the end of the Cold War has made it easier to sort out the relative importance of close-at-hand and distant loyalties, so have citizenries become increasingly able to construct scenarios that identify their local interests in distant events.

Although fragmegrative dynamics serve to challenge, if not to erode, the authority of states on most issues, an interesting twist in this process has occurred in France. Concerned about the surge of regional languages, the French government has sought to preserve national coherence and legitimacy by lending support to linguistic diversity. In effect, it has undertaken fragmegrative policies in order to offset the dynamics of globalization:

> For more than four centuries, the powers in Paris have disdained provincial tongues as vulgar and backward and fought to impose a standardized French on the rest of the nation. While few Western European countries have France's linguistic diversity – eight distinct languages and more than a dozen dialects – few states have also so systematically repressed regional speech in the name of national unity.
>
> But with English galloping across the Continent and a uniting Europe trying to brush away boundaries, the Government has concluded that France's regional languages enrich the national heritage rather than pose a threat to the country's identity. Now it wants to insure that they survive. All over Western Europe, minority languages are getting a new lease on life as regions take steps to preserve their traditions for fear of being swallowed up in a large, federal Europe.[29]

Fragmegrative dynamics are also conspicuous in the organizational explosion that has accompanied the ever greater interdependence of world affairs. As will be seen in chapter 17, the greater sensitivity to self-interests on the part of citizens and the greater complexity of global life have resulted in a proliferation of a wide range of organizations in every realm of activity. And in order to meet the challenges of greater complexity, ethnic groups, professional societies, subnational governments, social movements, and a host of other noneconomic actors have found it expedient to roam around the Frontier and enlarge their links abroad even as some of them have narrowed their scope and reinvigorated their activities at local levels. Even one of the world's most

---

[29] Marlise Simons, "A Reborn Provencal Heralds Revival of Regional Tongues," *New York Times*, May 3, 1993, pp. 1, A8. See also Marlise Simons, "France to Form New Body to Further Protect Culture," *New York Times*, February 25, 1996, p. 12.

nomadic peoples, the Gypsies, have organized to protect their collective interests.[30]

That globalizing processes in the social realm have contributed to fragmegrative processes is also evident in the xenophobic fervor of some territorial communities, a fervor that can reasonably be interpreted as a reaction to the complexities and challenges inherent in the rapid expansion of global interdependence. Recognizing that they are increasingly caught up in the globalization of national economies and cultural values, and thus feeling unprotected by their governments, the leaders and members of these communities have retreated behind perspectives and policies that highlight their distinct and separate subgroup identities. In some cases these retreats have even led to mass migrations, to searches for new and more friendly locales in which subgroup ties can be preserved and enhanced. In other cases they have fostered intense violence: a devastating Muslim raid on the western Philippine town of Ipil, for example, was interpreted as "definitely not just a criminal act. It's an assertion of a way of life that is being exterminated by the globalization of culture and the predominance of the Christian population."[31] Similarly, some part of the pervasive and worldwide alienation from national politics and politicians can be easily interpreted as localizing responses to globalizing processes.

Political sources of fragmegration

The causal links between globalizing and localizing dynamics are especially conspicuous in the political realm. Denmark's original rejection of the Maastricht Treaty is illustrative. Virtually by definition, the first Danish referendum pitted the virtues of centralization against those of decentralization, and as the campaign moved to its conclusion one could almost literally "see" individual concerns about sovereignty get converted into a collective outcome that favored localizing dynamics. The idea of a supranational authority proved to be, for a majority of Danes in the first referendum, unacceptable. That is, they resisted centralization and, in so doing, created an authority crisis both for their country and the European Community. As such, as a process in which central authority was challenged and rebuffed, the Danish situation was

[30] David Binder, "European Gypsies Issue Call for Human Rights at Meeting," *New York Times*, May 5, 1993, p. A12.

[31] This observation was made by a political scientist, Alex Magno, quoted in Hong Kong's *Eastern Express*, April 7, 1995, p. 10

but another instance of a long-term worldwide trend, a pattern in which newly acquired skills and confidence on the part of micro actors underlie a shift from traditional to performance criteria of legitimacy and thereby give rise to stalemate and paralysis among macro actors. Authority crises of this sort are not only global in scope, but they also mark politics at all levels of governance, from the local to the national to the regional to the international. And as macro institutions at all levels become increasingly mired in crisis and conflict, so do these consequences exacerbate the concerns of individuals. The shift of enough people in the second referendum to reverse the outcome of the initial Danish vote is suggestive of how these feedback mechanisms can operate. Similarly, the strength of fragmegrative dynamics became readily evident in Iran when its parliament rejected a bill that would have separated the city of Qazvin from the province of Zanjan and extensive rioting immediately ensued in the former.[32]

And why are people challenging and resisting central authorities? The reasons are many, but a main one is that the dynamics of globalization are rendering conventional means of governance increasingly difficult. Neither national nor local governments can on their own cope with the fallout of the world's rapidly growing interdependence. Goods, services, money, ideas, polluted air and water, drugs, AIDS, terrorists, migrants, crime – to mention only the more obvious globalizing dynamics – move too quickly across established political boundaries for governments to control sufficiently to satisfy their constituents. The world has thus become witness to both the internationalization of conflict and the internationalization of cooperation, two contradictory forms of interaction which are inextricably tied to each other, with the inability of governments to solve major problems leading to cooperation among them even as it also results in their fragmentation. Both the Danish government's aspiration to European unity and their public's original rejection of the idea, in other words, are part and parcel of the same underlying global processes.

That fragmegrative dynamics are fostering conflict in diverse parts of the world is easier to describe than to explain. The description would stress the simultaneity, or at least the close temporal proximity, of crowds in far-flung parts of the world gathering in town squares to protest prevailing conditions and angrily to demand reforms. Starting

[32] "Iran Clamps Lid on Riot-Torn City," *International Herald Tribune*, August 6–7, 1994, p. 2.

late in the 1980s, a number of cities and countries in the world were the site of such scenes, of authority crises in which people aggregated their complaints and indicated they were no longer willing to settle for the status quo. While each of these authority crises doubtless flowered out of their own path-dependent roots, their occurrence at roughly the same moment in history suggests that they also had common sources, that globalizing dynamics were spreading conflict beyond national jurisdiction. But how to account for this spread? Clearly, subtle processes of emulation facilitated by the instruments of the microelectronic revolution lie at the heart of the explanation. The idea of challenging authority gets planted in people's minds by scenes on their television screens of groups and crowds elsewhere in the world successfully evoking responses, even compliance, from governments. And once the idea is planted in a micro soil of unease and discontent rendered especially fertile by the complexities of an ever more interdependent world noted above, similar action can follow. In such a soil it can take only a minor incident for people to convert their new-found, transnationally induced readiness to resort to conflict into street protests.[33] Although it may be more circuitous, the internationalization of conflict is no less dynamic than the internationalization of production or the internationalization of information.

Much the same can be said about the globalization of cooperation. It does not seem like mere coincidence, for example, that in 1988 alone some six wars, along with several long-standing situations endlessly on the brink of war, either came to a halt or moved significantly toward accommodation. On the contrary, as indicated in chapter 22, subtle indicators of emulative processes can again be discerned that point to the operation of globalizing processes. In these cases, however, the processes of emulation involved governmental elites, who perceived successful peace negotiations elsewhere as containing lessons for their own situations, more than it did mass publics, whose war-weariness

[33] A more elaborate discussion of how the communications processes through which the globalization of conflict occurs can be found in chapter 14. For an analysis of how such processes are not in themselves sufficient to precipitate challenges to authority – since the diffusion of ideas along this line must be supplemented by a widespread receptivity to them and a "triggering event" – see John Bohstedt and Dale E. Williams, "The Diffusion of Riots: The Patterns of 1766, 1795, and 1801 in Devonshire," *Journal of Interdisciplinary History*, vol. 19 (Summer 1988), pp. 1–24. A cogent case for viewing the globalization of conflict as having deep historical roots is provided in Sidney Tarrow, *Power in Movement: Social Movements, Collective Action and Politics* (Cambridge: Cambridge University Press, 1994).

was neither dependent upon stimuli from abroad nor conducive to the holding of protest rallies in town squares.

In addition, the globalization of cooperation has acquired momentum from institutional sources. It is no accident that increasingly the initiatives of the United Nations, Amnesty International, and other IGOs and NGOs cross national boundaries. Such activities – not to mention the conduct of internationally supervised elections or of the international regimes that process environmental, wildlife, oceanic, and many other interdependence issues – can be readily interpreted as globalizing responses to localized conditions. The availability of these transnational mechanisms has made it possible for localized impulses toward cooperation to find external support, thereby further expanding the internationalization of cooperation.

Continuing tensions

If the economic, social, and political sources of fragmegration are seen as interactive and thus as mutually reinforcing, it seems reasonable to conclude that collectively they serve as the deeper tendencies at work in world affairs that account for the simultaneity of so many striking developments in recent years. Whatever their unique, path-dependent sources, and however they may differ in the issues and institutions they embrace, these diverse changes that have surfaced from northern Eurasia to southern Africa since 1988 have one major characteristic in common: they are all expressive of major external inputs, of both blatant and subtle dynamics that emanated from elsewhere and then moved so widely along the Frontier as to infuse situations everywhere with both globalizing and localizing dimensions. This suggests that the future is unlikely to be a mere extension of the present, that more surprises lie ahead as the tensions inherent in fragmegration continue to play themselves out and intensify the challenges of governance along the Frontier.

7   Boundaries

Borders are drawn in blood.

Bosnian Serb General Ratko Mladic[1]

"I am a citizen of a nonexistent state, and I don't know where I live. Is it the Commonwealth of Independent States, or is it the Russian federated Republic? Is it Siberia, and is it the Sovereign Republic of Altai?"

Letter in a Russian newspaper following the collapse of the Soviet Union[2]

What, after all, makes powerplant pollution in one part of North America a "transboundary" problem even as, in another part of the same continent, it is a domestic one? By the same token, if toxic wastes are generated by an electronic firm whose products are sold around the world, is their disposal strictly a local matter?

Ronnie D. Lipschutz[3]

Indian programmers in Bangalore work on systems in New York and London through "real time" satellite linkages. There is no question that value is being added, but it is impossible to specify where the transaction takes place: in India, in the United States, or in both at the same time. Is the very concept of geographic space and geographic markets relevant to transactions which take place in cyber space?

Stephen J. Kobrin[4]

[1] Quoted in the *New York Times*, June 3, 1995.
[2] Quoted in Celestine Bohlen, "'What Country Do I Live In?' Many Russians Are Asking," *New York Times*, June 14, 1992, p. 1.
[3] "Learning of the Green World: Global Environmental Change, Global Civil Society and Social Learning," paper presented at the Annual Meeting of the International Studies Association, Acapulco (March 23–27, 1993).
[4] "Back to the Future: Neomedievalism and the Post Modern World Economy," paper presented at the Annual Meeting of the International Studies Association, San Diego (April, 1996), pp. 8–9.

Identities and boundaries, these epigraphs suggest, are likely to be high on the personal and political agendas of individuals and communities in the years ahead. This is hardly surprising, given a turbulent world undergoing profound parametric transformations and racked by fragmegrative tensions. While the Cold War may have established the "inviolability of borders"[5] – as illustrated by the inner-Korean border and the Taiwan strait – so has the end of that historical period revealed wide chasms along the domestic-foreign Frontier. And just as the Frontier has become increasingly permeable, so have the boundaries that separate individuals from their collectivities and collectivities from each other entered a period of flux. Perhaps more than ever, collectivities have become preoccupied with their jurisdictional boundaries and individuals have become especially sensitive about their identities and affiliations. With the advent of terrorism in the Tokyo subway and the streets of Oklahoma City, people have tended to replace their national security concerns with apprehension over personal security.[6] With US soldiers being court-martialed for refusing to wear UN insignias,[7] with sports franchises relocating in new cities,[8] with star athletes giving higher priority to their salaries than their team loyalties and others refusing to stand for the national anthem on religious grounds,[9] with Olympic athletes changing the countries for which they compete,[10] and with long-time employees losing their jobs

---

[5] Ian Gambles, "Lost Time – The Forgetting of the Cold War," *The National Interest*, no. 41 (Fall 1995), p. 29.

[6] Tim Weiner, "Finding New Reasons to Dread the Unknown," *New York Times*, March 26, 1995, sect. 4, p. 1.

[7] "U.S. Convicts G.I. Who Refused to Serve Under U.N. in Balkans," *New York Times*, January 25, 1996, p. A4, and Marc Fisher, "War and Peacekeeping," *Washington Post*, March 4, 1996, p. D1.

[8] Leonard Shapiro, "For Fans, It's A Dawg's Life: In Cleveland, Faithful Bemoan Team's Move," *Washington Post*, November 20, 1995, p. A1.

[9] Jason Diamos, "The Anthem Resolution: Abdul-Rauf Will Stand, Pray, and Play," *New York Times*, March 15, 1996, p. B1.

[10] For an extensive analysis of the large number of competitors representing different countries at the 1996 Olympics than they had in earlier games, see Christopher Clarey, "When a Change of Address Comes with a New Anthem," *New York Times*, July 14, 1996, special supplement, p. 15. These shifts in affiliation were explained by one coach as easy to understand: "I think first of all, the athletes are in the Olympics for themselves, not their coaches, not their families, but themselves. Only if they are in a medal ceremony and see that flag and see that hymn do they get the feeling of the team or the nation. But this is not the first point, not anymore."

to downsizing[11] and company towns losing their companies[12] – to cite but a few recent trends – the traditional ties of people to their country, community, and employer have been increasingly cross-pressured.

Both the foci and intensity of these new preoccupations and sensitivities have added to the complexity of the larger contexts in which the tasks of governance must be undertaken. Most notably, the growing concern with boundaries and identities highlights the micro–macro links between individuals and their collectivities. If the former are impelled to rethink their personal, group, and national identities and loyalties, what are the consequences for the latter? Will people begin to imagine new communities as the bases of new orientations toward their salient boundaries and identities? How, in short, is governance along the Frontier shaped by the interaction of the tensions between micro and macro actors on the one hand and between localizing and globalizing tendencies on the other?

This chapter is organized around these questions. It seeks to trace and assess the processes whereby the interplay of events may reconfigure identities and redraw boundaries as they cascade into and through every community, country, and region of the world, sometimes resulting in a globalizing transnationalism that embraces popular forces as well as governments, sometimes culminating in a localizing individualism, and sometimes (though with decreasing frequency) remaining confined to the interactions of governments in the interstate system.

There are two fundamental ways in which the causal webs are established and maintained. One involves the interaction processes whereby collectivities at the macro level and individuals at the micro level shape each other. The other consists of those strands of the causal webs that result when the clashes between the globalizing and localizing practices at work in macro institutions, organizations, and collectivities persist, worsen, get resolved, or otherwise condition the viability and volatility of the processes through which governance occurs. Table 7.1 maps these dynamics. It identifies some of the primary differences between the

---

[11] In the words of a bank clerk, "Chase has always been my identity. Chase is part of my name. But I'm not going to roll over and die because I don't work for the new Chase. Yet if this keeps up, who's going to go to work anymore. Why bother? Why get out of bed?" N.R. Kleinfeld, "The Company as Family, No More," *New York Times*, March 4, 1996, p. A1.

[12] Sara Rimer, "A Hometown Feels Less Like Home," *New York Times*, March 6, 1996, p. A1, and Rosabeth Moss Kanter, "AT&T, Call Home," *Washington Post*, January 14, 1996, p. C1.

Table 7.1. *Micro–macro interactions in globalizing and localizing contexts*

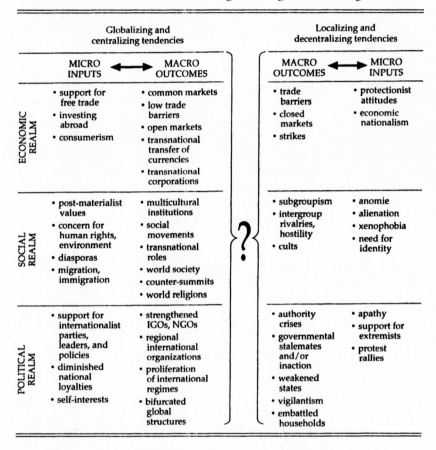

	Globalizing and centralizing tendencies		Localizing and decentralizing tendencies	
	MICRO INPUTS	MACRO OUTCOMES	MACRO OUTCOMES	MICRO INPUTS
ECONOMIC REALM	• support for free trade • investing abroad • consumerism	• common markets • low trade barriers • open markets • transnational transfer of currencies • transnational corporations	• trade barriers • closed markets • strikes	• protectionist attitudes • economic nationalism
SOCIAL REALM	• post-materialist values • concern for human rights, environment • diasporas • migration, immigration	• multicultural institutions • social movements • transnational roles • world society • counter-summits • world religions	• subgroupism • intergroup rivalries, hostility • cults	• anomie • alienation • xenophobia • need for identity
POLITICAL REALM	• support for internationalist parties, leaders, and policies • diminished national loyalties • self-interests	• strengthened IGOs, NGOs • regional international organizations • proliferation of international regimes • bifurcated global structures	• authority crises • governmental stalemates and/or inaction • weakened states • vigilantism • embattled households	• apathy • support for extremists • protest rallies

micro inputs and macro outcomes sustained by the tendencies toward globalization and localization in the economic, social, and political realms. The map's two-way arrows suggest the points at which micro phenomena condition – and are conditioned by – macro actors, institutions, and processes. The question mark represents the uncertainty infused into the course of events by fragmegrative dynamics, most particularly the uncertainties that are generated by the boundaries they span and the problematic nature of the identities they restructure. In effect, the two-way arrows and the question mark in the table serve as the foci of the chapter's effort to come to terms with the queries set forth above.

Of course, the map is hardly an exhaustive representation. A host of additional examples could be included in each cell of table 7.1, but those listed are sufficient to indicate how globalizing and localizing processes can get fashioned out of micro–macro interactions and then spread, become self-sustaining, and thereby contribute to the redrawing of boundaries, the redefining of identities, and the intensifying of tensions at work in the present stage of history.

Whatever else they may foster, these dynamics have a common characteristic: none is hindered by *established* territorial and jurisdictional barriers. Both the globalizing and localizing dynamics and the micro–macro linkages are capable of transgressing these barriers and redirecting the legitimacy sentiments on which new structures and processes get founded as people respond to new loci of authority and evolve new conceptions of territory. Globalizing dynamics can spread readily across the Frontier and are capable of reaching into any community anywhere in the world, just as localizing dynamics are capable of contracting energies and orientations within the limited confines of a subgroup that may or may not have a defined territorial jurisdiction. Whether any of these dynamics are sufficient to convert the new legitimacy sentiments into deep-seated and enduring structures and processes depends, in good part, on the capacity of people to adapt to the interplay of the contradictory changes that are now unfolding in their worlds.

The analytic challenge

Let us acknowledge at the outset the difficulty of empirically tracing the interactive effects of individuals and their collective institutions. Although these difficulties have been elaborated elsewhere,[13] the task becomes all the harder here because it is undertaken in the context of globalizing and localizing processes, all of which have a dynamic momentum of their own that is bound to be an amalgam of micro and macro factors so intertwined and complex as to pose a huge if not insurmountable analytic challenge. Some of the processes can be readily traced, but others – especially those that give structure to imagined communities – can be exceedingly difficult to identify and evaluate. The micro motives that sustain international finance and investment, for example, are easily grasped, just as is the ensuing swift and extensive

---

[13] James N. Rosenau, *Turbulence in World Politics: A Theory of Change and Continuity* (Princeton: Princeton University Press, 1990), Chap. 7.

macro movement of capital around the world. But once inquiry moves beyond self-interested motives and their quantifiable consequences, the analytic task becomes formidable. For then one not only has to comprehend the elusive micro orientations that foster imagined communities, but it is also necessary to estimate how these get translated into collective action and, in turn, are responsive to institutionalized patterns and requirements. Such causal webs are fashioned and sustained by a multiplicity of variables, each of which accounts for part of the variance and many of which involve contagion effects that are given impetus by the mental-emotional calculations of the people for whom the causal webs are relevant.

Furthermore, having long been mired in the presumptions of territoriality, we have few guidelines for proceeding to comprehend how the habits of peoples and the impulses of organizations will respond to conditions in which the spatial, temporal, and functional foundations of global life are undergoing turbulent transformations. As one astute observer suggests, noting that few changes have more transformative consequences than those which follow shifting conceptions of space and time, it is time to return to the tool-shed and fashion new conceptual instruments for probing the emergent global system: "It is truly astonishing that the concept of territoriality has been so little studied by students of international politics; its neglect is akin to never looking at the ground that one is walking on."[14]

So, even if observers come to recognize the presence of profound change, the analytic challenge is not trivial. On the other hand, meeting it may yield significant insights into the paradox of fragmegration wherein macro globalizing dynamics are fostering micro impulses to resist globalization and thereby spreading the processes of localization.

Micro orientations and the territorial continuum

Controversy attaches to the premise that developments at the micro level contribute to the course of events. Some analysts take as given that members of publics are too uninformed, compliant, and passive to have significant consequence in public affairs. From this perspective it makes little sense to accord macro–micro interactions a central place in any analytic framework that undertakes to account for the global scene.

---

[14] John Gerard Ruggie, "Territoriality and Beyond: Problematizing Modernity in International Relations," *International Organization*, vol. 47 (Winter 1993), p. 174.

World affairs, such an approach presumes, is to be understood and explained by focusing on the activities of states, international organizations, transnational corporations, and perhaps some key domestic groups, all of which so fully condition what happens at the micro level as to render superfluous inquiries into the dynamics at that level. Put differently some analysts posit only a one-way flow of influence as operative in macro–micro interactions.

For a number of reasons elaborated at length elsewhere[15] and further extended here in chapter 14, this reasoning is rejected in the ensuing discussion. Developments at the micro level are here considered central to both day-to-day and long-term trends in world affairs. Accordingly, it is useful to set forth briefly at the outset exactly what micro phenomena are regarded as sufficiently interactive with macro institutions and processes to produce outcomes that are likely to shape the context of governance in the decades ahead.

While the turbulence model emphasizes the analytic skills and emotional capacities of healthy adults, the concern here with globalizing and localizing dynamics points to the orientations of people everywhere as another change at the micro level that contributes to the alterations at work on the global scene. The enlarged skills are conceived to have been supplemented by altered horizons, by substantive predispositions that are not so much a product of the new skills as they are a result of the other parametric transformations outlined in chapter 4.

One surge of new orientations among the world's citizens involves the openness of political institutions. The collapse of the Soviet empire and the abandonment of command economies in all regions of the world has produced considerable movement along an orientational continuum that ranges from acceptance of authoritarian regimes at one extreme to demands for democratic government at the other. Despite some concern that the movement is always subject to reversal and may be temporary, there is wide agreement that in the present era the movement is essentially unidirectional: away from authoritarian practices and toward democratic politics. Indeed, for some this movement is so thoroughgoing that it marks the "end of history."[16]

However, neither globalizing nor localizing dynamics are systematically affected by micro orientations that vary in terms of the degree to

---

[15] Rosenau, *Turbulence in World Politics*, pp. 141–51.

[16] Francis Fukuyama, "The End of History?" *National Interest*, no. 16 (Summer 1989), pp. 3–18.

which people share a commitment to democratic values. Rather, the processes of fragmegration highlight another orientational dimension along which micro orientations appear to be changing. It involves shifting notions about the nature, scope, and importance of territory, about what identity means, about where boundaries are drawn, about what home and the homeland is. At one extreme on this continuum territorial identity is paramount, whereas at the other it is essentially irrelevant. Persons who lean in the former direction attach meaning to geographic space, viewing it as part and parcel of their very being, an integral feature of their family's history, a land in which their dead are buried and from which they derive cultural and material nourishment. Those at the "nonidentity" extreme of the continuum, on the other hand, accord higher priority to their occupations, social values, spiritual commitments, or professional affiliations than to their homelands. Somewhere in the middle of the continuum are many people who have evolved a capacity for shifting from one identity to another and thus are able to "live happily with multiple identities."[17]

Furthermore, all along the continuum, including the two extremes, territory is not necessarily equated with nation-state boundaries. This is partly because huge migrations of people fleeing political persecution or seeking economic opportunities convey the message that ties to the land can be severed, partly because the expansion of their analytic skills has enabled people to disassociate their notion of valued territory from the historical space controlled by their states, and partly because the states themselves are undergoing a diminution in their ability to exercise effective control over their spaces, territorial attachments have become increasingly variable. In some cases the alienation from states and the dictates of cultural history have resulted in more precise specifications of the space regarded as precious (subgroupism). In other cases territorial attachments have become increasingly ambiguous as they extend well beyond national boundaries (transnationalism). In a declining number of still other cases, especially those where cultures are coterminous with the history of a nation-state, the territorial attachments have not changed and remain as strong as ever (nationalism).

That micro orientations toward territoriality are increasingly complex and subject to variability can be highlighted by a series of questions inherent in the images of the earth resulting from space photography: Is

---

[17] Mike Featherstone, *Undoing Culture: Globalization, Postmodernism and Identity* (London: Sage Publications, 1995), p. 9.

not the image of the earth as a small blue sphere likely to erode peoples' sense of geographic attachment? Will they not be less impressed with the thought that there are Chinese, Canadian, or any other national boundaries when they see the world through lenses located deep in outer space? Is it not probable that "when the consciousness of an individual, even if only briefly, has become like that of satellites – namely, cosmopolitan, eccentric, and sovereign – then its ability to think of itself, through a process of simple identification, as part of a piece of political property on the earth below, is permanently disturbed"?[18] Could it be that the technological, economic, social, and political dynamics of globalization have become endemic precisely because psychologically people now recognize that the world has come together as a world?[19] On the other hand, do not recent events in the former Soviet Union, Yugoslavia, and Czechoslovakia point to a retreat to subgroup identities and thus an ever greater value being attached to land?

These questions not only suggest the potential of shifts in micro orientations; they also point to the need to avoid being so blinded by the indicators of intense localizing fervor which sustain virulent subgroupism that we downplay, overlook, or otherwise ignore emergent signs of variability in the direction of the values individuals attach to geographic space. Most of all, they highlight the need to allow for movement in opposite directions on the territorial continuum, a coexistence of psychological dynamics that value the homeland and those that look beyond territorial boundaries.

In addition to some quantitative findings that "feelings of belonging are clearly structured around the local and international poles,[20] qualitative signs suggestive of such a coexistence can readily be noted. They can be traced, for example, in what numerous US workers do not do in response to the internationalization of production. The media spotlight

---

[18] Peter Sloterdijk, "Nationality – A View From Above and Within," *Bard College Bulletin* (Spring 1991), p. 5.

[19] The perspective of many analysts on the effect of globalization on culture has been summarized succinctly by Anthony King as follows: "despite their different positions, and very different conceptual languages, all share at least two perspectives: the rejection of the nationally-constituted society as the appropriate object of discourse, or unit of social and cultural analysis, and to varying degrees a commitment to conceptualizing 'the world as a whole.'" Quoted in Frederick Buell, *National Culture and the New Global System* (Baltimore: Johns Hopkins University Press, 1994), p. 120.

[20] Sophie Duchesne and André-Paul Frognier, "Is There a European Identity?" in Oskar Niedermayer and Richard Sinnott (eds.), *Public Opinion and Internationalized Governance* (Oxford: Oxford University Press, 1995), p. 208.

tends to focus on Japan bashers and America firsters, but millions of people in the labor force do not engage in such behavior. Indeed, many buy Japanese automobiles and other imported goods to their liking. Similarly, just as many in the United Kingdom opposed closer ties to the European Union, so did considerable numbers actively support (or not protest) the extension of ties to the Continent. Likewise, the shift to market economies and democratic procedures in many developing countries that long adhered to command economies and authoritarian procedures appears to have been acceptable to sizable publics that had their appetites for luxury goods and voting rights heightened by the globalization of information. And even in those parts of the former Soviet world that are now experiencing virulent subgroupism, not to mention loud complaints about the advent of inflation and unemployment, there are segments of the public who evidence an acceptance of the idea that market economies and democratic institutions are worth the hardships that have to be endured to move in the new directions.

Other indicators that the processes of globalization are making inroads into territorial conceptions can be adduced from the relatively minimal opposition to the recent surge of activities on the part of international organizations. From the very visible extension of UN peacekeeping operations to the unmistakable constraints imposed by the IMF in many countries, from the continued expansion of the European Union's scope to the silent consent of Middle Easterners to searching out and destroying Iraq's nuclear capabilities, from the shift in Panamanian attitudes toward the United States[21] to the acceptance of NATO forces in Bosnia – to mention but a few of the signs indicative of a psychological globalization that allows for a diminution of the territorial imperative – it seems clear that people have begun to accept a widening of the political space represented by the Frontier.

The new roles to which interdependence and the globalization of national economies have given rise provide further insight into the potential variability of micro orientations at the nonterritorial extreme on the continuum. It seems clear that the responsibilities inherent in such roles tend to loosen, if not to liberate, their occupants from the psychological constraints of territory and any other limiting perspectives: "Commercial pilots, computer programmers, international bankers, media specialists, oil riggers, entertainment celebrities,

---

[21] Shirley Christian, "Panama Now Has Doubts Over U.S. Withdrawal," *New York Times,* April 19, 1992, p. 6.

ecology experts, demographers, accountants, professors, athletes – these compose a new breed of men and women for whom religion, culture, and nationality can seem only marginal elements in a working identity."[22]

In contrast to the incentives to move toward the nonterritorial extreme of the continuum are those that undermine such tendencies and, in effect, heighten the sensitivity of individuals to the virtues of territoriality. Consider, for example, the plight of those Russians whose micro orientations toward geographic space were called into question by the collapse and subsequent fragmentation of the Soviet Union. Being a country composed of 130 nationalities and ethnic groups and 31 autonomous republics and regions but no longer held together by a common mission, many people were left "feeling robbed of a sense of place, of purpose and of identity,"[23] which has subsequently fostered a resurgence of Russian nationalism.

Nor need there be a loss of territorial identity when micro orientations are dislocated by the transformations at work in world affairs. Even as people benefit from the new worldwide flows of information, for instance, so can they be isolated by these flows and thereby realize that something important is lacking in a borderless world where the boundaries of community have become global in scope. The information revolution, in other words, can be a mixed blessing at the micro level. As one observer puts it,

> When people in villages traditionally got together to talk, they talked about what they had in common. What the weather was like and what it meant for the crops; what the people in the next village were up to and if they meant harm; who in town was causing trouble and who needed help. The talk had real content, and the smaller the village the deeper the content was because everyone could agree on what was important – the talk was rooted in the particular facts of its local existence. By contrast, it obviously makes little sense for the global village to talk about the weather, since while some are harvesting others are planting . . . Since we must restrict our conversations to what we have in common, our global-village campfires are not as productive as the old tribal ones. We can find subjects of interest to all only by erasing content, paring away information – the things that interest me may not interest, or even be comprehensible, to you.[24]

[22] Benjamin R. Barber, "Jihad vs. McWorld," *Atlantic Monthly*, March 1992, pp. 54–5.

[23] Bohlen, "'What Country Do I live In?' Many Russians Are Asking," p. 1.

[24] Bill McKibben, *The Age of Missing Information*, as reproduced in the *New York Times*, May 24, 1992, sect. 7, p. 27.

While systematic shifts may thus be underway in territorial orientations at the micro level, these changes can be volatile and contradictory. They can be supportive of and responsive to the dynamics of both globalization and localization, and as such they are both a source and a product of the tensions presently racking world affairs.

Imagined communities

In addition to not being hindered by established territorial barriers, there is a second, equally important characteristic that globalizing and localizing dynamics share: both are sustained by imagined communities, that is, by structures and processes that are desired and believed to be susceptible to creation as means of linking together the interests, values, and futures of people who do not know each other but who are nonetheless regarded as fellow members of the same collectivity. They are imagined communities in the sense that while they may not have achieved political autonomy, economic viability, and social coherence, the mental and emotional predispositions necessary to establish them are sufficiently widespread to foster hope that the imagined can be transformed into the real.

While nation-states continue to function as central political actors and, as such, maintain structures that have evolved across history as people and organizations went about their daily tasks and sought to realize their particular goals, the globalizing and localizing dynamics are sufficiently powerful to encourage imagining supranational, transnational, or subnational communities that can serve needs and wants better than do the unwieldy and paralyzed states to which history is heir. Such imagined communities may or may not replace states, and they may or may not acquire concrete, discernible form, but the dynamics presently at work in world affairs make these nascent communities formidable contenders as engines of change, redesigners of boundaries, and sources of power in the years ahead.

That imagination can underlie the formation of historic communities has been persuasively demonstrated by Anderson's account of how nations evolved over the last several hundred years.[25] Reinforced by the advent of print media, which in turn led to the refinement of distinct languages attached to particular cultures, nations existed initially in the

---

[25] Benedict Anderson, *Imagined Communities: Reflections on the Origin and Spread of Nationalism*, rev. edn. (New York: Verso, 1991).

imaginations of elites, who increasingly appreciated that their language and culture encompassed unknown others with whom they had much in common. With the passage of time these imagined communities gradually acquired specific form as the course of events was interpreted to be consistent with the values and aspirations of those believed to be the nation's membership. Such responses eventually became so patterned – so habitual as motives and so regular as behavior – as to eventuate in structures and processes that were historically grounded.

While the lessons of history provide ample evidence as to the shape of imagined national communities – their main components being the achievement of political autonomy, sovereignty, acceptance as a state in the interstate system, a viable economy, and a consensual society sharing in a distinctive culture – the main structures of supranational, transnational, and subnational communities envisioned by those caught up in globalizing and localizing processes are less clear-cut, marked by considerable variety, and, in some cases, so inchoate as to defy articulation. To map and evaluate the boundary-changing consequences of globalization and localization, however, we need to delineate at least the bare outlines of these communities as they are imagined by those whose jobs or life-situations have oriented them away from their national communities.

Subnational communities

Since the localizing processes are often propelled by imagined political autonomy and thus closely resemble the nationalism that sustains nation-states, the imagined communities at the subnational level are more easily outlined than are those underlying globalizing processes at the supranational and transnational levels. At least three different forms of community are imagined as the culmination of localizing processes. One – what can be called the "territorial community" – involves ethnic, linguistic, and/or cultural ties that are linked to a historically specific territory imagined as the homeland of a nation with sovereign statehood. A second – the "subgroup" – derives its coherence in the imagination less from territorial and cultural attachments and more from shared interests that can be advanced or protected without the establishment of statehood. A third community imagined in the context of localizing dynamics is the "household" – that small, face-to-face unit organized around family ties that imagines itself as closely knit and surviving in the face of economic adversities and political upheavals. It is important to emphasize that while the household consists of few individuals, it is nevertheless a form of community in the sense that it is founded on a vision of enduring bonds sustained by cooperation among its members.

The territorial community is the most pervasive and conspicuous of those that drive localizing dynamics. Recent history offers a plenitude of examples of how the tendencies toward decentralization can convert imagined communities into concrete entities. Consider Croatia. It persisted through centuries of time as a politically autonomous entity in the imaginations of Croatians and recently took advantage of localizing dynamics in the Balkans to establish itself as a state with membership of the United Nations. Or consider the fact that "all along the southern fringe of the former Soviet empire, brush fires that sprang up with the collapse of central authority have resisted all efforts at mediation and control." These are fed by "warring nationalities" whose members "die for lands much of the world has never heard of . . . or for causes lost in the fog of history."[26] That is, territory and shared culture ("the fog of history") are central to some localizing processes, just as they lie at the core of imagined and actual national communities.

It follows, too, that the conversion of imagined communities into functioning territorial communities is highly problematic. Croatia successfully passed through the complex stages that lead to a concrete, relatively autonomous existence, but others are unable to move much beyond the imagination and still others get stalled somewhere in the conversion process. A quintessential insight into these processes whereby some get stalled in traversing the path to concrete status is available in the current case of the former Yugoslav republic of Macedonia. Although it managed to gain its independence, contain ethnic frictions, and maintain social tranquillity despite a Greek blockade and Serbian threats of invasion, Macedonia remained, until 1993, more imaginary than real – a "phantom nation" in diplomatic limbo – because it was unable to gain international recognition, thus preventing its citizens from traveling, trading, exchanging money, or using credit cards abroad. For a long time these last steps in the conversion of an imagined community were denied as a result of a Greek veto on recognition by the European Community (EC). Greece offered to withdraw its objection if Macedonia would change its name. Macedonian leaders indicated a willingness to call their community "New Macedonia" or "North Macedonia," but they were firm in not giving up the word

---

[26] Serge Schmemann, "Ethnic Battles Flaring in Former Soviet Fringe," *New York Times*, May 24, 1992, p. 7.

Macedonia. It had been so firmly planted in the imagination that, in the words of one official, an altered name would "erase our own identity . . . we would have to change everything, from schoolbooks to our poetry to our entire history" – that is, all the symbols through which culture and community live on in the imagination. And why did Greece insist on a name change? Because it feared Macedonia had territorial ambitions to incorporate Macedonians in Bulgaria and the northern Greek province of the same name into a single political entity.[27] Put in the analytic terms used here, a national community maintained a territorial community in a semi-imaginary state in order to prevent the realization of a perceived threat from an imagined transnational community.[28]

It is too simple, however, to assume that the dynamics which drive localizing processes are limited to an attachment to a widely shared culture located in a specific territory. The activities and aspirations of territorial communities are commonplace today, but, as noted, they are not the only outcomes envisioned by those who promote decentralization. Subgroups and households can also dominate imaginations. In the case of the former, the fragmentation of Mafia organizations and the splintering of religious organizations exemplify movement toward imagined communities that are stimulated less by territoriality and more by alienation from a parent group. Indeed, wherever organizational fragmentation occurs in other than an ethnic or nationality context, neither land nor shared cultural premises serve as prime stimuli to localizing processes as long as the fragmented unit's activities are permitted to unfold without undue interference and direction from outside. Such subgroups tend to take territoriality and culture for granted and to focus, instead, on the preservation and enhancement of their activities.

---

[27] Carol J. Williams, "Greeks Keep Macedonia a Phantom Nation," *Los Angeles Times*, May 27, 1992, p. 1.

[28] This situation was eventually resolved in Macedonia's favor as members of the EC agreed to recognize the national community as a territorial community and it was admitted to membership in the United Nations. In 1994 its independence was recognized by the United States. In so doing, however, the Clinton administration continued to try avoiding offense to either side by announcing that it was recognizing "the Former Yugoslav Republic of Macedonia." *New York Times*, February 10, 1994, p. A8. On the other hand, official status proved to be no panacea for Macedonia, as it became increasingly caught up in the tensions of the region. See Raymond Boner, "Balkan Conflict's Spread to Macedonia Is Feared," *New York Times*, April 9, 1995, p. 12. For a penetrating analysis of these developments, see Loring M. Danforth, "Names, Nationalism, and the International Recognition of the Republic of Macedonia," paper presented at the Annual Meeting of the International Studies Association, San Diego (April 1996).

What, then, are the characteristics of imagined subgroups not associated with jurisdiction over a particular geographic space? The answer varies, depending on the nature and purposes of the fragmenting subgroup. In some instances – e.g., a breakaway union local – the community is imagined to have more effective control over, or representation by, a subset of the original collectivity's membership. In other cases – such as the transfer of responsibilities to the field offices of a bureaucracy – the local entity may be imagined as more capable of managing the available resources than is the parent organization. In still other situations – such as the splitting off of a rival political party – an ideological cleavage may lead to imagining a more "pure" subgroup through the accomplishment of a successful break with the existing hierarchical arrangements. Whatever the particular structures conceived as worthy of fragmentation, however, the result is a diversity of localizing processes at various stages of evolution, some of which may be destined to achieve fruition while others continue unresolved for long stretches of time.

Perhaps the most elaborately imagined culmination of localizing dynamics is the household. Where the pragmatic orientations of subgroups do not compel grand formulations, the difficult, often precarious position of households in an ever more interdependent world appears to be grist for philosophical contemplation. Defined as "the smallest unit of civil society," and conceived "as both a polity and an economy," the household has been posited as a subnational community on which imaginations can focus with some hope of realization: they

> are miniature political economies that have a territorial base (life space) and are engaged in the production of their own life and livelihood. Households are *political* because their members arrive at decisions affecting the household as a whole and themselves individually in ways that involve negotiating relations of power. They have a *territorial base* because people have to have a place to live even if it is only a cardboard shack or a bit of pavement under the open sky. Their life space may be only temporary and neither very secure nor properly their own, and it may be shared with others. But every household activity requires such a space, and households that have continuity in time also claim and defend a life space of their own. Finally, households are conceived as *producers* and thus as a collective actor on behalf of their own (and sometimes others') material interests.[29]

---

[29] John Friedman, *Empowerment: The Politics of Alternative Development* (Cambridge, MA: Blackwell Publishers, 1991), pp. 46–7 (italics in the original).

Viewed in this way, households are seen as an alternative to main-stream models of economic development in national communities. Where the mainstream models are urban-centered and emphasize rapid growth and industrialization, the alternative model "places the emphasis on autonomy in the decision-making of territorially organized communities, local self-reliance (but not autarchy), direct (participatory) democracy, and experiential social learning . . . Centered on people rather than profits, it faces a profit-driven development as its dialectical other."[30] Stated more conceptually, "just as the paradigm in dominance approaches the question of economic growth from the perspective of the firm, which is the foundation of neoclassical economics, so an alternative development, based as it must be on the life spaces of civil society, approaches the question of an improvement in the conditions of life and livelihood from a perspective of the household."[31] Accordingly, the alternative model has been labeled the "empowerment approach,"[32] a term that highlights how micro–macro interactions may be relevant to the dynamics of fragmegration.

Supranational and transnational communities

Perhaps because of the diversity and rapidity of globalizing dynamics, outlines of imagined supranational and transnational communities that drive these dynamics are not so easily set forth. They range from communities that have been the subject of repeated articulations to others that are only barely discernible in the actions and words of disparate leaders. More precisely, imagined supranational communities – those in which states are subordinated to higher authorities created and sustained by the interstate system – have long been clearly articulated, whereas imagined transnational communities – those that span national boundaries but are essentially independent of the interstate system – are more often than not ill-defined and marked by contradiction.

Four types of supranational communities stand out as examples of how globalizing dynamics are imagined to culminate in authority structures that subsume states. One rests on the notion that some form of world government – more likely a confederation or a loose federation than a unitary system – can and ought to be created, an idea that has been the subject of an extensive literature even though few concrete steps have ever been taken that might eventuate in the supranational

---

[30] *Ibid.*, pp. vii, 9.   [31] *Ibid.*, p. 31.
[32] *Ibid.*, chap. 2.

authority necessary to the governance of such a system. A second type of imagined supranational community, also the focus of considerable analysis but much more developed insofar as the evolution of concrete institutions and practices is concerned, is the international regime, of which many have moved toward a modicum of realization in such issue-areas as oil, money, oceans, nuclear proliferation, and arms control. Regional political unions are a third type of imagined supranational community, with the steps toward continent-wide authority structures in Europe offering the most obvious illustration in this regard. Despite substantial progress in the economic realm, recent developments in Europe suggest that political unification of the continent faces severe obstacles; but the idea still lives on in many imaginations and may yet prove to be a quintessential instance of an imagination-driven spread of globalizing dynamics that culminate in an empirically observable transnational entity. The fourth example is the United Nations system, its charter and its many agencies, all of which have expanded their activities since the end of the Cold War even as there are also many ways in which the UN remains merely an instrument of the collective will of its member states.[33]

In comparison to the clarity with which schemes for world government, international regimes, regional unity, and the UN have been articulated in the imagination of analysts and the efforts of political leaders, those that envision transnational communities are mostly obscure and ambiguous. In some cases, to be sure, such communities are readily manifest. Consider diasporas – those "ethnic minority groups of migrant origins residing and acting in host countries but maintaining strong sentimental and material links with their countries of origin."[34] The Greek, Irish, Jewish, Armenian, and many other diasporas have evolved a number of ways of reinforcing their shared symbols and cultural ties, operating clear lines of communication, distributing financial and material assistance to their more beleaguered compatriots, and otherwise maintaining their bonds and contacts across

---

[33] For an analysis of the shifting role of the United Nations, see below (chap. 20), and James N. Rosenau, *The United Nations in a Turbulent World* (Boulder, Co: Lynne Rienner, 1992).

[34] Gabriel Sheffer, "A New Field of Study: Modern Diasporas in International Politics," in G. Sheffer (ed.), *Modern Diasporas in International Politics* (New York: St. Martin's Press, 1986), p. 3. For an extensive assessment of the role diasporas play in global life, see Joel Kotkin, *Tribes: How Race, Religion and Identity Determine Success in the New Global Economy* (New York: Random House, 1993).

national and generational boundaries. In effect, some diasporas stand out as having successfully exploited diverse globalizing dynamics in such a way as to convert their imaginations into tangible realities.

But diasporas are essentially exceptions to a general pattern in which the outlines of imagined transnational communities reek of inarticulate premises, ambiguous goals, inchoate structures, and irregular processes. Whether it be the environmental, feminist, peace, or Islamic movement (to cite only the more conspicuous of those presently extant), the symbols, memberships, modes of interaction, and hierarchical arrangements are, at best, variable and informal. Such movements tend to improvise from issue to issue, sometimes circumventing national governments and sometimes working with them, but at all times eschewing efforts to develop and intrude formal structures into their deliberations and activities. These qualities are readily discernible in this effort to generalize across social movements and posit them as culminating in "the Third System":

> We called this the "third system" not just by analogy with the Third World. The state and the market are the two main sources of power exercised over people. But people have an autonomous power, legitimately theirs. The "third system" is that part of the people which is reaching a critical consciousness of their role. It is not a party or an organization; it constitutes a movement of those free associations, citizens and militants, who perceive that the essence of history is the endless struggle by which people try to master their own destiny – the process of the humanization of man. The third system includes groupings actively serving people's aim and interests, as well as political and cultural militants who, while not belonging directly to the grassroots, endeavor to express people's views and to join their struggle. This movement tries to assert itself in all spaces of decision making by putting pressure on the state and economic power and by organizing to expand the autonomous power of people.[35]

None of the foregoing is to imply that the drift away from nation-states stimulated by localizing and globalizing dynamics is likely to lead to their ultimate replacement by other types of political structures. Some imagined communities may eventually become observable realities, but the empirical processes of spread that lead to the conversion of

---

[35] International Foundation for Development Alternatives (Nyou, Switzerland): dossier no. 17, pp. 69–70, as quoted in Friedman, *Empowerment*, p. 3. Another formulation along these lines can be found in Paul Ekins, *A New World Order: Grassroots Movements for Global Change* (New York: Routledge, 1992).

ideas into historic structures and processes are conceived as only *capable* of being local or global in scale. Events such as the break-up of Yugoslavia and of the former Soviet Union may feed the imaginations of other groups seeking political autonomy and thereby maintain the spread of localizing dynamics, but most states can employ their quasi-monopoly over the use of force to prevent imagined subnational communities from getting established as autonomous entities. Russia's attempted crushing of the independence movement in Chechnya is a quintessential example in this regard.

Whatever may be the limits on the processes of localization and globalization, the actual limits are less relevant for analytic purposes than the potential of an unlimited spread. What matters is the perceived emergence of new political space and/or the absence of established territorial and jurisdictional barriers. Such perceptions nourish the motives and sustain the pressures to move toward the realization of imagined communities. As long as technological developments and economic, political, and cultural processes encourage the belief that further spread is feasible, so will the momentum of globalizing and localizing dynamics be a major feature of the historical landscape. Their spread may be restricted by a lack of facilities, interests, or markets, but they are nonetheless relevant dynamics if they are theoretically extendable to any imagined community that develops the facilities, interests, or markets.

In short, from global television to wide-body jets, from fax machines to overnight mail deliveries, from VCRs to the Internet, from fiber optic telephone cables to orbiting satellites and the dishes to receive their signals[36] – to mention only the more conspicuous technological dynamics that have facilitated the coming together of the world as a world[37] – peoples everywhere have acquired the capacity to roam the Frontier with ease, often without pausing for permission to do so. Indeed, some have even settled on the Frontier and are, "in a very real sense, neither

---

[36] For a general assessment of the depth and breadth of the consequences of the microelectronic revolution, see Walter B. Wriston, "Technology and Sovereignty," *Foreign Affairs*, vol. 67 (Winter 1988–9), pp. 63–75.

[37] One observer notes that because of the technology-driven capacity of data to flit around the world defying territorial boundaries and having no jurisdictional home or final resting place, "globalization is partly shorthand for information abundance and improved communication – the internationalization of information flow." Derek Leebaert, "Innovations and Private Initiatives," *Washington Quarterly*, vol. 15 (Spring 1992), p. 114.

here nor there," but instead constitute phenomena of "growing importance – communities that span national borders."[38] Populated mainly by
immigrant workers and small entrepreneurs, these Frontier communities consist of people who travel back and forth so frequently between
their countries of origin and their income-producing locales that, in
effect, they "lead dual lives . . . [and] are at least bilingual, move easily
between different cultures, frequently maintain homes in two countries,
and pursue economic, political, and cultural interests that require a
simultaneous presence in both."[39] Described as "labor's analog to the
multinational corporation," these Frontiersmen and women do not
"thwart the operations of large corporations. As more common people
become involved in transnational activities, however, they subvert one
of the premises of globalization, namely that labor stays put and that its
reference point for wages and working conditions remains local."[40]
What repercussions are likely to flow from the proliferation of Frontier
communities? Perhaps none of consequence; on the other hand, "in this
context, transnationality and its political counterpart, dual citizenship,
may not be a sign of imminent civic breakdown but the vanguard of the
direction that new notions of community and society will be taking in
the next century."[41]

Not all of them may be interested in extending across conventional
boundaries – and depending on their historic ethnic or cultural commitments, some may even prefer to narrow the boundaries and resist external intrusions upon their communal ties – but the microelectronic and
transportation revolutions have made it possible for people, ideas,
goods, money, and services to pass through, circumvent, or otherwise
ignore the jurisdictions of states with relative impunity. Thus can diasporas and social movements quickly coordinate with counterparts
abroad. Thus can members of the European Union readily share each
others' produce and practices. Thus can opposition groups watch and
learn from the activities of citizens challenging authority in distant continents.

Stated more generally, there are powerful interaction effects between
the imagined and the real – between future-oriented aspirations and
prevailing economic, social, and political practices. Hence it is not sufficient to downplay the prospects for the imagined communities by

[38] Alejandro Portes, "Global Villagers: The Rise of Transnational Communities," *The
American Prospect*, no. 25 (March/April 1996), pp. 74, 77.
[39] *Ibid.*, p. 76.   [40] *Ibid.*   [41] *Ibid.*, p. 77.

calling attention to the localizing dynamics as evidence that globalization is an exaggerated fantasy or by highlighting global dynamics to demonstrate that worldwide localization is a mirage. To repeat: both are at work, both feed off the other, and these fragmegrative dynamics are likely to persist as long as the potential for supranational or subnational interaction sequences readily traversing the Frontier is woven into the fabric of the prevailing human condition.

Inhibited imaginations

While the power of imagined communities cannot be discounted, attention also needs to be paid to the possibility that some globalizing dynamics are not conducive to envisioning larger communities, that they can inhibit as well stimulate community formation and maintenance. It is hardly surprising, for example, that imagined transnational communities are sparse and ill-defined. Many globalizing processes are driven by technology and material concerns, with the result that they generate few incentives to frame goals that outline desired authority arrangements, much less aspire to cultural bonds and visions of new community structures. Less conspicuous, but surely no less important, are the ways in which technological dynamics have also contributed to individualizing processes. As indicated by the way in which television stations quickly become the focal point of mass uprisings, the products of the microelectronic revolution are crucial to the focusing of publics on their own private concerns. Just as television brings the world into the living room, in other words, so does it offer pictures of interest groups in action, thereby highlighting the virtues of action designed to advance personal goals. In addition, the spread of transnational crime networks[42] and the advent of computer viruses[43] are illustrative of how the very same technologies that have fostered globalization can also operate to dampen the imagination and suppress the inclination to form bonds to a community.

[42] For a succinct analysis of the dynamics of globalized crime, see Jessica Matthews, "We Live in a Dangerous Neighborhood," *Washington Post*, April 24, 1995, p. A19.

[43] A virus entitled Michelangelo, for instance, was anonymously introduced into IBM personal computers as a program designed to erase data and programs on the artist's 517th birthday, March 6, 1992. While Michelangelo's globalizing effects were not so virulent as feared, neither were they trivial. Some 750 personal computers used by South African pharmicists were struck, as were those of the New Salem Baptist Church in Kennesaw, Georgia, a magazine distributor in Edison, New Jersey, a newspaper in Argentina, the library of Boston University, the intelligence information system of the Uruguayan army, two companies in Great Britain, etc. Cf. *New York Times*, March 7, 1992, p. A6.

Multinational corporations and professional societies are still another realm in which the dynamics of globalization can curb the spirit of community and encourage the narrowing of horizons to oneself and the advancement of one's expertise. Such organizations are major players in the transnational world, but their interests are largely material and confined to short-term expectations. To be sure, multinational corporations can be models of organizational efficiency, both in terms of enhancing internal coherence and maneuvering around the boundaries of the interstate system. Yet, being primarily concerned with economic matters and thus not offending any potential markets, they eschew giving voice to imagined communities. They do, of course, devote energy to insuring cooperative relations with any political authorities who have some jurisdiction over the production and distribution of their products, but they are not otherwise inclined to enter the political realm. Accordingly, where members of social movements rely on their imaginations to give direction to their conduct, the diverse organizations that populate the world of international business and finance find inspiration in the bottom line and the concrete figures that depict profits and losses.

Transnational entities without imagined communities

Is this to say that the imaginations of people who occupy roles in the transnational world are dormant and untapped, that they lack a vision of the future other than that of servicing the bottom line or advancing their professional interests? If neighborhoods form vigilante groups and militia to defend their households when localizing processes become stressful, to what units of authority do those whose community ties have been undermined or severed by globalizing dynamics revert when their well-being is under siege? Is it possible that the undermined ties are not replaced by new authority structures, that powerful transnational processes can span borders without giving rise to either Frontier settlements or the imagined ties of new and enlarged communities? Can the dynamics of globalization foster transnational economic, political, and social entities that are connected by material and empirical links which transcend but do not alter established territorial boundaries?

Such questions seem to defy our understanding of how large-scale and distinguishable sociopolitical entities are formed and sustained. Although the historical formation of states tells us a great deal about the links between political organization and territoriality, these questions suggest there are still large gaps in our understanding, that the modern state has been so successful that we have difficulty grasping how it might some day be supplanted by competing entities.[44] Our social-scientific maps all depict communities that are sustained by a modicum of cohesion, that have at least a semblance of legitimacy, that are able to enact and implement policies, and that have members who are sufficiently linked to a shared history or a current plight to appreciate the symbiosis of mutual benefit. How, then, to frame a new map that allows us to probe the foregoing questions? How to allow for important and coherent transnational entities that emerge and thrive without the support of imagined visions of an eventual community?

One basis for extending our maps along these lines is provided by the plethora of transnational economic entities that have recently become salient on the world scene and appear to flourish independently of the policies of states. Variously called "micro regions," "natural economic territories (NETS)," "growth circles," "growth triangles," or "subregional economic zones," these entities are distinguished by extensive flows of trade, investment, and technology among contiguous localities or territories that span national boundaries. Such flows are, of course, not new, but today these economic interactions are so broad and deep as to be quite unlike the historical patterns of earlier periods. In effect, they consist of patterns readily discernible in an unfamiliar political terrain, in a geographic space that is not bounded by a sovereign state, that does not embrace an integrated economy, that may not partake of a common culture, that does not consist of a formal international relationship, and that lacks any kind of authority structure for making decisions on behalf of those who fall within its scope. Indeed, as will be seen in the next chapter's discussion of micro regions, these entities are flourishing so intensely as to permit an argument that "trade boundaries are superseding political boundaries . . . [I]n some cases, sub-regions of nation-states are developing economic links with neighbors that may be more vital than links with the political centers of power that govern them. This has raised the question of whether there is an emerging disjuncture between economic relations generated 'from below' and political authority administered 'from above.'"[45]

---

[44] For a cogent discussion of the links between territoriality and the state as well as the conditions under which competing entities might evolve to coexist with, if not replace, the state, see Hendrik Spruyt, *The Sovereign State and Its Competitors* (Princeton: Princeton University Press, 1994).

[45] Amos A. Jordan and Jane Khanna, "Economic Interdependence and Challenges to the Nation-State: The Emergence of Natural Economic Territories in the Asia-Pacific," *Journal of International Affairs*, vol. 48 (Winter 1995), p. 433.

That such transnational entities are increasingly relevant phenomena is indicated by the estimate that more than 180 have emerged in Europe and 9 have been identified in the Asia-Pacific region.[46] And such quantified data have been supplemented by analyses of particular cases. The entity forming across the border separating California and Mexico, for instance, has been extensively researched and shown to be vitally alive and growing.[47] For present purposes, the relevance of these emergent units is that they appear to function and thrive even though there are no indications that imagined communities are evolving at either the micro or macro levels to embrace, justify, and extend them. They are, rather, empirical systems that encompass communities but are not in themselves a community, that occupy a specified territory but are not in themselves bound together by the deep bonds normally associated with territoriality, that subsume a host of social, economic, and political structures but are not in themselves coherent structures. On the contrary, more often than not they are founded on numerous layers of authority, overlapping economies, discrepant cultures, migrating populations, and tension-filled border areas.

Conclusion

Whatever else the transnational entities that persist without the support of imagined communities may demonstrate, they are surely still another illustration of the large extent to which turbulent conditions are rendering traditional borders increasingly obsolete and encouraging the emergence of new forms of governance along the Frontier. With the basic foundations of organized human systems thus in continuous flux, every person and every group becomes both a potential adversary and a potential ally of every other person and every other group, a circumstance that aptly describes the tensions which underlie and sustain fragmegration. Thus security and stability at the individual and societal levels appear more elusive than ever and tending toward an all-time low as political systems fail to keep sufficiently abreast of the pace of change to redefine territorial and nonterritorial boundaries. People still need to attend to daily tasks and act out long-standing routines; but

---

[46] The data for Europe have been collected by the European Commission and those for Asia by Jordan and Khanna, "Economic Interdependence and Challenges to the Nation-State," pp. 433–62.

[47] Cf. Abraham F. Lowenthal and Katrina Burgess (eds.), *The California-Mexican Connection* (Stanford: Stanford University Press, 1993).

they have to do so with different and shifting conceptions of how the world is organized, how it works, and where they are located in it. In order to cope with the dynamism of fragmegration, and as the ultimate battleground on which conflicts between globalizing and localizing tendencies are waged, people have to evolve a balance between the values they attach to a homeland and those that look beyond territorial horizons.

It follows that with boundaries increasingly indeterminate and identities increasingly ambiguous, the tasks of governance in a turbulent world seem so daunting and severe to engender concern that perhaps they cannot be performed adequately under present global and local conditions. Before exploring this possibility, however, we need to specify more precisely what governance along the Frontier entails and then assess what the potential contribution of various actors may be for either ameliorating or deepening what is surely a worldwide crisis of governance. The next chapter wrestles with the challenge of identifying and clarifying the diverse activities that sustain governance along the domestic-foreign Frontier, while succeeding chapters probe in depth the roles played by various institutions, norms, practices, and actors in these processes.

8   Governance

Moody's is the credit rating agency that signals the electronic herd of global investors where to plunk down their money, by telling them which countries' bonds are blue-chip and which are junk. That makes Moody's one powerful agency. In fact, you could almost say that we live again in a two-superpower world. There is the U.S. and there is Moody's. The U.S. can destroy a country by leveling it with bombs; Moody's can destroy a country by downgrading its bonds.

Thomas L. Friedman[1]

As this epigraph suggests, to assess the nature of governance along and across the domestic-foreign Frontier is to focus on powerful tensions, profound contradictions, and perplexing paradoxes. It is to search for order in disorder, for coherence in contradiction, and for continuity in change. It is to confront processes that mask both growth and decay. It is to look for authorities that are obscure, boundaries that are in flux, and systems of rule that are emergent. And it is to experience hope embedded in despair.

This is not to imply the task is impossible. Quite to the contrary, one can discern patterns of governance along the Frontier that are likely to proliferate, others that are likely to attenuate, and still others that are likely to endure as they always have. No, the task is not so much impossible as it is a challenge to one's appreciation of nuance and one's tolerance of ambiguity.

Conceptual nuances

It follows that we need to start by drawing a nuanced set of distinctions among the numerous processes and structures that fall within the

---

[1] "Don't Mess With Moody's," *New York Times*, February 22, 1995, p. A19.

purview of governance along the Frontier. As a point of departure, governance is here conceived at a very abstract level as spheres of authority (SOAs) at all levels of human activity – from the household to the demanding public to the international organization – that amount to systems of rule in which goals are pursued through the exercise of control. The reason for this broad formulation is simple: in a turbulent and ever more interdependent world, where what happens in one corner or at one level may have consequences for what occurs at every other corner and level, it seems a mistake to adhere to a narrow definition in which only formal institutions at the national and international levels are considered relevant SOAs. The United Nations system and national governments are surely central to the conduct of governance today,[2] but they are only part of the full picture. In the words of the Council of Rome,

> We use the term governance to denote the *command* mechanism of a social system and its actions that endeavor to provide security, prosperity, coherence, order and continuity to the system. . . . Taken broadly, the concept of governance should not be restricted to the national and international systems but should be used in relation to regional, provincial and local governments as well as to other social systems such as education and the military, to private enterprises and even to the microcosm of the family.[3]

Governance, in other words, encompasses the activities of governments, but it also includes any actors who resort to command mechanisms to make demands, frame goals, issue directives, and pursue policies. In today's fragmegrated world these nongovernmental actors are extraordinarily varied and numerous, and their activities along and across the Frontier are considered no less central to the processes of governance than are the policies of governments. With ever greater interdependence corroding long-established boundaries and enabling the consequences of actions by individuals and groups as well as those launched by governments to spread well beyond the communities in which they originate, governance along the Frontier has come to be

---

[2] See chapters 18 and 20.

[3] Alexander King and Bertrand Schneider, *The First Global Revolution: A Report of the Council of Rome* (New York: Pantheon Books, 1991), pp. 181–2 (italics added). For other inquiries that support the inclusion of small, seemingly local systems of rule in a broad analytic framework, see John Friedmann, *Empowerment: The Politics of Alternative Development* (Cambridge, MA: Blackwell, 1992), and Robert Huckfeldt, Eric Plutzer, and John Sprague, "Alternative Contexts of Political Behavior: Churches, Neighborhoods, and Individuals," *Journal of Politics*, vol. 55 (May 1993), pp. 365–81.

marked by density and complexity. Indeed, as implied in table 3.3, it is precisely this density that underlies an upsurge of concern with governance on a global scale[4] and a widely shared recognition that the common sense of the epoch is changing.

Command and control

But the concept of command mechanisms can be misleading. It implies that hierarchy, perhaps even authoritarian rule, characterizes governance systems. Such an implication may be descriptive of many forms of governance, but hierarchy is certainly not a necessary prerequisite to the framing of goals, the issuing of directives, and the pursuit of policies. Indeed, a central theme of the ensuing analysis is that often the practices and institutions of governance can and do evolve in such a way as to be minimally dependent on hierarchical, command-based arrangements. Accordingly, while preserving the core of the Council of Rome formulation, here we shall replace the notion of command mechanisms with the concept of *control* or *steering* mechanisms, terms that highlight the purposeful nature of governance without presuming the presence of hierarchy. They are terms, moreover, informed by the etymological roots of "governance": the term "derives from the Greek 'kybenan' and 'kybernetes' which means 'to steer' and 'pilot or helmsman' respectively (the same Greek root from which 'cybernetics' is derived). The process of governance is the process whereby an organization or society steers itself, and the dynamics of communication and control are central to that process."[5]

To grasp the concept of control one has to appreciate that it consists of relational phenomena which, taken holistically, comprise systems of rule. Some actors, the controllers, seek to modify the behavior and/or

---

[4] See, for example, a new journal, *Global Governance*, published by Lynne Rienner in cooperation with the Academic Council on the United Nations (ACUNS) and the United Nations University. Recent books and reports on the subject include The Commission on Global Governance, *Our Global Neighborhood* (New York Oxford University Press, 1995); The Commission on Global Governance, *Issues in Global Governance: Paper Written for The Commission on Global Governance* (London: Kluwer Law International, 1995); Richard Falk, *On Humane Governance: Toward a New Global Politics* (University Park: Pennsylvania State University Press, 1995); Jan Kooiman (ed.), *Modern Governance: New Government–Society Interactions* (London: Sage Publications, 1993); and Yoshikazu Sakamoto (ed.), *Global Transformation: Challenges to the State System* (Tokyo: United Nations Press, 1994).

[5] Steven A. Rosell *et al.*, *Governing in an Information Society* (Montreal: Institute for Research on Public Policy, 1992), p. 21.

orientations of other actors, the controllees, and the resulting patterns of interaction between the former and the latter can properly be viewed as a system of rule sustained by one or another form of control. It does not matter whether the controllees resist or comply with the efforts of controllers; in either event, attempts at control have been made. But it is not until the attempts become increasingly successful and compliance with them increasingly patterned that a system of rule founded on mechanisms of control can be said to have evolved. SOAs and control mechanisms, in other words, are founded on a modicum of regularity, a form of recurrent behavior that systematically links the efforts of controllers to the compliance of controllees through either formal or informal channels.[6]

It follows that systems of rule can be maintained and their controls successfully and consistently exerted even in the absence of established legal or political authority. The evolution of intersubjective consensuses based on shared fates and common histories, the possession of information and knowledge, the pressure of active or mobilizable publics, and/or the use of careful planning, good timing, clever manipulation, and hard bargaining can – either separately or in combination – foster control mechanisms that sustain governance without government.[7]

But if governance is conceptualized at a very abstract level to include any system of rule at any level of human activity, in an ever more interdependent world how is a distinction to be drawn between control

[6] Rule systems have much in common with what has come to be called the "new institutionalism." See, for example, Robert O. Keohane, "International Institutions: Two Approaches," *International Studies Quarterly*, vol. 32 (December 1988), pp. 379–96; James G. March and Johan P. Olsen, "The New Institutionalism: Organizational Factors in Political Life," *American Political Science Review*, vol. 78 (September 1984), pp. 734–49; and Oran R. Young, "International Regimes: Toward a New Theory of Institutions," *World Politics*, vol. 39 (October 1986), pp. 104–22. For an extended discussion of how the concept of control is especially suitable for the analysis of both formal and informal political phenomena, see James N. Rosenau, *Calculated Control as a Unifying Concept in the Study of International Politics and Foreign Policy* (Princeton: Research Monograph no. 15, Center of International Studies, Princeton University, 1963).

[7] One observer suggests that the "idea of governance without government is easy enough to grasp. It refers to the role that social institutions or governance systems, in contrast to organizations or material entities, play in solving the collective-action problems that pervade social relations under conditions of interdependence." Oran R. Young, *International Governance: Protecting the Environment in a Stateless Society* (Ithaca: Cornell University Press, 1994). For a series of diverse essays along this line, see James N. Rosenau and Ernst-Otto Czempiel (eds.), *Governance Without Government: Order and Change in World Politics* (Cambridge: Cambridge University Press, 1992).

mechanisms that do and do not involve governance along the Frontier? The answer seems obvious: if the Frontier encompasses the legal, political, economic, and cultural spaces where domestic and foreign affairs converge or overlap, then only those rule systems with jurisdictions or consequences across such spaces can be regarded as aspects of its governance.

Viewed in this way, it might seem that delineating the processes of governance occurring along the Frontier is a relatively simple task. Presumably such processes are not operative with respect to those matters that are strictly local in nature and have no goals, foci, or repercussions that link domestic and foreign actors or institutions. An election in a Wyoming town, a court decision in rural China, a labor rally in downtown Lima, a property dispute in Naples, a budget crisis in Kiev, an educational experiment in Malaysia – such events are surely expressive of governance, but they normally do not foster or sustain consequences that span the nexus where domestic and foreign affairs converge. And much the same can be said about a hanging in Singapore, an ambassadorial appointment in Indonesia, an announcement of prospective cabinet members in Thailand, and a terrorism trial in Peru – *except* that in all these 1995 or 1996 cases the ensuing developments quickly spread across the Frontier and became, at least briefly, controversial foci of governance.[8]

If seemingly local events resulting from the behavior of single individuals can quickly become contested international issues, it follows that tracing governance across and along the Frontier is not as simple a task as it might seem at first glance. Given a mismatch between the world's political structures on the one hand and its economic, social, cultural, and normative structures on the other, there are bound to be complex and unexpected challenges which cannot be easily discerned, much less overcome, by organizing inquiry as if the distinction between domestic and foreign affairs is universally applicable and meaningful. Rather, the Frontier must be approached as an inherent source of tension among national governments intent upon preserving their boundaries and other types of actors who seek to expand, by-pass, ignore, or otherwise transgress the boundaries. These tensions take many forms, including most notably those among national governments (i.e., the

[8] The hanging involved a Philippine maid, the ambassadorial appointment was of an Indonesian general offensive to many Australians, the Thai nominees were thought to be involved in the drug trade by the United States, and the trial in Peru involved an American woman.

realm of international politics and foreign policy), those that stem from efforts of nongovernmental organizations to affect people, organizations, institutions, or governments across the Frontier (i.e., the realm of transnational relations), and those that arise out of unintended boundary-spanning consequences precipitated by strictly domestic activities (what have been called "cross-border spill-overs")[9] on the part of either governmental or nongovernmental actors. What distinguishes the following chapters is that while they allow for the involvement of states in transnational relationships and cross-border spill-overs, they concentrate on the second and third of these tension areas. The first has already been developed in a huge literature and, indeed, it is precisely the insufficiency of that literature that provoked the ensuing attempt to extend our understanding of governance beyond the well-established SOAs so exclusively dominated by states.

Interdependence and proliferation

Implicit in broadening the concept of governance to include transnational relations and cross-border spill-overs is a premise that interdependence involves not only flows of control, consequence, and causation within systems, but that it also sustains flows across systems. These dynamics whereby values and behaviors at one level get converted into outcomes at more encompassing levels – outcomes which in turn get converted into still other consequences at still more encompassing levels – highlight the large extent to which governance along the Frontier is not confined by standard geographic, social, cultural, economic, or political boundaries.[10] If major changes occur in the structure of households, if individual greed proliferates at the expense of social consciences, if people become more analytically skillful, if crime grips neighborhoods, if schools fail to provoke the curiosity of children, if racial or religious prejudices become pervasive, if resources get consumed faster than they are replenished, if the drug trade starts distributing its illicit goods through licit channels, if defiance comes to vie with compliance as a characteristic response to authority, if new trading partners are established, if labor and environmental groups in

---

[9] "Preface," in Susan L. Shirk, *How China Opened Its Door: The Political Success of the PRC's Foreign Trade and Investment Reforms* (Washington, DC: The Brookings Institution, 1994), pp. xvi–xviii.

[10] For an interesting analysis that posits an evolution to systems of governance without ties to identifiable territories, see Bruce E. Tonn and David Feldman, "Non-Spatial Government," *Futures*, vol. 27, no. 1 (1995), pp. 11–36.

different countries form cross-border coalitions, if cities begin to conduct their own foreign commercial policies – to mention only some of the more conspicuous present-day dynamics – then the consequences of such developments can ripple across and fan out within provincial, regional, national, and international levels as well as across local communities. Such is the crazy-quilt nature of modern interdependence. And such is the staggering challenge of tracing governance across the Frontier.

And the challenge continues to intensify as control mechanisms proliferate at a breathtaking rate. For not only has the number of UN members risen from 51 in 1945 to 184 a half-century later, but the density of nongovernmental organizations (NGOs) has increased at a comparable pace. With the continuing growth of the world's population, projected to exceed 8 billion by 2025, increasingly people will need to concert their actions to cope with the challenges and opportunities of daily life, thus giving rise to more and more organizations to satisfy their needs and wants. Chapter 17 highlights the large extent to which the organizational explosion of our time is no less consequential than the population explosion. And it is an explosion that is pervasive at all levels of human activity – from neighborhood organizations, community groups, regional networks, national states, and transnational regimes to international systems. As long ago as 1962 and in one country alone, for example, "an astonishing total of over 63,000 local governments with some autonomous authority over specific parcels of US space" were identified,[11] and presumably this and comparable figures for other countries have multiplied many times over in the intervening years. Indeed, to cite more up-to-date figures, the significant contribution that NGOs make to governance across the Frontier can be readily inferred from the fact that over 17,000 international nongovernmental organizations in the nonprofit sector were active in the mid-1980s and that in excess of 35,000 transnational corporations with some 150,000 foreign subsidiaries were operating in 1990.[12]

Not only is global life marked by a density of populations, in other words; it is also dense with organized activities, thereby complicating and extending the processes of governance along the Frontier. For while organizations provide decision-points through which the steering

[11] Edward W. Soja, *The Political Organization of Space* (Washington, DC: Resource Paper no. 8, Association of American Geographers, 1971) , p. 45.
[12] Jan Aart Scholte, *International Relations of Social Change* (Philadelphia: Open University Press, 1993), pp. 44–5.

mechanisms of governance can be carried forward, so may they operate as sources of opposition to any institutions and policies designed to facilitate governance. Put in still another way, if it is the case that global life late in the twentieth century is more complex than ever before in history, it is partly because the world is host to ever greater numbers of organizations in all walks of life and in every corner of every continent. As a consequence, it is possible to note an "upsurge in the collective capacity to govern": despite the rapid pace of ever greater complexity and decentralization – and to some extent because of their exponential dynamics – the world is undergoing "a remarkable expansion of collective power," an expansion that is highly disaggregated and unfolds unevenly but that nevertheless amounts to a development of rule systems "that have become 1) more intensive in their permeation of daily life, 2) more permanent over time, 3) more extensive over space, 4) larger in size, 5) wider in functional scope, 6) more constitutionally differentiated, and 7) more bureaucratic."[13]

Disaggregation and innovation

It follows from the foregoing that there is no single organizing principle on which governance across the Frontier rests, no emergent order around which communities and nations are likely to converge. Viewed on a global scale, governance is the sum of a myriad – literally millions – of control mechanisms driven by different histories, goals, structures, and processes. Perhaps every mechanism shares a history, culture, and structure with a few others, but there are no characteristics or attributes common to all mechanisms. This means that any attempt to trace a hierarchical structure of authority which loosely links disparate sources of governance to each other is bound to fail. In terms of governance, the world is too disaggregated for grand logics that postulate a measure of coherence along the Frontier.

Indeed, the continuing disaggregation that has followed the end of the Cold War suggests an extension of the anarchic structures that have long pervaded world politics. If the absence of an ultimate authority signified the presence of anarchy during the era of hegemonic leadership and superpower competition, such a characterization of global affairs is all the more pertinent today. It might be said that a new form of anarchy has evolved in the current period – one that involves not only the

---

[13] Martin Hewson, "The Media of Political Globalization," paper presented at the Annual Meeting of the International Studies Association, Washington DC, (March 1994), p.2.

absence of a highest authority, but also encompasses such an extensive disaggregation of authority as to intensify the pace at which transnational relations and cross-border spill-overs are permeating the Frontier, even as it also allows for much greater flexibility, innovation, and experimentation in the development and application of new control mechanisms.

Emergence and evolution

Underlying the growing complexity and continuing disaggregation of governance across the Frontier are the obvious but often ignored dynamics of change wherein control mechanisms emerge out of path-dependent conditions and then pass through lengthy processes of either evolution and maturation or decline and demise. In order to acquire the legitimacy and support they need to endure, successful mechanisms of governance are more likely to evolve out of bottom-up than top-down processes. As such, as mechanisms that manage to evoke the consent of the governed, they are self-organizing systems, steering arrangements that develop through the shared needs of groups and the presence of developments that conduce to the generation and acceptance of shared instruments of control.

But there is no magic in the dynamics of self-organization. The SOAs that sustain governance do not just suddenly happen. Circumstances have to be suitable, people have to be amenable to collective decisions being made, tendencies toward organization have to develop, habits of cooperation have to evolve, and a readiness not to impede the processes of emergence and evolution has to persist. The proliferation of organizations and their ever greater interdependence may stimulate felt needs for new forms of governance, but the transformation of these needs into established and institutionalized control mechanisms is never automatic and can be marked by a volatility that consumes long stretches of time. Yet, at each stage of the transformation, some form of governance can be said to exist, with a preponderance of the control mechanisms at any moment in time evolving somewhere in the middle of a continuum that runs from nascent to fully institutionalized mechanisms, from informal SOAs where goals are framed, directives issued, and policies pursued, to formal instruments of decision-making, conflict resolution, and resource allocation.

No matter how institutionalized rule systems across the Frontier may be, in other words, governance is not a constant in these turbulent times. It is, rather, in a continuous process of evolution, a becoming that fluctuates between order and disorder as conditions change and emergent properties consolidate and solidify. To analyze governance by freezing it in time is to insure failure in comprehending its nature and vagaries.

The relocation of authority

As previously indicated, central to governance across the Frontier are major shifts in the location of authority and the site of control mechanisms on every continent and in every country, shifts that are as pronounced in economic and social systems as they are in political systems. In some cases the shifts have transferred SOAs away from the political realm and into the economic and social realms even as in still other instances the shift occurs in the opposite direction.

Partly these shifts have been facilitated by the end of the Cold War and the lifting of the constraints inherent in its bipolar global structure of superpower competition. Partly they have been driven by a search for new, more effective forms of political organization better suited to the turbulent circumstances that have evolved with the shrinking of the world by dynamic technologies. Partly they have been driven by the skill revolution that has enabled citizens to identify their needs and wants more clearly as well as empowering them more thoroughly to engage in collective action.[14] Partly they have been stimulated and sustained by subgroupism – the fragmenting and coalescing of groups into new organizational entities – that has created innumerable new sites from which authority can emerge and toward which it can gravitate.[15] Partly they have been driven by the continuing globalization of national and local economies that has undermined long-established ways of sustaining commercial and financial relations.[16] And, no less, the shifts have been accelerated by the advent of interdependence issues that have fostered new and intensified forms of transnational collaboration as well as new social movements that are serving as transnational voices for change.[17]

---

[14] For an analysis of how the skill revolution has empowered people to engage more effectively in collective action, see chapters 14 and 15.

[15] The dynamics of subgroupism are outlined in chapter 4.

[16] See, for example, Peter F. Drucker, *Post-Capitalist Society* (New York: HarperCollins, 1993).

[17] For cogent analyses of the emergent role of new social movements, see Ron Eyerman and Andrew Jamison, *Social Movements: A Cognitive Approach* (Cambridge: Polity Press, 1991); and Leslie Paul Thiele, "Making Democracy Safe for the World: Social Movements and Global Politics," *Alternatives*, Vol. 18 (1993), pp. 273–305; R.B.J. Walker, *One World, Many Worlds: Struggles for a Just World Peace* (Boulder, CO: Lynne Rienner, 1988). For a discussion of the impact of new interdependence issues, see chapter 4.

In short, the numerous shifts in the loci of governance stem from interactive tensions whereby processes of globalization and localization are simultaneously unfolding on a worldwide scale. In some situations the foregoing dynamics are fostering control mechanisms that extend beyond national boundaries and in others the need for the psychic comfort of neighborhood or ethnic attachments is leading to the diminution of national entities and the formation or extension of local mechanisms. The combined effect of the simultaneity of these contradictory trends is that of lessening the capacities for governance located at the level of sovereign states and national societies.[18] Much governance will doubtless continue to be sustained by states and their governments initiating and implementing policies in the context of their legal frameworks – and in some instances national governments are likely to work out arrangements for joint governance with rule systems at other levels – but the effectiveness of their policies is likely to be undermined by the proliferation of emergent control mechanisms both within and outside their jurisdictions.[19] In the words of one analyst, "the very high levels of interdependence and vulnerability stimulated by technological change now necessitate new forms of global political authority and even governance."[20]

Put more emphatically, perhaps the most significant pattern discernible in the criss-crossing flow of transformed authority involves processes of bifurcation whereby control mechanisms at national levels are, in varying degrees, yielding space to both more encompassing forms of governance and narrower, less comprehensive forms. Analyzed in terms of the resulting structures of authority, four very different types

---

[18] These contradictory trends are elaborated in chapters 5, 6, and 18.

[19] None of this is to imply, of course, that the shifts in the loci of authority occur easily, with a minimum of commotion and a maximum of clarity. Far from it: the shifts derive from delicate bargaining, and usually they must overcome extensive opposition, with the result that the "[t]ransfer of authority is a complicated process and it seems there no longer is one single identifiable sovereign, but a multitude of authorities at different levels of aggregation and several centres with differing degrees of coercive power (not all of them public and governmental!) . . . [I]t becomes increasingly difficult to differentiate between public and private institutions, the State and Civil Society, domestic and international." Kaisa Lahteenmaki and Jyrki Kakonen, "Regionalization and Its Impact on the Theory of International Relations," a paper presented at the Annual Meeting of the International Studies Association, Washington, DC (March 1994), pp. 32–3.

[20] John Vogler, "Regimes and the Global Commons: Space, Atmosphere and Oceans," in Anthony G. McGrew *et al.*, (eds.) *Global Politics: Globalization and the Nation-State* (Cambridge: Polity Press, 1992), p. 118.

of SOAs can be discerned: (1) those in which the interstate system's hierarchical structure of authority remains essentially unchanged and governance is sustained by the interactive policies of states (what we shall refer to as "established" SOAs); (2) those in which the loci of authority have undergone transformation in ways that are accepted by both national governments and other actors to the extent that the transformed loci of authority are sufficiently clear-cut to enable all concerned to contain their differences and accommodate to each other ("accommodative" SOAs); (3) those in which the loci of authority are so vigorously contested that accommodation is not a goal and the threat or use of force is not precluded ("contested" SOAs); and (4) those in which the loci of authority are unclear as a result of cross-border spill-overs that stem from strictly domestic activities and may prove transient once the consequences of a spill-over get resolved ("transient" SOAs).

The virtue of this fourfold scheme for analyzing governance along the Frontier is that while it does not preclude institutionalized governmental mechanisms, it orients attention to dynamic and evolving processes rather than to the routinized procedures of national governments. Every SOA must deal with rapidly changing, ever more complex challenges to governance in which people, information, goods, and ideas are in continuous motion and, thus, endlessly reconfiguring social, economic, and political horizons. All four types of SOAs may be faced with the instabilities and disorder that derive from resource shortages, budgetary constraints, ethnic rivalries, unemployment, and inflation. All of them may need to contend with the ever greater relevance of scientific findings and the epistemic communities that form around the findings. All of them may be subject to the continuous tensions that spring from the inroads of corrupt practices, organized crime, and restless publics that have little use for politics and politicians. All of them must cope with pressures for further fragmentation of subgroups on the one hand and for more extensive transnational links on the other. And many of the last three types of SOAs, given the fragility of their legal status and the lack of long-standing habits of support for them, may have severe adaptive problems and some of them may fail to maintain their essential structures intact.[21] Governance along the Frontier, it seems reasonable to anticipate, is

---

[21] For a conception of political adaptation in which adaptive systems are posited as being able to keep fluctuations in their essential structures within acceptable limits, see James N. Rosenau, *The Study of Political Adaptation* (London: Frances Pinter, 1981).

likely to consist of proliferating mechanisms that fluctuate between bare survival and increasing institutionalization, between considerable chaos and widening degrees of order.

Governance along the frontier

SOAs and their control mechanisms are spurred into existence through several channels: through the sponsorship of states, through the efforts of actors other than states at the transnational or subnational levels, or through states and other types of actors jointly sponsoring the formation of rule systems. They can also be differentiated by their location on the aforementioned continuum that ranges from full institutionalization on the one hand to nascent processes of rule-making and compliance on the other. Although extremes on a continuum, the institutionalized and nascent types of control mechanism can be causally linked through evolutionary processes. It is possible to trace at least two generic routes that link the degree to which rule systems are institutionalized and the sources that sponsor these developments. One route is the direct, top-down process wherein states create new institutional structures and impose them on the course of events. A second is much more circuitous and involves an indirect, bottom-up process of evolutionary stages wherein nascent dynamics of rule-making are fostered by publics or economies that experience repeated interactions and generate organizational activities which, in turn, eventually get transformed into institutionalized control mechanisms.[22] Stated more generally, whatever their sponsorship, the institutionalized mechanisms tend to be marked by explicit hierarchical structures, whereas those at the nascent end of the continuum develop more subtly as a consequence of emergent interaction patterns which, unintentionally and without prior planning, culminate in fledgling control mechanisms for newly formed or transformed systems.

Table 8.1 offers examples of the rule systems derivable from a combination of the several types of sponsors and the two extremes on the continuum. The matrix suggests the considerable variety and complexity out of which the processes of governance along the Frontier

[22] For a cogent analysis in which this bottom-up process is posited as passing through five distinct stages, see Bjorn Hettne, "The New Regionalism: Implications for Development and Peace," in Bjorn Hettne and Andras Inotai (eds.), *The New Regionalism: Implications for Global Development and International Security* (Helsinki: UNU World Institute for Development Economics Research, 1994), pp. 7–8.

Table 8.1. *The sponsorship and institutionalization of control mechanisms*

		Nascent	Institutionalized
Not state-sponsored	Transnational	Nongovernmental organizations → Social movements → Epistemic communities Multinational corporations	The Internet European Environmental Bureau Credit rating agencies
	Subnational	Ethnic minorities → Micro regions → Cities	American Jewish Congress The Greek lobby Crime syndicates
State-sponsored		Macro regions → European community → GATT →	United Nations System European Union World Trade Organization
Jointly sponsored		Cross-border coalitions → Issue regimes	Election monitoring Human rights regime

evolve. In the table, moreover, there are hints of the developmental processes whereby nascent mechanisms become institutionalized: as indicated by the dotted arrows, some of the control mechanisms located in the right-hand cells have their origins in the corresponding left-hand cell as interdependence issues generate pressures from the nongovernmental world for intergovernmental cooperation which, in turn, lead to the formation of issue-based transnational institutions. The histories of more than a few control mechanisms charged with addressing environmental problems exemplify how this subtle evolutionary path can be traversed.

However rule systems not sponsored by states may originate, and whatever pace at which they may evolve, it is useful to note one fundamental distinction between those that arise out of subnational sources and those that have transnational roots. Relatively speaking, the former mechanisms of governance are usually (though not always) energized by despair, by frustration with existing systems that seems best offset by contracting the scope of governance, by a sense that large-scale cooperation has not worked and that new subgroup arrangements are bound to be more satisfying. Thus subnational systems of rule often (though not always) evolve contested SOAs. On the other hand, transnational mechanisms tend to be essentially forward-looking. They may be propelled by dissatisfactions over existing (national or subnational) arrangements, but the evolution of transnational systems is likely to be marked less by despair over the past and present and more by hope for the future, by expectations that an expansion beyond existing boundaries will draw upon cooperative impulses which may serve to meet challenges and fill lacunae that would otherwise be left unattended. To be sure, globalizing dynamics tend to create resistance and opposition, since any expansion of governance is bound to be detrimental to those who have a stake in the status quo. Whether they are explicitly and formally designed or subtly and informally constructed, however, on balance transnational rule systems tend to evolve in a context of hope and progress, a sense of breakthrough, an appreciation that old problems can be circumvented and moved toward either the verge of resolution or the edge of obsolescence. It follows that such systems tend to evolve accommodative SOAs.

Many of the rule systems listed in table 8.1 are subjected to intensive examination in subsequent chapters, but it is useful to differentiate among them here in terms of the four types of SOAs outlined above. In so doing the enormous delicacies that attend governance along the Frontier can be readily discerned.

Established spheres of authority

While the foreign policies of states and the organizations of the inter-state system are major features of governance along the Frontier, an account of how they function as established SOAs in this regard need not detain us here. As previously noted, they are the focus of the realist and liberal worldviews and thus the subject of a huge literature that can be readily consulted, whereas the purpose of this analysis is to focus on the emergent worldview and how transformative dynamics are foster-ing new types of SOAs that are not presided over exclusively by states and their international organizations. But it must be emphasized that "one does not have to do away with the 'state' to establish the influence of transnational relations in world politics,"[23] that in not pausing to elaborate on the role played by established SOAs, there is no intent to suggest they are increasingly peripheral. Indeed, there is no better illustration of the widening of the Frontier than the continuing salience of the interstate system's European Union and its growing capacity to govern. Furthermore, chapters 18 and 20 examine, respectively, the various ways in which states and the UN have had to adjust to the expansion of the Frontier and, in so doing, they make clear that such actors still perform central functions in global affairs.

Accommodative spheres of authority

Although the following discussion of a sample of accommodative SOAs highlights the cooperative foundations on which they rest, this is not to say, of course, that such SOAs are free of conflict. On the contrary, like any political arena, their actors often differ persistently and extensively on how problems should be managed. On balance, however, accom-modative SOAs derive their integrity and staying power from the incen-tives for cooperation to which the dynamics of globalization give rise. Such is the case, for example, when both national governments and diverse NGOs are driven by particular issues to seek solutions across

---

[23] Thomas Risse-Kappen, "Bringing Transnational Relations Back In: Introduction," in Thomas Risse-Kappen (ed.), *Bringing Transnational Relations Back In: Non-state Actors, Domestic Structures, and International Institutions* (Cambridge: Cambridge University Press, 1995), p. 15.

the Frontier, a process which leads to the creation of regimes that in any one of a number of ways evolve regularized forms of authority designed to manage the conflicts embraced by their sphere.[24] That is, interdependence issues not only impel governments to work with counterparts abroad, but also so fully embrace the interests of diverse NGOs that the latter often participate in the decisional processes through which values are allocated. In trade, oil, the environment, whaling, and many other issue areas, such regimes have become standard features of the global landscape. The literature on world affairs refers to them as "international regimes," but this is a misnomer because the rules, norms, principles, and procedures of many regimes (to cite a widely accepted definition)[25] often involve a sharing of authority among NGOs as well as national governments. To be sure, the more institutionalized regimes become, the more are intergovernmental organizations likely to acquire the formal authority to make decisions; but movement in this direction is likely to be accompanied by preservation of the joint sponsorship of states and NGOs through arrangements that at least accord formal advisory roles to the relevant NGOs. No issue regime, it seems reasonable to assert, can prosper without control mechanisms that allow for some form of participation by all the interested parties. As one observer put it with respect to several specific issue regimes,

> Increasingly, this transnationalization of civic participation is redefining the terms of governance in North America, not only in the commercial arena but also on issues such as the environment, human rights, and immigration. Nongovernmental organizations, particularly grassroots groups, located throughout these societies are playing a growing role in setting the parameters of the North American agenda, limiting the ability of public officials to manage their relation-

---

[24] The case for regime analysis is cogently advanced in Stephan Haggard and Beth A. Simmons, "Theories of International Regimes," *International Organization*, vol. 41 (Summer 1987), pp. 491–517; Robert O. Keohane, *After Hegemony: Cooperation and Discord in the World Political Economy* (Princeton: Princeton University Press, 1984); Stephen D. Krasner (ed.), *International Regimes* (Ithaca: Cornell University Press, 1983); Volker Rittberger (ed.), *Regime Theory and International Relations* (Oxford: Clarendon Press, 1993); Oran R. Young, *International Cooperation: Building Regimes for Natural Resources and the Environment* (Ithaca: Cornell University Press, 1989); Mark W. Zacher, "Toward a Theory of International Regimes," *Journal of International Affairs*, vol. 44 (1990), pp. 139–57; and Mark W. Zacher with Brent A. Sutton, *Governing Global Networks: International Regimes for Transportation and Communications* (Cambridge: Cambridge University Press, 1996).   [25] Krasner (ed.), *International Regimes*, p. 2.

ship on a strict government-to-government basis, and setting the stage for a much more complex process of interaction.[26]

As indicated in table 8.1, it follows that not all the steering mechanisms of issue regimes are located at the nascent end of the continuum. Some move persistently toward institutionalization – as was recently the case in the human rights regime when the UN created a High Commissioner for Human Rights – while others may be stalemated in an underdeveloped state for considerable periods of time. However, given the ever greater interdependence of global life, it seems doubtful whether any issue area that gains access to the global agenda can avoid evolving at least a rudimentary control mechanism. Once the problems encompassed by an issue area become widely recognized as requiring attention and amelioration, it can hardly remain long without entering at least the first stage of the evolutionary process toward governance. This process is manifestly evident in the cumulating institutional practices whereby the deliberations of NGO-sponsored conferences around particular issue areas – on the environment in 1992, human rights in 1993, population in 1994, the human habitat in 1995, and women, also in 1995 – impact on those of comparable UN-sponsored gatherings convened at the same time and, so to speak, down the street from each other in the same locale.

In short, the control mechanisms of some regimes may be informal, disorganized, and often ineffective in concentrating authority – that is, so rudimentary and nascent that governance is spasmodic and weak. In other cases, as illustrated by this chapter's epigraph depicting the powerful role that Moody's and other crediting agencies play in the global economy,[27] the rule systems may be formalized, well organized, and capable of effectively exercising authority. But in all regimes, regardless of their stage of development, "the interaction between the parties is not unconstrained or is not based on independent decision making."[28] All

[26] Cathryn L. Thorup, "Redefining Governance in North America: Citizen Diplomacy and Cross-Border Coalitions, " *Enfoque* (University of California, San Diego), Spring 1993, pp. 1, 12.

[27] For a cogent elaboration of this role, see Timothy J. Sinclair, "Investment, Knowledge and Governance: Credit-Rating Processes and the Global Political Economy" Ph.D. dissertation, York University, Toronto, 1995.

[28] Arthur Stein, "Coordination and Collaboration: Regimes in an Anarchic World," in David A. Baldwin (ed.), *Neorealism and Neoliberalism: The Contemporary Debate* (New York: Columbia University Press, 1993), p. 31.

regimes, that is, have control mechanisms to which their participants feel obliged to accede even if they do not do so repeatedly and systematically.

Regional concerns, both within and among countries, underlie another type of accommodative SOA fostered by incentives to cooperation embedded in globalizing processes. Although more haltingly and less self-consciously than is the case for issue regimes, actors in a geographic region are often drawn into cooperating with each other by shared economic interests that, in turn, become the basis for new forms of authority. As one observer put it,

> The process of regionalization from within can be compared with the historical formation of nation states with the important difference that a coercive centre is lacking in processes of regionalization which presuppose a shared intention among the potential members . . . The difference between regionalism and the infinite process of spontaneous integration is that there is a politically defined limit to the former process. The limitation, however, is a historical outcome of attempts to find a transnational level of governance which includes certain shared values and minimizes certain shared perceptions of danger. Like the formation of ethnic and national identities, the regional identity is dependent on historical context and shaped by conflicts. And like nations and ethnies, regional formations which have a subjective quality . . . [are] "imagined communities" . . . [D]espite enormous historical, structural, and contextual differences, there is an underlying logic behind contemporary processes of regionalization.[29]

Nor are the processes of regionalization confined to the convergence of countries in the same geographic space. Even more conspicuous are the accommodative SOAs that are emerging as "micro" regions organized around cities. An insightful example along these lines is provided by the developments that have flowed from the success of a cooperation pact signed in 1988 by Lyon, Milan, Stuttgart, and Barcelona, developments that have led one analyst, noting that "surveys show Europeans are now more inclined to link their identities and allegiances to cities and regions,"[30] to the conclusion that "a resurrection of 'city states' and

---

[29] Hettne, "The New Regionalism," pp. 2–3. For another formulation that also differentiates between the old and new regionalism, see Lahteenmaki and Kakonen, "Regionalization and Its Impact on the Theory of International Relations," p. 9. For a contrary perspective, see Stephen D. Krasner, "Regional Economic Blocs and the End of the Cold War," paper presented at the International Colloquium on Regional Economic Integration, University of São Paulo (December 1991).

[30] William Drozdiak, "Regions on the Rise," *Washington Post*, October 22, 1995, p. A22.

regions is quietly transforming Europe's political and economic land-scape, diminishing the influence of national governments and redraw-ing the continental map of power for the 21st century."[31] All four cities and their surrounding regions have an infrastructure and location that is more suited to the changes at work in Europe.[32] They have attracted sizable investments and enjoyed a prosperity that has led to new demands for greater autonomy. Some argue that, as a result, the emerg-ing urban centers and economies are fostering "a new historical dynamism that will ultimately transform the political structure of Europe by creating a new kind of 'Hanseatic League' that consists of thriving city-states."[33] One specialist forecasts that there will be nine-teen cities with at least 20 million people in their greater metropolitan areas by the year 2000, with the result that "Cities, not nations, will become the principal identity for most people in the world."[34] Another offers a similar interpretation based on

> the coastal rim of maritime Asia. Cities such as Tokyo, Hong Kong, Bangkok, Seoul, Singapore, Osaka, and Taipei are the hubs for most of Asia's air and sea transportation, its international entrepreneurship, its pattern of direct overseas investment . . . As a rough approximation, we can say that less than a dozen urban centers in Asia (representing perhaps 4% of the total population) are the locus of 90% of the interna-tional finance, of international transportation, of trade oriented manu-facturing, and international information networks. To underscore the fact that capitalistic growth centers on a small selection of Asia's cities, is to highlight their contrast with the national societies that make up the bulk of Asia's geography and population. Certainly the intensity of international activities are tens to hundreds of times higher per

---

[31] William Drozdiak, "Revving Up Europe's 'Four Motors,'" *Washington Post*, March 27, 1994, p. C3.

[32] For an analysis which conceives of these "four motors" of Europe in terms of micro regions rather than cities – the Rhône Alps instead of Lyon, Lombardy instead of Milan, Baden-Württemberg instead of Stuttgart, and Catalonia instead of Barcelona – see Lahteenmaki and Kakonen, "Regionalization and Its Impact on the Theory of International Relations," p. 15.

[33] Drozdiak, "Revving Up Europe's 'Four Motors,'" p. C3.

[34] Pascal Maragall, quoted in Drozdiak, "Revving Up Europe's 'Four Motors,'" p. C3. For extensive inquiries that posit the transnational roles of cities as increasingly central to the processes of global governance, see Saskia Sassen, *The Global City: New York, London, Tokyo* (Princeton: Princeton University Press, 1991), and Earl H. Fry, Lee H. Radebaugh, and Panayotis Soldatos (eds.), *The New International Cities Era: The Global Activities of North American Municipal Governments* (Provo, UT: Brigham Young University Press, 1989).

capita in these cities than in the nation states that we typically focus on.[35]

Still another observer anticipates that a desire to bring government closer to the people could make nationhood obsolete. By the middle of the next century, he believes there could be multinational security alliances while real government is carried out by what he calls "the international metropolitans":

> In just a few decades, nation states such as the United States, Japan, Germany, Italy and France will no longer be so relevant. Instead, rich regions built around cities such as Osaka, San Francisco and the four motors of Europe will acquire effective power because they can work in tandem with the transnational companies who control the capital.[36]

Needless to say, since the borders of regional SOAs are determined by the "naturalness" of their economic zones and thus rarely coincide with the boundaries of political units, the clash between the incentives induced by markets and the authority of governments is central to the emergence of transnational governance mechanisms. Indeed, it is arguable that a prime change at work in world politics today is a shift in the balance between these two forces, with political authorities finding it increasingly expedient to yield to economic realities. In some instances, moreover, political authorities do not even get to choose to yield:

> Regional economic interdependencies are now more important than political boundaries. In Seattle ... Japan is seen as neighbor and valued trading partner, while New York and the East Coast are regarded as distant. Illustrating this point is the regional economic community that developed across the US–Canadian border among five American states and two Canadian provinces without the approval of Washington, D.C., or Ottawa.[37]

---

[35] Thomas P. Rohlem, "Cosmopolitan Cities and Nation States: A 'Mediterranean' Model for Asian Regionalism," paper presented at the Conference on Asian Regionalism, Maui, HI (December 17–19, 1993), pp. 1–2.

[36] Riccardo Petrella, as quoted in Drozdiak, "Revving Up Europe's 'Four Motors,'" p. C3. For an analysis by the same author which indicates concern over the trend to city-like states, see Riccardo Petrella, "Techno-racism: The City-States of the Global Market Will Create a 'New Apartheid,'" *Toronto Star*, August 9, 1992.

[37] Michael Clough and David Doerge, *Global Changes and Domestic Transformations: New Possibilities for American Foreign Policy: Report of a Vantage Conference* (Muscatine, IA: The Stanley Foundation, 1992), p. 9. For indicators that a similar process is occurring in the Southwest without the approval of Washington, DC, or Mexico City, see Cathryn L. Thorup, *Redefining Governance in North America: The Impact of Cross-Border Networks and Coalitions on Mexican Immigration into the United States* (Santa Monica, CA: The Rand Corporation, 1993).

Put differently, "The implications of region states are not welcome news to established seats of political power, be they politicians or lobby-ists. Nation states by definition require a domestic political focus, while region states are ensconced in the global economy."[38] This potential clash, however, need not necessarily turn adversarial. Much depends on whether the political authorities welcome and encourage foreign capital investment or whether they insist on protecting their noncompetitive local industries. If they are open to foreign inputs, their economies are more likely to prosper than if they insist on a rigorous maintenance of their political autonomy. But if they do insist on drawing tight lines around their authoritative realms, they are likely to lose out:

> Region states need not be the enemies of central government. Handled gently, region states can provide the opportunity for eventual prosper-ity for all areas within a nation's traditional political control . . . Political leaders, however reluctantly, must adjust to the reality of eco-nomic regional entities if they are to nurture real economic flows. Resistant governments will be left to reign over traditional political ter-ritories as all meaningful participation in the global economy migrates beyond their well-preserved frontiers.[39]

It seems clear, in short, that cities and micro regions are likely to become major control mechanisms in world politics in the years ahead. Even if the various expectations that they replace states as centers of power prove to be exaggerated, their SOAs seem destined to emerge as either partners or rivals of states as their crucial role becomes more widely recognized and they thereby move from an objective to an inter-subjective existence.

Still another set of accommodative SOAs can be discerned when members of NGOs operate outside of regimes and apart from govern-ments. Impelled by a felt need to enhance their influence either at home or abroad by reaching out for support to counterparts across the Frontier, such actors often form coalitions which then evolve new rules for pooling resources and advancing their causes. Whether they be alliances among multinational corporations or transnational arrange-ments among volunteer organizations with common tasks such as those analyzed in chapter 17, these SOAs are sustained by their shared pur-poses to adopt procedures that enable them to resolve conflicts among their components in different countries.

[38] Kenichi Ohmae, "The Rise of the Region State," *Foreign Affairs*, vol. 72 (Spring 1993), p. 83.   [39] *Ibid.*, pp. 84–5.

The history of some of these SOAs, especially those that eventuate in NGOs founded on volunteerism, provides a keen insight into the evolution of accommodative SOAs. Usually referred to as social movements, these SOAs have evolved as wellsprings of governance across the Frontier in recent decades. Indeed, they are perhaps the quintessential case of nascent control mechanisms that have the potential of spawning institutionalized rule systems. Their nascency is conspicuous: they have no definite memberships or authority structures; they consist of as many people, as much territory, and as many issues as seem appropriate to the people involved; they have no central headquarters and are spread across numerous locales; and they are all-inclusive, excluding no one and embracing anyone who wishes to be part of the movement. To the extent they are organized, social movements evolve around a salient set of issues – like those that highlight the concerns of feminists, environmentalists, or peace activists – and as such they serve transnational needs that cannot be filled by either national governments, organized domestic groups, or private firms. Social movements are thus constituent parts of the globalizing process. They contribute importantly to the noneconomic fabric of ties facilitated by the new communications and transportation technologies. They pick up the pieces, so to speak, that states and businesses leave in their wake by their boundary-crossing activities: just as the peace movement focuses on the consequences of state interactions, for example, so has the ecological movement become preoccupied with the developmental excesses of transnational corporations.

However, despite the lack of structural constraints, which allows for their growth, social movements may not remain permanently inchoate and nascent. At those times when the issues of concern to their members climb high on the global agenda, they may begin to develop organizational arrangements through which to move toward their goals. The International Nestlé Boycott Committee is illustrative in this regard: it organized a seven-year international boycott of Nestlé products and then was dismantled when the Nestlé Company complied with its demands.[40] In some instances, moreover, the organizational expression of a movement's aspirations can develop enduring features. Fearful that the development of organizational structures might curb their spontaneity, some movement members might be aghast at the prospect of

[40] Kathryn Sikkink, "Codes of Conduct for Transnational Corporations: The Case of the UWH/UNICEF Code," *International Organization*, vol. 40 (Autumn 1986), pp. 815–40.

formalized procedures, explicit rules, and specific role assignments, but clearly the march toward goals requires organizational coherence at some point. Thus have transnational social movement organizations (TSMOs) begun to dot the global landscape.[41] Oxfam and Amnesty International are two examples among many that could be cited of movement spin-offs that have evolved toward the institutionalized extreme of the continuum. While the European Environmental Bureau (EEB), which was founded in 1974, has moved less rapidly in this direction, it now has a full-time staff quartered in a Brussels office and shows signs of becoming permanent as the environmental movement matures.[42]

Further insight into the potential of accommodative SOAs is provided by the procedures for election monitoring that have evolved in recent years. As will be seen in chapter 13, it has become established for the "international community," often led by NGOs with considerable support from the UN, to move into the Frontier and station "foreign observers" such that they can render judgments about the fairness of domestic elections in countries where appropriate institutions for conducting elections have yet to become institutionalized. That some domestic authority has shifted to the foreign monitoring teams is evident on those occasions when they have issued negative judgments and the elections have then been rescheduled or canceled.

In contrast to the monitoring of elections, the authority of epistemic communities – those ties across the Frontier through which experts on issues share findings and offer conclusions – derives not from actions undertaken in the political arena, but from their influence as specialists. As one analyst notes, "Members of an epistemic community . . . are primarily and overtly concerned with claims of substantive knowledge about whatever issue or problems attracts them to public organizations and political decision makers. Their knowledge about communicable diseases, deep-sea mineral deposits, nuclear fission, or exchange rate stability gives them their claim to be heard."[43]

---

[41] Janie Leatherman, Ron Pagnucco, and Jackie Smith, "International Institutions and Transnational Social Movement Organizations: Challenging the State in a Three-Level Game of Global Transformation," a paper presented at the Annual Meeting of the International Studies Association, Washington, DC, (March 1994).

[42] Leatherman, Pagnucco, and Smith, "International Institutions and Transnational Social Movement Organizations," p. 20.

[43] Ernst B. Haas, *When Knowledge Is Power: Three Models of Change in International Organizations* (Berkeley: University of California Press, 1990), p. 42.

In sum, although marked by enormous diversity, accommodative SOAs are increasingly salient on the global scene and provide substantial evidence that governance along the Frontier is undergoing substantial transformation. More than that, they clearly point to the adaptive capacities of governmental and nongovernmental actors and, in so doing, demonstrate that the relocation of authority does not necessarily lead to the collapse of coherent and cooperative approaches to the challenges posed by change.

Contested spheres of authority

While accommodative SOAs highlight the ability of present-day actors to adapt to transformative dynamics that are widening the Frontier, there remain many SOAs where the existing or emergent lines of authority are not accepted and serve as the foci of intensely waged debates and rivalries. Ethnic minorities and other subgroups that seek to secede from the SOA in which they are located are illustrative in this regard. Such collectivities reject the authority to which they are subject and seek to have the boundaries dividing them from other collectivities redrawn. The uprising of the Zapatistas in Mexico and the meticulous and prolonged efforts to redraw the boundaries separating Serbs, Croatians, and Muslims in Bosnia are not atypical of how the Frontier itself can serve as the focus of conflict. And these examples also suggest that contested SOAs are especially prone to collapsing into violence if issues over the scope of authority cannot be resolved peacefully.

But ethnic conflicts are by no means the only basis for the emergence of contested SOAs. The efforts of Greenpeace to prevent France from nuclear testing in the South Pacific on the grounds that nuclear matters have come under the jurisdiction of the Frontier are also illustrative of how violence can accompany conflicts over the Frontier's scope. Protests against the French plans came from governments and NGOs all around the world, but Greenpeace sailed its vessels into French waters to stop the tests and evoked the use of force by the French. Even as French authority prevailed when force was employed, however, so was the presence of nongovernmental authority in this contested SOA revealed when the protests and boycotts of French products around the world impelled the French to reduce the number of scheduled nuclear tests from eight to six.

Another type of contested SOA has evolved out of the world's addiction to drugs. Run by drug lords whose authority along the Frontier remains undiminished despite the cooperative efforts of national governments to end it, the drug combines exercise control over considerable land and air space in certain parts of the world.[44] In some cases, moreover, public officials get coopted by the drug organizations and, in effect, become subject to their authority. The recent forced resignation of a Colombian president offers an insight into the nature of these SOAs and their ability to persist alongside governments.

Closely related to, and often sustained by, the drug trade are contested SOAs along the Frontier founded on crime. Facilitated by the dynamics of globalization, numerous crime syndicates have evolved institutional forms known as "transnational criminal organizations" (TCOs). While their conduct violates all the norms that are considered to undergird the proper exercise of authority,[45] at the same time their "complexity . . . does not permit the construction of simple generalizations."[46] Yet, it is reasonable to assert that they have evolved contested SOAs: they control their affairs in patterned ways that often involve strategic alliances between themselves and national and local criminal organizations, alliances that "permit them to cooperate with, rather than compete against, indigenously entrenched criminal organizations."[47] Yet, while TCOs have evolved independent authority structures, they have not succumbed to excessive bureaucratization. On the contrary, "they are highly mobile and adaptable and able to operate across national borders with great ease . . . partly because of their emphasis on networks rather than formal organizations."[48] Thus it is hardly surprising that, "with the globalization of trade and growing consumer demands for leisure products, it is only natural that criminal organizations should become increasingly transnational in character," that they have been "both contributors to, and beneficiaries of, . . . a

---

[44] Phil Williams, "International Drug Trafficking: An Industry Analysis," *Low Intensity Conflict and Law Enforcement,"* vol. 2 (Winter 1993), pp. 397–420.

[45] It is noteworthy, though hardly surprising, that the more pervasive violations of widely shared norms become, the more do contested SOAs provoke the evolution of accommodative rule systems which seek to contain, if not to end, the activities of TCOs. Cf. Ethan A. Nadelman, "Global Prohibition Regimes: The Evolution of Norms in International Society," *International Organization*, vol. 44 (Autumn 1990), pp. 479–526.

[46] Louise I. Shelley, "Transnational Organized Crime: An Imminent Threat to the Nation-State?" *Journal of International Affairs*, vol. 48 (Winter 1995), p. 464. See also, Peter Andreas, "The Retreat and Resurgence of the State: Liberalizing and Criminalizing Cross-Border Flows in an Integrated World," paper presented at the Annual Meeting of the American Political Science Association, Chicago, (Sept. 1995).

[47] Phil Williams, "Transnational Criminal Organizations and International Security," *Survival*, vol. 36 (Spring 1994), p. 106.   [48] *Ibid.*, p. 105.

great increase in transactions across national boundaries that are neither initiated nor controlled by states,"[49] and that

> Not only is transnational activity as open to criminal groups as it is to legitimate multinational corporations, but the character of criminal organizations also makes them particularly suited to exploit these new opportunities. Since criminal groups are used to operating outside the rules, norms and laws of domestic jurisdictions, they have few qualms about crossing national boundaries illegally. In many respects, therefore, TCOs are transnational organizations *par excellence*. They operate outside the existing structures of authority and power in world politics and have developed sophisticated strategies for circumventing law enforcement in individual states and in the global community of states.[50]

A good measure of how new opportunities have facilitated the explosiveness of TCOs in the present era is provided by the pattern of criminal activities that have evolved in the former Soviet Union since the collapse of the Soviet empire. "More than 4,000 criminal formations comprising an estimated 100,000 members now operate in Russia alone" and, of these, some "150 to 200 . . . have international ties."[51]

Transient spheres of authority

As interdependence shrinks the world and undermines boundaries, more and more occasions are likely to arise in which the actions of individuals become cross-border spill-overs and serve to generate transient SOAs designed to cope with unexpected repercussions along the Frontier. Normally the individual actions become cross-border spill-overs by evoking widespread public reactions that then compel national governments to interact and respond to the demands to which the spill-overs gave rise. The rape of a retarded young Okinawan by three American soldiers, the caning of an American for painting graffiti on walls in Singapore, and the Nigerian hanging of an activist who sought

---

[49] *Ibid.*, p. 97. For another dimension of transnational criminality, see Victor T. Levine, "Transnational Aspects of Political Corruption," in Arnold J. Heidenheimer, Michael Johnston, and Victor T. LeVine (eds.), *Political Corruption: A Handbook* (New Brunswick, NJ: Transaction Publishers, 1989), pp. 685–99.

[50] Williams, "Transnational Criminal Organizations and International Security," p. 100.

[51] Rensselaer W. Lee III, "Post-Soviet Organized Crime and Western Security Interests," testimony submitted to the Subcommittee on Terrorism, Narcotics and International Operations, Senate Committee on Foreign Relations, Washington, DC (April 21, 1994). For another, more elaborate discussion along these lines, see Stephen Handelman, *Comrade Criminal: Russia's New Mafiya* (New Haven: Yale University Press, 1995).

to bring an end to drilling by the Shell Oil Company in his province are conspicuous examples of individuals who recently precipitated wide repercussions among publics, NGOs, and governments that became the basis for relocated forms of authority until jurisdictions become clear and the repercussions get played out. In these cases the jurisdiction of local courts was at issue and the sphere of authority thereby contested for a relatively brief time.

Other transient SOAs involve collective actions by previously disparate people who are brought together by nonrecurrent issues that eventually get resolved, with the result that the rule systems generated to resolve them no longer serve any purposes and come to an end. A case in point was the campaign to protest apartheid in South Africa by getting corporations to withdraw their investments from that country: the transient SOA lasted several years, but ended when apartheid was overturned. In still other instances, such as the UN's control over Iraq's oil shipments, the transgression of the Frontier still persists, although it is doubtful whether such an arrangement will eventuate in a permanent SOA.

Perhaps the most common type of transient SOAs consist of cross-border coalitions generated by momentary issues that link subnational collectivities immediately adjacent to national boundaries. During the debate over the North American Free Trade Agreement (NAFTA), for example, coalitions of American, Canadian, and Mexican groups with one or another stake in the outcome of the debate came together to pursue their common causes with respect to, say, trade, labor, or environmental issues. In creating their networks they had to evolve systems of rules for framing and implementing joint policies. Interestingly, many of the rules were fashioned through e-mail and electronic conferencing that enabled the groups' members to keep in continuous touch with each other even though they rarely came together in face-to-face meetings. Put more dramatically, "[r]ather than be represented by a building that people enter, these actors may be located on electronic networks and exist as 'virtual communities' that have no precise physical address."[52] Even more relevant to governance along the Frontier, this form of communication also facilitated a bypassing of state authorities. Some of the cross-border coalitions involved local governments located near national boundaries that

---

[52] David Ronfeldt and Cathryn L. Thorup, *North America in the Era of Citizen Networks: State, Society, and Security,* (Santa Monica, CA: The Rand Corporation, 1993), p. 22.

found it more expedient on a variety of issues to form coalitions with counterparts across the border than to work with their own provincial or national governments. Such coalitions may even be formed deliberately in order to avoid drawing "unnecessary or premature attention from central authorities to local solutions of some local problems by means of informal contacts and 'good neighborhood' networks. Often it [is] not a deliberate deception, just an avoidance of unnecessary complications."[53]

While cross-border coalitions may move on to form enduring NGOs, most are likely to disband as the issues that gave rise to them wane. Being networks rather than organizations, their rule systems are too issue-specific to encourage movement beyond transciency. Nonetheless, "the new local and cross-border [coalitions] are a potential wild card. They may be proactive or reactive in a variety of ways, sometimes working with, sometimes against, state and market actors who are not accustomed to regarding civil society as an independent actor."[54] Transient SOAs, in short, are based in issues rather than regimes. They are expressive of the unexpected in world affairs, the *ad hoc* arrangements that are necessary to cope with a fast-moving course of events that engulfs the Frontier in a variety of ways. And they are also indicative of the fluidity and fragility on which the foundations of SOAs can rest.

Conclusion

In an ever more interdependent world the need for control mechanisms outstrips the capacity or readiness of national governments to provide them. There are a variety of types of situation where national governments are unwelcome, or where they fear involvement will be counterproductive, or where they lack the will or ability to intrude, or where they find it expedient to participate in rule systems jointly with organizations from the private sector. As the Frontier widens, in sum, so are a variety of new spheres of authority likely to evolve and become landmarks on the global scene.

None of this is to imply, of course, that national governments and states are no longer central loci of control in the processes of governance.

---

[53] Ivo D. Duchachek, "The International Dimension of Subnational Government," *Publius*, vol. 14 (Fall 1984), p. 25.

[54] Ronfeldt and Thorup, "North America in the Era of Citizen Networks," p. 24.

To repeat (and as will be seen more elaborately in chapter 18), they are very central indeed. No account of global affairs can ignore them or give them other than a prominent place in the scheme of things. Nevertheless, the preceding analysis should make clear that, considered in a fragmegrative worldview, not only have states lost some of their earlier dominance of the governance system, but also the lessening of their ability to evoke compliance and govern effectively is in part due to the growing relevance and potential of control mechanisms sustained by transnational and subnational systems of rule.

9 Norms

> The society is caught between values. The old ones are gone, and the new ones are not yet formed.
>
> Lt. Roman G. Fyodorov[1]

As the Frontier widens, so do traditional norms become less applicable to the new fragmegrative situations. Confronted with unfamiliar issues, new claims to loyalty, and a multiplicity of messages received from ever greater numbers of disparate sources, both citizens and officials are likely to feel deprived of the normative anchors to which they have long been accustomed. Systems of rule cannot persist unless they enjoy the support of most of those they encompass, and underlying the support for particular goals and specific policies are norms about the processes of governance to which people subscribe. If such norms are widely shared, governance is undertaken relatively easily; but if there is considerable division over who is entitled to make policy decisions, what constitutes the legitimate procedures for making policy, and whether the regulations that flow from the adopted policies are to be obeyed, then governance becomes very difficult indeed.[2] Thus it is that many forms of governance at the local and national levels have enabled organiza-

---

[1] Quoted in Steven Erlanger, "Images of Lawlessness Twist Russian Reality," *New York Times*, June 7, 1995, p. A10.

[2] For succinct and clarifying discussions of the nature of norms and their relevance to the kinds of issues that form the Frontier's agenda, see Abram Chayes and Antonia Handler Chayes, *The New Sovereignty: Compliance with International Regulatory Agreements* (Cambridge, MA: Harvard University Press, 1995); Ann Florini, "The Evolution of International Norms," *International Studies Quarterly*, vol. 40 (September 1996), pp. 363–89. Judith Goldstein and Robert O. Keohane (eds.), *Ideas and Foreign Policy: Beliefs, Institutions, and Political Change* (Ithaca: Cornell University Press, 1993); and Friedrich V. Kratochwil, *Rules, Norms, and Decisions: On the Conditions of Practical and Legal Reasoning in International Relations and Domestic Affairs* (Cambridge: Cambridge University Press, 1989).

tions, communities, and societies to preserve their coherence and move toward their goals. It is the extent to which the same can be said about governance along the Frontier that is the prime focus of this chapter.

Important queries can be raised about governance under conditions of turbulent change: Have the processes of globalization generated at least some transcendent values that find expression across time, space, and culture? Is there bound to be, as the above comment of a Russian police officer implies, a period of global normlessness – of growing crime rates, alienation, corruption, and flourishing black markets – that marks the transition from old to new normative premises? Or is the transition likely to endure, with governance along the Frontier continuously riven by conflicts between adaptive norms that facilitate new systems of rule and deviant and self-serving norms that undermine systemic coherence and a concern for the dignity of people, the value of life, and the well-being of marginal groups?

Since the present era can fairly be described as tumultuous and pervaded with uncertainties, such questions cry out for exploration, for attempts to clarify where normative concerns fit in the welter of swift-moving, calamitous events. The danger is twofold. On the one hand, links to fundamental values may be lost as citizens, officials, and governments alike get swept up by the many challenges to their traditional routines and procedures. On the other, fundamental values can seem so threatened that people, organizations, and societies cling to them tenaciously and fail to seize whatever opportunities may be available in the new turbulent circumstances.

Both of these dangers are acute in this post-Cold War period of fragmenting countries, troubled economies, fragile polities, and restless publics. They highlight the normative implications of the ever greater civic responsibilities that turbulent conditions are imposing on individuals and the ever sharper choices leaders have to make between the whole group and the subgroup, between order and autonomy, between centralized power and decentralized authority. Individuals, leaders, and societies may be capable of facing up to these challenges, but it remains to be seen whether they can cope with the unfamiliar normative challenges that have arisen in the widening space of the domestic-foreign Frontier.

Normative responses to a turbulent world

Four challenges seem particularly relevant to the processes of governance. One concerns the implications of the speed with which normative choices have to be made. A second involves the possibility that the tensions inherent in fragmegration may have rendered the traditional precepts of Western civilization unreliable as guides to individual and group conduct. A third focuses on traces of some worldwide norms that can be discerned in both the state- and multi-centric worlds. Finally, attention needs to be given to those arenas in which the cleavages may be so deep as to prevent the evolution of widely shared norms.

Norms in a fast-moving world

Perhaps nothing is more evocative of normative reactions than dramatic and instantaneous change. When events move slowly, culminating only as a number of pieces fall into place over long stretches of time, citizens and officials alike do not readily appreciate that new values may be at stake as situations unfold. They have time to yield to their belief in rational reasoning, to weigh the evidence, to ponder, to exchange views, to consider alternative perspectives, and then to move carefully to judgment. But when developments occur suddenly, seemingly from nowhere, in rapid-fire succession, recorded on television screens in minute, often horrendous and gory detail, the normative challenges are unmistakable and enormous. The pictures compel reactions deep within the core of viewers, responses that cannot be rationalized away or coated over by extenuating circumstances. Rwandans desperately drinking muddy water and dying of cholera, a market and its customers in Sarajevo scattered by bursting shells, a dead American soldier dragged through the streets of Mogadishu, students mown down by army troops in Tiananmen Square – these recent scenes are new to most eyes and, as such, they evoke deep-seated responses that are new because such sights have never before been witnessed in motion, in color, in unrelenting horror. They are scenes that have reversed the policies of governments, modified conceptions of national interest, intensified charitable impulses, and hardened the resolve of activists and isolationists alike.

In short, the new normative challenges are enormous because the information revolution has so speeded up the processes of world affairs as to infuse an immediacy into the choices they pose that renders them different in kind from those earlier generations had to confront. The bare outlines of the choices – between self and community, between home and abroad, between group and subgroup, between compliance and defiance, between order and freedom – are perhaps no different than those faced in the agrarian and industrial eras, but in this postindustrial era of high-speed communications the choices are stark and cannot be postponed or avoided. Resort to norms, be they grounded in shock or cynicism, is propelled by the time it takes for the eyes to take in the unfolding atrocities or the heroic deeds. Even bureaucracies and hesitant cabinets cannot readily dawdle, else the course of events moves on and leaders have to live with the consequences of being excessively deliberative.

Put in another way, norms stand out in bold relief in the present era because their presence and dimensions are so instantaneously evident and so obviously indicative of a common fate. Under the harsh gaze of the television camera, some situations are so appalling, so utterly grue-some, that it is unimaginable the world will not eventually develop control systems to prevent their persistence and reoccurrence. Already the world is discovering a new moral compass and rediscovering sub-tleties that were lost to the normative certainties of the Cold War. Precisely because the new stimuli come so quickly and pierce so deeply, moreover, the emergent norms have a uniquely genuine quality in the sense that the immediacy of events denies time for dithering and weigh-ing alternative responses. Governments may not move as decisively as some would wish, or they may not move at all, but the scenes that occa-sioned humanitarian responses in Africa or anguished reactions to Bosnia will not go away. They are permanently etched in the minds of this generation and tapes of them can always be replayed. Thus, to the extent that norms are developing on a global scale, their evolution is partly the result of the intense way in which today's turbulent situations have jolted people and officials out of their long-accepted normative premises.

It seems likely, moreover, that local and national situations further reinforce the jarring and norm-generating nature of tragedies abroad. Whether it is because the television camera now takes people much deeper into the depravities of human affairs than ever before, or whether it is because of the fatigue of modernity and the disarray and dislocations thereby produced, the present era is marked by startling circumstances at home that tap into new normative responses. From presidential resignations to powerful earthquakes, from holocaust sur-vivors to crime victims, from exploding spaceships to accused Supreme Court nominees, from drug smugglers to AIDS carriers, from a celebrity's flight on a Los Angeles freeway to a trail of corruption through the upper echelons of the Italian elite, from a devastated build-ing in Oklahoma City to poisonous gas in Tokyo's subways – all recorded in detail, played on television and replayed on VCRs – the air-waves are pervaded with unfamiliar and intimate scenes that once were remote and now serve to stimulate untapped core reactions and a subsequent rush to judgment. People may feel they have become hardened by the spate of excesses and thus can no longer be surprised, much less jolted; but time and again either new situations arise with which existing value systems are ill-prepared to cope or standard conflicts reoccur with such new twists as to be normatively challenging. And the more involved people become in absorbing and handling newly stirred feelings, the more they feel themselves participants in the situations at home and abroad which seem to cry out for condemnation, cynicism, or some other form of judgment.

Traditional guides to normative choices

No less important to the evolution of norms shared along the Frontier are the ways in which long-established and core values associated with the notion of community have frayed as a result of the dynamics of fragmegration. If new challenges contribute to the forging of shared norms by upending or bypassing old ways of responding to situations, then the assaults on community identities and boundaries that derive from the tensions between globalizing and localizing dynamics may be as stimulative of broad value consensuses as the detailed and intimate media coverage of previously distant events. Paradoxically, that is, even as fragmegrative tensions call into question long-established values associated with the notion of community, so may the disarray they foster add to the search for new normative bases with which to assess issues that sustain governance along the Frontier.

Challenges to the concept of community are inherent in the possibility that the traditional precepts of Western civilization through which people appreciated the necessity of compromise in order to preserve both individual and community values may no longer be reliable as guides to resolving the dilemmas thrust upon them by a world that is simultaneously both increasingly interdependent and increasingly fragmented. That is, the history of the nineteenth and most of the twentieth century is the story of convergence around ever more encompassing political entities in order to preserve individual values in the context of collective needs and wants; but today the processes of community-building have been reversed. Today the story is in good part one of fragmentation, of rights overriding responsibilities, of people opting for individual and subgroup needs and wants. But neither citizens nor leaders have any experience in adapting their traditional values to the demands of subgroupism and the increasing ineffectiveness, even the break-up, of whole systems. How, for example, does one give expression to a morality that values the commons when everywhere there is evidence that others have narrowed their conception of the commons to their own particular set of subgroup loyalties? If one's fellow citizens are pressing for subgroup autonomy, how does one stand firm for a balance in which whole-group needs are also served? And how do political leaders champion the virtues of the larger community when their followers insist it is unresponsive to their needs and demand that their leaders give voice to subgroup aspirations? How do leaders seek to manage an authority crisis when efforts at accommodation are viewed as betrayal?

Let us be more specific. If one lives in Quebec, Belgrade, or Chechnya and recognizes that the political unions called Canada, Yugoslavia, and Russia have served collective needs, how does one conduct oneself as others mobilize to press for complete separation and autonomy? Or if one is a leader in these multi-ethnic situations who sees the virtues of forfeiting a measure of autonomy for institutions that facilitate collective effort, how does one resist the demands of those who place autonomy ahead of any schemes founded on political union, be it of a confederative or federative kind? Or consider the problem of environmental pollution. Suppose citizens can see ahead to the day when the ozone gap will be a threat to the well-being of their grandchildren, how do they give expression to this normative conclusion when they observe many of their fellow citizens opting for the comforts of the present? If leaders perceive the growing gap as posing severe long-term threats to future generations, how do they press the choices inherent in this perception upon their followers when the latter are concerned only with short-term benefits? And how do citizens learn to ignore those leaders who offer short-term gains and downplay long-term dangers?

How, in short, can citizens and leaders adhere to the middle of the road paved by traditional values when the course of history is moving groups and nations toward narrowly defined, self-serving solutions? Put even more starkly, how can that sense of community from which norms shared along the Frontier must emerge be served in an era of rampant subgroupism, a time when the ultimate subgroup is the individual?

Such questions can seem quite abstract in comparison to the immediacy of swift-moving events. Thus for leaders and analysts to raise them, and thereby imply that new normative standards are needed if future calamities are to be avoided, is to risk seeming naive and idealistic. After all, many will argue, it is the powerful forces of subgroupism that are in the ascendant and any efforts to promote normative standards that do not allow for their realization are bound to fall on deaf ears. The most that wise leadership and citizenship can accomplish, such reasoning asserts, is a governance that moderates these forces so that human rights and dignity are not trampled. To go further, to press for a temporal expansion of the standards so that they encompass long-run considerations, is to invite charges of being impractical and out of touch.

Compelling as this reasoning may be, it falls down in failing to appreciate that countervailing forces are at work. For not only has subgroupism flourished with the breakdown of the values associated with the whole community, but the breakdown is also having the consequence of clearing social space for new norms to evolve, a space that the dynamics of globalization are filling no less than are those of subgroupism, and in some respects the tensions between the two sets of dynamics favor the global expansion of normative horizons. Leaders may not single-handedly be able to arouse concern for the long-run well-being of the whole community, but they are not alone. They can count on the course of events to arrest attention to global dangers and needs.

The evolution of shared norms

In other words, paradoxical as it may seem, the dynamics of fragmegration and the impact of television have at least one dimension in common: they are both unsettling and, as such, they are both norm-generating. Fragmegration may highlight new norms pertaining to subgroupism and selfish individualism, but the media offer brutal reminders that distant others need help. It is not a long step from being aghast over scenes in Oklahoma City, Rwanda, Bosnia, and many other remote places pervaded by disaster, to a sense of vulnerability as a human, a feeling that the well-being – perhaps even the fate – of the species is at stake and that some kind of action has to be taken.

Perhaps the most conspicuous indicator of norms shared along the Frontier is the large degree to which it has become commonplace to refer to the concerns and interests of an entity called "the international community." Sometimes the reference is made with the United Nations in mind, but frequently it is voiced in the context of a less organized but no less specific actor, as if there is now a community, no less real for its lack of organization, that is bound to protect and serve the decency of humankind. In the mind of those who speak of the "international community," this is not an imagined entity that ought to be nursed into being; it is, rather, conceived to be an empirical reality, an actor that has obligations, responsibilities, and capabilities even if it lacks describable structures.

To be sure, reliance on the "international community" as a vehicle for normative expressions may stem in good part from the inadequacies of the UN, and for some it may also serve as a code-word for US or Western dominance. Yet, to stress its role as a substitute for an ongoing institution or a hegemonic leadership underestimates its importance. Today the term is widely used because such an entity is regarded as part of the global landscape. It gives voice to the collective nature of shared challenges. Criticisms expressed in its name are directed as much toward the developed as the developing world. And thus, amorphous as it may be, the international community is urged to focus attention on a particular situation; or it is seen as worried by a series of events; or it is called upon to act – to note but a few of the many ways in which this increasingly salient entity pervades public discourse. And for those who have served on election-monitoring teams, equipped only with a badge indicating they represent the "international community," this term has a concrete as well as an abstract meaning. One need merely wave the badge and mumble that its bearer represents the "international community" and the doors, registration records, and ballot boxes within countries are opened for inspection.

Of course, this is not to ignore those locales along the Frontier where cynicism and alienation flourish. Nor is it to imply that conflict has been surmounted in those areas where traces of normative evolution are visible. Reference is not being made to a world society that has consolidated its shared values and relegated to the status of a small minority those who oppose the values around which consensuses appear to be forming. Rather the point is that enough evolution has occurred for traces of widely shared norms to be noticeable. In each case opposition or controversy is also evident and there is still a long evolutionary process to unfold before it can be said that the Frontier is marked by norms approaching full acceptance. But the degree of acceptance is not trivial. It is discernible and it appears to be widening.

The loci of normative consensuses

So it is not nearly so paradoxical as it may seem at first glance that traces of norms shared on a global scale can be discerned midst the tensions that are racking local and national communities. The emergence of five of these traces is sufficiently pronounced to warrant singling out as underpinnings of rule systems along the Frontier. One is humanitarian issues, those horrendous circumstances that bring famine, disease, and genocide to huge numbers of underprivileged people. A second and closely related area is human rights. Another concerns the integrity of democratic institutions, and a fourth involves values pertaining to invasions launched by the military forces of states. In a fifth area, the environment, the traces of evolving norms are somewhat more elusive as a consequence of the long-run nature of the issues involved.

Humanitarian issues

Although droughts and ethnic conflicts that result in fleeing refugees have long been part of the human condition, situations that involve mass suffering, starvation, and death have filled some of the vacancies high on the global agenda left by the end of superpower competition. During the Cold War such situations tended to be addressed by the superpower in whose domain they arose, with the result that they never reached the point where television could record horrendous scenes of human misery. But in the absence of superpower rivalry, ethnic and tribal conflicts have become so intense as to create a form of havoc that seems so new and different as to challenge – with the help of orbiting satellites and global television – the consciences of people everywhere. And it seems clear that the consciences of those in wealthier parts of the world have risen to the challenge, or at least they have done so sufficiently to justify regarding the response to humanitarian situations as a widely shared norm. The operation of the norm is evident not only in the response of governments and the United Nations to suffering in Rwanda, Bosnia and a host of other similar calamities, but also in the donations of individuals and private charities throughout the world. The amount of giving is often not adequate to the need and there are occasional signs of a disaster fatigue that fosters a decline in the amounts of money raised, but there has been no narrowing of the places from which donations come. That remains global in scope. Clearly, there are limits to the self-centered orientations of individuals and groups. For many people there is a point beyond which human degradation leads them to put aside their private preoccupations and either make donations or accept the efforts of their governments to alleviate such situations.[3]

An insight into the power of this global norm is provided by the reac-

[3] For an incisive discussion of this point, see Martha Finnemore, "Contrasting Norms of Humanitarian Intervention," paper presented at the Third SSRC Workshop on Norms, Identity, and International Security, Stanford University (October 7–9, 1995).

tion of the United States to the 1994 tragedy in Rwanda. Having failed to ameliorate comparable circumstances in Somalia and then accompanying its withdrawal from Somalia with statements that it would not again become so enmeshed in such situations, the pressure generated by television coverage of unspeakable suffering in Rwanda led the United States to reverse itself and lend its resources to an effort to limit the scope of the tragedy.

One can regret, of course, that unimaginable horror is required before the conscience of humankind is stirred to action, but there may be comfort in knowing that it can be stirred. And there is further comfort in knowing that humanitarian issues are not the only kind that are the focus of emergent global norms, as the ensuing discussion suggests.

Human rights

While countries differ as to whether human rights are composed of socio-economic or political dimensions, the continuing worldwide dialogue about one or the other formulation suggests the emergence of global norms with respect to the basic rights of individuals. To be sure, some of the attention to political rights is mere lip service, voiced by governments whose policies can hardly be regarded as liberal with respect to the rights of free speech and assembly, but the fact that they feel obliged to talk about such matters and to defend their record in terms of socio-economic rights is surely an indicator that such issues are considered to have a worldwide legitimacy. Indeed, with some governments honoring human rights through their policies, with Amnesty International and other groups relentlessly drawing attention to incidents and countries where widespread violations of rights occur, and with the UN having established a High Commissioner for Human Rights, it seems clear that such issues have not only achieved a high place on the global agenda, but also that they are backed by a momentum that will keep them in the public eye for a long time to come.[4]

Democratic institutions

Linked closely to human rights issues are the institutions that sustain the processes whereby such rights are preserved even as the will of majorities is realized. That norms associated with democratic institu-

---

[4] For a good summary of the emergence of human rights as a global concern, see Jack Donnelly, "State Sovereignty and International Intervention: The Case of Human Rights," in Gene M. Lyons and Michael Mastanduno (eds.), *Beyond Westphalia? State Sovereignty and International Intervention* (Baltimore: Johns Hopkins University Press, 1995), pp. 115–46.

tions are also spreading on a global scale is perhaps most conspicuous with respect to the number of countries which have recently shifted from closed to open political regimes.[5] Their spread is also evident in the emergence of norms that justify calling in the "international community" to observe domestic elections and report on the fairness of their procedures. As will be seen at greater length in chapter 13, despite occasional claims that the privileges of national sovereignty are being violated, election monitoring by outside observers is now an established practice in all parts of the world where balloting procedures may be in question. Likewise, the UN Security Council's support of an American-led military force to restore a democratically elected president of Haiti who had been ousted by a *coup d'état* is still another trace of emergent global norms in this area. To be sure, two members of the Council, China and Brazil, abstained from voting on the issue, but it is not unreasonable to view abstentions as an acquiescence to the norms in the sense of not publicly acting in opposition to them.

Freedom from conquest

As indicated by the involvement of thirty-two countries in the UN-sanctioned, American-led operation to push the Iraqi forces out of Kuwait and restore that country's self-governing capacities, it can be argued that another set of global norms is evolving that focuses on the right of peoples to be free of conquest by other states. There is, of course, a countertrend in which conquest is ignored by the international community or otherwise defined as intrastate conflict, but today the central tendency appears to be in the direction of condemning through words and actions outright violations of national boundaries. A number of reasons for the normative resurgence in this direction can be identified (see chapter 22) and they seem sufficiently cumulative to justify the expectation that the momentum will continue to mount in favor of implementing collective actions to restore conquered borders.

Ecological issues

As will be seen in chapter 10, there are several reasons to anticipate a growing consensus around issues of environmental degradation. The probabilities along this line are conceived to be greater the more such issues are threatening or overtaken by disaster. Accordingly, since most

---

[5] Samuel P. Huntington, *The Third Wave: Democratization in the Late Twentieth Century* (Norman: University of Oklahoma Press, 1991).

of the threats are in the distant future and since severe disasters cannot be anticipated, individuals and governments alike are inclined to focus on the benefits of economic development and thus to postpone action, perhaps even suppress their concerns, relevant to the dangers of ecological deterioration. In the absence of catastrophe, therefore, it seems unlikely that the pace of convergence around common ecological norms will quicken in the short run.

Continuing cleavages

All of this is not to imply the absence of limits on the emergence of boundary-spanning norms. Major cleavages that presently seem unbridgeable can be readily identified. Four are especially noteworthy. One involves the fault lines that separate cultures or, as one formulation has it, the clash of civilizations.[6] While it is questionable whether these cultural divisions will ever result in outright military conflicts, they do seem to be founded on mutually exclusive premises that make them irreconcilable. Orientations toward God, science, women, and modernity are so different in, say, Muslim and Western countries that it is reasonable to presume the differences will still be in place many decades from now.

A second, somewhat overlapping cleavage is the long-standing set of disputes that have divided the developing world from its counterpart.[7] The two differ on a wide range of issues – most of which revolve around the distribution and redistribution of wealth which, in turn, get reflected in arguments over governance in a variety of areas – that also seem unlikely to ameliorate in the coming years, or at least as long as the income disparities between (and within) the two worlds remain so high and the standard of living in the developing world remains so low. It is difficult to conceive of widely shared norms evolving around issues of wealth and welfare while the world's wealth is concentrated in relatively few hands. Some analysts even contend that as the gap between rich and poor grows among and within countries, so does the likelihood of one or another form of class warfare.

---

[6] Samuel P. Huntington, "The Clash of Civilizations," *Foreign Affairs*, vol. 72 (Summer 1993), pp. 22–49.

[7] North–South divisions are the subject of a vast literature. A point of departure for probing it can be found in many of the chapters in Yoshikazu Sakamoto (ed.), *Global Transformation: Challenges to the State System* (Tokyo: United Nations University Press, 1994).

Third, the problem of when, how and under what auspices the international community should intervene in the internal conflicts of countries poses seemingly intractable issues as long as the prerogatives of sovereignty are considered inviolable. As will be seen in chapter 11, these prerogatives appear to be undergoing subtle changes, but until such time that the changes emerge as full-fledged global norms – and that may still be in the distant future – the question of intervention is likely to be a major cleavage around which various actors vigorously differ.[8] This fault line was conspicuous in the recurring question of whether and how to intervene in Bosnia, more than once reaching the point where it divided the UN from NATO and the United States from its European allies, and in all probability it will continue to be evident in a number of other situations as the tendencies toward subgroupism and fragmentation remain strong.

Related to all the other cleavages is a fourth set that revolves around the priorities individuals, groups, and societies attach to the aforementioned choices they must endlessly confront between whole systems and subsystems, between the benefits of globalization and the merits of localization. Whether they surface in the developed or developing worlds, in Muslim or Christian countries, or in societies tending toward division or those tending toward underlying consensus, cleavages over where to allocate resources, direct loyalties, and draw boundaries are bound to remain intense under present conditions. Thus it is possible that the pervasiveness of fragmegration will hinder the evolution of widely shared norms well into the future. This is not a cleavage that has obvious fault lines, but it does embrace issues that divide groups and societies in important and seemingly enduring ways.

Are world politics at a standstill?

The finding that shared values appear to be evolving on a worldwide basis in several issue areas even as an equal number of cleavages seem likely to inhibit this normative evolution is, of course, consistent with the dynamics of a world undergoing turbulence and fragmegration. The normative foundations of the fragmegrative worldview are no less pervaded with contradictions and ambiguities than are its practices and

---

[8] Again a voluminous literature is available on the nature of humanitarian issues and the problem of external interventions into them. See, for example, the various essays in Lyons and Mastanduno (eds.), *Beyond Westphalia?*

institutions. Humankind is moving in opposite directions and it has developed the moral bases for doing so. How long can such profound contradictions persist? Probably a long time, given the deep sources of subgroupism on the one hand and the imperatives of globalization on the other.

If that is the case, are world politics at a standstill? Or are there reasons to believe that the areas of consensus along the Frontier can be expanded and the cleavages bridged? The first question is easier to answer than the second. There is too much change at work within and among societies for the politics of the Frontier to be at a standstill. The dynamics of fragmegration, not to mention the material realities of population growth, resource utilization, and ecological fragility, are giving rise to new attitudes, behavior, and institutions that will doubtless make the world different in the coming decades than it is today.

But will these transformations result in a normative convergence that supersedes, or at least minimally reconciles, the localizing and globalizing patterns that pervade the Frontier? One observer offers an affirmative answer by outlining a normative scenario in which the seemingly contradictory dynamics of fragmegration are both confronted and reconciled:

> Humane governance . . . is as concerned with equity and human distress as it is with stability and sustainability. It is sensitive to the claims of the unborn for undiminished life prospects. Shaping the structures and practices of governance in human directions is the core task of democratizing processes. It involves not only the deepening of democracy in state/society settings, but the outward extensions of democracy to transnational arenas fashioned by states, corporations, and banks and the inward extensions of human rights to villages, rural areas, as well as to schools, homes, the workplace . . . This view of humane governance is one that *links the global and regional to the national and personal.* The aggregation of the various sites of governance from the local and personal to the global and bureaucratic cumulatively constitute humane governance.[9]

Another observer, "overwhelmed by the complexity and apparent hopelessness of what I had seen" during a lengthy trip through the developing world, hints at a negative answer to the question of reconciling fragmegration's contradictions:

---

[9] Richard Falk, *On Humane Governance: Toward a New Global Politics* (University Park: Pennsylvania State University Press, 1995), p. 17 (italics added).

if the past is any guide, in too many places there will be a time lag between extreme social deterioration and strategies which might have prevented it. The long-range future may be bright, but the next few decades will be tumultuous. Keep in mind that the collapse of just a few small countries scattered around the globe has overwhelmed policymakers in the West . . . [T]he banal truth is that economic and social development is generally cruel, painful, violent, and uneven – and humanity is developing more dramatically than ever before.[10]

A more cautious response to the question posits the world as deeply ensconced in a choice-point, a period of time when the clash between humane and exploitative governance on a global scale is unfolding as tendencies toward democracy, human rights, and environmental protection vie with those fostering virulent nationalism, personal greed, and the exhaustion of nature's bounty. How the choice will play out is best assessed after the ensuing analyses of the processes and actors through which rule systems are sustained and governance achieved. Pieces of the puzzle are identified at a number of points in subsequent chapters and consideration of whether they form a coherent pattern is undertaken in the concluding chapter.

---

[10] Robert D. Kaplan, *The Ends of the Earth: A Journey at the Dawn of the 21st Century* (New York: Random House, 1996), p. 437.

10   Environments

> It is necessary to acquire a full understanding of the increasingly global context of political interaction, not conceived as simply "world-wide", but rather as the relationship between local issues addressed in a global context and global issues addressed in a local context – local environmental problems (land, water, air pollution) may demand a global strategy, and global environmental problems (ozone depletion, the greenhouse effect, and climate change) may demand local action.
>
> Hugh C. Dyer[1]

> Environmental sovereignty says my home, my space, isn't just limited to my borders on a map. It includes the air I breathe, the water off my shore and the whole extended food chain upon which I rely. Environmental sovereignty is not confined either by conventional borders or by conventional time.
>
> Thomas L. Friedman[2]

> Environmental issues represent the paradigmatic transboundary challenge and thus serve as a prime focus for studies of global governance.
>
> Paul Wapner[3]

As these epigraphs imply, in climbing high on the global agenda environmental issues have eroded boundaries within as well as between societies. Pollution is carried by winds and currents across provinces as well as countries, thus cutting a wide swath along the

---

[1] Hugh C. Dyer, "Environmental Ethics and International Relations," *Paradigms*, vol. 8 (Summer 1994), pp. 61–2.

[2] "The Bomb and the Boomerang," *New York Times*, August 27, 1995, sect. 4, p. 15.

[3] "Bringing Society Back In: Environmental Governance and World Sociology," paper presented at the Annual Meeting of the International Studies Association, San Diego (April 1996), p. 24.

Frontier. Clearly, if the many challenges of nature that presently beset humankind are to be met in the future, actions will have to be undertaken at all levels of community. Some of the challenges – such as ozone depletion, pollution of the oceans, loss of biodiversity, and potential climate changes – are global in scope and thus require international collaboration to limit or alter their consequences. For such challenges, "It will not help, the way it sometimes does, to break the problem into smaller, more manageable, pieces. Only a comprehensive global approach to managing environmental resources and coordinating sustainable development will work."[4] Still, a preponderance of the threats to land, air, water, and species have their roots within communities and thus can only be surmounted through the cumulation of actions at the local and societal levels, at those points where people conserve, exploit, or otherwise come into contact with nature.

The implications of this perspective for governance in a turbulent world are obvious. The task of achieving and maintaining sustainable development in which life on earth is improved without long-term damage to the environment is in reality a complex of multiple challenges, each of them serious in itself and all of them overlapping such that they are to be found everywhere along the Frontier. Thus the burdens of governance are likely to be shouldered by diverse SOAs that are widely dispersed, that are located at all levels of collective activity, and that may take new as well as traditional forms.[5]

The challenges of environmental governance

An insight into the full scope of the problem can well start with stress on the interactive foundations of environmental and social systems. It is clear, for example, that even as the processes of nature provide contextual limits and opportunities for the conduct of social, economic, and political life, so do human situations serve as context for the natural environment.[6] More than that, the two are so profoundly interactive that oft-times both nature and humankind blend together into a single

---

[4] Lawrence E. Susskind, *Environmental Diplomacy: Negotiating More Effective Global Agreements* (New York: Oxford University Press, 1994), p. viii.

[5] An elaborate formulation along these lines is developed in Paul Wapner, *Environmental Activism and World Politics* (Albany: State University of New York Press, 1996).

[6] See, for example, Andrew Goude, *The Human Impact on the Natural Environment* (Cambridge, MA: MIT Press, 1990), and Joy Tivy and Greg O'Hare, *Human Impact on the Ecosystem* (New York: Longman, 1981).

causal stream. People consume resources, thereby transforming nature; in turn, nature's transformations alter the conduct of community and world affairs, leading to changed patterns of consumption and a continuing cycle of interaction. Today this cycle is distinguished by its fast pace. The causal stream has become a rushing river, swollen by the melting snows and bursting dams of endlessly dynamic technologies. And as the pace of interactive change accelerates, so do the tasks of governance become ever more delicate and the processes of nature ever more threatening.[7]

The approach taken here to the question of whether humankind can come to terms with the dangers that lie ahead is to identify the multiplicity of environmental challenges and to suggest how singly and together they both provide opportunities and pose obstacles that are in continuous tension and that, taken together, demand daring, diligent, and disciplined governance if the future is to be marked by success in moving toward the widely shared goal of sustainable development.[8] Anticipating the central thrust of what follows, again it is found that the analysis is rooted in contradiction: the opportunities for improvement are judged to have never been better and the obstacles to progress are assessed to have never been greater! And what is the key to whether improving or worsening patterns will unfold in the coming decades? Relevant as both may be, the answer involves neither the vagaries of nature nor the pressures of change; rather, the key determinants will likely be found in the processes of governance through which people collectively confront the multiplicity of environmental threats that loom on the horizon. Whatever may be the interactions between humankind and nature that our grandchildren inherit, the key to whether their lives will be marred by continuing environmental degradation or enhanced by a progressive trend toward effective environmental management depends on the degree to which a worldwide consensus on the nature of effective management can be fashioned and, thus, on how well the challenges of environmental governance are met. To a large extent these are the same challenges set forth in the general analysis of governance

---

[7] A succinct but thorough assessment of these tasks and how well they have been undertaken is provided in Peter M. Haas, "The Future of International Environmental Governance," paper presented at the Annual Meeting of the International Studies Association, San Diego (April 1996).

[8] For a skeptical perspective on the prospects for sustainable development, see Peter M. Haas, "Is 'Sustainable Development' Politically Sustainable?" *Brown Journal of World Affairs*, vol. 3 (Summer/Fall 1996).

presented in chapter 8, but the ensuing discussion stresses that allowance has to be made for how the environment may modify and reshape the control mechanisms through which order is maintained and movement toward goals sustained.

To appreciate why the prospects for effective environmental management teeter between being more favorable and more horrendous – and where governance fits in the resolution of these tensions – it is useful to highlight the various contexts in which the dynamics that interactively link natural and human systems are located. Each type of system serves as a source of change for the other, but both are also responsive to other transformations at work in the world which serve as boundary conditions within which the links between human systems and nature evolve. One obvious condition, for example, is the state of the global economy. As it fluctuates back and forth between booms and busts, so do the resources available for addressing nature's challenges move back and forth between larger and smaller amounts.

Environmental contexts

Although many aspects of the environment are relevant to the interaction between nature and humankind, three are treated here as especially salient. One involves the large extent to which our understanding of the dynamics of environmental change derive from the application of scientific methods. Another is the unique time frame within which environmental issues get identified, addressed, and resolved. The third pertains to the important ways in which disasters can shape the salience of environmental challenges and the readiness of polities to consider them. Table 10.1 summarizes how these phenomena are interactively linked and how the linkages can lead to both opportunities and obstacles insofar as the tasks of governance are concerned.

The scientific context

Notwithstanding the ever increasing degrees of complexity that distinguish the postindustrial era in all walks of life and at every level of politics, environmental issues are perhaps more fully pervaded by complex technical dimensions than any other type on the global agenda. Rooted in the processes of nature and its responses to human intervention, such issues are inescapably embedded in a scientific context. Unlike the cases of the economy, education, housing, labor, and other conventional foci of controversy, the outcomes of environmental issues are located in the ups and downs of nonhuman processes rather than the behavior of people. What people do or fail to do, of course, shapes nature's processes, but ultimately the latter adhere to their own laws and not to those of organized society. As such, they give rise to objective outcomes in the sense that what happens is not vulnerable to the vagaries of motivation, chance encounters, institutional lapses, or any of the other uncertainties that attach to social dynamics. In short, environmental issues may be rife with uncertainties, but these derive as much from the mysteries of nature as from the variability of human affairs.

Thus it is that environmental issues turn centrally on the scientific method and its applications. Politicians cannot exercise control over environmental outcomes without recourse to scientific findings. They may claim that the findings are not clear-cut or remain subject to contradictory interpretations, but they are nonetheless dependent on what the practices of science uncover about the laws of nature.

It follows that criteria of proof are at the heart of environmental politics, that the outcomes of environmental issues depend as much on the persuasiveness of evidence as on the various dimensions of power that sustain or resolve other types of issues. To be sure, the exercise of power is not irrelevant to the conduct of environmental politics, and it is surely the case that deft politicians can manipulate support in favor of one or another environmental policy, but ultimately the outcomes will be shaped by the proofs that are brought to bear on the dictates of nature.[9] Development-minded groups – and the scientists affiliated with them – can argue for the exploitation of nature for only so long if that exploitation continues to lead to discernible and measurable deterioration; at some point the data become too telling to ignore and interest-group politics is compelled to yield ground to the politics of science. How long it takes for nature to unfold in these ways, for scientists to converge around shared consensuses, and for the findings then to force change in the conduct of politics is, of course, an open question. Indeed, this temporal question serves as another contextual factor worthy of notation.

The temporal context

Leaving aside for the moment large-scale disasters, a preponderance of the world's environmental challenges normally cumulate slowly in

---

[9] For an extensive discussion of the role of scientific proof in the conduct of global affairs, see James N. Rosenau, *Turbulence in World Politics: A Theory of Change and Continuity* (Princeton: Princeton University Press, 1990), pp. 198–209, 425–9.

Table 10.1. *Attributes of environmental issues and world politics that pose opportunities and obstacles for environmental governance*

	Opportunities	Obstacles
Attributes unique to environmental issues		
SCIENTIFIC FOUNDATIONS OF ENVIRONMENTAL CHALLENGES They are observable, quantifiable, and measurable.	Studies of nature's changes tend to be authentic and thus increase the chances of persuading publics to alter their behavior.	Comprehension of scientific findings is not easily acquired and publics may resist them, especially when scientists disagree about their meaning.
TEMPORAL FOUNDATIONS OF ENVIRONMENTAL CHALLENGES Threats posed by environmental uses and abuses normally evolve slowly in small increments across long stretches of time; they are recognized by experts long before publics and long before they become immediate problems.	There is plenty of time to frame policies and educate publics before the long-term challenge becomes a short-term threat; also, experts and politicians can proceed relatively free of harassment by aroused publics.	Politicians, political systems and publics are oriented toward short-term problems and thus to avoiding hard choices and postponing action; immediate environmental crises may be required to arouse short-run concerns and mobilize remedial actions.
DISASTERS AS CONTEXTS Ecological events (e.g., Three Mile Island, Bhopal, and Chernobyl) periodically surface with such force as to be widely perceived as disastrous and to quickly become global events.	Disasters offer a glimpse into the future, a chance to perceive how long-term processes can culminate in short-term horrors, and thus an opportunity to educate elites and publics alike on the need for environmental diligence and an early confrontation of long-term threats.	The implications of disasters can be so threatening as to evoke either excessive or insufficient, head-in-the-sand responses; they can also lead to exaggerated forecasts and thence to public apathy.

Changing attributes of world politics

THE SKILL REVOLUTION Everywhere people are becoming more capable of constructing scenarios of world affairs that culminate in their pocketbooks and homes than were their grandparents.	Publics and elites will increasingly have respect for scientific findings, long-term processes, and the fact that what is distant is also proximate, thus making them more ready to adapt to environmental necessities.	Being better able to see where they fit in global, regional, and community processes, people may become more aware of their self-interests and more ready to perceive them in selfish ways that have little regard for their consequences for society.
AUTHORITY CRISES FOSTERING: (a) WEAKENED GOVERNMENTS AND DIMINISHED SOVEREIGNTY National governments can still evoke compliance by resorting to coercion, but they are less and less capable of framing effective policies and maintaining their sovereign prerogatives.	It has become increasingly evident that national governments can no longer go it alone with respect to ecological issues; their diminished capacities thus require an increased readiness to cooperate with counterparts abroad.	Being caught up in stalemate, if not paralysis, states are less and less able to make or implement the financial and diplomatic commitments needed to carry out negotiated international ecological agreements.
(b) AUTHORITY REDISTRIBUTED UPWARD TO SUPRANATIONAL LEVELS The advent of transnational or interdependence issues requiring intergovernmental cooperation has led to a proliferation of international governmental organizations (IGOs) and regimes.	Since many ecological issues are boundary-spanning in their scope, it is only at supranational levels that they can be addressed, thus giving IGOs and regimes a potential for effectively dealing with ecological challenges that regularly extend across the borders that separate states.	While governments are ready to conclude international ecological agreements, the authority they thereby cede to IGOs and regimes may not invoke their compliance when the agreements are subsequently implemented.

Table 10.1. (*cont.*)

	Opportunities	Obstacles
(c) AUTHORITY REDISTRIBUTED SIDEWARD TO SOCIETAL-LEVEL INSTITUTIONS The spread and increased capabilities of social movements, non-governmental organizations (NGOs), multinational corporations, and other transnational entities has fostered a further relocation of authority and decentralization of the global system.	NGOs and the environmental movement stimulate concern, provide technical studies, offer alternative policies, format grass roots activism, and otherwise heighten the salience of ecological issues, with the result that they "have affected the political cultures of almost every nation"[a] and made possible the coordination of diverse interests at such gatherings as the Rio Global Forum in 1992.	Some NGOs and some parts of the environmental movement turn to extremism in their demands and actions, thus complicating the processes through which ecological negotiations are sustained.
(d) AUTHORITY REDISTRIBUTED DOWNWARD TO SUBNATIONAL ENTITIES A vast proliferation of organizations and subgroupism has further weakened state authority and contributed to the disaggregation of global politics and governance.	Both local governments and NGOs have avenues through which to express and act on their environmental concerns, thus bringing ecological issues closer to the level at which their resolution will ultimately be either improved or worsened, i.e., to the level of citizenries.	Pro-development groups and officials at the local level are able to voice opposition to conservation policies and engage in organizational activities that inhibit or prevent meeting ecological challenges.
BIFURCATION OF GLOBAL POLITICS Where world affairs were once managed by an anarchic system of states, today this state-centric world has been paralleled by a multi-centric world consisting of a wide variety of	As indicated by the parallel conferences at Stockholm (1972) and Rio (1992), the bifurcation of global structures into two worlds of world politics provides a structure for spreading involvement and responsibility with respect to	The decentralization represented by the bifurcation of global structures may make it more difficult for regimes in the state-centric world to frame and carry out ecological agreements as diverse interests and opposition groups in the

other actors whose interactions are patterned and structured.

efforts to address diverse ecological problems; it facilitates keeping the state-centric system in close touch with thinking and aspirations in the private sector.

multi-centric world are heard and accommodated.

EVER EXPANDING DEGREES OF GLOBAL INTERDEPENDENCE
Dynamic communications and transportation technologies continue to shrink geographic and social distances, rendering peoples and events everywhere in the world ever more subject to what happens in every other part of the world.

Citizens will be able to feel increasingly in touch with the consequences of their own environmentally relevant behavior as they realize that the actions of others in distant places affects their own well-being; groups and social movements will increasingly benefit from the shrinkage of physical and social distances as their members and activities are ever more closely linked across national boundaries.

Individuals and groups with noxious goals (such as crime syndicates) will be better able to maintain their coherence and thwart efforts at governing them.

GROWING TENSIONS BETWEEN GLOBALIZING AND LOCALIZING DYNAMICS
The centralizing and decentralizing forces at work on a global scale are profoundly interactive with each increment of the one tending to foster an increment of the other.

Citizens will be increasingly faced with choices between proximate and distant preferences, thus adding to their analytic skills and their grasp of the dynamics of world affairs; local communities will be increasingly inclined to reach out to counterparts for information and support.

Some individuals, communities, and states will resolve the tensions by withdrawing and establishing more rigid lines dividing them from outside influences; globalization is seen as pervaded with threats rather than opportunities; some states may intensify stress on sovereign rights.

Note: [a] Ron Eyerman and Andrew Jamison, *Social Movements: A Cognitive Approach* (Cambridge: Polity Press, 1991), p. 77.

small increments that, in the absence of corrective measures, are likely to be increasingly detrimental over the long term. As a result, environmental politics tends to be organized around a continuous struggle between the few experts who recognize the need for corrective measures to offset the long-term dangers and the many producers, consumers, and citizens who are concerned with maximizing short-term gains and minimizing short-term losses. That is, more often than not, the political processes of communities and states tend to be loaded against the long run. People and politicians readily reason that long-term outcomes are too uncertain and too distant to worry about when the current scene is so pervaded with immediate needs and difficulties. So the impulse to avoid hard choices and postpone action is deeply embedded in the structure of environmental politics. All concerned are aware that their generation will be followed by others, that their children will grow to have children, but somehow the problems of unborn grandchildren seem minimal compared to those that beset people seeking to preserve or improve their welfare today.

It follows that in addition to its scientific foundations, the politics of the environment is by its very nature temporally different from, say, the politics of the economy or the politics of agriculture. The collapse of a stock market or the failure of a crop are, so to speak, instantaneous events with enormous and obvious immediate consequences that cannot be ignored, that require unqualified responses, and that quickly come to dominate the concerns, headlines, and agendas of the day. Environmental developments, on the other hand, are easily relegated to peripheral status. With the rare exception of when they connote disaster (see below), such developments do not pose a need for instant reactions, altered policies, or restless preoccupations. Usually they are developments in the sense that a government agency has issued a report or a nongovernmental organization has called attention to an ominous trend, events which tend neither to capture headlines nor to evoke efforts to place their implications high on the relevant agenda. Only as interest groups keep environmental issues alive, therefore, do they come before the public. Otherwise their long-term horizons consign them to short-term oblivion.

Politicians and groups anxious to protect or enhance the quality of the environment are thus destined to be mired in an uphill struggle. Using tentative findings, they face the difficult task of delivering disturbing and onerous messages that are neither immediately relevant nor easily rejected. They have to press policy options that require altered processes of production, revised modes of consumption, and a host of other sacrifices to which the body politic is not accustomed.[10] And perhaps most difficult of all, they cannot promise early and satisfying benefits in exchange for the sacrifices. Inescapably, therefore, support for sound environmental politics is bound to be fragile and reluctant, ever susceptible to erosion and distortion.

Disaster as context

But there is one condition under which the widespread predisposition to postpone or avoid the implications of environmental degradation are disrupted and replaced with a restless urgency that swiftly moves such issues from the periphery to the center of the political stage: namely, when environmental threats become realities and collapse into a single, dramatic, unexpected, and devastating disaster. Each marginal increment in a detrimental trend can be easily rationalized as just a temporary blip in an otherwise benign or murky pattern. But even the most adroit politician committed to dodging the taint of untoward events cannot evade the fallout of environmental disasters. Chernobyl, Three Mile Island, Bhopal, and other such disasters thus become turning points in politics. They are profoundly transformative. They arouse those who survive but are contaminated by the fallout into making demands and undertaking actions that are shrill, insistent, and durable. Nor are the fears engendered by disasters confined to those immediately exposed to them. Such events can be readily imagined by people everywhere as occurring at comparable facilities near their homes. As a consequence, major disasters quickly become globalized and thereafter deeply embedded in the memory banks on which future officials and publics draw for guidance in conducting their affairs.

To be sure, some individuals in communities far removed from the site of disasters may manage to remain oblivious to them; others may soon repress, forget, or otherwise act as if they never occurred; and still others may uneasily reason that such lightning never strikes twice. Memories can be short in politics as immediate needs press for attention. From a systemic perspective, however, things are never quite the same again. The consequences of the disaster pervade the speeches of politicians, legal precedents get adopted by courts, parties pledge

---

[10] For a good example of an effort to cope with this dilemma, see Sam Fulwood III, "Study Urges 'Revolution' Dedicated to Global Cleanup," *Los Angeles Times*, January 12, 1992, p. A4.

"never again" in their platforms, editorial pages take note of the disaster's anniversary, interest groups remind followers and adversaries alike of its portents, and so on through all the channels whereby societies adapt to systemic shocks.

Chernobyl is perhaps the quintessential example of how disasters stand out as exceptions to the temporal processes that sustain environmental threats as peripheral problems to be dealt with in the long run. When the reactor at the Chernobyl plant blew in 1986, it fostered rallies sponsored by marginal protest movements. The event "began to attract impressive crowds of people who were becoming aware of the carelessness with which bureaucrats had adulterated their food, poisoned their air, and contaminated their drinking water. The authorities were acutely embarrassed by the protests . . . It was difficult to deny the facts of ecological degradation, and environmental health is like motherhood: you can't be opposed to it."[11] Indeed, so significant was the disaster that Ukrainians began "to think of the Chernobyl explosion . . . as a product of a Russian policy of genocide, directed against the Ukrainian people – a continuation, in fact, of Stalin's elimination of the kulaks and his purges of the Communist Party."[12]

The conscious-raising effects of disasters, however, are not necessarily salutary. The very real repercussions they initiate can lead to distortions as well as correctives in the political process. Knowledge that a disastrous situation can quickly convert long-run uneasiness into short-run urgency may tempt pro-environment activist groups to over-interpret available data as indicating that ominous circumstances lie just ahead or, worse, to manipulate the data so that the likelihood of such circumstances developing seems beyond question. And the more activists yield to these temptations, the more are publics likely to become apathetic, much like the reactions to the boy who cried wolf too often. Similarly, given the potential disasters have for precipitating reform, some extremists (like the Unabomber) may be tempted by a dispirited cast of mind to believe they can engineer a major calamity that wreaks so much havoc in a community or region as to transform the temporal context and permanently elevate environmental issues to the top of the global agenda.

[11] Geoffrey Hosking, "The Roots of Dissolution," *The New York Review of Books*, vol. 39 (January 16, 1992), pp. 35–6.
[12] Hosking, "The Roots of Dissolution," p. 36.

Political contexts

Still another set of contextual factors, perhaps the most pervasive of all, involves the conditions under which environmental developments and problems are perceived, framed, addressed, and managed at every level of politics. For even as the scientific and temporal dimensions of the physical environment shape political structures, so is it the case that the latter operate as crucial determinants of how environmental opportunities are seized and environmental constraints heeded, ignored, or otherwise handled. In addition to the situation-specific variables that infuse dynamism into environmental issues, in other words, there is a larger political context, a set of structural constraints within which the interaction of human and nonhuman dynamics occurs.

Put in still another way, just as aspects of both the environment and the political arena can operate as independent and dependent variables, so can some dimensions of both be viewed as constants, as parametric boundary conditions that enhance and/or limit the management or mismanagement of nature's processes. Some resources in the environment are finite and others require centuries to replenish. Some processes of degradation feed on themselves and others are reversible. In a like manner, some basic structures that mark politics in any era of history cumulate to an invariable setting within which efforts to exploit, utilize, or otherwise respond to environmental conditions are sustained. As indicated in table 10.1, the major parametric transformations that underlie the present-day turbulence of world politics have had substantial consequences for the way in which environmental challenges are recognized and processed in the political arena.

In the case of the skill revolution, the consequences can be readily anticipated. Most notably, the expansion of citizens' skills is likely to render such issues as pollution, waste, resource depletion, and global warming increasingly less mysterious and remote to the body politic. Many people will doubtless continue to feel in awe of the experts who issue findings and make pronouncements about nature's tendencies, but their ability to absorb information, discern contradictions, and play out scenarios is likely to grow to the point where proofs will have to be increasingly precise and elaborate. In the face of a skill revolution at mass levels, it can reasonably be hypothesized, the locus of environmental politics is likely to shift, encompassing more alert and attentive citizens who press their leaders more vigorously and effectively. As noted below, recent poll data indicate that such a shift may already be underway.

While this is not to say that time horizons will be greatly narrowed and the long run substantially collapsed into the present, it is to suggest that opponents of conservation and environmentally sensitive policies are likely to find it increasingly difficult to dismiss the contentions of those who stress the dangers inherent in the prevailing practices of production and consumption. Similarly, the transformation of the micro parameter seems likely to add to and extend the repercussions of environmental disasters. The more skillful citizens are, the less are they likely to repress or otherwise forget events which highlight the precarious vulnerability of their own circumstances.

The transformation of the macro–micro parameter has also had wide implications for environmental governance. With authority crises besetting governments, their voices and policies on environmental issues are likely to be undermined and, correspondingly, the findings and interpretations of science seem bound to acquire greater legitimacy. To be sure, while the counter-culture and post-modern perspectives are expressive of reactions against the excesses and failures of science in recent decades,[13] for most segments of the publics science is one arena that has yet to be engulfed by the pervasive cynicism in which governments, corporations, universities, and most other societal institutions have become embedded. Thus it can be anticipated that politicians and bureaucracies will be ever more eager to turn to relevant scientific communities both for the guidance and, even more, for the legitimacy necessary to frame and sell their environmental policies. Such efforts may not halt the erosion of their authority, but they may well serve to insulate environmental politics from the destabilizing effects of the transformative dynamics of the macro–micro parameter.

Equally noteworthy, weakened governments are likely to undertake efforts to manage environmental problems by reaching out to counterparts abroad. That is, since the processes of nature tend to span political jurisdictions as quickly as currents carry pollution downstream, the built-in need for cooperation on environmental issues is likely to be augmented by the lessened authority of states and governments. For the same reason it can be anticipated that, increasingly, environmental issues will be centered in international organizations and other

---

[13] For a succinct discussion of these reactions, see Pauline Rosenau, *Postmodernism and the Social Sciences* (Princeton: Princeton University Press, 1992).

transnational actors which, while not necessarily endowed with sufficient authority to resolve the issues, will at least have the scope to address the cross-border foundations of such problems. Signs of a seepage of environmental politics away from exclusively national jurisdictions are already evident in the work of the United Nations on such matters.

As for the ways in which the context of authority crises may affect the repercussions of disasters, it seems reasonable to assume that the probability of calamitous environmental events will increase as governments and their bureaucracies become less able to frame effective policies designed to monitor and prevent tendencies toward severe environmental breakdowns. To a large extent disasters of this sort are rooted in administrative laxity that cumulates across time and that weakened governments lack the capacity to recognize, the will to address, or the authority to correct. At the same time the repercussions of disasters seem likely to erode further the authority of national governments inasmuch as occurrences of the former are likely to be ascribed, at least in part, to poor performances on the part of the latter.

In short, the role of domestic authorities in environmental challenges seems bound to become unraveled in the years ahead. The closer environmental issues climb to the top of political agendas, the greater is the likelihood that national governments will be eclipsed by transnational organizations and movements.

In a like manner the transformation of the macro parameter points to far-reaching consequences for environmental governance. The bifurcation of global structures and the expanded autonomy of actors in the multi-centric world mean that environmental groups – both the protesters and the exploiters of nature – have wider opportunities to mobilize support for and exert pressure on behalf of their goals. It is no mere coincidence, for example, that the environmental movement gained momentum during the very decades that the decentralizing dynamics at work in global politics weakened states and strengthened subnational, transnational groups, and other actors whose legitimacy claims derived from conspicuous performances not encumbered by the responsibilities of formal authority. Concerns about the environment that surfaced in earlier periods, when the state-centric system was predominant and states were able to ignore the evidence of potential problems, never had a chance to cohere and widen their bases of support. Inchoate and disparate as environmental groups may still be, their evolution into a discernible and influential social movement can be traced to the transformation of the macro parameter.[14] Indeed, as will be seen in chapter 17, it can easily be argued that the developing momentum of the environmental movement also served as a stimulus to the processes of bifurcation whereby states ceded some of their space on the global stage to counterparts in the multi-centric world.

In sum, the decentralized structures of world politics allow greater leeway for linkages among diverse types of environmental groups in different parts of the world to be established and evolve as transnational organizations. Presumably these processes of coalition formation will be speeded up as scientific findings reveal distant environmental threats to be moving closer to present-day realities.

Environmental governance on a global scale

It thus seems clear that successful management of environmental challenges will depend on effective governance along the Frontier. An understanding of the challenges can be further clarified by looking more closely at the question of whether control can be established over those environmental issues that are truly global in scope. Thus far the analysis suggests that it is misleading to separate out the global challenges, because they are so inextricably tied to developments at other levels of collective action. But suppose this premise is tightened and variables not operative on a global scale are held constant. What can then be said about the prospects for environmental governance? Is it plausible to anticipate a system of rule comprised of UN agencies, international regimes, NGOs, and other relevant actors that achieves effective control over such truly global situations as ozone depletion, ocean pollution, loss of biodiversity, and potentially devastating climate changes? Indeed, given the many recent efforts to assess the prospects for global environmental governance,[15] what can be said that is new and useful?

The literature on these questions is ambivalent. On the one hand, it is marked by a pervasive sense of gloom and doom, by a long parade of

---

[14] For a cogent discussion of the impact of the environmental movement, see Wapner, *Environmental Activism and World Civic Politics.*

[15] Summaries of some recent efforts can be found in Sheldon Kamieniecki (ed.), *Environmental Politics in the International Arena: Movements, Parties, and Policy* (Albany: State University of New York Press, 1993), and Ronnie D. Lipschutz and Ken Conca (eds.), *The State and Social Power in Global Environmental Politics* (New York: Columbia University Press, 1993).

horribles which seem to imply that things can only get worse. The main components of this parade are diverse and numerous: states fall back on their sovereignty when they oppose control measures, or they approve the measures but either do not comply with them or falsely report compliance; the money and resources needed to address the challenges are not available; national leaders attach higher priority to stimulating their economies than to environmental management; more than a few multinational corporations are inattentive to the environmental degradation that results from their production processes; multilateral aid programs have not stressed sustainable development and thus are marked by failure; the North–South divide continues to be deep and unbridgeable; most developing countries lack the staff, information, and equipment to monitor environmental practices and enforce environmental standards; the UN and its agencies have yet to demonstrate a capacity to grab hold of the challenges, much less to ameliorate them; compromises lead to deadlocks or, worse, to watered-down common denominators that neither protect the environment nor clearly identify threats; key treaties on the environment have yet to be ratified and those that have do not seem to have induced substantial reductions in environmental deterioration; and perhaps most discouraging of all, prior efforts to institute effective control mechanisms have come to naught as the international system remains immune to alterations of its anarchic ways.

Despite these severe and huge obstacles, on the other hand, the literature is also upbeat, pervaded with suggestions for reform, and marked by an optimism that can be quite infectious. One observer vigorously contends that the various accounts of the obstacles are all exaggerated;[16] another sees a growing role for NGOs that is bound to be beneficial;[17] a third devotes five chapters to parading the horribles, only to amplify in the last chapter on the ten recommendations for reform of the governance process made by the Salzburg Initiative in 1991;[18] a fourth anticipates the emergence of a new set of ethics to enable people to work through the dilemmas posed by environmental issues;[19] a fifth notes that increasingly "national leaders are aware of the need to reduce

---

[16] Christopher D. Stone, *The Gnat is Older than Man: Global Environment and Human Agenda* (Princeton: Princeton University Press, 1993).

[17] Kal Raustiala, "States, Civil Actors, and Participation in International Efforts for the Environment," paper presented at the Annual Meeting of the International Studies Association, Washington, DC (March 1994).

[18] Susskind, *Environmental Diplomacy*.

[19] Dyer, "Environmental Ethics and International Relations".

pollution and use resources more efficiently while spurring the economy";[20] a sixth stresses the growing importance of international environmental governance, noting that both new institutions and institutional reforms (including an agreement to institutionalize procedures for monitoring compliance with treaty obligations) flowed from the 1992 UN Conference on Environment and Development (UNCED);[21] and a seventh discerns a "new international environmental politics" emerging since the 1992 Rio meeting that is founded on more informed and committed publics, a proliferation of environmentally minded NGOs and a greater readiness on their part to monitor governments, "a shift in the burden of proof for international environmental protection," a convergence of environment groups from the North and the South under the banner of sustainable development, and the advent of new UN agencies such as the Commission on Sustainable Development (CSD) and the Global Environment Facility (GEF) which may more effectively address the challenges than did other, differently structured agencies in the past.[22]

How to evaluate these contradictory lines of thought? Do the optimistic assessments derive from that strain of the human spirit which has to plow ahead despite insurmountable odds? Or are there subtle bases for anticipating that the gloom and doom perspective is premature and that many, if not all, the challenges of global environmental governance will ultimately be met?

At least four bases for avoiding a premature pessimism can be identified. One is rooted in the relative rapidity with which environmental issues have climbed high on the global agenda. A second is linked to a focus on sovereignty as a behavioral variable rather than as a cherished principle. A third reconsiders the skill revolution in the light of the Earth Summit. The fourth reverses again the premise which holds constant the local and regional levels and stresses that developments at these levels may facilitate the tasks of governance at the global level.

The salience of environmental issues

Despite the difficulties of achieving wide consensuses on many environmental issues, and quite apart from the deep cleavages that rage

---

[20] The World Resources Institute, *World Resources, 1994–95* (New York: Oxford University Press, 1994), p. 235.

[21] The World Resources Institute, *World Resources, 1994–95*, pp. 223–6.

[22] Peter M. Haas, "International Environment Politics After Rio," paper presented at the ACUNS/ICRA Symposium, Tokyo (January 7–9, 1993).

around some of these issues, there can be little doubt that the challenges inherent in humankind's interactions with nature have become a central concern in the politics of communities and nations everywhere. This is not a trivial development. Issues at the top of political agendas are there because of deep-seated concern and not out of peripheral curiosity. They are there because both citizenries and their officials restlessly perceive problems requiring resolution. And they remain at the top of agendas because the resolutions are either slow to evolve or are deemed insufficient. Being high on the list of priorities, moreover, means that the talents and energies of the groups and communities affected by the issues will be engaged and that publics can be mobilized on behalf of proposed solutions. High salience also means that the level of citizen awareness is likely to be much greater than is the case for most issues on the agenda, and, in turn, this awareness suggests politicians cannot long avoid seeking ameliorative policies in areas where compromises can be reached.

When issues climb to the top of political agendas, in short, the momentum is in favor of their being addressed and policies being adopted. Thus it is not surprising that, ever since their lunge to near the top in 1972, environmental issues have been the focus of frequent studies, recommendations, disputes, and policy innovations in local communities, among national factions, and at the international level. And in the absence of clear-cut resolutions of any of the major issues, there is every reason to anticipate the momentum to continue to mount. The importance of this continuing build-up can be readily glimpsed if one pauses to imagine what circumstances would be like if somehow environmental issues were to slip back to a peripheral place on – if not off – political agendas.

Some part of the momentum stems from that attribute of environmental issues that inclines observers not to hesitate in giving voice to their visions of a better tomorrow and to do so with more than a little creativity in the search for concrete changes and practical solutions that would inch the world toward sustainable development. Both hard-nosed environmentalists and committed developers share a readiness to think afresh about policy alternatives, and this readiness helps sustain the momentum in favor of attending to environmental challenges.

The high salience of environmental issues – the notion that, like motherhood, everyone supports some form of progress toward resolution – has another attribute worthy of note. It allows for the politics of shame to be employed to good advantage. Much as politicians, parties, and bureaucracies may be disposed not to devote time and energy to environmental matters, and much as they might want to adopt delaying tactics, the nature of the issues makes them vulnerable to being shamed into addressing them. President Bush's clear preference not to attend the 1992 Earth Summit in Rio, followed by his reluctant commitment of three days to an appearance there, offers a good example of how the politics of shame can evoke behavior that would not otherwise occur. NGOs and others eager to sustain the salience of environmental issues and focus thought around policy proposals can hardly lose if they counter bureaucratic inertia and political stonewalling by resorting to shame as a means of exerting pressure.

Sovereignty as a variable

To be high on the world's agenda is not, of course, to assure that progress toward sound and global environmental policies will ensue. The momentum in this direction is encouraging, but it does not guarantee successful outcomes. For success to occur, other factors must be in place and conducive to maintenance of the momentum. Happily, a good case can be made for changes in the sovereignty principle that lessen its capacity to redirect or reverse the momentum.

By all accounts, sovereignty is a prime barrier to progress in developing collective responses to environmental challenges. States have the exclusive right, it is alleged, to reserve to themselves the final say on any proposed policies and, accordingly, they can veto any internal or external proposals with which they disagree. That is their sovereign right derived from their recognized membership in the society of nations, and it is a right that many of their business enterprises urge them to act upon. Thus, it is said, the fact that they have and exercise this right means that policies designed to meet environmental challenges can succeed only to the extent that the policies do not violate the interests of the states involved. For if they do run counter to state interests, the policies will fall victim to the exercise of the state's classic right to reject them. As one observer put it, "when the crunch comes" the individual state will resort to an insistence on its sovereign privileges and thereby prevail over the collective will.[23]

---

[23] Kenneth Waltz, *Theory of International Politics* (Reading, MA: Addison-Wesley, 1979), p. 94.

Formally and legally speaking, this formulation is telling. But considered informally and nonlegally, it is deeply flawed and highly misleading. As will be seen in the next chapter, it is a perspective which treats sovereignty as a dichotomous variable – either sovereignty exists or it does not – rather than as a continuous variable encompassing many diverse types of actions that can be regarded as expressive of sovereign behavior. Put differently, the crunch rarely comes, and the key questions thus involve the reasoning and behavior by which states accept intrusions upon their sovereign rights while also retaining the right to have the ultimate judgment. The inclination to dichotomize sovereignty makes it difficult to appreciate that there are many points on the sovereignty continuum between its presence and its absence. Yet, for a variety of reasons associated with the dynamics of change that are transforming world affairs, an appreciation of the variability of sovereignty principles is growing. A key point, highlighted in chapter 18, is that while states can ignore dictates originating in international organizations, pressure by other states, or demands of NGOs, they are increasingly inclined to conclude that the better part of wisdom is not to exercise their sovereign privileges and, instead, to bargain their way through to a satisfactory or satisficing conclusion. To the extent this orientation has replaced the classic one – and the evidence along this line is considerable, ranging from the many instances in which the UN Secretary-General has used the politics of shame to get his way with member states to the even more numerous instances in international regimes when member states feel obliged to go along rather than be responsible for scuttling a policy – the alleged barriers to sound environmental policies posed by the sovereignty principle are weakened, if not overcome. Put differently, the many ways in which states have converged around common policies in the environment field – including the more than 113 environmental treaties that have been adopted since 1972[24] – could never have happened if the classic conception of the sovereignty principle still held sway.

This is not to imply, of course, that states will never again call upon their sovereignty to block policies they deem to be threatening. Obviously, the existence of the classic conception renders it ever-avail-

---

[24] Hillary E. French, *After the Environmental Summit: The Future of Environmental Governance*, Worldwatch Paper no. 107 (Washington, DC: Worldwatch Institute, 1992), p. 6.

able. But a distinction has to be drawn between possessing an acknowledged privilege and adhering to a pattern of its nonuse. Recent history suggests that as states have become weaker relative to the demands made upon them, so have they become increasingly ready to adhere to the pattern even as they affirm the privilege.

The skill revolution revisited

The continuing evolution of analytic skills at the micro level of citizenries appears to be another factor conducive to the momentum favoring environmental issues. Recent findings suggest that people are increasingly sensitive to such issues, that they are ever readier to perceive the ways in which the environment may impact on their well-being. A 1992 opinion poll conducted by the Gallup organization in twenty-two Northern and Southern countries, for example, "demonstrated increasing widespread concern about environmental contamination, in both the North and South, and growing demands for international action. Most striking is the universal doubling in the percentage of respondents who felt that their own health was more seriously affected by environmental contamination than ten years ago."[25] Remarkably similar results were uncovered in an earlier poll conducted by the Louis Harris Organization for the UN Environmental Programme (UNEP). Although the samples were not large, this poll found that concern with environmental problems has become global in scope. A majority – and, in some cases, a large majority – of people in thirteen countries perceived a worsening of their environments over the previous ten years. Only in Saudi Arabia did a majority report it had gotten better, and one suspects this finding might be quite different if the Saudis had been polled subsequent to the environmental degradations unleashed by Iraq during the Gulf War. More important, most respondents anticipated that the processes of environmental degradation would worsen and thus looked to their governments to attach higher priority to the need for environmental protection. Indeed, huge majorities of 75 to 100 percent in each surveyed country agreed that more should be done by national and international organizations to address environmental problems. And perhaps most notable of all, as Harris put it, " alarm about the deterioration of the environment and support for much tougher environmental programs are not confined to Western countries, but are found in the

[25] Quoted in Haas, "International Environment Politics After Rio," pp. 7–8.

210

East and West, in the South and North, and in the rich and poor countries of the world."[26]

Growth in the number, membership, and resources of environmental NGOs is so pronounced as also to suggest the presence of greater involvement and skills with respect to such issues. More than 1,400 environment groups sent representatives to the 1992 Earth Summit and Global Forum meetings in Rio, a statistic that reflects how "their membership and resources grew dramatically" in the late 1980s, so much so in fact that "many larger groups became increasingly professionalized by hiring scientists and lobbyists. Greenpeace International's annual budget of 100 million dollars is well in excess of that of UNEP's!"[27]

Reports on "the status of programme implementation" of Global Environment Facility (GEF) small grants to diverse communities in some fifteen countries also highlight the spread of relevant environmental skills to individuals at the micro level.[28] Indeed, often they are compelling accounts of how the 127 projects (selected out of over three times that number of applications) encourage broad participation and, for very little money, focus on specific challenges relative to global warming, destruction of biological diversity, pollution of international waters, depletion of the stratospheric ozone layer, or land degradation (particularly desertification and deforestation). To be sure, the GEF's small-grants programme is not without its critics and self-acknowledged faults;[29] and it is also the case that the perused reports were prepared by the programme itself; but even after allowance is made for a full array of criticisms and the distortions inherent in self-reported accounts, the potential for transforming environmental situations and attitudes at local levels throughout the world seems very impressive

---

[26] For discussions of these data and alternative interpretations of the openness of publics to learning about environmental challenges, see Lester W. Milbrath, "The World Learns About the Environment," *International Studies Notes*, vol. 16 (Winter 1991), and *Environmental Problems, a Global Threat* (Muscatine, IA: Stanley Foundation, 1989), pp. 6–7 (the Harris quote is reproduced from p. 6).

[27] Haas, "International Environment Politics After Rio," p. 8.

[28] United Nations Development Programme, "Global Environment Facility: The Pilot Phase and Beyond, Working Paper Series Number 1," May 1992; United Nations Development Programme, "The GEF NGO Small Grants Programme, Progress Report, 1992," January 29, 1993; and United Nations Development Programme, "The GEF NGO Small Grants Programme, Progress Report No. 3," October 29, 1993.

[29] The World Resources Institute, *World Resources, 1994–95*, pp. 229–31.

indeed. The accounts of projects in fifteen countries convey a clear sense that environmental challenges can be addressed, that citizens and their leaders in local communities can be trained and mobilized to shoulder the tasks of environmental management, and that such work at the grass roots need not be unduly expensive. Consider this apparently typical report from the host NGO in Nepal:

> Dealing with over 300 NGOs scattered through the length and breadth of the geographically difficult country is a unique experience that no other NGO has so far gone through. As such, it is the feeling that in spite of great difficulty in transport and communication the programme is satisfactorily proceeding. A number of NGOs receiving GEF funding are already demonstrating their ability to achieve their goals with very little resources. The greatest lesson that those of us who are involved with the GEF/SGP in Nepal is that this type of small-scale efforts [sic] by local NGOs is the solution both to global problems and to the problem of environment and sustainable development in the country. The resources provided under the programme is [sic] really very small compared to the zeal with which projects are undertaken and the communities are mobilized for achieving specified goals.[30]

In sum, there are reasons to believe that the bumper sticker which urges people to "think globally and act locally" is more than a vacuous slogan. Those five words appear to be descriptive of an ever-widening experience in ever-wider areas of the world.

The relevance of local and regional efforts at environmental management

As the GEF experience makes clear – if it was not otherwise self-evident – any attempt to hold constant environmental developments at local and regional levels is ill-founded. It is a procedure that encourages a focus on global governance, but maintaining such a focus is difficult as one encounters continual reminders that activities and orientations at all levels are inextricably pieces of the same whole cloth. Analysts can assess the roles played by the UN, international regimes, and national governments in meeting environmental challenges, and they can do so without references to developments at the level of local and provincial communities; but such inquiries are likely to seem conspicuously incomplete and their findings needlessly insufficient. Why? Because

---

[30] United Nations Development Programme, "The GEF NGO Small Grants Programme, Progress Report No. 3," p. 19.

control exercised at the global levels is too dependent on the participation and cooperation of actors in local communities. States can hold international conferences and agree on terms that constrain environmental pollution, the waste of resources, the maintenance of biodiversity, and many other control mechanisms, but the implementation and success of such agreements falls largely to people and organizations at the national and local levels. A GEF funding criterion nicely summarizes the high degree to which all the levels of governance are interdependent: "In general, GEF should fund projects when domestic costs are greater than domestic benefits, but global benefits are greater than domestic costs."[31]

In short, whatever may be their disruptive consequences, the decentralizing tendencies at work in the world seem destined to facilitate governance of the environment. They are bringing governance closer to the level at which "ecological consciousness" can evolve and people are able to "see themselves as being the *cause* for the environmental *effect*."[32] Put differently, the more the momentum toward environmental governance builds, the more will citizens everywhere be caught up in its ripple effects; and the more enmeshed they become, the more will support for appropriate control mechanisms be generated.[33] After all, "People do not, other things being equal, pollute and damage those natural systems on which they depend for life and livelihood if they see directly what is happening; nor voluntarily use up a resource under their feet and before their eyes if they perceive that it is precious, needed, vital; nor kill off species they can see are important for the smooth functioning of the ecosystem."[34]

[31] United Nations Development Programme (UNDP), "Global Environment Facility: The Pilot Phase and Beyond," p. 31.

[32] Kirkpatrick Sale, *Dwellers in the Land: The Bioregional Vision* (San Francisco: Sierra Club Books, 1985), p. 54 (italics in the original).

[33] Viewed from this perspective, a proposal that people may be ready to pay special taxes in return for a cleaner environment is anything but far-fetched. See Mary Durfee, "Increasing Citizen Participation: The Virtues of an Ecosystem Tax for the Great Lakes," unpublished paper, Michigan Technological University, September 15, 1993.

[34] Sale, *Dwellers in the Land*, p. 54.

Part III
Societal contexts

11   Sovereignty

The time of absolute and exclusive sovereignty . . . has passed; its theory was never matched by reality.

UN Secretary-General Boutros Boutros-Ghali[1]

Like all relationships, political balances are endlessly in a process of becoming. Sometimes the process is erratic and sometimes it is unerring, but it is always evolving and is never fixed as each point on the evolutionary trend-line subsumes dynamics that generate immediate or eventual movement on to the next point. To assess the nature of a prevailing political balance is thus to focus on a convergence of diverse causal streams, a convergence that is bound to change as the streams sustain their momentum into the future.

The law introduces a degree of intermittency into the evolutionary nature of political balances. When a particular balance is codified and legally sanctioned, the evolutionary process enters a period of intermittent pause, a period that lasts as long as the new legal codes are effective and sustain the balance between the opposing forces that press for a resumption or reversal of the prior trend-line. Viewed in this way, codified legal arrangements are end-points of numerous and diverse non-legal developments. Their codification reflects the premises that underlie those moments of convergence wherein past changes are synthesized in the hope of achieving a respite from uncertainty and a measure of stability. And for a while the law does stabilize relationships and institutions as its precepts evoke compliance and introduce regularity into public affairs. But eventually the political side of the balance resumes its evolution, at which point habits of compliance begin to attenuate, ambiguity begins to spread, and the legal arrangements begin to undergo recodification.

---

[1] *An Agenda for Peace: Preventive Diplomacy, Peacemaking and Peacekeeping* (New York: United Nations, 1992), p. 9.

This conception of political balance serves as a backdrop for this chapter's inquiry into the ways in which the sovereign rights of states are undergoing diminution in the face of the many forces that are widening the domestic–foreign Frontier. For it is sovereignty – those political and legal prescriptions that accord states supremacy over the affairs of their country – that has long served to define the uncontested space beyond which lies the Frontier. Viewed in this way, this book's premise that the Frontier is expanding necessitates an analysis of how the principles of sovereignty are lessening their hold over officials, organizations, and citizens who move into and around the Frontier.

Conceiving of sovereignty as caught up in an endless process of becoming facilitates the task. It is a conception which enables us to treat sovereignty as the culmination of complex psychological and sociopolitical processes rather than as simply an unwavering legal principle. It allows us to stress that the present state of the state – of sovereignty's reach – is in flux and that a variety of signals point to a decline in the capacity of states to prevent the expansion of the Frontier and a corresponding increase in the competency of other actors to ignore, override, or otherwise circumvent the long-standing claims of states to full jurisdiction over their own affairs. More than that, the conception of sovereignty as intermittently ensconced in a process of becoming highlights a perspective in which both the aspiration to maintain collective legitimacy through statehood and the impulse to serve human needs through collective intervention are acknowledged as powerful determinants of behavior, neither one morally superior to the other and both deeply rooted in the human psyche.[2]

The analytic challenge

Precisely because it is so subject to change, achieving clarity on the concept of sovereignty is extremely difficult. Its use can be traced back to Aristotle, but its formulation in subsequent eras has varied widely.

[2] The shift from the sovereignty of kings to the sovereignty of the people provides a good measure of the time-scale that may be involved in the processes whereby conceptions of sovereignty undergo transformation between periods in which a widely shared consensus prevails. Popular sovereignty can be fairly said to have originated with the American and French Revolutions, but it did not achieve worldwide acceptance until 1945, when it was incorporated in Article 1 of the United Nations Charter. For a cogent analysis of how the protection of the "sovereign's sovereignty" underwent change in international law to protection of the "peoples' sovereignty," see W. Michael Reisman, "Sovereignty and Human Rights in Contemporary International Law," *American Journal of International Law*, vol. 84 (October 1990), pp. 866–76.

And many of the formulations have been marked by ambiguity, contradiction, and the lack of a consensual perspective. For some purposes sovereignty is exclusively a legal concept that can be understood by probing the materials of international law. It is also a political concept that requires focusing on the conduct of states. For other purposes it can be treated as a psychological concept with which to explore the behavior of ethnic groups, nationalism, and peoples' sense of community and territoriality. Within each of these analytic traditions, moreover, the sovereignty concept has taken on diverse meanings at different historical junctures as different elites evolve different stakes in the contents and applications of the concept.

The ambiguities and difficulties inherent in the analysis of sovereignty seem especially challenging at this time of profound and rapid change.[3] For not only do states and their sovereign prerogatives seem ever more vulnerable to the demands of both domestic constituents and international organizations, but they also have to contend with the advent of new global actors and processes that confound their roles, constrain the limits of their authority, and undermine their territorial appeal. As previously stressed, the sovereignty of states no longer confines the flow of information, goods, money, and people.[4] Markets are worldwide, ozone gaps are hemispheric in scope, multinational

---

[3] Thus it is hardly surprising that the present era has been marked by a veritable flood of interpretations of what the concept means and encompasses. Among the more recent works are Thomas Biersteker and Cynthia Weber (eds.), *State Sovereignty as Social Construct* (Cambridge: Cambridge University Press, 1996); Jens Bartelson, *A Genealogy of Sovereignty* (Cambridge: Cambridge University Press, 1995); Abram Chayes and Antonia Handler Chayes, *The New Sovereignty: Compliance with International Regulatory Agreements* (Cambridge, MA: Harvard University Press, 1995); Michael Ross Fowler and Julie Marie Bunck, *Law, Power, and the Sovereign State: The Evolution of the Concept of Sovereignty* (University Park: Pennsylvania State University Press, 1995); Siba N'Zatioula Grovogui, *Sovereigns, Quasi Sovereigns, and Africans: Race and Self-Determination in International Law* (Minneapolis: University of Minnesota Press, 1996); Hurst Hannum, *Autonomy, Sovereignty, and Self-Determination: The Accommodation of Conflicting Rights*, rev. edn. (Philadelphia: University of Pennsylvania Press, 1995); David B. Knight, "People Together, Yet Apart: Rethinking Territory, Sovereignty, and Identities," in George J. Demko and William B. Wood (eds.), *Reordering the World: Geopolitical Perspectives on the 21st Century* (Boulder, CO: Westview Press, 1994), pp. 71–86; Thom Kuehls, *Beyond Sovereign Territory: The Space of Ecopolitics* (Minneapolis: University of Minnesota Press, 1996); Gene M. Lyons and Michael Mastanduno (eds.), *Beyond Westphalia? State Sovereignty and International Intervention* (Baltimore: Johns Hopkins University Press, 1995); and Daniel Philpott, "Sovereignty: An Introduction and Brief History," *Journal of International Affairs*, vol. 48 (Winter 1995), pp. 353–68.

[4] Cf. Walter B. Wriston, "Technology and Sovereignty," *Foreign Affairs*, vol. 67 (Winter 1988–9), pp. 63–75, and David Webster, "Direct Broadcast Satellites: Proximity Sovereignty and National Identity," *Foreign Affairs*, vol. 62 (Summer 1984), pp. 1161–74.

corporations provide global services, CNN offers the same news to all, tourists and human migrations are everywhere, fax machines ignore national boundaries, as do computer modems, satellites, and the Internet. In some deep and significant sense, in short, the authority of states has, like money, moved offshore.

Yet, just as the foundations of sovereignty have been eroded by the centralizing processes of globalization, so have they been reinforced by decentralizing tendencies wherein people are shrinking "we" to like-minded others and enlarging "they" to everyone else. Subgroupism, tribalism, nationalism, ethnicity – however they are labeled, these simultaneous inclinations to resist globalization by reverting to close-at-hand ties have the consequence of further challenging those who aspire to clarifying the bases of modern-day sovereignty. In some deep and significant sense, in other words, the authority of states has also, like shopping malls, devolved toward the local community.

Normatively, too, sovereignty has long been varyingly appraised. For some it is a dangerous illusion that inhibits international cooperation and conduces to conflict. For others it is a positive stimulus to a shared sense of community, a feeling of collective independence. For still others it is mostly a neutral means of specifying legal and geographic jurisdictions. There is some utility to all three of these perspectives. To the extent that states hide behind their sovereign prerogatives as a reason for resisting or avoiding collaborative international projects, then to that extent sovereignty does become dangerous, either by serving as an illusionary symbol of independence that blocks a full accommodation to the realities of interdependence or by providing an excuse for responding aggressively to neighbors who are said to be a "threat." Likewise, to the extent that people have a need for community and a sense of independence, then to that extent the achievement and maintenance of sovereignty for their nation does serve important human longings.[5] And to the extent that governments, courts, and philosophers need a framework for differentiating among political entities with competing claims to ultimate authority, then to that extent the sovereignty concept has proved its worth for centuries. Whatever the merits of these diverse normative perspectives, the problem is that they all derive from very different purposes and thus arrive at very different interpretations of the same phenomenon.

[5] For a discussion of how sovereignty serves deep-seated psychological needs, see Gordon Pocock, "Nation, Community, Devolution and Sovereignty," *Political Quarterly*, vol. 61 (July–Sept. 1990), pp. 318–27.

Unfortunately, we are ill-equipped to sort out these various understandings of sovereignty and treat it as ensconced in a process of becoming. Our habitual forms of analysis are so state-centric that we are more inclined to view the dynamics of globalization as problems for states to manage than as undermining their sovereignty. For globalization is not so much a product or extension of the interstate system as it is a wholly new set of processes, a separate form of world politics, initiated by technologies that have fostered new human needs and wants. Confronted with unfamiliar processes stemming from unfamiliar sources, we have been slow to make the necessary theoretical adjustments. It is much easier to fall back on the tried and true, on the notion that no change is so sharp as to render obsolete long-standing analytic traditions. One analyst, for example, acknowledges that the sovereignty claims of states "have changed across time and over countries," but nevertheless concludes that the institution of sovereignty is presently so entrenched in world politics that it is "difficult to even conceive of alternatives" to it, "regardless of changed circumstances in the material environment."[6] If this is so, if it is the case that our imaginations are paralyzed by the sovereignty concept, there are good reasons to pause and ponder the implications of the observation that since "no shared vocabulary exists in the literature to depict change and continuity, . . . we are not very good as a discipline at studying the possibility of fundamental discontinuity in the international system."[7]

The sovereignty continuum

In order to accommodate the conception of sovereignty both as an expression of the widespread need to maintain community through the preservation and advancement of statehood and as a porous boundary ever more vulnerable to the dynamics of globalization, the ensuing

---

[6] Stephen D. Krasner, "Sovereignty: An Institutional Perspective," *Comparative Political Studies*, vol. 21 (April 1988), pp. 88, 90. For another expression of the difficulty of envisioning "a politics *sans* sovereignty," see Jean Bethke Elshtain, "Sovereignty, Identity, Sacrifice," *Social Research*, vol. 58 (Fall 1991), pp. 545–64.

[7] John Gerard Ruggie, "Territoriality and Beyond: Problematizing Modernity in International Relations" *International Organization*, vol. 47 (Winter 1993), pp. 140, 143–4. For another extended discussion of the problems involved in employing the concept of sovereignty in the context of rapid change, see R. B. J. Walker and Saul H. Mendlovitz, "Interrogating State Sovereignty," in R. B. J. Walker and Saul H. Mendlovitz (eds.), *Contending Sovereignties: Redefining Political Community* (Boulder, CO: Lynne Rienners, 1990), pp. 1–12.

analysis focuses on a subtle attitudinal shift from a perspective in which, say, humanitarian interventions occur at the "convenience-of-the-states" toward a "states-are-obliged-to-go-along" orientation.[8] The former orientation rests on the presumption that states are free to intervene across the Frontier at their own discretion, while the latter posits states as under heavy pressure to accommodate to global consensuses by going along with widely shared multilateral postures toward the Frontier. In the former context sovereignty remains inviolable, while in the latter its inviolability is relaxed and made subject to modification. Both attitudinal contexts, it should be stressed, presume the continued viability of states and their sovereignty, but they are differentiated by the degree to which sovereign prerogatives are considered to predominate.

In other words, sovereignty is treated as a continuous rather than as a dichotomous variable. And its movement along the continuum between the convenience-of-the-states extreme and the states-are-obliged-to-go-along extreme is conceived as shaped by situational, domestic, international, and legal determinants. Consequently, all states are seen as having become subject to movement along the continuum, with the extent to which they are able to husband their rights or international organizations are able to set aside those rights being as variable as the numerous permutations and combinations inherent in the four sets of determinants.

Viewing sovereignty in this way, i.e., conceiving of it as a continuous variable determined by a multiplicity of sources, not only serves to inhibit the tendency to regard the relative rights of states and their international communities as stable and constant, but also facilitates an appreciation of the dynamism of the processes in which sovereignty is embedded. Among other things, it suggests the possibility that each increment of diminished (or enhanced) sovereignty – of successful (or unsuccessful) humanitarian intervention that sets aside (or moves forward) the rights of states – may alter the global context and thereby pave the way for subsequent increments.

Sovereignty in a turbulent world

Given a world with new parametric values represented by the skill revolution, the relocation of authority, and the bifurcation of global

---

[8] The distinction between these two contexts is elaborated in James N. Rosenau, *The United Nations in a Turbulent World* (Boulder, CO: Lynne Rienner, 1992), pp. 61–4.

structures, what kinds of movement can be expected on the sovereignty continuum? Answers to this question can be readily derived from the turbulence model. In all likelihood, for example, the advent of the skill revolution has moved issues pertaining to possible compromises of the sovereignty principle beyond elite circles in many societies to where they are now being pondered more widely by mass publics.

The transformation of the macro–micro parameter may have even greater consequences for movement along the sovereignty continuum. Presumably the onset of pervasive authority crises undermines commitments founded on the existence of an ultimate arbiter whose decisions evoke unquestioned compliance.[9] The disciplined, unhesitating obedience that sustains organizations expressive of this idea is bound to dissipate once authority gets associated with performance and other nontraditional criteria. Such a process is already evident in perhaps the most disciplined organization extant today, the Mafia,[10] and it can also be discerned in military establishments, many of which are encountering serious difficulties in recruiting, disciplining, and retaining their personnel.[11] Thus it is hardly surprising that the authority crises may be eroding the principle that under all circumstances states have the right to refuse to comply with the directives of external authorities or the demands for autonomy from internal authorities. While states more often than not enjoy continued success in exercising their sovereign privileges, the idea that such a practice is questionable has been planted wherever the transformation of the macro–micro parameter has reached crisis proportions.

Similarly, it is not difficult to anticipate how the diffusion of power and authority in a bifurcated world occasioned by the transformation of the macro parameter has also intensified movement along the sovereignty continuum. With players in the global economy able to ignore

---

[9] For an extensive discussion of how the undermining of the sovereignty principle began, of how "decolonization amounted to nothing less than an international revolution . . . in which traditional assumptions about the right to sovereign statehood were turned upside down," see Robert H. Jackson, *Quasi-states: Sovereignty, International Relations and the Third World* (Cambridge: Cambridge University Press, 1990), chap. 4 (the quotation is from p. 85).

[10] "The Columbo family civil war . . . is solid evidence of a widespread phenomenon: the breakdown of autocratic leadership and dissension in the lower ranks . . . The system of dictatorial control and unflinching loyalty in all of the families . . . is fracturing in the same way that the Soviet Union suddenly collapsed." Selwyn Raab, "In the Mafia, Too, a Decline in Standards," *New York Times*, January 19, 1992, sect. 4, p. 6.

[11] See chapter 19 below.

and move freely beyond the scope of traditional political jurisdictions, the idea that states have the right to make final decisions has become increasingly problematic. The more bifurcated structures underlie the practices of organizations and the activities of producers and consumers, the less are state authorities inclined to exercise, or even be aware of, their right to withhold or apply ultimate sanctions. To be sure, states continue to maintain large bureaucracies designed to monitor transgressions of their traditional political jurisdictions, and transnational actors continue to adhere to the rules and procedures required by national bureaucracies; but the existence of the monitoring activities and the obeisance paid them by organizations in the multi-centric world is not necessarily a measure of sovereignty's continued effectiveness. History is replete with bureaucracies that survive even though their original purposes have been rendered obsolete by the course of events. Put differently, this lag time stems from "rapid and continuing changes ... which have eroded national boundaries and the powers of government but left the structure – and the rhetoric – of national politics in place."[12]

Situational determinants

Let us look more closely at how the parametric transformations that have brought turbulence to world politics may be affecting the ways in which sovereignty's situational, domestic, international, and legal determinants impact on the relative rights of states and their international communities. For a number of reasons, the advent of a bifurcated world has tended to deepen the severity of the situations around which the question of possible external humanitarian intervention arises. Such situations have always been distressing and eye-catching, else collective intrusion would not have become an issue, much less a reality; but as stressed in chapter 4, today the crisis conditions within societies that catch the world's eye and encourage international intervention are likely to seem far more severe and ominous than was the case in pre-turbulent times. Partly this greater severity can be traced to the breadth and depth of the revolution in microelectronic technology. Now more people see and hear more about the desperate circumstances of their fellow humans than ever before, and the messages they receive are qualitatively as well as quantitatively different as the detail of close-up tele-

---

[12] William Wallace, "What Price Independence? Sovereignty and Interdependence in British Politics," *International Affairs*, vol. 62 (Summer 1986), p. 367.

vision pictures relentlessly tells stories on a scale of horror not matched in earlier eras. Indeed, both the content and horror of televised coverage can be so relentless and severe as to give rise to compassion fatigue, to the "crisis of crisis awareness,"[13] which in turn can add to the urgency of calls for amelioration through international intervention.

The severity of humanitarian situations has also been intensified by the continuing proliferation of global interdependencies. As the course of events in any part of the world becomes increasingly dependent on developments anywhere else, so can increasingly explosive humanitarian situations cascade their repercussions well beyond the locale in which they originated.[14] Put more succinctly, people flee starvation, violent repression, and civil war, and in the very act of fleeing they extend the scale and severity of the circumstances that may call for international intervention. The advent of mass migrations cascading across the fault lines of interdependence are illustrative in this regard. The dislocations unleashed by the spread of turbulent conditions has led huge numbers of people to seek economic and political surcease from calamity and, as a consequence, humanitarian situations seem bound to become ever more compelling and severe. Haitians fleeing to the United States and Rwandans fleeing to Zaire are only recent instances of how the severity of a humanitarian situation can feed on itself.

There is, of course, a difference between those situational determinants that arise out of human conflict or neglect and those that have their roots in famines, earthquakes, and nature's many other ways of intruding disaster. As indicated by the role played by the International Red Cross, the latter situations compel humanitarian intervention irrespective of their severity. It is only when situations are driven by human aggression, such as those in which genocide or mass migrations are at issue, that varying degrees of severity are likely to evoke correspondingly different shifts in the balance between the rights of states and their international communities.

It follows that situational determinants do not necessarily conduce to movement away from the convenience-of-the-states end of the sovereignty continuum. To the extent that governments can demonstrate

---

[13] Piotr Sztompka, "The Global Crisis and the Reflexiveness of the Social System," *International Journal of Comparative Sociology*, vol. 25 (1984), p. 45.

[14] For an extended discussion of how the "cascade" has superseded the "event" as the central process of world politics, see James N. Rosenau, *Turbulence in World Politics: A Theory of Change and Continuity* (Princeton: Princeton University Press, 1990), pp. 298–395.

their competence to maintain minimal living conditions and resist undertaking aggression against their own peoples, the less will they attract television coverage and the more will the propriety of their sovereign rights seem compelling. However, while the severity of domestic situations can lessen as well as increase, the prevalence of turbulence on a global scale suggests that situational determinants are more often likely to heighten the legitimacy of humanitarian interventions and sustain movement along the sovereignty continuum away from the convenience-of-the-states extreme and toward the states-are-obliged-to-go-along extreme.

Domestic determinants

At any moment in time the balance between the rights of states and their international communities is partially shaped by the aggregate receptivity of publics and policy-makers around the world. There are numerous ways in which such a global sum of domestic orientations – world opinion, so to speak – is crucial to movement along the sovereignty continuum, but for analytic purposes the worldwide status of sovereign prerogatives is treated here as a dimension of international and legal determinants. On the other hand, allowance needs to be made for the possibility that orientations toward the propriety of humanitarian interventions vary depending on whether the action is directed toward other societies or one's own. It is one thing to support intrusions upon the sovereignty of other states, but it may be quite another to be receptive when such actions occur at home. The idea that one's own internal affairs justify outside intervention is likely to evoke far more powerful reactions than will any general principles about sovereignty to which one adheres. To probe the domestic determinants of movement along the sovereignty continuum, therefore, is to focus on the nature of patriotism in a society, the ability of its officials to mobilize public resistance to intervention, the coherence of opposition groups, and the many other internal dynamics whereby societies respond to external pressures.

This is not to imply, however, that people necessarily oppose interventions within their own societies even as they may support them elsewhere. Not only may those oppressed or victimized by the circumstances that pose the issue of external intervention welcome such actions, but the rally-around-the-flag phenomenon has been undermined by the parametric transformations that have brought on global turbulence. To be sure, the lessened effectiveness of states, the challenges to their authority, and the advent of more intensive subgroupism has fostered among publics a heightened sense of territoriality, a search for shared identity, and an inclination to press for exclusive jurisdiction over their internal affairs. Yet, to the extent that citizens are more analytically skillful and thus more resistant to being mobilized by vague symbols of sovereign authority, or to the extent that their expanded skills induce confusion over the appropriateness of traditional state prerogatives, then to these extents political leaders cannot rely on wholesale and unquestioned support for their opposition to humanitarian interventions which intrude upon their country's sovereign rights.

Viewed in this way, it is no accident that everywhere appeals to sovereignty appear to be mouthed less and less often by public officials. Whereas once such appeals were central to the lexicon of politics, today they are conspicuous by their relative absence from the dialogues of world affairs. And where they are voiced, they do not necessarily silence those whose analytic skills have led them to assess whether benefits necessarily inhere in territorial and sovereign values. The experience of Matt Darcy, a 31-year-old car salesman in Michigan, is illustrative in this regard: he got himself into trouble (and out of a job) by commenting in a nationally televised interview that, "If America makes a good product, I buy it. If they don't, I buy what's good for my money. I don't have to spend money [on a domestic car] because it's American."[15] Similarly, while Japanese and Americans have been bashing each other's cultures and trading practices with an intensity that implies a sense of violated sovereignty, for every bashing there are leaders on both sides who publicly question the merits of such conduct.

Movement along the sovereignty continuum, of course, is anything but a smooth trend-line. Halting and punctuated as it may be, however, the movement does appear to favor humanitarian interventions insofar as domestic determinants are concerned. Indeed, it seems likely that internal societal dynamics will continue to agitate such movement well into the future. The discrepancy between the simple symbols of national sovereignty and the realities of governmental and economic crises is so great that both publics and their leaders are likely to be increasingly disillusioned by the symbols as the realities worsen. The symbols do provide psychic satisfactions -- "The fact of sitting around the table with the most important states in the world is a reaffirmation of sovereignty,"

---

[15] Adam Bryant, "Views on Foreign Cars Cost Salesman His Job," *New York Times*, February 23, 1992, p. 16.

said the Foreign Minister of San Marino on the occasion of the UN Security Council's approval of his 24-square-mile country's admission to membership[16] – and they are also vague enough to allow for diverse segments of a population to converge and cooperate:

> Before the beginning of 1991 nearly all [the former Soviet republics] were demanding "sovereignty." This was a capaciously ambiguous concept – it might mean anything from full independence to the right to run your own refuse collection; but it had the advantage of providing an issue on which intellectuals and the local apparatchiks could cooperate. For the former the word stood for their dreams of national self-determination and democracy; for the latter, it meant they would at last have real power . . .[17]

In Quebec, too, support for independence has been sought by infusing the sovereignty concept with a measure of ambiguity that allows for a diversity of meanings to be attached to it. One news account, for example, reported that the then leader of the Parti Quebecois, Jacques Parizeau, "muddied the waters . . . by telling Quebecers a `sovereign Quebec' would continue to use the Canadian dollar and its citizens would keep their Canadian passports, regardless of whether Ottawa approved."[18]

To repeat, however, the psychic and consensus-building virtues that attach to the symbols of sovereignty are unlikely to sustain their appeal in the face of either projected or actual problems. In Quebec, for example, a projection that the economy would slump by as much as 15 percent if voters chose independence appeared to induce slippage in support for the proposal.[19] In Ukraine second thoughts about sovereignty began to emerge as "many of those who voted for statehood . . . did so only because they thought they would be better off in an independent Ukraine and not out of strong nationalist feelings."[20] Similarly, Estonians discovered that independence and the privileges of statehood offer no magic solutions to the problems of hunger, inflation, and ethnic conflict.[21] Such realities, on the contrary, can emerge as products of sov-

---

[16] Alan Cowell, "Now, After 1,600 Years, Time to Join the World," *New York Times*, February 26, 1992, p. A4.

[17] Geoffrey Hosking, "The Roots of Dissolution," *New York Review of Books*, January 16, 1992, p. 36.

[18] John F. Burns, "Sovereign Quebec Needn't Be Separate," *New York Times*, February 21, 1992, p. A4.   [19] *Ibid.*

[20] Serge Schmemann, "With Seeds of Nation Slow to Flower, Ukrainians Blame Shadow of Russia," *New York Times*, March 9, 1992, p. A4.

[21] Serge Schmemann, "Free, Yes, But Estonians Are also Shivering," *New York Times*, January 24, 1992, p. 1.

ereignty, in which case the inclination to cling to the inviolability of territory and statehood may well erode, thereby inducing further movement away from the state's rights extreme of the continuum. The more harsh economic and political conditions prevail, in short, the more are claims to exclusive jurisdiction likely to fall on deaf ears or become, in the words of Ivan Kapitanets, the deputy commander of the Black Sea fleet, expressions of the "childhood illness of sovereignty and state independence."[22]

International determinants

While situational and domestic determinants of the values that attach to sovereignty consist of deep-seated, slow-moving, and fluctuating societal processes that slowly cumulate to an increasing acceptance of external interventions, those that originate in the international arena tend to acquire momentum through specific acts in which interventionary efforts are initiated. As such, as the bases of successful or failed attempts to intervene in the domestic affairs of states, international determinants are readily discernible in trend-setting events which sustain an aggregative process. More precisely, each interventionary act, whatever its outcome, is so much of a break with historic conventions that it serves as an explicit stimulus to subsequent events of a comparable nature. Every time a national election is supervised by impartial observers brought in from abroad, for example, the norm that affirms such an intervention in domestic affairs is reinforced, making it harder subsequently for authoritarian regimes elsewhere to prevent such intrusions and easier for their opponents who fear repression to appeal successfully for outside supervision. Likewise, each occasion on which the UN is able to intrude peace-keeping forces into domestic conflicts serves to legitimate international concern and action with respect to such conflicts that arise elsewhere. In the same manner, as the IMF or the World Bank achieves, case by case, compliance to their demands that domestic adjustments be made in exchange for needed financial resources, so do they facilitate adherence to comparable policies in subsequent situations and thereby supplement the appropriateness of external involvement in domestic economies.

And this appears to be exactly what has occurred in this turbulent, post-Cold War era. Calls for supervised elections, for international peace-keeping forces, and for IMF involvement have acquired increas-

---

[22] "Russia and Ukraine Try to Settle Military Dispute," *New York Times,* January 12, 1992, p. 3.

ing degrees of legitimacy. It is no accident that supervised elections, UN peace-keeping efforts, and IMF-induced adjustments tend to occur in rapid-fire succession. Each such event is part of an aggregative global process that undermines traditional interstate norms and sets precedents for future interventions. This momentum has been cogently documented with respect to the vulnerability of domestic economies to international management,[23] but it can also be discerned as operative in the election and peace-keeping arenas. And it also appears to have spread from global to regional organizations. While neither the recent intrusion of the Organization of American States into the domestic politics of Haiti nor the European Community's involvement in the internal affairs of Yugoslavia were immediately successful, their simultaneity highlights how quickly the momentum favoring external intervention can gather steam.[24]

Furthermore, with the bifurcation of the macro parameter and the advent of a multi-centric world capable of supporting challenges to the authority of states, the aggregative processes that undermine traditional conceptions of national jurisdictions have come to be championed by active and innovative actors who need not pay heed to the responsibilities and constraints of sovereignty.[25] The human rights movement, the ecological movement, the women's movement, and the peace movement, whatever else they may be and whatever else they may accomplish, occupy crucial roles as mobilizers and stimulators of change in this regard. They make it possible for Amnesty International to claim that "Human rights are now part of the working agenda of every government on earth – not by their *own* choice but because of the persistent pressure of the world's citizenry."[26] Indeed, in the United States

---

[23] Thomas J. Biersteker, "The 'Triumph' of Neoclassical Economics in the Developing World," in J.N. Rosenau and E.-O. Czempiel (eds.), *Governance Without Government: Order and Change in World Politics* (Cambridge: Cambridge University Press, 1992), chap. 4.

[24] For an analysis of how the momentum surged with respect to monetary union in Europe, see Ian Harder, "Sovereignty and the Eurofed," *Political Quarterly*, vol. 61 (Oct.–Dec. 1990), pp. 402–14.

[25] For an example of how one nongovernmental organization has successfully championed movement toward the states-are-obliged-to-go-along extreme of the sovereignty continuum, see Howard Tolley, Jr., "Popular Sovereignty and International Law: ICJ Strategies for Human Rights Standard Setting," *Human Rights Quarterly*, vol. 11 (November 1989), pp. 561–85.

[26] Fund-raising letter from John G. Healy, Executive Director, Amnesty International USA, December 5, 1991, p. 3 (italics in the original).

leaders of Amnesty International and other human rights groups are now regularly consulted by public officials: "We see assistant secretaries and desk officers all the time. Even if we don't get what we want, we're in the mix now. The relationships are warm. They seek, we give. They call, we help."[27]

Supplemented by situational and domestic determinants, in short, the international milieu also appears to be contributing to movement toward the states-are-obliged-to-go-along extreme of the sovereignty continuum. The wide and rapid success of the human rights movement highlights the way in which the international milieu – that amorphous complex of attitudes, sentiments, and predispositions that underlies how governments and publics approach specific situations in which the rights of states and those of their international communities are pitted against each other – can gather momentum and become an agent of change. Indeed, it has been cogently argued that in international law "the sovereign had finally been dethroned" when the United Nations adopted the Universal Declaration of Human Rights in 1948,[28] a contention that is empirically discernible in the fact that even those states most resistant to such intrusions have had to accept, or at least acknowledge, the legitimacy of outside interventions in their affairs. As a Latin American specialist has put it, "It would be hard to find a country in this hemisphere in which raised consciousness of human rights has not had any effect. Even in the most extreme case of Cuba, Fidel Castro has had to deal with the United Nations Human Rights Commission, and he has had to respond to questions posed not by the United States or the Cuban-American community but by Latin Americans."[29]

Just as heads of states find it increasingly difficult to resist the momentum inherent in the changing international milieu, so are officials of international communities likely to be increasingly emboldened by it to allow themselves to move from a traditional convenience-of-the-states perspective to one in which they are imbued by the states-are-obliged-to-go-along orientation. Traces of this attitudinal shift can be detected in the conduct of top UN officials. Their shifts are nuanced and incremental rather than bold assertions, but they nonetheless appear to

---

[27] John G. Healy, quoted in Barbara Crossette, "State Department's Human Rights Office Grows in Influence," *New York Times*, January 19, 1992, p. 9.

[28] Cf. Reisman, "Sovereignty and Human Rights in Contemporary International Law," p. 868.

[29] Robert Pastor, as quoted in Crossette, "State Department's Human Rights Office Grows in Influence," p. 9.

be patterned and, as such, significant. Their readiness to bring governance to Afghanistan by convening a conference of rival factions was
prompted not only by circumstances in that troubled country, and the
success of their plan was due not only to the war-weariness of the factions, but both the initiative and the success of the UN in the situation
also stemmed from memories – i.e., the momentum – of recent interventions successfully carried out by the UN that rendered mute the question of Afghanistan's sovereign prerogatives.[30] In a like manner the
International Atomic Energy Agency (IAEA) approved a plan to
conduct nuclear inspections in countries that have accepted the Nuclear
Non-Proliferation Treaty but that are suspected of developing nuclear
weapons in secret. The IAEA has always had the right to intervene in
this way, but only lately has it exercised the right.[31] Likewise, while the
UN Secretary-General is an employee of states and the chief spokesper-
son for the state-centric world, there are signs – as indicated by the epigraph opening this chapter – that a recent occupant of the post,
Boutros-Ghali, saw the organization as more than the sum of its parts
and was thus willing to make decisions which can be construed as
intruding upon the sovereignty of the UN's members.

But taking note of an international milieu and momentum that is
tipping the balance between states and their international communities
in favor of the latter is not to imply a wholesale shift that will one day
culminate in the obsolescence of the sovereignty principle. After all, the
bifurcation of world politics posits a continued viability for the state-
centric world. And, after all, the psychic needs that accord high value to
community ties and territoriality are not about to attenuate.
Accordingly, the shifting balance needs to be viewed as a limited one, a
trend-line favoring movement on the sovereignty continuum that takes
the form of a gentle, if ragged, slope which differentiates among issue
areas and allows for states to retain their rights on a wide range of issues
involving substantive rather than symbolic interests. Put differently,
while it seems excessively simplistic to argue that at present "there is no
greater authority than the sovereign, egoistic nation-state,"[32] and while
"no doubt one should resist the idea that [the nation-state] is becoming

[30] Edward A. Gargan, "Afghan President Agrees to Step Down," *New York Times*, March 19, 1992, p. A3.

[31] Paul Lewis, "U.N. Says Iraq Defies Order to Destroy Weapons," *New York Times*, February 28, 1992, p. A5.

[32] Paul Kennedy, *The Rise and Fall of the Great Powers: Economic Change and Military Conflict from 1500 to 2000* (New York: Random House, 1987), p. 440.

dissolved," it is also the case that "the character of states, and their inter-relations, are being quite dramatically influenced by factors operating both below and above the level of the nation state itself."[33]

But again caution is in order. Conceivably the momentum favoring modifications of the sovereignty principle will be brought to a halt and movement on the sovereignty continuum reversed. This is hard to imagine in a world composed of ever more analytically skillful citizens whose sensitivities and institutions place a high value on human rights, survival and dignity; but given the uncertainties that attach to turbulent conditions, long pauses in the movement away from sovereign rights are not beyond the realm of possibility.

Legal determinants

Given the common tendencies fostered by situational, domestic, and international determinants, what can one say in response to the question of whether international communities have the right to intervene in the affairs of member countries? The question is deceptive.[34] It addresses the murky space where law and politics converge, where legal precepts prevail that may no longer limit or guide behavior. Surely there is a large body of international law, bulwarked by the conventions of the interstate system, which points to the conclusion that international communities do not have the right to intervene, that sovereignty is inviolable and not open to qualification. Yet, as the preceding analysis suggests, there is welter of practice that suggests otherwise, that points to violations of sovereignty which are accepted without vigorous protest. Even the UN member with the most vociferous history of reliance on the sovereignty theme, The People's Republic of China, voted to abstain in the Security Council when the UN intruded upon Iraq's sovereignty.

Thus it would seem that, irrespective of the prevailing legal order, the odds are against international law retaining its viability with respect to the prerogatives of statehood. As stated at the very outset, the dictates of the law provide no more than an intermittent pause in political relationships. The present pause has lasted some 400 years, but that is not

---

[33] Anthony Giddens, "Review Symposium: Comments on Paul Kennedy's *The Rise and Fall of the Great Powers*," *British Journal of Sociology*, vol. 40, no. 2 (June 1989), p. 331.

[34] For another formulation that also challenges the question as deceptive, even as "a red herring," see Jarat Chopra and Thomas G. Weiss, "Sovereignty Is No Longer Sacrosanct: Codifying Humanitarian Intervention," *Ethics and International Affairs*, vol. 6 (1992), pp. 95–117.

to say it is beyond being undermined. All the indicators point to the contrary. They all suggest that the legal status of sovereignty rights is bound to be subverted by the transformative dynamics currently at work in world affairs.

Some might argue with this conclusion on the grounds that there is a wide gap between a raised consciousness and a legal precept, that people may believe that humanitarian interventions are justified even as states effectively ward off interventionary actions by adhering to their legal rights. The record, however, belies this line of reasoning. The sensitivity to genocide, human rights violations, and mass migrations is not confined to publics and nongovernmental groups. So many governments have evidenced a readiness – through their participation in peace-keeping operations – to contribute to the enforcement of minimal humanitarian standards that emergent norms in this area come close to having the clout and prestige of law.

Nor is there much force to the realist argument that the pattern wherein international communities intervene in the domestic affairs of their members is misleading, that such interventions occur not because states feel obliged to accept them, but because it is in their interest to allow them to take place. In this view the widespread acceptance of interventionary behavior derives from convenience rather than law, and thus the sovereignty of states is seen to remain intact because lately states have chosen not to exercise it. If push ever came to shove, if a state ever got faced with an unwanted intervention, this reasoning concludes, it would surely protest that its sovereignty has been violated. But recent history does not support this conclusion: one could cite innumerable occasions when states might have been expected to register such protests but either did not do so or did so half-heartedly without any real conviction.

Furthermore, the realist contention suffers from a flawed conception of law in relation to change. To view international law as continuing to favor states because the precedents underlying claims to sovereign privilege have not been specifically abrogated and thus continue to prevail even though states do not claim them is to cling to such a narrow, technical, and formal conception of the law as to render inquiries into the dynamics of social change virtually impossible. The test of change is to be found in behavior and not legal sanctions.

Conceivably, of course, the World Court and other judicial bodies, not to mention foreign offices and multilateral agencies, may take actions that run counter to the prevailing momentum and reassert the unqualified nature of sovereignty. Again, however, such developments seem highly unlikely. In a "borderless" world of "global webs," "global factories," "off-shore banks," "de-nationalized inter-corporate alliances," and inter-societal "connections" that span national boundaries and evolve institutions such as the European Union, which is "neither a state nor an international organization,"[35] it is difficult to construct a scenario wherein the sovereignty of states remains fixed.

This is not to say that a wholesale reversal of the historic foundations of international law is under way. Even as profound transformations unfold, so do long-standing habits, bureaucratic inertia, and historic continuities persist. The foregoing discussion has dealt with the question of whether sovereignty is likely to protect states from external intervention when humanitarian concerns are at issue. On a variety of other issues, clearly, the legal status of states is unlikely to be significantly jarred or alterations made in the sanctity they enjoy under treaties and the many other formal instruments of international communities.

Sovereignty's future

If it is assumed, as seems reasonable, that the parametric transformations sustaining turbulence in world politics are not transitory phenomena,[36] the continuing advance of the skill revolution, the persistent deepening of authority crises, and the unending processes of structural bifurcation seem destined to cumulate to a threshold point where the relocation of values on the sovereignty continuum becomes irreversible for the foreseeable future. The key to this threshold lies in the public's acceptance of authority structures and the ways in which the crises enveloping them undermine the integrity and prerogatives of national institutions. For sovereignty highlights the extent to which people can

[35] For inquiries that focus on these new forms of global structure, see Kenichi Ohmae, *A Borderless World* (New York: Harpers, 1990); Robert B. Reich, *The Work of Nations: Preparing Ourselves for 21st-Century Capitalism* (New York: Alfred A. Knopf, 1991); Joseph Grunwald and Kenneth Flam, *The Global Factory: Foreign Assembly in International Trade* (Washington, DC: The Brookings Institution, 1985); Jonathan Aronson and Peter Cohey, *When Countries Talk: International Trade in Telecommunications Services* (Cambridge, MA: Ballinger, 1987); Katrina Burgess and Abraham F. Lowenthal (eds.), *The California–Mexico Connection* (Stanford: Stanford University Press, 1993); and Joel Havemann, "Neither a State nor International Organization," *Los Angeles Times*, February 4, 1992, p. H9.

[36] The expectation that the future of world politics will continue to be marked by turbulence is set forth in Rosenau, *Turbulence in World Politics*, pp. 453–4.

exercise control over their own lives, and now that citizens have a growing capacity to link the acts of leaders to the degree of freedom they can exercise on their own behalf, they are likely to be acutely sensitive to any movement toward the convenience-of-the-states extreme on the sovereignty continuum that jeopardizes their well-being. Thus do efforts to reassert the privileges and benefit of sovereignty seem destined to founder, caught up in the entangling networks of competence and agitation woven by newly empowered masses.

12   Constitutions

> The question is: Does constitutional structure cause a political condition and a state of public opinion or does the political condition and a state of public opinion cause the constitutional structure? This sounds at first like the chicken and egg problem in which there is no causal direction; but I think that usually there is a cause and that constitutional forms are typically derivative. It seems probable to me that public opinion usually causes constitutional structure, and seldom, if ever, the other way around.
>
> William H. Riker[1]

In a fast-paced world of alert publics, troubled economies, and deep cleavages, what roles, if any, can constitutional arrangements play in controlling, modifying, or adapting how communities and societies adapt to a widening Frontier? If it is the case that centralizing tendencies are fostering the formation of transnational authorities, that decentralizing tendencies are relocating legitimacy in the direction of subnational authorities, and that as a result the scope of national governance is undergoing erosion, to what extent can the dynamics of change be absorbed and directed by the legal arrangements through which peoples accommodate to each other? Indeed, with the identities of people and the boundaries of their systems undergoing transformation, are formal constitutions tending toward obsolescence and thus increasingly in need of extensive revision?

In one form or another, these questions have come to occupy central positions on the agendas of international, national, and subnational systems, each struggling to find a proper role for itself that allows for the maintenance or enhancement of its legitimacy in swift-moving, fluid

---

[1] "Comments on Vincent Ostrom's Paper," *Public Choice*, vol. 27 (1976), p. 13.

political situations along the Frontier. Whatever may be the particulars of the struggle – whether it be the European Union searching for the limits of transnational authority over historic nation-states, the treaty arrangements through which Serbs, Croats, and Muslims in Bosnia undertake to reverse their downward spiral, the fragmenting republics of the former Soviet Union lurching toward new relationships with each other, the people of Germany adjusting to a reunion that all thought they desired and no one anticipated, the two Koreas inching toward a return to an earlier unity, the two Chinas sparring over control mechanisms that would alter their present estrangement, the people of Hong Kong preparing for a treaty-mandated reunion with the People's Republic of China, the United Nations pondering whether to enlarge its Security Council and add to its permanent members, the two main cultural groups and Eskimos of Canada seeking both coherence and autonomy, the factions of strife-ridden countries trying to evolve new legal bases for living together, or the boards of corporations seeking to placate more demanding stockholders by adjusting their charters – a prime issue is how to establish new constitutional arrangements that can work, that can enlist the support of diverse peoples accustomed to an earlier constitutionality that is recognized to have become archaic. Confederation, federation, integration, unification, continentalism, secession, self-government, independence, multisystem nations, dual recognition – these are among the concepts offered and debated by jurists and politicians as constitutional solutions for governance along the Frontier.

Just as sovereignty has undergone redefinition as the Frontier has widened, in other words, so have constitutions, formal or informal, come into question as the basis for rule systems across the Frontier. Recent years have witnessed a veritable explosion in the number of new constitutions contemplated, pursued, and eventually approved. During the period from 1960 to 1988, between two and ten new constitutional charters were approved each year and the figure for all the years since 1989 exceeds sixty.[2] The world may not be an orderly place, but that is not for lack of an effort to make it so, to base governance on explicit and accepted rules of the political game.

This is not the place to undertake an extended probe into the juridical

---

[2] A. P. Blaustein (ed.), *Constitutions of the Countries of the World* (Dobbs Ferry, NY: Oceania Publications), cited in Fred W. Riggs, "Viable Consitutionalism: Towards a Manifesto," unpublished paper, University of Hawaii, 1993.

issues involved, but at the same time no inquiry into the foundations of governance in a turbulent world can ignore the role that constitutional arrangements can and do play in the wake of the parametric transformations that are presently under way. In so doing, two somewhat different approaches to the task are possible. One can either analyze them with a view to recommending feasible schemes for resolving particular types of constitutional conflicts, or one can probe the fertility of the subsoil into which any schemes will have to be planted. Eventually, of course, the two foci have to be brought together if workable schemes are to evolve. But initially they tap different skills, one those of the jurist concerned with legal and equity issues, and the other those of the social scientist concerned with the underpinnings of change and the limits within which law can be effective in periods of profound transformation. As the above epigraph indicates, it is the latter concerns that are the main focus of this chapter.[3]

But, it might be asked, how is it possible to generalize across all the situations in which constitutional issues have arisen? The response is obvious: while an understanding that obtains across diverse situations – from secessions to unifications, from aspirations to autonomy to those for integration, from subnational arrangements to supranational ones – must allow for path-dependent, historically specific orientations and for institutions that are unique to every community, country, and region, nevertheless one can presume that the dynamics of globalization have infused the subsoils of all political systems with some of the same ingredients. In all situations involving the adoption of new constitutional arrangements, for example, the subsoil will consist of at least three strata, each of which is necessary, but none of which is sufficient, to any arrangements that take root and eventually flower: (1) a deep stratum made up of those underlying orientations, norms, and ideas through which people join together in a shared acceptance of the basic rules and procedures that enable governance to occur; (2) a mid-level stratum composed of those historical precedents and institutional flexibilities that allow for an accommodation to proposals for new constitutional provisions; and (3) a surface layer pervaded by the immediate circumstances of history – say, a particularly creative leader, a failed coup, or an external threat – that facilitates a recognition of the need for a new

---

[3] For a similar approach, see Alec Stone, "What Is a Supranational Constitution? An Essay in International Relations Theory," *Review of Politics*, vol. 56 (Summer 1994), pp. 441–74.

legal order. Only when all three of these subsoil strata are present can it be anticipated that old constitutional arrangements will successfully give way to a new and coherent system of effective rule along the Frontier.

It follows that a cogent assessment of any specific proposal for bringing a measure of legal order out of overlapping jurisdictions, separated countries, fragmenting empires, or competing subnational factions requires digging deep into the subsoils of present-day world affairs for an understanding of the conditions under which newly planted constitutional arrangements are likely to flourish or fail. Some of their subsoils may have richer nutrients than do others, but all of them have to draw strength from, or yield to weaknesses in, the same commons. Hence to develop an understanding of the difficulties faced by, say, the European Union is also to begin to grasp the problems that confront the fashioning of a multisystem nation out of the two Chinas. Stated differently, wherever basic constitutional arrangements have surfaced on political agendas, the central concern is nothing less than the creation of effective authority in response to the widening Frontier, either where none has existed previously (as in regional international organizations), or where a prolonged period of time has elapsed since an effective authority structure prevailed in the past (as in the two Germanys, Koreas, and Chinas), or where the existing structures are deemed noxious and in need of replacement (as in countries that abandoned communist regimes in favor of democratic arrangements).

Some conceptual distinctions

At first glance it may seem obvious what is meant by the constitution of a rule system, but there are different ways of using the term that need to be noted. In the most generic sense of the term, a constitution is the rules of the game by which the members of a community or society interact with each other. It sets the boundaries within which officials must confine their actions and it specifies to a lesser or greater degree the procedures that the government and its citizens must follow as they relate to each other in the public arena. These basic components of constitutions can either be formally recorded in writing, in which case reference is usually made to the Constitution, or they can be more comprehensive than the written document and include statutes, judicial decisions, executive orders, and informal practices issued or evolved subsequent to the adoption of the Constitution. This broader, uncodified notion of a constitution is often referred to as "the living constitution" of the polity, by which is meant the full array of rules and procedures (including those of the Constitution) that govern its day-to-day life.

Attention needs to be called to another, closely related concept that is often used to embrace an even more comprehensive game and set of rules than those encompassed by living constitutions. The latter are designed to govern the internal procedures and relationships of a system, but in an ever more interdependent world procedures are also needed to govern outsiders who cross the Frontier and pursue their affairs within the system. The rules of this game have usefully been called "the framework of law" that a polity develops for its members as well as for those from abroad who conduct business with them. The degree to which a country is able to attract foreign investments, for example, can be significantly affected by the framework of law it has evolved to assure investors that they will be treated fairly and that their investments will be protected from other than market forces. Whatever terms may be used, in other words, the dynamics of globalization have enlarged the scope of the legal and constitutional provisions through which societies govern their affairs. In this sense it may be more clarifying to think of the title of this chapter as "Law" rather than "Constitutions."

Formal and informal procedures

Important as Constitutions surely are, it is all too easy to exaggerate their capacity for bringing a measure of stability to the conduct of public affairs. More accurately, unless care is taken, one can readily slip into presuming that the wording of the preambles, articles, and clauses of charters, by-laws, and Constitutions can shape the course of events. They are, after all, just words – sometimes eloquently recorded, but nonetheless just words. What counts is whether the words express and reflect an underlying agreement to live by the rules they specify. Governance cannot occur without consensual foundations, but the mere recording of the procedures to be followed is no guarantee that all concerned will live by the rules and accept decisions that go against their immediate interests. The origins and sources of a social order are located only secondarily in charters, constitutions, legislative decrees, or any other founding documents; their primary source is the ideas, orientations, predispositions, memories, habits, and belief systems of a people and their leaders. In short, even as the specific phrasing of Constitutions cannot be ignored, the social scientist must probe beneath the wording to the attitudes and commitments out of which they emanated.

But it is also possible to lean too far in the opposite direction and treat wrangling over phraseology as pettiness, as stalling, or as an evasiveness in which politicians or diplomats engage so as to avoid decisions or provoke their adversaries into either leaving the bargaining table or agreeing to clauses they might not otherwise accept. Such a perspective may exaggerate the dynamics at work. For it may well be that the more intensely the competing parties wrangle over the rules, and the longer it takes for them to draft and ratify the specific procedures to which they agree, the greater is the likelihood that they will have made compromises with which they can subsequently live in the event their deliberations reach a successful conclusion. What often may seem like nit-picking in legislative debates or judicial proceedings about the meaning and limits of clauses is in fact a necessary part of the process through which workable procedures are drawn up to fashion a living constitution.

As noted, moreover, whatever may be the formal rules they specify, effective constitutions must allow for implementation through informal procedures that evolve as their provisions get enacted in the daily routines of the governed communities. At best, constitutions are only broad outlines. They cannot possibly cover in detail all the conflicts that may arise. They have to be interpreted and informal rules have to evolve to give their formal clauses meaning. This is why constitutions may be fragile at their inception. They require time for the habits of living under them to cumulate. They leave much to be interpreted and only as time elapses is it possible to know whether the original consensus on which the Constitution was founded extends to the interpretations that are subsequently rendered by chief executives, legislatures, bureaucracies, or courts. Thus inevitably there are tensions between the formally specified rules and the informal ones that citizens and groups live by. To be sure, the more extensively a constitution's procedures are formalized, the more is it likely to be effective; but it is nonetheless also the case that the ultimate key to success is the extent to which informal procedures develop to meet day-to-day contingencies and prevent differences of opinion from escalating into constitutional crises.

The need for formalized rules is especially acute with respect to the framework of laws that a polity offers its investors, tourists, and professionals from abroad. Foreign actors are likely to keep their boundary-spanning activities to a minimum the less clear-cut is the framework of law. If they cannot be sure they and their investments are covered by equitable laws, instead of being subject to the whims of bureaucrats, they will surely be discouraged from initiating border-crossings. The record of foreign investments in China is a good example in this respect. Until such time as the Chinese develop a known and effective framework of law to embrace foreign businesses, the flow of direct investments will be much less than what the size of its market suggests would be the case if proper legal arrangements were in place. Much the same can be said about the US–Japanese trade relationship: for some time now both countries have been trying to get the other to change its fundamental rules of the trading game, interactions that have been pervaded with friction because the frameworks of law that each has developed are so fundamentally different and so deeply embedded in their cultures and historic practices.

New constitutional arrangements in a turbulent world

Keeping in mind the diversity of constitutional situations that presently command attention, let us return to the questions raised at the outset and add to their specificity: Given a world with new parametric values represented by the skill revolution, the relocation of authority, and the bifurcation of global structures, what kinds of opportunities and limitations are likely to attach to the processes through which demands for new legal arrangements either achieve fruition or prove fruitless? How might the transformation of these parameters shape the capacity of political systems to frame and/or sustain viable constitutions that, other things being equal, facilitate governance in the face of the multiple challenges of the postindustrial world? To what extent, that is, are the new subsoils of politics receptive to the planting of new constitutional seeds and conducive to the flowering of meaningful and durable foliage? Are the dynamics of fragmegration likely to consign most constitutions to the dust-heap of history?

The answers are mixed. In the case of the skill revolution the increasingly analytic capacities of citizens seem likely to enable them to be more fully appreciative of constitutional issues and to grasp how the proposed legal arrangements will affect their well-being. It may take some time, to be sure, for those who have never known free elections to understand the fine points that differentiate single-member from proportional-representation electoral systems. Yet, they do not need cognizance of the technical details in order to have a preference and act intelligently. They need only know that a single-member system will best serve them if they are likely to be in the majority, while proportional representation is preferable if their party leanings are those of a small minority. And this understanding can be developed rather quickly as leaders of various factions argue about the merits of alternative systems. Beyond the specifics of most constitutional issues, in other words, are core values that do not require advanced training to grasp.

Conceivably the enhanced skills of citizens that enable them to perceive the implications of constitutional issues will also have the consequence of making it more difficult for leaders and legal experts to engage in the compromises that are necessary to enrich the subsoils out of which effective rules of the game must grow. Those who seek to govern in public affairs have long been hampered by poverty, resource shortages, internal conflicts, and a host of other problems that make it difficult to develop coherent policies and sustain progress toward a better life. But now, with citizens ever more sensitive to their own well-being, with publics ever more capable of forming quickly to press their demands in downtown squares, and with the lenses of global, regional, and local television cameras ever more ready to record leadership performances, the tasks of constitutional revision are bound to be delicate and ever more susceptible to disarray and relocation. That is, when the newly developed skills of citizens are trained on the restructuring of system-wide governance – on territoriality, political inclusion and exclusion, decision-making procedures, judicial rights, and all the other explosive issues that constitutional arrangements seek to settle – the authority that attaches to political institutions seems likely to become especially tenuous. Thus might authority crises deepen, and thus might proposals for multisystem nations, unified polities, federated states, and any other new constitutional arrangements founder and get caught up in the entangling networks of competence and agitation woven by newly empowered masses.

And even as new constitutional arrangements are adopted and new procedures put into place, there remains the problem that many publics with their newly empowering skills lack experience with the workings of their unified polities, multisystem structures, democratic constitutions, or whatever may be their new institutional arrangements. In the case of the democratic procedures quickly adopted by countries fashioned out of the former Soviet Union, for example, the lack of experience apparently tended to offset the newly acquired skills. People grasped the new procedures, but they had no bases for knowing that democratic processes unfold slowly, circuitously, and often with a seeming lack of direction, if not an unseemly disarray. Hence they tended to count on changes being quickly fashioned and then underwent disillusionment when not much seemed to happen. When the first open legislative debates in Russian history were first televised the audiences were huge, but as the debates dragged on without much apparent resolution the number of viewers dropped off substantially. People learned first-hand that while democracy involves open and free discussion, it is not a particularly efficient form of governance.

It follows that the transformation of the macro–micro parameter has further complicated the task of constitutional revision. The greater readiness of publics to link their compliance with authority to the performances of their leaders is likely to heighten their impatience with public affairs at those times when constitutional issues are high on the political agenda. Precisely because such issues take awhile to get resolved, these are the times when performances are least likely to appear successful. At such times authority crises do not readily allow for procedures that are slow to evolve and move communities toward their goals. To revert to the geological metaphor, if the deeper subsoils lack the proper nutrients – as is likely if time does not permit the habits of democratic followership to take root – the new authority structures may well wither on the vine.

In other words, if even the most sturdy authority relations are delicately balanced and susceptible to erosion in a time of profound and global transformation, it is difficult to imagine newly established authority structures functioning smoothly at the outset. Thus the transformation of the macro–micro parameter, and especially the replacement of traditional compliance habits with performance criteria of legitimacy as a basis for relating to authorities, seems destined to operate as a continuing limitation on the success of newly proposed constitutional arrangements. Whatever the new arrangements may be, their success depends on the building up of appropriate habits in which the newly installed authorities are accepted and heeded, a requirement that is often highly problematic under fluid conditions where citizens are more impelled to question than to comply with authority. Habitual responses are distinguished by their unthinking character, and people do not act or refrain from acting unthinkingly unless they have had repeated experiences which support their readiness not to give second thought to their own conduct. In the absence of repeated affirming experiences, fledgling habits can readily be undermined, even extinguished, by contrary events, by televised scenes of authority being challenged elsewhere in the world, by policy failures at home, and by a host of other intervening developments.

Interestingly, the subsoils that allow new constitutions to grow and flourish do not always require the nutrients of a common culture and language. Sometimes these may even hinder the formation of appropriate political habits. The two Germanys, for example, had a shared culture and language as well as more than a half-century of political and economic unity prior to their separation at the end of World War II. Despite these commonalities, however, the habits that sustain effective authority have not quickly moved into place since they were reunited in 1990. In both the former western and eastern halves of the country strong voices can be heard which suggest that the old habits of a divided system linger and inhibit the formation of new orientations that would make for effective authority relations. Similarly, the fears and demands expressed in one of the Koreas or Chinas with respect to their historic counterpart often seem more powerful as sources of continued division than do the cultural and linguistic dynamics they share.

It is perhaps instructive to note that there is one set of circumstances which does seem to conduce to the quick development of appropriate political habits that facilitate the swift evolution of new and acceptable constitutional arrangements; namely, when war leads to the full destruction of a country's authority structures and leaves it no choice but to adopt the new ones imposed and (initially) implemented by its conquerors. More specifically, there are at least two glaring cases of situations where victors and vanquished internationally negotiated constitutional provisions that were far more easily integrated into the habit structures of the peoples involved than is usually the case when negotiations require accommodation and cooperation among subgroups within states who have long distrusted each other. The enmities that divide subgroups within states are intimate and endlessly buttressed by a wide range of issues, whereas the antipathies that separate states are distant and not so subject to continual reinforcement as to withstand erosion through time. To appreciate the significance of this difference one need only compare how the "free world's" deep hostilities toward Germany and Japan during World War II have changed in the last fifty years with the unremitting animosities of Serbian, Croatian, and Bosnian subgroups in the former Yugoslavia. The comparison sug-

246

gests it is much easier for former enemies in interstate wars to make up, converge, and start afresh in a constitutional context than it is for peoples long ensconced in the same domestic conflicts.[4]

Considered in the context of this difference, it is hardly surprising that movement toward new constitutional arrangements in the European Union is less tumultuous and more promising than is the case for proposals that would restructure the relations of subgroups pressing for autonomy in the former Soviet Union, India, Korea, and China. Similarly, it has been less divisive for Canadians to develop new legal provisions for their trade with the United States than it has been for them to work out the relations of Quebec to the other Canadian provinces.

The bifurcation of the global system underlies another set of limitations that obtain wherever new constitutional arrangements may be sought. The evolution of a multi-centric system with a great diversity of autonomous transnational actors not only adds to the density and complexity of the setting in which such arrangements have to develop, but also offers alternative foci of loyalties and legitimacy for the individuals and groups which the proposed arrangements are designed to encompass. Whether it is proposed to aggregate separate subsystems into a larger constitutional jurisdiction, or disaggregate an existing system into lesser jurisdictions, the diversity of emotional ties, contractual agreements, and habitual relationships of those affected have become so extensive and far-reaching that extraordinary political creativity will be needed to evolve new jurisdictional schemes that retain rather than replace these transnational links and thereby generate enough support to be adopted and durable. Any such scheme that actually comes into being and endures will have accomplished a transnational version of gerrymandering that is likely to make politicians in the United States who rearrange voting districts seem amateurish by comparison.

This is another way of saying that the bifurcation of world politics seems bound to hinder the scope and competence of newly created authorities. The autonomy of actors in the multi-centric world militates against the development of clear-cut jurisdictional lines and political boundaries. Such actors are likely to resist – and to do so effectively – any arrangements that intrude upon the hard-won autonomy they gar-

---

[4] For a lengthy discussion of this point, see the essays in James N. Rosenau (ed.) *International Aspects of Civil Strife* (Princeton: Princeton University Press, 1964).

nered out of the declining competence of states. At best the newly created authorities will have to move cautiously, mollifying and pleading, if they are to survive and nurse new habits of compliance into being. Such an initial perspective, however, is likely to foster a shadow of reticence and circumspection that is not well suited to launching a new constitutional venture. But not to proceed in this way, and instead to seize upon whatever power the new constitution seems to afford, is to bring about a situation comparable to the many years in Beirut that witnessed each new attempt at coalitional arrangements quickly collapse whenever efforts to exercise authority were undertaken.

As for the ways in which the tensions between globalizing and localizing dynamics affect constitutional issues, there is evidence that efforts have been made lately to adjust frameworks of law to both of these opposing pressures. Subsequent to the end of the Cold War, for example, the newly independent countries in the former Soviet bloc evolved their living constitutions so as to allow for their interdependence with the rest of the world. Just as Poland's framework treated former Polish citizens living abroad as an election district and thus accorded them a vote in Poland's first open election, so did Yugoslavia's constitution allow for the appointment of a prime minister who was a citizen of the United States as well as a former resident of Yugoslavia. Similarly, a number of other countries altered the immigration procedures and the laws governing foreign investments in such a way as to reflect the opportunities as well as the pressures of a shrinking world. Not only have boundaries become increasingly porous as interdependence has mounted, in other words, but so have efforts to keep living constitutions abreast of the dynamics of globalization and the widening of the Frontier.

In sum, if the multiple impacts of parametric transformations are considered in the context of the need to weather tides pulling political processes in both globalizing and localizing directions, it seems clear that living constitutions can be sufficiently flexible to retain their effectiveness as rules to which actors adhere. Their vulnerability to fragmegrative conditions is readily evident, but in some cases so is their capacity to make the most of their legal opportunities.

Multisystem nations in a turbulent world

The implications of the foregoing analysis for the special case of divided countries serve to clarify further where constitutions fit in a rapidly changing world. Precisely because their separation is presently so thoroughgoing, countries like the two Chinas and the two Koreas allow for a probe of key variables that are located at the far extremes of any legal continua that may be relevant. They provide, as it were, an incisive glimpse into the quintessential nature of the main constitutional problems that all countries bordering on stalemate or sociopolitical deterioration must confront.

Consider the proposal that the People's Republic of China (PRC) and the Republic of China (ROC) coalesce in a multisystem nation.[5] In it considerable importance is attached to the historical foundations of the Chinese nation, while the advent of its separation into two distinct, separate, and autonomous political systems is regarded as a transitional phenomenon that is capable of eventually giving way to the more powerful undercurrents of shared language and culture. After all, it is argued, the systemic differences are sustained by abstract economic and political ideologies, and in the long run these are surely no match for the deep emotional impulses, ingrained habits, and cultural ties that derive from long membership in the same nation. Those who advance the proposal are keenly aware of the obstacles that have to be surmounted for a multisystem nation to become politically viable – not the least problem being that the PRC conceives of a one-country, two-systems arrangement as one in which it is the central government and the ROC is a subsidiary or local government, whereas the ROC proposes that the arrangement involve a sufficient degree of decentralization for the two governments to be equals – but their reasoning rests on an underlying presumption that the commonalities of nation are far more powerful than systemic discrepancies and that thus political viability under a single set of constitutional arrangements can ultimately be achieved.

Given the main themes of this chapter, however, there are sound reasons to question the assumption that the values that attach to nation are likely to prevail, even in the long run, over those that derive from systemic properties. The assumption suffers from an ignoring of the possibility that long experience in a system can be just as habit-forming as having deep roots in a nation. Systems develop their own cultures,

---

[5] For one of the many formulations of this proposal, see Yung Wei, "The Unification and Division of Multi-System Nations: A Comparative Analysis of Basic Concepts, Issues, and Approaches," in Hungdah Chu and Robert Downen (eds.), *Multi-System Nations and International Law: The International Status of Germany, Korea and China* (Occasional Papers/Reprints Series in Contemporary Asian Studies, no. 8, School of Law, University of Maryland, 1981), pp. 59–74.

their own norms for relating to others, their own conceptions of how conflicts should be resolved, their own premises about the value of human life, and so forth. Just because the two Chinas or the two Koreas are differentiated along a communist–capitalist dimension does not mean that such differences are superficial in terms of the strength of their underlying attitudinal and behavioral patterns; nor does it necessarily follow that their common languages, histories, and cultures are strong enough to survive the prolonged persistence of huge economic and political discrepancies. One need only observe the resistance of Russian bureaucrats and masses to capitalist techniques of production and investment, their inclination to perceive profit as evil and hard work as fruitless, to appreciate that economic cultures can exercise a powerful hold on people.

Stated differently, fundamental economic systems have histories and cultures of their own and, given the passage of enough time, these can supersede, or at least blend with, the norms and traditions of the prior civilization. The more time passes, moreover, the more does the new systemic culture become embedded in the mores and practices of those it encompasses. And as the systemic culture becomes increasingly entrenched, of course, the more are its premises likely to spread to the noneconomic dimensions of life, with the result that the residues of nation – of common language and ancient history – may become increasingly less powerful as forces for successful convergence. Indeed, at some distant point in the future, any efforts to frame a new constitution for a single nation that embraces two discrepant economic systems will seem more like an artificial contrivance – a structure without authority, a psychic palliative – than an integrative mechanism for achieving a modicum of reunification.

No less important, the vast interdependencies fostered by the globalization of world affairs are bound to further complicate any attempt to nurse a multisystem nation into being. For each of the systems in the nation, and especially those that have pursued policies that allow for the globalization of capital, production, labor, and markets, will have to make sure its ties to the international community and its links to the world economy are not upended by re-establishing the single nation. We will know much more about the extent to which the requirements of a world economy do or do not dominate efforts to construct new constitutional arrangements for domestic polities as the links between Hong Kong and the Chinese mainland evolve in the future.

Some bases for optimism

Notwithstanding the many diverse reasons to be dubious about the chances of multisystem nations establishing effective constitutional arrangements, there are two reasons to temper pessimism with a degree of optimism. One concerns the passage of time and the emergence of new generations of elites for whom the arguments in favor of separate, autonomous nation-systems may be less compelling than they were for the generations that engineered and lived through the separation in the first place. It is no mere coincidence that the first signs of movement toward renewed interactions between both the two Chinas and the two Koreas occurred as the leaders who presided over the division of their countries gave way to successors who never directly experienced the animosities that accompanied the parting of the ways after World War II. To be sure, as previously noted, the newer generations have acquired stakes in their different economic and political systems that are likely to limit their readiness to seek a restoration of their common heritage in a multisystem nation. Nevertheless, the later generations are also likely to be more open to efforts to achieve an integration of their historical cultures and their economic systems than are their predecessors. This is not to say that they will quickly rearrange their priorities so as to support national values over systemic values, but it is to note that they may not be averse to considering constitutional arrangements designed to synthesize the two sets of values.

More importantly, an optimistic note can be sounded by focusing on the possibility that the very parametric changes that have sustained the decentralizing tendencies in world affairs may eventually facilitate the emergence of centralizing directions. More skillful citizens may come to appreciate that while their autonomous subgroups have provided a variety of benefits, there remain large, crucial problems that lie beyond their competence as subgroups to resolve. Most notably, the persistence of authority crises and governmental stalemates to which the autonomy of subgroups inadvertently or otherwise contributes may come to be viewed as deleterious to the realization of subgroup aspirations. If, for example, the downward spiral of an authority crisis leads to extensive disorder, the need for centralized institutions capable of restoring a semblance of stability may begin to seem as appealing as the need for subgroup autonomy. Under these circumstances a search for whole systems that achieve a better balance between centralizing and decentralizing dynamics is likely to ensue, at which point the idea of a multisystem nation may take on greater credence for those societies that were split apart in the aftermath of war.

Indeed, if it is the case that the turbulence of world politics has weakened states and rendered them less and less viable as whole-system entities, the search for a balance between autonomy and interdependence could even lead peoples who did not experience a postwar separation to find the idea of a multisystem nation compelling. Conceivably, the multisystem nation may come to be viewed as embodying a set of constitutional arrangements comparable and preferable to those that comprise federal systems. Whereas federations concentrate some authority in central institutions, those of multisystem nations may provide psychic unity through the symbols of a shared culture while at the same time maintaining political autonomy for the units that comprise the various systems of the nation.

Put differently, the idea of a multisystem nation is quite consistent with the bifurcated structure of world politics. It involves constitutional arrangements that acknowledge the dispersion of authority across several worlds and, as such, it allows for a legal context in which the continuing proliferation of subgroups can occur.

Of course, the tensions between centralizing and decentralizing tendencies are as old as politics itself. People yearn for order (a centralizing tendency) even as they also value their freedom (a decentralizing tendency), and the problem of how to reconcile the two aspirations has yet to yield its place as the number one issue on every political agenda. In the present-day context of a globalized world economy and far-reaching world politics, these fundamental aspirations are being reconciled through the processes of bifurcation. Today the yearning for order takes the form of recognizing the pervasiveness of interdependence and the valuing of freedom takes the form of pressing for greater autonomy. The result is a conception of politics as the arena in which autonomy is achieved so as to freely chose the manner in which interdependencies will be established and sustained.

To take note of bases for optimism, however, is not to ignore all the uncertainties and potential threats to which our turbulent world is presently heir. Nor is it to forget that in the absence of fertile subsoils can any amount of tinkering with constitutional arrangements achieve a workable balance between order and autonomy. Indeed, given the fast-moving cascades that roil global politics today – not to mention the numerous ways in which the two Chinas are unlike – to pose the question of whether such a balance can be translated into a multisystem nation with acceptable constitutional arrangements is to invite a return to pessimism. At the very least such a nation is bound to encounter enormous birth pains, with the odds being stacked against a successful outcome.

Prospects for governance

Irrespective of whether multisystem nations are actually coming into being, the dilemmas they face highlight the challenge of fashioning and maintaining rule systems along a widening Frontier. They point yet again to the question of whether constitutions are simply a product of underlying social, economic, and political realities and thus constrained by them, or whether constitutional arrangements can operate as causal agents and shape the ways in which politics is conducted and policies are framed. And they also accent how much depends on the breadth of the underlying consensus out of which a constitution evolves. Only if a widespread conviction evolves among the groups encompassed by proposed constitutional arrangements that their distinctive economic and political needs will not be endangered by an elevation of their common language and culture into constitutional principles can a measure of effective governance develop, and even then the range of effectiveness is likely to be confined to those issue areas which focus on the shared symbols of culture and history. Under these circumstances, it is possible to imagine, given the passage of enough time, the authority of a new constitution expanding to the point where it could operate as a stimulus to change and further accommodation, thereby operating as a causal agent. Of course, for such an expansion to occur, the constitutional arrangements would have to allow for a blend of autonomy and interdependence that sustains public acceptance and proves capable of withstanding the strong, contradictory currents of a turbulent world.

13   Elections

We are witnessing a sea change in international law, as a result of
which the legitimacy of each government someday will be measured
definitively by international rules and processes. We are not quite
there, but we can see the outlines of this new world in which the citizens of each state will look to international law and organization to
guarantee their democratic entitlement.

Thomas M. Franck[1]

As increasing numbers of countries have sought to evolve living
constitutions based on democratic processes, so have elections emerged
as delicate instruments of governance along the Frontier. Many systems
have had little or no experience in the conduct of elections or the pre-
liminary campaigns and registration procedures that culminate in the
voting booth. In more than a few other instances, prior experience has
been confined to the rituals of one-party elections which offer little
guidance for participating in open and free elections. Accordingly, a
major institution of modern governance is still very much in the process
of evolution and, in an increasing number of cases, it is being shaped by
the parametric transformations that have brought turbulence and the
dynamics of globalization to world affairs. As the epigraph suggests,
however, there can be little doubt as to where the path of this evolving
institution is leading.

Perhaps the most conspicuous impact of the skill revolution, authority crises, and bifurcated structures on electoral institutions is the recent
surge of occasions whereon the international community, represented

Parts of this chapter were adapted from a paper originally co-authored with Michael
Fagen.
[1] Thomas M. Franck, "The Emerging Right to Democratic Governance," *American Journal
of International Law*, vol. 86 (January 1992), p. 50.

by any one of numerous organizations, has monitored, supervised, or otherwise participated in the elections of developing countries in Africa, Asia, the Caribbean, Latin America, and the former Soviet empire. Put more challengingly, the pattern appears to involve the violation of traditional sovereign rights. Lately it has become commonplace for persons from abroad, equipped only with a badge certifying they are observers entitled to watch and report on voting procedures, to cross the boundary separating international from domestic politics and become enmeshed in local or national electoral processes. In effect, the Frontier has widened to the point where many domestic elections have become international events.

It should be noted that the pattern to be explained is not external involvement in domestic elections, but the surge in such occasions. Instances of international involvement occurred in Europe as long ago as 1857[2] and the United States involved itself in a number of Central American and Caribbean elections between 1900 and 1940;[3] but it was not until the post-World War II period that the pattern gathered momentum: "Since 1948, the number of elections held under international auspices has increased both in terms of quantity and geography. In the past 40 years, governments, intergovernmental organizations, and nongovernmental organizations have increasingly sponsored missions to observe elections."[4] Indeed, noting that in 1991 the General Assembly of the United Nations established a standing electoral commission to help member states that ask for assistance to guarantee that their elections will be free and fair, one observer anticipates that "requesting international electoral monitoring . . . will likely become an increasingly routine part of national practice . . . "[5] Put differently, "one can convincingly argue that states which deny their citizens the right to free and open elections are violating a rule that is fast becoming an integral part of the elaborately woven human rights fabric."[6]

While there appears to be wide agreement that the momentum has reached a point where the emerging electoral pattern is on its way to becoming an established feature of world and national politics, the

---

[2] Marilyn Anne Zak, "Assisting Elections in the Third World," *Washington Quarterly* (Autumn 1987), p. 178.   [3] *Ibid.*, p. 176.

[4] *Ibid.* In addition to the monitoring missions, there is a "trend among industrialized nations to include election support assistance in aid packages to promote democratization." "Japan to Help Pay Election Costs Overseas," *Daily Yomiuri*, September 5, 1994, p. 1.   [5] Franck, "The Emerging Right to Democratic Governance," p. 77.

[6] *Ibid.*, p. 79.

same cannot be said with respect to the meaning of the pattern. Queries such as the following yield a variety of answers: What does the pattern tell us about the effectiveness of states, the competence of citizens, and governance and politics in this turbulent era? Is it expressive of world-wide impulses toward democratic forms of government or merely the result of weak states acquiescing to outside pressures for the adoption of democratic procedures? Does the emergent pattern reflect the evolution of new global norms?

The variety of answers that such questions evoke can be traced to differences in the theoretical perspectives that analysts employ. Those convinced that the principle of national sovereignty is still vitally alive, for example, are likely to wonder whether the pattern exists at all, stressing that each electoral situation is so marked by unique features that discerning in them the early stages of an emergent pattern accords more significance to the spread of global practices and norms than is warranted. After all, this line of reasoning stresses, states are still in charge and they can bring an end to the presence of outside observers any time they want. On the other hand, for those who adhere to the consensual view that the rash of internationally monitored elections can be fairly judged to form a pattern, such a conclusion only serves to raise still other questions. Does the pattern have any staying power? Is it merely a transitional phenomenon generated by the dislocations of a world in flux, a temporary deviation from the long-established rights of states to maintain exclusive control over their own domestic affairs? Alternatively, if the pattern is judged to be more enduring than transitional, what are its likely consequences? Is each successful internationally monitored election likely to enhance the probabilities of success in future elections, thus solidifying the emergence of new global norms? Or are the vagaries of electoral politics such that the successes occur at random and the central trend is bound to be one of failure and eventual disengagement by the international community?

The perspective on governance in a turbulent world employed here offers a response to such questions derived from the core premise that internationally monitored elections are not simply instances of local political systems choosing their leaderships; they are also instances of global politics, of the international community crossing sovereign boundaries to participate in the internal affairs of states. To be sure, observing or monitoring elections is a mild, unspectacular, and non-authoritarian form of boundary-crossing participation, but the turbulence model suggests that nonetheless it may well be yet another significant reflection of central tendencies at work in world affairs, an instance of the international community's increasing involvement in the daily routines of its constituent parts, a clear-cut case of the continuing dissolution of the boundaries that have long divided local, national, and international systems.

With few exceptions,[7] however, the growing literature on externally monitored elections does not proceed from a perspective that treats domestic elections as international events. The roles and consequences of the outside observers are not ignored, but the significance of their presence is obscured as most analysts focus on national systems and how their achievement or maintenance of democracy can be served through electoral processes. Consequently, scant are the interpretations that posit the electoral process as part of the larger global dynamics presently transforming how local and national communities conduct their affairs. It is precisely this gap in the literature that the turbulence model addresses. Whatever its flaws, the model has the virtue of focusing on both the domestic and international dimensions of modern-day political processes. It highlights the implications of elections for the countries in which they are held even as it focuses on them as instances of more encompassing global dynamics, thereby compelling reflection on the circumstances under which the international community moves into the contested space that constitutes the Frontier.

Three underlying premises

Although it serves as the main perspective underlying what follows, the turbulence model is supplemented by three additional premises that guide the analysis:

(1) No matter how they may be conducted or whatever the consequences to which they give rise, elections in any political system are turning-points, defining moments that create, transfer, or maintain legitimacy and tell all concerned how the forces at work in the system are arrayed and the extent to which it is capable of sustaining continuities and adapting to changes.

[7] Conspicuous exceptions include Dennis J. Amato, "Elections Under International Auspices, 1948–1970," unpublished Ph.D. dissertation, Johns Hopkins University (1971); David Stoelting, "The Challenge of U.N. Monitored Elections in Independent Nations," *Stanford Journal of International Law*, vol. 28 (Spring 1992), pp. 371–424; and Franck, "The Emerging Right to Democratic Governance," pp. 46–91.

(2) Elections monitored by teams of diverse foreign observers are part and parcel of the processes of globalization that are widening the Frontier.

(3) Given an ever more interdependent world in which information about elections is rapidly and widely distributed beyond the countries in which they are held, no election is simply a local event; rather, every election becomes part of the world's memory bank and, as such, may contribute to the way in which later elections are conducted.

Elections as defining moments

So much of what happens in politics derives from the decisions and policies of governments that elections tend not to be preoccupying. Election periods are brief compared to those of governance that follow and, besides, neither the campaign nor the vote may have much to do with the policies pursued by the newly elected officials. Whether their mandates are broad or narrow, the realities of governance are so much more complex than the issues framed during the campaign that policymakers can readily rationalize the necessity of straying from the pledges they made in the heat of the electoral contest. And supplementing the sense that elections may be peripheral to the conduct of government is a widespread cynicism that posits politicians as so eager to win that they buy votes or otherwise corrupt the electoral process.

Despite their brevity and seeming irrelevance, however, elections are critical events in the life of any polity. Whether assessed in terms of the turbulence model or any other theory, all political systems have to create wellsprings of legitimacy that allow their leaders to act on behalf of their publics, thus enabling them to maintain sufficient coherence for the polity to persist intact through time. Elections are the means through which virtually all modern polities generate those elements of political legitimacy that ensure the compliance of citizens with the directives of officials. Where legitimacy once derived from the divine right of kings or popes, today it is rooted in the collective judgments rendered in the voting booth. This is why democrats are ever ready to press for elections and why autocrats are ever ready to postpone, evade, or tamper with them. It also explains why even the most autocratic regimes feel obliged to hold elections periodically. Even though they may use coercion or otherwise rig electoral outcomes, they too need a measure of legitimacy.

Elections also lie at the heart of the political process in the sense that the day of their occurrence is one moment in the life of the polity when its control becomes system-dominant – that is, when no individual or group can determine what happens. At all other times polities are subsystem-dominant as officials, elites, the military, and other influential factions shape the course of events. But on election day the playing field is leveled as all concerned, the powerful along with the powerless, await the collective outcome of thousands or millions of separate actions.[8] And when all the votes are tallied, the hierarchical array of forces within the polity are revealed for all to ponder and adjust to – a defining moment that, for better or worse (depending on whether the results are accepted or contested), informs leaders and publics alike that they are inextricably linked to each other, that they share a collective fate, and that they are facing the future together as a coherent or divided society. Put differently, irrespective of the degree to which the outcome is tainted by fraud, apathy, or violence, and quite apart from who wins and who loses, an election is the one moment when all citizens engage in the same behavior (i.e., they all relate to the polity by entering or avoiding the voting booth), with the result that their society undergoes a collective experience that reaffirms or alters its prior course. In addition, elections serve to create many of society's heroes and villains, to enhance its unity or intensify its divisions, to resolve its differences or perpetuate its stalemates – all outcomes which serve to provide citizens with an opportunity to register their sense of participation in, alienation from, or apathy toward the symbols and practices which differentiate their society from all others.

Of course, the performance of these electoral functions varies from society to society. Under some circumstances – such as those that do not allow for competing parties or candidates, that do not guarantee the secrecy of ballots, or that do not otherwise permit the electorate to make a free choice – they are performed badly and the playing field is anything but level. Yet, even when they are held under the most autocratic and fraudulent circumstances, elections are defining moments. They may not foster or transfer legitimacy in such a system, but they still reveal the prevailing array of societal forces and, being system-dominant, they always offer hope that cracks in autocratic regimes will be exposed.

Elections as global events

Owing to the shrinkage of social and geographic distances as a result of dynamic technologies and the evolution of global norms, it now matters

---

[8] Since they cannot be 100 percent certain that their fraudulent schemes will be effective, even those who seek to intimidate voters, buy votes, or otherwise steal the election must experience the system-dominant character of elections on the days they are held.

to people and groups around the world if the internal affairs of countries violate the rights and safety of their citizens. The result has been a globalization of domestic politics – or at least the advent of a readiness of both opposition groups at home and concerned parties abroad, no longer inhibited by the historic barriers posed by sovereignty, to press for the presence of international observers to facilitate the holding of fair and open elections in those countries which have yet to evolve cultures and institutions that insure close adherence to democratic procedures. Equally important, the new political calculus is such that the leaders who preside over autocratic regimes tend to feel obliged to yield to the pressures to invite and certify foreign observers. They may try initially to resist the idea of external assessments of their electoral procedures, but more often than not they eventually discover that their links to the international system are too extensive to risk the loss of support that would follow a refusal to admit impartial election observers from abroad. In short, international monitoring of domestic elections has become a new and key strand in the world's political fabric.

This is not to say, however, that states are so weakened that they accede readily to international monitors and conduct fair elections. Quite to the contrary, those leaders and factions who fear their rule will come to an end if a fair election is held can and do resort to a variety of subterfuges in order to obtain a favorable outcome of the vote. Lest they be caught engaging in illegitimate practices, however, they go to considerable lengths to hide their devious manipulations and give the appearance of accommodating the foreign observers. Internationally monitored elections are thus marked by a continuous struggle – a political dance, as it were – between local election officials and external monitors.

And it is a struggle that does not necessarily end on election day. Charges and counter-charges of fraud can last well into the post-election period even if the outside monitoring team judges the election to have been conducted fairly. The key question is whether the protests that the election was stolen eventually cease. That is the test of a fair election and, as such, the primary goal of international election monitoring. An outside team may pronounce an election to have been fairly held, but if those who lost the election do not accept the final tally of votes as accurate, if they contest the results verbally or otherwise, the external pronouncement will have little meaning or, worse, will seem like an external validation of the unfair practices which the losers claim caused their defeat. In short, legitimacy must attach to an election for it to be a significant event in the life of any polity, and international intervention in electoral processes can be acclaimed only when the legitimacy is measured by the participation in the election of all the society's major groups and their acceptance of the final tally.

Elections as international sequences

Norms and practices that develop on a global scale, like those that evolve within countries, are not created by a single defining event; rather, they are the product of repetition, of numerous occasions when new circumstances and structures call forth the same new responses. The more these responses cumulate and become patterned, the more do they acquire an independent life of their own and eventually come to be widely recognized as legitimate standards of conduct. Accordingly, given a shrinking world in which worldwide publicity attaches to significant domestic events, it is reasonable to proceed from the premise that every internationally monitored election may be part of a global norm-building sequence. Presumably each such election augments the legitimacy of the interventionary norm that accepts external involvement in domestic politics if the outside observers perform their tasks impartially and avoid the appearance, much less the fact, of favoring one or another party to the election. And presumably the norm is also reinforced if the monitors depict the election as having been conducted fairly or if they discern sufficient fraud to withhold their approval of the outcome.[9]

The impact of turbulence

That the onset of turbulence in world politics has had consequences for the conduct of elections can be readily discerned. In the case of the macro parameter, the emergence of the multi-centric world and the bifurcation of global structures has led to a decline in the capacity of the state-centric world to manage its affairs. Intergovernmental cooperation has never been easily accomplished, but it has become all the more difficult with the added layers of organization and special interests that have accompanied the growing density and dynamism of the multi-

---

[9] Nor is the norm necessarily undermined when a revolt or *coup d'état* negates the results of an election shortly after its procedures have been labeled as fair by one or more teams of foreign observers. Much will then depend on the reactions of the international community to the negation of the election. If it does not accept the negation and acts to keep it high on the global agenda of issues that remain unresolved, as it did with respect to negated elections in Burma, the Philippines, Haiti, Nigeria, and Panama, then the interventionary norm may actually be strengthened.

centric world. In addition, with the sovereignty of states now less secure, the state-centric world has become more vulnerable to any pressures exerted by coalitions formed in the multi-centric world. The bargaining position of those state leaders who prefer to avoid international monitoring of their elections has thus been increasingly weakened as more and more transnational actors converge around the idea of sending election-monitoring teams. The way has been paved, in other words, for actors in the multi-centric world and governments in the state-centric world to evolve practices and norms, either by invitation or otherwise and either individually or collectively, wherein they routinely engage in boundary-crossing activities that involve them in domestic elections.

The transformation of the micro parameter is no less relevant. Viewed in the context of a pervasive skill revolution, voters are likely to comprehend ever more fully the degree to which elections can serve as turning-points for their polities. They may be cynical about politicians and they may be dubious that their single vote can make any difference; but in this era of military regimes and paralyzed governments being toppled by the collective actions of publics, they are likely to be increasingly aware that elections can offer an opportunity for change and renewal. Their newly enlarged skills enable them to discern where, when, and how the aggregation of individual votes can serve their interests and establish conditions under which political leaders can be constrained and new policies initiated.

It follows that in societies which have yet to establish firmly grounded institutions that accord value and legitimacy to procedures for the people to choose openly among parties and candidates seeking to govern them, the implications of external observers being in their country to monitor their elections are likely to be more widely understood as the electorate becomes more skillful. In particular, voters who have felt deprived of fair elections in the past, or those who have accumulated grievances against the existing regime, are likely to grasp that the presence of outside observers increases the chances of obtaining a change in government. Cynicism may continue to prevail as past experience leads people to construct diverse scenarios in which the monitors are outwitted by those who would keep the regime in power, but at the same time their expanded skills are likely to facilitate an appreciation that the regime, faced with monitoring from abroad, will have to be more ingenious in its resort to fraud than was the case in earlier elections. In addition, more than a few voters may be led to attach greater importance and legitimacy to their election upon learning that groups abroad view the occasion as worthy of monitoring. And some may even become more hopeful for their future as they ponder the meaning of the international community's involvement in their domestic politics and conclude that the world cares about their country and the accessibility of its political institutions.

The presence of outsiders may even contribute to a lessening of cynicism and alienation within the electorate. It has been noted that in many parts of the developing world people have no confidence in their political institutions and thus are merely inhabitants rather than citizens of their countries.[10] Their experience tells them that the state is not to be trusted, that the courts are rigged, that officials are more responsive to bribes than mandates, and that the likelihood of meaningful political reform is thus virtually nil. But such deep and underlying attitudes may begin to shift when the alienated learn that groups abroad are ready to intrude in their politics and check on the degree to which their regime engages in corrupt practices at election time. Several generations may be needed for civil societies to evolve, but the transition from being inhabitants to being citizens of a country may well begin with elections that acquire legitimacy through external validation.

Viewed in the context of expanded skills and the prospects for fairer elections, it is hardly surprising that strangers from abroad wearing badges certifying their international observer status tend to be warmly greeted by voters as they perform their monitoring tasks.[11] And the more prestigious the sponsorships and leaders of their delegations, the more are voters pleased about their presence, seeing the delegations less as an intrusion upon their country's sovereignty and more as a mechanism for improving the chances of an honest campaign, an even-handed counting of the ballots, and an accurate reporting of the results. In effect, therefore, the combination of enlarged skills on the part of voters and the presence of international observers has served to strengthen the political will of electorates.

The implications of transformations of the macro–micro parameter

---

[10] For a useful discussion of the differences between inhabitants and citizens, see Tina Rosenberg, "Beyond Elections," *Foreign Policy*, vol. 84 (Fall 1991), pp. 78–9.

[11] The warm welcome often extended by voters is not, of course, always matched by the officials and military personnel who fear being voted out of power. Yet, while case histories report vivid instances of international observers being hassled at election stations, they are even more fulsome in their accounts of the friendly responses of those standing in line to cast their ballot.

263

are equally numerous. The pervasive authority crises have heightened the salience of citizenries as a source of legitimacy, strengthened the demands of opposition groups for opportunities to demonstrate their support through the ballot box, and intensified the sensitivities of those possessing formal authority to the need for a periodic renewal of their legitimacy. Thus even in Latin America, where authoritarian traditions have deep historic roots, once quiescent electorates are experiencing a magnified readiness to achieve a meaningful voice in the affairs of their polities and to insist that fair and open procedures be employed to guarantee the expression of their preferences.[12] Stated differently, the transformation of the macro–micro parameter has created a receptive political climate for international monitoring teams seeking to assist transitional societies revise and solidify their electoral institutions.

The evolution of collective election monitoring

Using the turbulence model, it is not difficult to transform an erratic path of norm-building events into a historical logic that accounts for the legitimacy which now attaches to external interventions in domestic elections. As the bifurcation of world politics gathered momentum and multiplied the number of actors concerned about the rights of publics to what has felicitously been called their "democratic entitlement,"[13] so did the norm justifying external intervention become broadly multilateral in scope and high-minded in purpose. In earlier decades and centuries election monitoring was generally limited to decolonization, hegemonic supervision, or the maintenance of international peace, concerns which did not focus on the domestic rights of publics and thus did not require the participation of teams of observers who fanned out across the political landscape. It was not until recent years that an erratic norm-building process began to introduce wide cracks in the armor of national sovereignty. As recently as 1989, for example, when the UN broke its unblemished "hands-off" record by sending an election team to Nicaragua, it deferred to the sovereignty concept and justified the action as protecting the international peace of the *region* in response to the Sandinista request and the initiative of all the Central American presidents. Only with the Haitian ONUVEH mission of October 1990,

---

[12] Abraham F. Lowenthal, "Latin America: Ready for Partnership?" *Foreign Affairs*, vol. 72, no. 1 (1992–3), p. 76.

[13] Franck, "The Emerging Right to Democratic Governance."

did the UN undertake a precedent-setting involvement in a situation without a clear threat to the maintenance of international peace.[14]

Just as the immediate past has witnessed a broadening of the scope of external involvement to include acceptance of outside monitors in the internal electoral procedures of individual states, so has the interventionary rhetoric changed. Justification for "collective involvement" has been expanded to include peace-keeping or peace-making – not only between nations but within nations as well (e.g., in El Salvador, Angola, and Cambodia). Increasingly such justification has come to be based on global norms and notions of the defense of human rights and the democratic entitlement.

Thus it is under the rubric of fundamental human rights – to freedom of expression and association, and to the right to freely elect one's government – explicitly enunciated in the several international instruments, that international organizations base their "moral imperative"[15] for insertion into the electoral process of sovereign states. Article 21, paragraph 3 of the Universal Declaration of Human Rights, for example, specifically calls for the basic human right of representative government: "The will of the people shall be the basis of the authority of government; this will shall be expressed in periodic and genuine elections which shall be by universal and equal suffrage and shall be held by secret vote or by equivalent free voting procedures."

Nor are international organizations alone in being moved by the moral imperative. A number of nongovernmental organizations (NGOs) such as the Council of Freely Elected Heads of Government, the National Democratic and Republican Institutes, the International Human Rights Law Group, the Catholic Church, and many others have increasingly served in key roles not only as election monitors, but as promoters and guarantors of democracy and the civic institutions and support structure upon which it depends. So extensive has this NGO practice become that oft-times the election scene can seem overrun by observer teams.

To stress the momentum that seems likely to transform international election monitoring into an established global procedure is not to say that the norm-building process is uncontested. Not only are those who

---

[14] *Ibid.*, pp. 72–3.

[15] This terminology was employed by Mary McGrory in the *Washington Post* in describing Jimmy Carter's electoral monitoring initiatives and is quoted by Canadian Senator B.A. Graham in his *The Seeds of Freedom: Personal Reflections on the Dawning of Democracy* (Clementsport, Nova Scotia: The Canadian Peacekeeping Press, 1996).

subscribe to the *real politik* perspective dubious about the solidity of the norm (on the grounds that the more powerful states have compelled less powerful ones to acquiesce in the presence of foreign election observers), but there also continue to be some states – from Mexico and Cuba in the Western Hemisphere to China and Myanmar in the Eastern – that adamantly cloak themselves in the sovereignty shield when it comes to the issue of elections and observers. Such countries have consistently voted against international election monitoring and the dictates of electoral "rights" in various types of international fora.

To repeat, however, the central tendency clearly favors collective intervention in the domestic affairs of countries when democratic and humanitarian values are under assault. The predominance of the new interventionary norms may not always lead to humanitarian values prevailing over nationalistic ones – as indicated by the failure of several externally observed elections – but the evolution of the norms, halting and circuitous as it may be, seems bound to continue as the complex bifurcation of world affairs becomes ever more ingrained.

A multiplicity of players

As the interventionary norms have solidified, so have the procedures for conducting monitored elections become increasingly institutionalized. Successful monitoring has now come to involve a multiplicity of actors who play a variety of key roles in the processes whereby election procedures are prepared in advanced, implemented on election day, and followed up in subsequent months.[16] One inquiry identifies sixteen types of collective actors – the United Nations, regional international organizations, the United States, other interested governments, non-governmental organizations (NGOs), international personalities, external observer teams, internal observer teams, voters, host governments, military elites, opposition factions, election bureaucracies, social scientists, computer specialists, and the media – and assesses how the dynamics inherent in each of the three parameters are likely to condition their attitudes, impose constraints on their freedom of action, and provide opportunities for them to affect the electoral process.[17] An

[16] See, for example, Larry Garber, *Guidelines for International Election Observing* (Washington, DC: International Human Rights Law Group, 1984).

[17] James N. Rosenau and W. Michael Fagen, "Domestic Elections as International Events," in Carl Kaysen, Robert A. Pastor, and Laura W. Reed (eds.), *Collective Responses to Regional Problems: The Case of Latin America and the Caribbean* (Cambridge, MA: American Academy of Arts and Sciences, 1994), pp. 29–68, 165–74.

insight into both the competition and cooperation – as well as the complexity and magnitude – inherent in these diverse efforts is discernible in the role played by NGOs and the external observer teams.

As wearers of badges that identify them as bearers of the authority of the international community, members of the external observer teams may not see themselves as momentarily endowed with a unique form of legitimacy, and they may never have occasion to flash their badges on behalf of the larger community's interest in free and fair elections, but that is exactly the circumstance in which they conduct their responsibilities. More often than not the performance of these tasks generated by the bifurcation of world politics and the global spread of democratic norms does not involve the exercise of this transient and ambiguous authority as the team members go about the routine work of observing voting booths, interviewing party poll watchers and election officials at their stations, hearing and coping with complaints, and witnessing the counting of ballots; but in virtually every monitored election since 1989 some team members became enmeshed in delicate situations in which they were confronted by armed or unarmed officials and/or party functionaries who sought to divert, inhibit, or otherwise prevent them from performing their duties. In some instances the flashing of their badges resulted in the desired resolution of a confrontation, but occasionally they had to bow to the potential threats, walk away, and subsequently report the harassment to those who compiled the full record of the team's endeavors.

In short, while international personalities such as former US president Jimmy Carter and other Latin American presidents play crucial roles as spokespersons for the external observer teams and legitimators of their findings, they are by no means the only individuals whose work can have significant consequences. The other members of the teams, drawn from a wide range of professions in diverse parts of the world,[18] perform the mundane and yet crucial work of infusing sufficient substance into the monitoring process as to make it politically meaningful. They receive no pay for their efforts, but they receive ample remuneration in the form of satisfaction that they have contributed to the advance of cherished values. They are not the unsung heroes of the process – that honor goes to the voters – but their emergent role and the badge that

---

[18] In order to enhance the legitimacy of the monitoring teams, those who form them try to select members from a broad sample of people from as many countries as possible. The National Democratic Institute's team sent to the 1993 Paraguayan elections, for example, consisted of some thirty-one members from some fifteen countries.

attaches to it has become a symbol of the changing balance between national sovereignty and international responsibilities.

The significance of this role can be discerned in the growing number of persons and teams sent to observe critical elections. As the participation of external observers in elections all over the world has become commonplace, so has the need to send teams large enough to visit a significant number of polling sites on election day. Only with large delegations that can be deployed systematically around a country can the observers check against fraudulent practices and be in a position to publicize the cumulative finding that the election was conducted freely and fairly. Thus it is hardly surprising that in the 1990 Nicaraguan election, 2,578 accredited observers from 278 organizations were present on election day, with 435 observers fielded by the Organization of American States visiting 3,064 voting sites (some 70 percent of the total) and 237 UN monitors visiting 2,155 sites.[19] Even more indicative, the 1993 election in Cambodia was said to involve more than 20,000 UN personnel.[20]

Consistent with the shifting norms induced by the bifurcation of the global system is the fact that the recent surge in externally monitored elections has been accompanied by a shift from passive to active modes of observation. Traditionally the election teams, lacking any legal authority to intervene and correct observed imperfections, played a limited role of passive onlooking. But with the surge in monitored elections have also come new activities, ranging from active questioning of officials to denouncing and rejecting the electoral procedures as so rooted in fraud as to distort the outcome. "Notwithstanding their circumscribed juridical role, international observers sometimes become mediators between ruling and opposition parties or between election authorities and domestic monitoring groups."[21] Viewed from a long-term perspective, moreover, the impact of external monitoring teams can hardly be understated: "The international observers [can help] expand the boundaries of civility in a country filled with mistrust."[22]

---

[19] In addition, some 1,500 members of the international press corps were on the scene. Cf. Robert A. Pastor, "Nicaragua's Choice: The Making of a Free Election," *Journal of Democracy*, vol. 1 (Summer 1990), pp. 18, 21.

[20] Larry Garber, "A New Era of Peacemaking: United Nations and Election Monitoring," unpublished paper, National Democratic Institute for International Affairs, Washington, DC (no date), p. 16.

[21] Larry Garber and Eric Bjornlund, "Election Monitoring in Africa," a report of the National Democratic Institute for International Affairs, Washington, DC (September 1992), p. 9.   [22] Pastor, "Nicaragua's Choice," p. 19.

Conclusion

Externally monitored elections, of course, offer no guarantee that democratic institutions will become so well entrenched as to be impervious to the many challenges that lie ahead in a fragmegrated era. The holding of elections is only one of a complex set of delicate premises and processes that sustain democratic governance. It is a necessary but not a sufficient foundation for the development and maintenance of any democracy. But as such, as a necessary cause, it does appear to be ever more prevalent on the global scene. And internationally monitored elections add further to the tendencies favoring the holding of free and fair elections because, in the words of one astute observer, they serve as "an assault on discouragement."[23] That is, they can have consequences that extend well beyond election day. Among other things for example, the training of internal monitoring teams "not only improves the quality of a particular election, but also creates a cadre of citizens committed to supporting nascent democratic institutions."[24]

It might be argued that these encouraging prospects are diminished by the fact that the conduct of an election is so costly for both the electing society and the actors abroad who monitor it that the will to sustain such processes will eventually attenuate. While this is surely an era of severe financial constraints, such an argument suffers from the misconception that holding elections is regarded as a luxury that can be afforded only when spare resources are available. All the evidence indicates to the contrary. One may be hard put to specify where the money for monitored elections will come from in the future, but all the relevant actors and motives make it seem highly probable that somehow the resources will be found when tensions rise in developing societies over whom they want to lead them in the future. Put differently, officials and publics in the international community are likely to appreciate that the expenditures incurred promoting elections and democracy is money better spent than the funds required in reconstructing peace when societies collapse into prolonged violence.[25]

Nor is this to imply that externally monitored elections have (or are

---

[23] Graham, *The Seeds of Freedom.*

[24] Garber and Bjornlund, "Election Monitoring in Africa," p. 13.

[25] It is noteworthy, for example, that the Japanese foreign ministry announced a plan of election support assistance "to provide grants of about 50 million yen to several nations annually, supplying ballot boxes, election campaign vehicles and computers." *Daily Yomiuri*, September 5, 1994, p. 1.

likely to) become routine and therefore easily undertaken. Quite to the contrary, all the literature suggests that despite the cumulation and codification of considerable experience in such matters, elections do not automatically get monitored. They entail a meticulous attention to myriad details, to coordination tasks that depend on exact timing, and to the training of large numbers of volunteers. Just because decent values are served through external election monitoring, this does not mean that such values will be served simply by having observers present on election day. Rather, in order to render meaningful judgments and report them to the international community, the monitoring teams have to engage in "a sustained observation effort that considers the quality of the election laws, voter registration, the election campaign, the balloting and counting processes, and the degree to which the results are respected."[26] Successful elections do not simply happen; they require work, dedication, cumulated wisdom, and political will, attributes that, happily, appear to be abundantly available.

But does external monitoring constitute a mechanism of governance along the Frontier? Most certainly. Whatever hesitations the host countries may have about the presence of outsiders who judge the fairness and propriety of their election procedures, and irrespective of their attempts to circumvent the monitors and load the electoral outcome, now they yield both to the pressure for external monitoring and to the judgments the outsiders make during and after election day. Elections have been postponed because of irregularities in voter lists detected by the external monitors, "dirty tricks" uncovered during the balloting have been terminated at the insistence of monitors, and the verdict of outsiders that the final tallies were fraudulent have resulted in the holding of new elections. To be sure, a few countries still adamantly refuse admission to outside monitors or do not allow them to be present on a scale sufficient to allow for legitimation of the electoral outcome, but the monitoring process has become so fully institutionalized that normally the host countries overcome their reluctance as they begin to recognize the problems they cause for themselves by refusing to acquiesce in the monitoring process. Furthermore, while the monitoring process may not be free of friction and competition among the numerous teams, the more procedures have been institutionalized, the greater has been the collaboration among the teams.

---

[26] Jennifer McCoy, Larry Garber, and Robert A. Pastor, "Pollwatching and Peacemaking," *Journal of Democracy*, vol. 2 (Fall 1991), p. 107.

Put differently, the advent of established procedures for the external monitoring of elections demonstrates the large extent to which control mechanisms derive their effectiveness from information and reputation even if their actions are not backed up by constitutional authority. It might even be said that governance in an ever more complex and interdependent world depends less on the issuance of authoritative directives and more on the release of reliable information and the legitimacy inherent in its detail.

This conclusion is further reinforced by evidence that a global momentum in the direction of monitored elections has been building for several years. The literature is full of examples of monitoring practices developed in one election and then tried and perfected in subsequent elections.[27] The downfall of Marcos in the Philippines, the peaceful transfer of power in Nicaragua, the tumultuous transfer in Panama, and the circuitous transfer in Haiti were defining events for each of these countries, but they were also part of a cumulative process whereby citizens, NGOs, publics, and officials everywhere have acquired the value orientations, the technical capacities, and the political will to contribute their share to future elections in the developing world.

During periods of turbulence, in short, the people and collectivities of the world are capable of innovative and rapid learning. Shaken out of their traditional modes by profound parametric transformations, they appear increasingly ready to evolve new patterns and institutions that are expressive of a new balance between the interests of the international community and those of sovereign states.

---

[27] It is noteworthy in this regard that the International Human Rights Law Group, having observed some twenty-five elections since 1983, has developed guidelines widely used by other actors.

Part IV
Actors

14 Individuals

What I have lost is my home – that quality of life, that degree of security, that easy camaraderie that cut across religious lines. That loss is irreparable.

Vibhuti Patel[1]

The sheer quantity of learning taking place in the world is already many times greater than in the past.

Seymour Papert[2]

Even if the government wanted to control us, we are stronger than they are right now, and our guns are normally much better than the ones carried by the Public Security Bureau

unnamed women in Western province of China[3]

We have to work 12 hours a day. Why should we give any of our money to the Government? They'll only steal it.

Tannis Patakis, grocery store owner in Athens[4]

The worldwide pervasiveness of turbulent conditions has extended both the number and types of actors who play key roles on the global stage. The skill revolution has heightened the importance of individuals as citizens, authority crises have altered the competence of states, and the bifurcation of global structures has led to a proliferation of non-

---

[1] "India's Days of Rage," *New York Times*, February 27, 1993, p. 19.

[2] *The Children's Machine: Rethinking School in the Age of the Computer* (New York: Basic Books, 1993), p. vii.

[3] Quoted in Patrick E. Tyler, "In Rural China 'Gold Lords' Challenge the State," *International Herald Tribune*, July 20, 1995, p.2.

[4] Quoted in Marlise Simons, "Enforcing One of Life's Certainties Has Problems," *New York Times*, May 26, 1995, p. A4.

governmental organizations. Taken together, these transformations have made ever more consequential the way in which people in all walks of life conduct themselves. Accordingly, this and the next six chapters focus on the diverse actors who have come to exert a commanding presence on the global stage.[5]

Citizenship

Narrowly conceived, citizenship is rooted in territoriality. It refers to individuals who belong to a polity, local or national, that has specified geographic boundaries, the authority to enforce its policies within its borders and to claim the loyalty and compliance of its citizens. In addition, polities evolve expectations, some formal and some informal, that their citizens will take on responsibilities which, through civic action, will contribute to the polity's well-being. Thus people are citizens of a state, a province, or a city, and in exchange for abiding by its laws they receive its protection against physical, social, and economic harm.

The concept of citizenship has been deeply embedded in the territorial system of states that has organized world affairs for several hundred years. Idealists often refer to themselves as "citizens of the world," but this designation is also a reflection of the territorial foundations of citizenship in the sense that it gives voice to an aspiration for a global polity to replace those of states. That a territorial perspective underlies the conventional notion of citizenship is further evident in the fact that people do not regard themselves as citizens of an ethnic minority, a multinational corporation, a political party, a social movement, or any other type of large-scale organization that does not derive its existence from the politicization of a specified geographic space. Rather, to designate the voluntary nature of involvement in such nonterritorial groups a more encompassing concept, that of membership, is used, even though their members also have obligations and are expected to shoulder responsibilities that will contribute to the group's well-being.

Spurred by the politics of the Frontier, recent years have witnessed individuals in all parts of the world loosening (or tightening) their notions of civic responsibility to extend beyond (or contract within) the

---

[5] For an analysis which posits the advent of diverse actors as a long-term process, see Yale H. Ferguson and Richard W. Mansbach, "Multiple Actors and the Evolution of International Society," paper presented at the Annual Meeting of the American Political Science Association, Chicago (September 1992).

borders of polities. Accordingly, the ensuing discussion enlarges the narrow concept of legally acquired citizenship to include that of voluntary membership. The terms are used interchangeably to refer to political activities undertaken by individuals in relation to any large-scale organization, territorial or not, with which they identify.

Through decades and centuries the narrow, territorial foundations of citizenship have served well the psychic need of individuals to identify with a community of like-minded others, a sense of belonging to a larger political entity that can provide the protection and security necessary to the conduct of daily routines. This emotional tie is poignantly evident in the first epigraph above, which was expressed by a woman who witnessed her beloved city, Bombay, collapse into vicious religious strife. In the industrial era such emotional ties have found expression in patriotism and loyalties that have enabled states to raise revenue, resolve group conflicts, negotiate treaties, mobilize armies, and otherwise enhance welfare through the maintenance of sovereign authority. Indeed, the narrow, polity-bound conception of citizenship reached a zenith of intensity during and after World War II, when first a wartime enemy and then a Cold War enemy were seen to threaten the very existence of states and the communities they served. By 1945 and during the early years of the Cold War rivalry between the United States and the Soviet Union, people everywhere experienced impassioned levels of national patriotism that infused their citizenship with fervent emotional meanings and focused their loyalties on a narrow set of polity-enhancing values. Relatively speaking, during the 1940s and 1950s national leaders had little difficulty mobilizing their citizenries on behalf of the goals of their states. Whether they headed superpowers or developing countries, leaders could exhort their citizens to make the sacrifices needed to maintain their policies.

The transformation of citizenship

Starting at various points in the postwar years, however, the foundations were laid for a broadening of the concept of citizenship. The sources of this transformation were multiple, some leading to a slow expansion of the civic skills of individuals, others more rapidly altering their attitudes toward states and their role in an ever more interdependent and complex world, and still others fostering either a "devaluation of citizenship" as a result of "the increasing importance of international human rights codes, with its promise of universal 'personhood,'" or an erosion of citizenship as a consequence of huge cross-border migrations undermining "the distinction between 'citizen' and 'alien.'"[6]

The second epigraph above suggests that education has been a prime stimulus to the enhancement of people's skills, but there are many other sources and rank ordering their importance is neither easy nor necessary.[7] It suffices to stress that all of them interactively contributed to the onset of the skill revolution that, by the 1990s, resulted in individuals around the world being increasingly able to grasp the global nature of their circumstances and to collectively demand they be heard and heeded by their leaders. Indeed, as the last two epigraphs above incisively indicate, today's news is filled with accounts of citizens not only engaging in collective demands on their leaderships, but in so doing increasingly appearing, for better or worse, to be ready to defy their leaders.

It is important to amplify the above phrase "for better or worse." In highlighting the large degree to which the skill revolution has enlarged the role of citizenries, there is no implication that the world is therefore better off or that governance is thereby facilitated. To the extent the skill revolution has led to the evolution of globally shared values, to people having become less self-centered and more civic-minded, and thus to more self-conscious and responsible behavior on the part of citizens, then to that extent it can be said that their new roles improve the prospects for a saner, more easily governed world. But the skill revolution does not necessarily conduce to "better" citizenship. As will be seen, the enlarged skills can also lead in "worse" directions – to more self-interested and thus more selfish conduct in which the welfare of larger systems is ignored while that of close-at-hand subsystems is accorded the highest priority. In short, to contend that recent years have witnessed citizens becoming more analytic, active, committed, and wiser is only to say that they are better able to serve their values, whatever these might be.

---

[6] David Jacobson, *Rights Across Borders: Immigration and the Decline of Citizenship* (Baltimore: Johns Hopkins University Press, 1996), p. 9. For a useful discussion of what is regarded as "an explosion of interest in the concept of citizenship," see Will Kymlicka and Wayner Norman, "Return of the Citizen: A Survey of Recent Work in Citizenship Theory," in Ronald Beiner (ed.), *Theorizing Citizenship* (New York: State University of New York Press, 1995), pp. 283–322 (the quote is from p. 283).

[7] For a full discussion of the many sources of the skill revolution, see James N. Rosenau, *Turbulence in World Politics: A Theory of Change and Continuity* (Princeton: Princeton University Press, 1990), chap. 13.

Challenging the skeptics

But the impact of the skill revolution is not self-evident. To argue that individuals at the micro level are central to the course of events at the macro level of global politics is to evoke doubt and disbelief on the part of many analysts. They reject the proposition on the grounds that it does not really matter what individuals do at the micro level, that macro-level processes can be described, analyzed, and predicted without recourse to the conduct of citizens, that in world affairs the latter are, in effect, mere servants of the former. In effect, some contend, accounting for the behavior of citizens only adds unnecessary complexity to our mental pictures of governance along the Frontier. The attribution of causal power to individuals, such reasoning concludes, serves our moral consciences, but that is a far cry from servicing the requirements of cogent empirical inquiry.

The fact that this rejection of the micro-level proposition ignores the extensive case that can be advanced for treating citizens as key variables in world politics[8] suggests either that the case is flawed or that it has not been adequately made. Lest the latter is true, the initial task here is to restate briefly the core premises underlying the view that micro–macro interactions do matter and then to undertake further elaboration by identifying four kinds of citizenship that can introduce variability into the processes whereby micro dynamics contribute to macro outcomes on the world stage.

Put differently, it is time to turn the table on the skeptics, give them pause, make them so uncomfortable about their dismissal of the micro level that they are impelled to restate and defend more fully their strict macro perspectives. If they are resistant to probing the micro level empirically, at least they can clarify their theoretical bases for ignoring it. The case for taking individual behavior seriously may be flawed, but the flaws have not been persuasively advanced. It is not enough simply to assert that systemic processes at the macro level are sufficient to explain macro outcomes.

Stripped to its essentials, the case for viewing individuals as crucial to world affairs rests on three equally important premises. One is that citizens have become more analytically and emotionally skillful and a

---

[8] For an elaboration of the argument that citizens are key variables in world politics, see James N. Rosenau, "Citizenship in a Changing Global Order," in J.N. Rosenau and E.O. Czempiel (eds.) *Governance without Government: Order and Change in World Politics* (Cambridge: Cambridge University Press, 1992), pp. 272–94.

second is that this skill revolution at the micro level matters, that through perceptual and aggregative processes citizens are shaping macro outcomes more extensively than they have in the past.[9] The third is the presumption that the macro system of world politics has entered a period of prolonged turbulence that is especially vulnerable to micro inputs.

Perhaps through no fault of their own, skeptics have misconstrued these premises in several significant ways: they have equated skills with information; they have thought in terms of individuals acting alone rather than collectively; and they have underestimated the extent of the authority crises that are part and parcel of the transformations presently sustaining global turbulence. Accordingly, skeptics find it easy to dismiss the relevance of micro actors by highlighting the great gaps in peoples' information about world affairs (noting the proportion of poll respondents who are unable to identify the capital of Pakistan always seems a winning blow), and/or by stressing that the single person has neither adequate access to or influence in the political process to impact significantly upon it, and/or by noting the historical pattern wherein governmental authority has always been subjected to challenge. Accurate as these observations may be, however, they have little to do with the underlying argument.

Glaring information gaps do not necessarily prevent the acquisition of greater civic competence. To become more skillful is to be able to construct more elaborate scenarios, to discern more causal relationships, and to be readier to accept complexity – irrespective of the amount of information one may possess. What counts is not the capital of a country, but the capacity to trace events into and out of the capital regardless of its identity. One does not need to know the capital of Pakistan – indeed, one can be misinformed about its name and location – in order to grasp ominous stirrings in distant places and appreciate how these can trace a path to one's doorstep and pocketbook. To be sure, it may be the case that the more information people have, the more are they able to frame goals, sift alternatives, and make decisions; but analytic and emotional skills also derive from a host of sources unrelated to levels of information. Political wisdom can be acquired through families, work situations, and community crises – to mention only its more conspicuous sources. It is not difficult, therefore, to make a strong case for viewing "the judgment of the general public . . . under some conditions . . . [as] equal or superior in quality to the judgment of experts and

[9] Rosenau, *Turbulence in World Politics*, chap. 7.

elites who possess far more information, education, and ability to articulate their views."[10] To fall back on the skimpy-level-of-information reason for rejecting the relevance of micro phenomena in world politics is thus to avoid confronting the challenge. Compared to the impressive indicators of effective citizen activities that mark the recent history of most countries of the world, the alleged information barrier comes close to being a rationalization for elitist perspectives.

Similarly, reliance on the isolation of individuals in an ever more complex world is profoundly misleading as a basis for dismissing the micro level. The individual does appear to be increasingly removed from the centers of societal power, and his or her solitary actions such as voting may well not make much of a difference; but this isolation is besides the point. What counts are the processes whereby citizens join together to aggregate their preferences and actions through collective behavior. The presumption of increasing micro relevance rests squarely on the understanding that people, being better able to assess where, when, and how collective action can be effective, are increasingly ready to pool their resources on behalf of shared goals. The evidence for this greater readiness is considerable. In town squares throughout the world citizens have recently converged to concert their energies on behalf of one or another grievance.[11] Some analysts have questioned whether the spate of collective actions is a temporary phenomenon and soon to be followed by citizens lapsing back into an earlier passivity;[12] but the persistence of the authority crises should give skeptics pause and lead to an acknowledgment that this pattern may have become a permanent feature of a world rendered turbulent by the transformation of three of its prime parameters.[13]

It follows that the context in which citizenship is claimed and practiced is especially intrusive in the present era. With people, economies, cultures, and polities becoming ever more interdependent, the larger forces playing upon citizens everywhere are sometimes liberating and sometimes constricting; but at all times they are relentless, complex, and substantial, often demanding adaptive responses even as they also

---

[10] Daniel Yankelovich, "You Can Argue with Einstein," *The Responsive Community*, vol. 1 (Winter 1990–1), p. 78.

[11] The processes of convergence are subjected to further analysis in chapter 15 below.

[12] This query is fully explored in Sidney Tarrow, "The Globalization of Conflict: Isn't This Where We Came In?" paper presented at the Annual Meeting of the American Political Science Association, Washington, DC: (August 1991).

[13] Sidney Tarrow, *Power in Movement: Social Movements, Collective Action and Politics* (Cambridge: Cambridge University Press, 1994), pp. 195–8.

invite habitual acquiescence. The resulting crises of authority and legitimacy that pervade every region and continent pose difficult and unfamiliar challenges for modern citizens and their political identities. The
world impinges too closely for them to rely on the widely used strategy
which readily justifies "the rational ignorance of the typical citizen."[14]
Today their identity, their ethics, and their conduct are in question as the
dynamics of change alter the boundaries, norms, and goals through
which they relate to their fellow citizens.[15] In many countries more than
a few individuals appear to have lost their way politically, as if they are
practicing what might be called citizenship without moorings.[16]

It also follows that as the skill revolution enables citizens to have a
greater impact on the course of events, so does it accord them greater
responsibility for what happens – for the weakening of communal ties,
the persistence of political stalemate, the onset of violence, and the
many other instabilities at work in a turbulent world. Whether they are
able to shoulder the connections between their micro actions and macro
outcomes is, of course, another matter. It is one thing to be ever more
skillful in identifying and acting on behalf of one's self-interests, but it
is quite another to look at the world from the perspective of one or more
whole systems.

To appreciate what benefits or damages the collective welfare, and
then to act in such as way as to achieve a reasonable balance between per-

---

[14] The premises of this strategy are set forth in Mancur Olson, "Is Britain the Wave of the
Future? How Ideas Affect Societies," in M. Mann (ed.), *The Rise and Decline of the Nation
State*. (Cambridge, MA: Basil Blackwell, 1990), pp. 99–101. For a critique of this strategy, see Paul C. Stern, "Why Do People Sacrifice for Their Nations?" *Political Psychology*,
vol. 16 (1995), pp. 217–35.

[15] For discussions of how the dynamics of change may impact on individuals, see William
Alonzo, "Citizenship, Nationality and Other Identities," *Journal of International Affairs*,
vol. 48 (Winter 1995), pp. 585–99, and Carl May and Andrew Cooper, "Personal Identity
and Social Change: Some Theoretical Considerations," *Acta Sociologica*, vol. 38 (1995),
pp. 75–85.

[16] A cogent account of the many consequences that may follow when citizens are
deprived of their political moorings can be found in Bruce Weber, "Many in the Former
Soviet Lands Say They Feel Even More Insecure Now," *New York Times*, April 23, 1992,
p. A3. It is noteworthy, moreover, that the sense of disarray is global in scope, that "the
first international study of major depression reveals a steady rise in the disorder worldwide," so much so that "in some countries the likelihood that people born after 1965
will suffer a major depression – not just sadness, but a paralyzing listlessness, dejection
and self-depreciation, as well as an overwhelming sense of hopelessness – at some
point in life is more than three times greater than for their grandparents' generation."
Daniel Goleman, "A Rising Cost of Modernity: Depression," *New York Times*, December
8, 1992, p. 13.

sonal and public interests, is more an emotional than an analytic skill, more an application of values than a use of intellectual powers,[17] with the result that people develop an orientation in which they judge themselves in relation to the more encompassing systems they view as important. These "self–environment orientations" are pervasive. People everywhere, in all countries, are conceived to make such judgments in one way or another. They cannot act or remain passive without somehow seeing themselves in relation to their surroundings. Such judgments tend to be constant as long as continuity and stability mark the course of events, but they are subject to transformation in a period of turbulence. While people in some cultures may be more inclined toward themselves and in others predisposed to favor their whole systems, at some point in all cultures the dynamics of change can engender shifts in the way individuals evaluate their relative worth. Indeed, self–environment orientations can be a significant indicator of the processes of globalization: the more people in diverse countries converge around similar orientations, the more are core values spreading on a global scale.[18]

In short, by self–environment orientation is meant the appraisal people make of the relative worth of themselves and their most relevant macro collectivities. With globalizing and localizing dynamics undermining loyalties, shifting boundaries, and proliferating organizations, a variety of collectivities, e.g., societies, states, social movements, ethnic minorities, and transnational organizations, are candidates for greatest relevance. For purposes of simplicity, such entities are here lumped under the general heading of "most salient macro collectivity", a term which allows for the possibility that a major redistribution of self–environment orientations may occur when the course of events leads to the formation of new collectivities or the collapse of old ones.[19]

---

[17] The distinction between emotional and analytic skills is cogently presented in Daniel Goleman, *Emotional Intelligence* (New York: Bantam Books, 1995).

[18] The notion of "self–environment orientations" was initially formulated with respect to the orientations of states rather than individuals: see James N. Rosenau, *The Adaptation of National Societies: A Theory of Political Behavior and Its Transformation* (New York: McCaleb-Seiler, 1970). For another, more recent formulation organized around the links between self and society, see John P. Hewitt, *Dilemmas of the American Self* (Philadelphia: Temple University Press, 1989).

[19] For a discussion of some of the methodological difficulties involved in measuring self–environment orientations, see Harriette S. McCaul, Verlin B. Hinsz, and Keven D. McCaul, "Assessing Organizational Commitment: An Employee's Global Attitude Toward the Organization," *Journal of Applied Behavioral Science*, vol. 31 (March 1995), pp. 80–90.

Table 14.1. *Four types of citizenship*

	Priority attached to self	
	Low	High
Priority attached to most salient collectivity **Low**	APATHETIC or ALIENATED	SELF-CENTERED
High	ALTRUISTIC or IDEOLOGICAL	DEMOCRATIC

Alternative citizen roles

Several basic citizen roles can be derived by distinguishing among self–environment orientations in which individuals attach either high or low priority to themselves or their most salient collectivity. As can be seen in table 14.1, those who are inclined to treat their own needs as far more important than those of their collectivity practice what can be called *self-centered* citizenship. Persons who have the opposite tendency and place their collectivity's needs well ahead of their own practice either of two forms of citizenship: those who have an incremental approach to the collectivity's problems practice *altruistic* citizenship, whereas those who proceed from an inflexible image of what collectivity life ought to be practice *ideological* citizenship. People who are cynical about the responsiveness of macro politics to micro inputs or for other reasons attach little political significance either to their own or their collectivity's needs and are thus disinclined to enter the public arena, practice what can be termed *apathetic* or *alienated* citizenship. Finally, individuals who invest deeply in the realization of both their own and their collectivity's needs are likely to practice a *democratic* form of citizenship. This balanced form approaches the democratic ideal in the sense that citizens are not unmindful of their own interests even as they recognize the necessity of also accommodating to the processes and goals of the larger collectivities to which they attach salience.[20]

While self–environment orientations derive primarily from the way in which people assess the value of their interests relative to those of collectivities, they are also shaped by a crucial perception, namely, how individuals perceive the interactive processes that sustain micro–macro relationships. The causal strength of micro factors relative to macro dynamics is never self-evident. Whatever may be the objective bases of micro–macro interactions, the interpretation of them can vary widely, from the total cynic who believes individuals can exercise no influence over the course of events to the unmitigated optimist who sees macro institutions as keenly responsive to micro inputs. Cynics are thus likely to be attracted to forms of citizenship wherein minimal consequence is attached to actions at the micro level; they just cannot believe that anything they may do in the political arena matters, a belief that may well be so powerful as to offset the values they attach to their own or society's interests. Contrariwise, optimists are likely to be drawn to citizenship practices consistent with their view that societal institutions are malleable, that what they do counts. Strong convictions about political issues, in short, can be moderated by views of how the political process functions.

It follows that self–environment orientations can never be more than subjective appraisals developed through personal experience, society's socialization processes, and the class, economic, political, and other objective circumstances that prevail at any moment in time. In a rapidly changing and dynamic era the objective circumstances are likely to foster new self–environment orientations, shifting practices of citizenship, and altered political identities. As the analytic skills of citizens expand, for example, so does their capacity to identify their own interests, to evolve scenarios of how the course of events will culminate on their doorstep, or to otherwise cope with the welter of complexity churned by the parametric transformations. For some of those mired in apathetic and ideological inclinations, their new-found skills are likely, other things being equal, to wrench them out of their habitual orienta-

---

[20] It should be noted that all these self–environment orientations are ideal types. As is evident in table 14.1, the varying forms of citizenship represent extremes on continua. In fact, of course, people tend to combine their self and societal concerns and are thus located at various points along each continuum. It is only for analytic purposes that the focus here is on the ideal types formed by the extremes.

tions and render them more ready to engage in either self-interested or democratic forms of citizenship. In some cases, on the other hand, the expanded skills may foster a greater sense of futility over the ability of micro actors to shape macro outcomes and thus move some self-interested and democratic citizens away from politics and into passivity and apathy.

In a like manner the worldwide authority crises that mark the present era are likely to have micro consequences irrespective of the type of citizenship people practice. Other things being equal, for example, the more citizens get caught up in the volatility of such crises, the more are they likely to redefine their self–environment orientations, revise their political identities, and undertake new forms of behavior in the public arena. In effect, the shifting lines of authority along the Frontier leave them with little choice but to reconsider how they want to conduct themselves.

New conceptions of territoriality are still another consequence of global turbulence that can be traced in all the citizenship types. As stressed in chapter 7, with authority undergoing relocation "upward" toward transnational organizations, "sideward" to social movements, and "downward" toward subnational collectivities, the sense of who one is politically and the meanings of territory – of geographic space to which historical and cultural significance is attached – are no longer as compelling as they once were.[21]

In short, citizens of every orientation are subject to diminished claims on their loyalties and, other things being equal, are thus more ready to rethink the collectivities with which they identify and to redefine the balance between their own and society's interests.[22] But other things are rarely equal. Just as crises which lead to the relocation of authority can vary in their intensity, scope, and direction, so can the dynamics of the skill revolution be varyingly applied. Hence, in order to take note of the systematic underpinnings of such variabilities, we need to look more closely at how each of the citizenship types has been affected by the cascading changes brought on by global turbulence.

---

[21] For one example of how shifts in the meaning of territory have been altered, see Richard O'Brien, *Global Financial Integration: The End of Geography* (London: Chatham House, 1992).

[22] For a cogent discussion along this line, see Yale H. Ferguson and Richard W. Mansbach, "The Past as Prelude to the Future: Changing Loyalties in Global Politics," paper presented at the Annual Meeting of the International Studies Association, Acapulco (March 1993).

Self-centered citizenship

The distinguishing features of this manner of relating to the political arena are the high value attached to one's own interest and the low concern for the welfare of any larger collectivity. Most people are, properly, keenly attentive to their own needs and wants, ever ready to seek a minimum degree of comfort for themselves and their families. In this sense self-interests are a prime source of the power that propels political issues and sustains political processes. But many people are also preoccupied with the more encompassing systems to which they belong, partly because their own welfare is tied to the stability and progress of the larger system and partly because they also care about the values to which their collectivities are committed. For the most part, however, these larger concerns are essentially irrelevant to those who practice self-centered citizenship. Their focus on themselves is so extensive as to preclude appreciation of macro institutions.[23]

This is not to imply, however, that self-centered citizens are necessarily inclined to advance their interests by exploiting the larger system. Such individuals can certainly be found in every corner of the world. Whenever possible, they cheat on their taxes, avoid regulations, disregard efforts to conserve resources, and so on through a long list of actions that could make a contribution to the welfare of their communities. They are the free-riders of societies and, as such, their collective impact serves to exacerbate macro tendencies toward stalemate and fragmentation. If the larger society is unstable and incapable of addressing and resolving its major problems, self-centered citizens could not care less as long as the disarray does not undermine their livelihood. If their way of life is endangered by societal disarray, of course, their keen attention to their own goals will lead them into momentary concerns for the macro system and to actions designed to preserve the status quo through which they have benefited.

It follows that as economies founder and standards of living decline, and as societies become increasingly fragile and unable to retain an underlying value consensus or institutional coherence, so will more and more individuals be inclined to restructure their self–environment

---

[23] Self-centered citizenship is a recurring concern in several recent articles by Robert D. Putnam. See his "Bowling Alone: Declining Social Capital," *Journal of Democracy*, vol. 6 (January 1995), pp. 65–78, and "Tuning In, Tuning Out: The Strange Disappearance of Social Capital in America," *PS: Political Science and Politics*, vol. 28 (December 1995), pp. 664–83. For arguments against Putnam's thesis, see *The American Prospect*, no. 25 (March/April 1996), pp. 17–28.

orientations in the direction of self-centered citizenship. Indeed, the individual can be viewed as the ultimate subgroup, and it would not be difficult to amass evidence that this form of subgroupism has become increasingly rampant on a worldwide scale. Where students used to protest over issues of authority and democracy, for example, now they tend to engage in such actions for much more self-interested reasons such as career training and tuition fees.[24]

Nor are the tendencies toward self-centered citizenship confined to mass publics. Leaders in all walks of life are giving voice to subsystem values and neglecting to stress the virtues of whole-system cooperation and coherence. As emphasized in chapter 16, rare today are leaders who speak of the need to maintain balanced self–environment orientations or who articulate a vision which stresses that societies cannot move forward without compromises in which people give up some of their personal needs on behalf of larger aggregates. Put differently, gross leadership failures throughout the world have undermined socialization processes and contributed to the emergence of new generations lacking the values necessary for whole-system persistence and progress.

While global turbulence may well be swelling the ranks of self-centered citizens at an exponential rate throughout the world, it needs to be stressed that not all of them are free-riders. Some are self-centered, so to speak, by default. Due to the dynamics of turbulent change, they have no larger system for which they feel any attachment and to which they can devote their energies. They are not apathetic about the political arena, but either they are confused as to where they fit in it or they have been drawn into lines of work that transgress long-established boundaries. Instead of being free-riders, they are either lost riders whose political homes have been swept away by authority crises or jet-set riders whose political homes have been transformed by an ever more globalized economy and the expanding webs of an ever more intricate global interdependence. Indeed, with governments weakening and subnational groups becoming more demanding, and with the Frontier's boundaries thus being called into question or redrawn, it seems likely that more and more citizens will lose their bearings. They may be inclined to care about the well-being of a larger system, but they no

---

[24] Cf. Clyde Farnsworth, "For Youths, Fire That Drove Quebec Burns Low," *New York Times*, September 27, 1995, p. A4, and Julia Preston, "Mexico's New Rebel Students Just Want Careers," *New York Times*, October 3, 1995, p. A3.

longer know what that system is and thus are compelled, by default, to practice self-centered citizenship.

Similarly, although for entirely different reasons, jet-set riders have had to default to their own self-interests. In their case the larger national communities to which they have been attached are less and less salient the more they become ensconced in new, transnational roles that orient them to see the world as their bailiwick. The product of ever greater interdependence and the globalization of national economies, these roles require their occupants to focus on concerns that extend well beyond national boundaries and that obscure the values into which they were originally socialized. Since there are no reasons to anticipate a slowing down of the pace of globalization, the ranks of jet-set riders seem bound to become more numerous. Put in terms of self–environment orientations, the new global roles have not only loosened their occupants from the psychological constraints of territory, but to a large extent they have also liberated them from the responsibility of worrying about the welfare of political communities.[25]

Not all self-centered citizens, however, have been comfortable with their new roles in the global economy. For some the shedding of territorial commitments and responsibilities is worrisome. Consider, for example, the case of Americans who moved from long-time jobs in Detroit's automobile industry to comparable positions in Japanese firms producing Japanese cars in the United States. Consisting of designers, engineers, salespersons, public relations specialists, and manufacturing experts, these "Detroit expatriates" who committed their professional lives to the Japanese have apparently been increasingly confused by their citizenship as US–Japanese automotive competition intensifies. "Cast into a neutral space in terms of patriotism," they speak of "evenings when my wife and I look at each other and I think, `I wish I could be doing this for an American company.'"[26] Yet, despite their concern that their new positions may seem like a betrayal, most of the expatriates are eventually able to accept and rationalize the political implications of their new positions. Some regard themselves "as ground-floor participants in the borderless economy, their positions in the industry transcending such quaint notions as them-against-us."[27]

[25] Benjamin R. Barber, "Jihad vs. McWorld," *Atlantic Monthly*, March 1992, pp. 54–9.

[26] Gerald Hirshberg, former Buick design chief who is now Vice-President of Nissan Design International, quoted in Donald Woutat, "Detroit in Rearview Mirror," *Los Angeles Times*, March 11, 1992, p. 1.

[27] Woutat, "Detroit in Rearview Mirror," p. A7.

As one of them put it, "I could feel the shrinking of the globe in a very personal way. It's been overwhelmingly exhilarating."[28]

Whatever may be the extent to which self–environment orientations are turning in self-centered directions on a global scale, the result is a further weakening of governments and other institutional mechanisms for realizing collective goals and maintaining social order. Such is the central dynamic of micro–macro interactions in the present era. The macro arrangements work less and less well, thus turning micro actors inward, all of which further reduces the effectiveness of the macro arrangements. There is substantial evidence that this process is gathering momentum in the United States today.[29]

Altruistic citizenship

It will be recalled that this is one of two forms of self–environment orientations in which citizens treat the needs of their most salient collectivities as considerably more urgent and important than their own. It involves an incremental approach to the political arena, a focus on particular issues which come to be viewed as so important or threatening as to warrant putting personal concerns aside, or at least achieving a perceptual convergence in which personal satisfactions are equated with the goals and needs of the most salient collectivity. In the sense that such individuals come to focus so intensely upon larger problems that they ignore their own immediate interests, it is an altruistic form of citizenship. It is driven not by ideology in the sense of being a blueprint for society, but by a concern with one problem or issue at a time.

The quintessential expression of this form of citizenship is to found among those who participate in social movements. The feminists, the environmentalists, the anti-war activists – these are people for whom a single set of issues is all-encompassing. They tend to have enough personal resources, or to be so ready to place societal concerns over their own, that they have or make the time necessary to engage in a wide variety of activities on behalf of their issue-based goals. For some of them the issue-oriented incremental approach becomes so much a way of life that they turn to new issues if and when the old one is resolved. An example here is members of the peace movement who moved on to

---

[28] Hirshberg, quoted in Wovtat, "Detroit in Rearview Mirror," p. A7.

[29] Cf. James N. Rosenau, "Citizenship Without Moorings: Individual Responses to a Turbulent World," paper presented at the Annual Meeting of the American Sociological Association, Pittsburgh (August, 1992), and Richard Morin and Dan Belz, "Americans Losing Trust in Each Other and Institutions," *Washington Post*, January 28, 1996, p. A1.

environmental preoccupations when the end of the Cold War reversed the global arms race.[30]

To a large extent transnational rather than national or subnational concerns serve as the driving force of altruistic citizenship. All the issues that sustain modern social movements involve global problems and thus the movements become informal networks of like-minded citizens in different parts of the world who communicate and converge episodically as the issues that draw them together surge and wane on the global agenda. It follows that altruistic citizens, like some of their self-centered counterparts, tend not to be oriented toward specific societies. But unlike self-centered citizens, the altruistic types have no sense of loss with respect to their political homes. Rather, their home takes on a global cast as they develop allegiances to issue outcomes. And their convictions along this line, reinforced by movement members elsewhere in the world, lead them to believe that micro actions can have desirable collective outcomes, that governments can be moved if enough people share in their efforts to bring about change. Indeed, it is reasonable to presume that no other form of citizenship stimulates deeper beliefs in micro–macro interactive processes than does the altruistic form. The image of a movement member engaging in protest behavior that leads to them being physically removed by police exemplifies the depth of their perception that micro actions can have cumulative consequences.

It seems plausible that the transformative consequences of global turbulence have also greatly enlarged the ranks of altruistic citizens. With governments weakened and lines of authority obscured, social movements have flourished with the onset of turbulence.[31] People are attracted to them because the movements are, so to speak, picking up the slack brought on by the globalization of national economies and the bifurcation of world politics into multi-centric and state-centric worlds. Since interdependence issues cannot be addressed, much less managed, by governments alone, and since the informal structures of social movements are well suited to transgressing the boundaries that inhibit states from resolving these types of issues, individuals predisposed toward

---

[30] For an analysis of the psychological dynamics that underlie participation in social movements, see Ron Eyerman and Andrew Jamison, *Social Movements: A Cognitive Approach* (Cambridge: Polity Press, 1991).

[31] A cogent analysis of the global role of social movements can be found in R.B.J. Walker, *One World, Many Worlds: Struggles for a Just World Peace* (Boulder, CO: Lynne Rienner, 1988).

self–environment orientations that attach greater value to the environment than the self are likely to gravitate toward the transnational networks which social movements offer their members.

Ideological citizenship

Although doing so for very different reasons, there is a second type of person who attaches much greater importance to the needs of their most salient collectivities than to personal ones. Unlike the incremental approach of the altruistic citizen, the ideologue has a vision of the total society and is inflexible with respect to the basic principles on which the vision rests. Ideologues are more than ready to sacrifice their personal well-being on behalf of their larger blueprint. The image of an Iranian fundamentalist throwing himself into battle and seeking martyrdom on behalf of Islam captures well the extent to which the self–environment orientations of ideologues is skewed in favor of the environment.

Of all the citizenship types identified here, it is probably the ranks of the ideologues that have been most diminished by the onset of global turbulence. The ever greater complexity of societal life, the increasingly intractability of economic problems, the pervasiveness of authority crises and the unmistakable tendencies toward political stalemate – not to mention how the collapse of the Soviet Union revealed the falsities of communism – have all contributed to a flight from rigid ideological formulations and a worldwide readiness to cast self–environment orientations in a more pragmatic context. To be sure, some personality types still cling to the rigidities that sustain ideologues and all societies will thus always have their ideological wings. In the present era, however, it seems likely that these wings will be small even as they will doubtless continue to be vociferous.

And how have the disaffected ideologues restructured their self–environment orientations? As indicated by trends in the former Soviet Union, some have turned toward a balanced set of orientations and come to subscribe to democratic citizenship practices. But there is also considerable evidence that the transition to democratic practices has proven difficult, even impossible, for many in those lands that have thrown off the yoke of communist ideology. The heady first weeks and months of freedom have been followed by the realities of economies in shambles and the lures of ethnicity. Learning to accept the consequences of democracy – votes that produce undesired results, debates that seem interminable, competitive programs that seem confusing – is not easy under the best of circumstances and thus requires huge leaps of faith under horrendous conditions. And given the absence of an elite capable of articulating extensive experience in democratic procedures, it is hardly surprising that many in the former Soviet empire have moved quickly through democratic self–environment orientations and come to adhere either to apathetic or self-centered orientations.

Apathetic citizenship (passive and alienated)

Notwithstanding the incentives to active citizenship that the skill revolution and other dynamics of global turbulence have highlighted, there remain many people in all parts of the world who attach little importance to either their own or society's needs insofar as these can be served through action in the political arena. This self–environment orientation, however, derives from several contradictory sources, with the result that it is possible to differentiate between two basic types of apathetic citizenship, one that we shall call *passive citizenship* and another that can be labeled *alienated citizenship*. The former is, so to speak, the truly apathetic citizen who attributes no causal strength to collective action at the micro level and no readiness on the part of macro institutions to attend to his or her needs. Such people are, thus, oblivious to the political arena. They neither care about nor follow its developments. Alienated citizens, on the other hand, are no less ready to see themselves as lacking influence through collective action or to view their most salient collectivities as unresponsive to their needs, but they differ from the passive citizen in that they are not so much oblivious to the political arena as they are disgusted by it. That is, they care and at some level they tend to believe that their alienation conveys a message which may eventually be heard by the collectivity's leadership. The alienated citizen, in short, engages in a form of active passivity, contradictory as such a characterization may seem.[32]

A host of factors operates to encourage passive citizenship. The poor and downtrodden, long suppressed in the relentless rigors of poverty, have little reason to hope that society will be responsive to their needs and, thus, they have even less reason to believe they can do anything about their plight. Passivity thus becomes a way of life, not only because the resources needed to be active in politics are lacking, but also because the spirit flags. Under these circumstances, the skill revolution is of no consequence. Passive citizens have no reason to enlarge their skills and thus either resist or avoid the powerful stimuli of the skill revolution.

It may also be that passivity becomes a way of life for some people

---

[32] For an extensive discussion of these two forms of apathetic citizenship, see Tom DeLuca, *The Two Faces of Political Apathy* (Philadelphia: Temple University Press, 1995).

who live well above the poverty line but who have used their new-found skills to extend their belief that the world is too complex to change. Such people may have a modicum of the resources needed to participate in collective action even though they have become habituated to passivity by virtue of the assumption that collective action at the micro level is futile. Citizens of this sort do not become alienated in the sense of actively detesting the political arena. They are, rather, truly passive because they have long since presumed the political world is essentially irrelevant to their daily routines.[33]

In the case of alienated citizens, however, futility is moderated by caring and passivity is offset by indirect involvement. Normally their behavior consists, for all practical purposes, of inaction and detachment, but it is also a studied inaction and detachment because their orientation is to follow the course of events and derive therefrom reinforcement for their alienation. Most importantly, this form of caring can lead to staying away from the voting booth, casting blank ballots, avoiding rallies, or otherwise seeking to make known their alienation through nonparticipation.[34] Indeed, sometimes town squares remain empty because leaders have urged their followers to engage in collective action wherein the macro sum of micro actions is a conspicuous avoidance, a message that the political arena has gaps because they chose to remain outside it. In some cases citizens can be so alienated that they treat public officials as, in effect, enemies.[35]

Still another reason for the pervasiveness of apathetic citizenship is the worldwide dearth of effective leaders who can rouse people out of

---

[33] For US data along these lines, see R.W. Apple, Jr., "Poll Shows Disenchantment With Politicians and Politics," *New York Times*, July 12, 1995, p. 1, and Richard Morin, "Who's In Control? Many Don't Know or Care," *Washington Post*, January 29, 1996, p. A1.

[34] A clear-cut example of this form of alienation is provided by the 1993 presidential election in Iran, which resulted in some 13 million voters (or some 14 per cent more than in the 1989 election) abstaining from casting their ballots. As one observer put it, "If you do not have the stamp on your identity card showing that you voted, it is more difficult to find Government employment, obtain a passport or receive Government-subsidized food or assistance. If this many people were willing to take this risk, it can only be read as a broad political protest." Chris Hedges, "Rafsanjani Re-elected in Iran, but Without a Huge Mandate," *New York Times*, June 14, 1993, p. A8. Likewise, the number of Iranians who voted in the 1992 parliamentary elections was some 35 per cent fewer than the figure for 1980. Douglas Jehl, "Iran's Economic Plight Casts a Pall on Today's Vote," *New York Times*, March 8, 1996, p. A3.

[35] See, for example, Thomas B. Edsall, "Public Grows More Receptive to Anti-Government Message," *Washington Post*, January 31, 1996, p. A1, and Timothy Egan, "Federal Uniforms Become Target of Wave of Threats and Violence," *New York Times*, April 25, 1995, p. A1.

their doldrums. Confidence that micro actions can produce collective outcomes is, presumably, subject to variability, depending in part on whether the case for it can be persuasively voiced. Yet, such voices are hardly a salient aspect of the political landscape in this turbulent era. One observer argues that "[i]t is 200 years or more since the world had such a vacuum of purposeful authority."[36] Put differently, the ranks of leaders throughout the world are so pervaded with those who focus on narrow interests that few are concerned to make politics seem meaningful to those who either have lost hope or are alienated. To be sure, there is no dearth of leaders who seek to capitalize on fear, racism, and territorial attachments among apathetic citizens as means of enlarging the ranks of their followers, and to some extent such manipulations do result in stirrings among the apathetic. And there are also some leaders who seek support by offering themselves as no-nonsense outsiders who can break through governmental stalemates and produce effective cures to society's ills, and again these tactics can lead to momentary inroads into the ranks of the apathetic. But the messages of outsiders are not geared to an enduring break with apathy. They are only palliatives, temporary expedients that are ill-designed to initiate basic alterations in self–environment orientations.

Democratic citizenship

Since recent years have been witness to a widespread turn away from authoritarian toward democratic governments, it is tempting to conclude that there has been a corresponding tide in the direction of democratic citizenship. As previously implied, however, it is easier to establish formal institutions that adhere to democratic procedures than it is to evolve self–environment orientations which sustain and enlarge support for those procedures. Clarity about the intent and meaning of these procedures, and the processes of socialization through which they become habitual lines of thought for citizens, take decades to evolve. And in the course of their evolution a variety of intervening events can undermine the core values that need to be grasped. As indicated by numerous citizens in the former Soviet empire, it is far from certain that newly established democratic institutions at the macro level can take full root at the micro level.

Put differently, the values associated with achieving a balance between self and collectivity needs are complex and delicate. They

---

[36] Brian Beedham, "If Politicians Can't Decide, People have to Do It Themselves," *International Herald Tribune*, July 18, 1995, p. 8.

necessitate being prepared to favor process over outcome and thus to accept unwanted outcomes to which a majority subscribes. They require a readiness to be sensitive to the needs of the larger collectivity precisely at those times when one's own interests may be at stake. They demand an ability to resist corruption and other forms of self-interested behavior which might undermine equity and curtail deliberative forms of decision-making. And they are also founded on an understanding that the rights of minorities need to be protected. Such values are not easily maintained without any prior experience in democratic ways.

Nor is the preservation of balanced self–environment orientations a simple matter for those whose cultures have long inured to democratic principles. In times of economic downturns when the societal pie shrinks, even those most committed to democratic values can be sorely tempted to accept short-cuts, emergency measures, restricted liberties, martial law, and a host of other procedures which compromise their commitments to open and equitable procedures.

Given the authority crises fostered by the parametric transformations of this turbulent era, moreover, the practices of democratic citizenship can be subjected to enormous pressures. In the absence of clear-cut lines of authority and the presence of paralyzed or otherwise ineffective governments – not to mention a continuing flow of immigrants, legal and illegal, across national boundaries who compete for jobs and live by different cultural tenets – individuals in the majority can all too easily begin to forget the principles that accord protection to minorities. No less important, they can begin to lose touch with the democratic value that differentiates between being heard and being heeded by public officials and thus start to reject political processes that fail to yield their preferred outcomes. And all of this is especially the case if the leadership of democratic societies begins to compile a record of deception, self-serving corruption, and a host of other actions that can make micro actions seem irrelevant to macro outcomes and thereby erode public appreciation of democratic values and procedures.

In sum, while the challenges to democratic citizenship have always been severe, today they seem particularly intense and subtle. More than that, the challenges are everywhere, or at least wherever governments are faltering and change is overwhelming.

Citizenship without moorings

Assuming that the onset of global turbulence has thus had major consequences for the way in which people everywhere balance their own needs against those of their larger collectivities, it is hardly surprising that most citizens at every point on the self–environment continuum are in motion, either searching for a new balance or struggling to reaffirm the old one. Like their ships of state, the anchors that tie citizens to core values have become unhooked, leaving their commitments adrift and their orientations buffeted by cross-cutting winds. The inner need to maintain macro attachments and political identities persists, but the foci of the attachments and identities have been increasingly obscured by transformative events. There are no moorings on to which people can readily latch.

It is thus difficult to come to an overall conclusion as to what the foregoing analysis portends for governance along the Frontier. Does the restlessness among citizens everywhere – the unmooring of their ties to traditional authorities – point to a possibility that institutions designed for the exercise of supranational authority can develop adequate support among the world's publics to be increasingly effective? Or are such institutions bound to flounder as subgroupism, passivity, alienation, and rigid ideologies become ever more pervasive among citizenries?

This discussion of changing citizenship orientations and practices can be read to provide an affirmative answer to both these questions. The increasing readiness of individuals to challenge authority, the emergence of performance criteria of legitimacy, the hints that many people are newly appreciative of democratic self–environment orientations, the apparent expansion of the learning potential of publics, and the signs of greater commitments to social movements with global concerns all suggest that compelling, properly designed, and equitable arrangements for addressing and coping with, if not resolving, the challenges posed by the dynamics of worldwide change may receive a fair hearing among major segments of the world's citizens. Or at least these indicators suggest that there is a probability of sufficient public support for placing new governance proposals on the global agenda. Political leaders need not fear that airing ideas for new institutional arrangements will be immediately dismissed and cost them their political lives. They would appear to have the license to be forward-looking, whatever may be the fate of any proposals they introduce into the various political processes that must be cleared for new institutions to develop.

At the same time a gloomy case, in which the prospects for governance along the Frontier are bound to flounder, could readily be derived from the foregoing assessment. The skill revolution has had its downside with respect to the readiness of people to expand their horizons and allow for the well-being and governance of the world as a whole system. Subgroupism, passivity, alienation, and proclivities for ideological citizenship may be sufficiently widespread to doom any solid but imaginative proposals for constructive change that may be advanced.

In sum, the global scene is highly indeterminate insofar as future efforts to reform governance institutions are concerned. Surely, the ups and downs of the world economy are of major consequence – if for no other reason than the availability of adequate funding for the reforms is central to their success – as is the readiness of leaders in all walks of life to adopt whole-system thinking and thereby stake their futures on a commitment to the reform process. Yet, while such indeterminacies can be viewed as obstacles to reform, so can they be seen as opportunities. At the very least they afford creative leaders a chance to press for whole-system values that reduce indeterminacy in the global system and thereby enlist ever wider public support for the idea of institutional changes appropriate to the transformations unfolding at all levels of community life. As the next two chapters emphasize, while the world does not have a plethora of leaders and publics who give voice to whole-system values, neither is it wholly lacking in these respects.

15 Publics

> For a moment, [the leaders were caught by surprise. They] were not so much leaders as followers of a process of social combustion that raced forward spontaneously and uncontrollably: first came the mass movement; then came the demands and the negotiations . . . Suddenly, there was a power in society where none was supposed to be . . . Right in the heart of a totalitarian system, under which people are supposed to be at their most helpless, Solidarity gave the world one of the most startling demonstrations of the power of the people that it has ever seen.[1]

While it is hardly surprising that the fast pace of the skill revolution, the spread of authority crises, the emergence of the multi-centric world, and the further quickening of these patterns by the events surrounding the end of the Cold War have upended citizens everywhere, leading many into restructuring their self–environment orientations, it is less clear how and why these dynamics have resulted in the formation of publics capable of toppling governments or otherwise effecting change. Individuals are restless, their loyalties are in flux; their inclinations to shift to apathetic, self-centered, ideological, or democratic forms of citizenship have been intensified; but how and why these tendencies among individuals have been transformed into spontaneous and effective publics is not easily explained. How and why, for example, did the collapse of communism in the Soviet Union and the end of apartheid in South Africa occur so quickly, so thoroughly, and so successfully in the late 1980s and early 1990s? Why were the 1989 processes of spontaneous coalescence of great numbers of Poles, Czechs, Hungarians, East Germans, Bulgarians, and Romanians around actions and goals that would enlarge their voice in the affairs of their countries so similar to

---

[1] "Notes and Comments," *The New Yorker*, October 20, 1986, p. 35.

the upheavals that had occurred within the preceding few years in Sri Lanka, Soviet Georgia, Armenia, and Estonia, South Korea, Algeria, Haiti, Taiwan, Mexico, Ethiopia, Singapore, Tibet, Argentina, India, the Philippines, the West Bank and Gaza Strip, Chile, Burma, Panama, China, the Sudan, and Yugoslavia? Why, in short, has the lurch toward change and accommodation unfolded on a global scale and, equally important, why did so many historic breakpoints occur in and among so many countries in such a short span of time?

These questions point to puzzling phenomena not only because the upheavals were largely spontaneous, but in many cases they were also initiated and sustained by only a modicum of political organization. The communist parties of Eastern Europe and the former Soviet Union were not toppled by well and highly organized opposition parties. Rather, the prime movers were instantaneous coalitions of citizens facilitated by rudimentary instruments of mobilization. Faced with governments that controlled the media of communication as well as the military services, unarmed, leaderless, and minimally informed publics have nevertheless prevailed everywhere but in Burma and China. How has this happened? What underlies the perplexing globalization of patterns wherein the traditional loci of authority have been so undermined? Through what processes have so many micro actors been so fully converted into such competent macro actors?

Addressing this puzzle serves as the purpose of this brief chapter. The goal is to explore how the capacity for engaging in collective action has passed through a threshold whereat publics have become central actors on the world stage.

Insufficient answers

Doubtless there are numerous pieces to the puzzle. What might be called the "Cold War factor" looms large at first glance. The changes toward more open and less oppressive party control initiated in the USSR under Mikhail Gorbachev in the last half of the 1980s appear linked to the breakdown of the Soviet system and the ability of restless publics to assert themselves. Such an explanation, however, is not sufficient to account for the collective actions that mark recent world history. These upheavals would not have unfolded as they did without the Soviet Union pulling back from the Cold War, but neither would they have occurred if individuals and publics had not been ready to seize the openings, challenge the authorities, press their demands, and concert their actions.

Nor is it sufficient to look for a solution to the puzzle solely in the pressures for political expression that are generated by economic circumstances. Both the rich and the poor have evidenced a readiness to coalesce and claim authority for themselves. Part of the explanation might be found in the processes of rapid economic development – say, in such countries as Taiwan, South Korea, and China – but this is hardly a central piece of the puzzle inasmuch as there are too many poor countries, such as Romania, Burma, Tibet, and Soviet Georgia, where publics coalesced but where movement into the stages of economic development that foster mushrooming demands for political autonomy had yet to occur.

Similarly, it can hardly be said that widespread nationalism lies at the heart of the explanation. Ethnic loyalties were a factor in such places as Sri Lanka, Estonia, and the West Bank, but again there are a number of situations where authority crises were sustained by other than nationalistic fervor.

Nor can it be said that the solution of the puzzle lies in the lure of democratic institutions. To be sure, as illustrated by the placing of a replica of the Statue of Liberty in Tiananmen Square and the singing of "We Shall Overcome" in Wenceslas Square, the demand for such institutions, or at least for political autonomy and self-governance, has been global in scope. Except for Iran, none of the more recent upheavals involved a clamor to follow and support a single leader or an authoritarian ideology. Nevertheless, the notion that this period of turbulence has been sustained by global aspirations for more democracy also falls short of an adequate explanation. It fails to account for the timing of the upheavals, for why the surfacing of such aspirations occurred in the 1980s. If the desire for democracy has fueled the convergence of peoples in the central squares of diverse cities, why were the same squares empty in the 1970s? Why didn't they fill up in the 1960s? The answer, again, must be that other dynamics were at work. Important and heart-warming as the mushrooming of pro-democracy forces throughout the world has been, they are best viewed as agents of change, as products of even more fundamental sources that culminated in a single historical moment.[2]

Theoretically, of course, it is possible that the pervasive pattern is mere coincidence, that separate circumstances in each situation gave rise to the appearance of an overall pattern but that in fact those years

[2] For a cogent discussion of the complexity of the pro-democracy movements, see Dankwart A. Rustow, "Democracy: A Global Revolution?" *Foreign Affairs*, vol. 69 (Fall 1990), pp. 75–91. For a more general appraisal of the difficulties of identifying and explaining the sources that underlie public protests, see Mario Diani and Ron Eyerman, *Studying Collective Action* (London: Sage Publications, 1992).

were marked only by a series of country-specific and issue-specific episodes. Again, however, the argument is flawed. It suffers not only in the face of empirical indicators of causal chains wherein more than a few of the various challenges to authority were linked to each other, but it also falters when confronted with the extremely low probability of numerous historic upheavals unfolding *simultaneously* (or within a very short time frame) in diverse, widely separated countries in the absence of any overall sources that are operative on every continent.

Beyond the situation-specific pieces of the puzzle, in other words, must lie global dynamics that are the better part of the explanation. Most notably, the transformation of key global parameters, the advent of interdependence issues, the weakening of states and governments, the tendencies toward subgroupism, and the dynamism of electronic technologies are not only global in scope, but they can also be said to have converged and interacted in the late 1980s in such a way as to facilitate the activation of publics in response to the evolving historic circumstances.

The solution of the puzzle, in short, is subtle. It is not based on a single-cause model. All the dynamics may have initially been responses to the technological upheavals that underlay the ever-growing interdependencies of economic, political, and social life, but once the micro-level shifts began, alterations in the status of states, governments, and subgroups were bound to follow as people became receptive to the decentralizing consequences inherent in their growing capacity to locate their own interests more clearly in the flow of events.

Spontaneous authority

To trace, as previous chapters have, numerous stimuli to expanded analytic and emotional skills is not, of course, to demonstrate that in fact such an expansion has occurred. To discern that people are more able than ever to "see" how micro actions can aggregate to macro outcomes and thus to intrude themselves into the course of events is not to show they seize the opportunities to do so. Indeed, many observers are inclined to be skeptical that a relocation of authority sustained by a skill revolution has occurred. Yes, they would argue, regimes have been toppled in Eastern Europe and, yes, the streets of Rangoon, Beijing, Seoul, Manila, and elsewhere have been jammed with people giving voice to their demands. But such events have occurred before in history, only to be followed by publics retreating back to quiescence as the challenged authority structures get modified or reconstituted. Face it, the skeptics would conclude, the record of history well justifies positing citizens everywhere as remote from and uninformed about world affairs, as simplistic, as incapable of learning, as rabbles, as masses that are normally passive but that can be easily be manipulated and/or mobilized by state officials or opposition leaders.

But such reasoning is belied by the spontaneity of virtually all the uprisings of the 1980s, beginning in Kwangju, Korea, at the very start of the decade and running through the upheaval in Bucharest, Romania, at the very end of the decade.[3] This more recent history traces a record of citizens everywhere judging the performance of officials as unacceptable and then relocating authority in the direction of themselves.[4] In one case, Estonia, the history even includes a rally attended by one-third of the entire country.[5]

As the upheavals gathered momentum, to be sure, new organizations came into being – or old ones took advantage of the upheaval – and undertook leadership tasks that extended and enriched the aggregative dynamics.[6] Change could not have come to Poland

---

[3] Nor did the spread of spontaneous uprisings come to an end with the close of the decade. It continued apace in the 1990s in Kuwait, Mongolia, Nepal, Albania, the Ivory Coast, and several other countries of sub-Saharan Africa. See, for example, Youssef M. Ibrahim, "An Affluent Kuwait Joins an Arab Trend Toward Democracy," *New York Times*, March 11, 1990, p. 1; Nicholas D. Kristof, "Calls for Reform Widen in Mongolia," *New York Times*, March 11, 1990, p. 10; and Kenneth B. Noble, "Clashes and Unrest Grow Fiercer in Ivory Coast," *New York Times*, March 3, 1990, p. 3.

[4] Although the analysis focuses on how more competent citizens are intruding themselves into politics through collective actions that converge upon the public squares of the world, it must be stressed that such highly visible activities are not the only form of mass behavior to which their enhanced skills can contribute. The same capabilities can also underlie a readiness to avoid collective action in situations where restraint seems more appropriate to the accomplishment of desired outcomes. Consider, for example, this account of the mass restraint exercised in Lithuania during a key period of its drive for independence from the Soviet Union: "In Vilnius, the public's self-control has been phenomenal . . . Television suggested that the people were constantly on the streets, chanting national songs and weeping with joy under their tricolor. Lithuanians, however, are economical with political gestures. When the moment is right, they will turn out by the hundreds of thousands, but for the most part they have behaved as if an attempt to break out of the Soviet Union was a monthly routine." Neal Ascherson, "The Trial of Lithuania," *The New York Review*, April 26, 1990, p. 3.

[5] David K. Shipler, "Symbols of Sovereignty," *The New Yorker*, September 18, 1989, p. 52.

[6] Interestingly, the question of whether the spontaneous actions of citizens preceded or followed organizational effort can be of political as well as analytic concern. It became a central issue in Romania during the early days following that country's revolution, with spokespersons for small parties that emerged in opposition to the new, post-revolution ruling group, the Council for National Salvation, complaining that the Council

without Solidarity as a macro whole that gave voice and direction to the micro parts. Conversely, where the initial micro stirrings were not followed by organizational coherence – as was the case in Burma and China – the change processes have yet to culminate. Nevertheless, the fact that so many of the uprisings were marked by spontaneity amounts to cogent evidence that the analytic and emotional skills of people have expanded, that they seize upon as well as "see" the opportunities to contribute to collective outcomes. Hundreds of thousands – and in some instances, millions – of people do not suddenly converge in the same city square for the same purposes by chance. Either they are organized to do so or, in the absence of any coordinated mobilization, they do so because they have the skills which enable them to sense the urgency and virtue of converging. Since most of the uprisings originated well before organizations could be formed or activated, the spontaneity of the participants says a great deal about their analytic and emotional skills. Consider Tiananmen Square. The coalescence of pro-democracy forces there in May 1989, "happened with startling, and seemingly inexplicable swiftness,"[7] so much so that "without weapons, without communications other than *xiaodao xiaoxi*, or grapevine, without transportation other than bicycles, and trucks borrowed from farmers and work units, without even any agreement on what they are demonstrating for – except the right to demonstrate – the students and those protecting them are blocking a modern, well-equipped army."[8]

Similar accounts of leaderless uprisings elsewhere in the world during this period can readily be cited,[9] but Tiananmen Square serves as a quintessential case because it was the site of more than one million people converging at the same place at the same time without being mobilized by experienced leaders and an effective organizational hierarchy. Such a large scale captures well the likelihood that citizens have

had been in existence for some six months and was thus manipulating its perpetuation in power. The Council, on the other hand, was quick to assert that this was not the case, that the revolution had been unplanned and instantaneous. As the prime minister at the time, Petre Roman, put it, "We had no contact. It was spontaneous. The [popular] Front was created on the spot." Cf. *New York Times*, January 3, 1990, p. 1.

[7] Nicholas D. Kristof, "China Erupts . . . The Reasons Why," *New York Times Magazine*, June 4, 1989, p. 28.

[8] Fred C. Shapiro, "Letter from Beijing," *The New Yorker*, June 5, 1989, p. 73.

[9] See, for example, Robert Pear, "Burmese Revolt Seen as Spontaneous," *New York Times*, September 10, 1988, p. 3, and Flora Lewis, "The Czechs Start Over," *New York Times*, December 17, 1989, sect. 4, p. 21.

undergone an expansion of their skills and a restructuring of their orientations toward authority and legitimacy that are irreversibly transforming the conduct of politics. How else to explain the extraordinary convergence of humanity? How else to account for the systematic controlling of intersections, the blocking of streets, the clearing of passageways, the procuring of trucks, and the distribution of limited resources? These developments did not occur randomly. They did not happen because people suddenly discovered they were possessed of courage. They did not happen because seasoned leaders used a well-defined organizational network to get out their memberships. They did not happen because a national figure used a television platform to exhort a normally quiescent public into taking action. No, they happened because, in an environment enriched by pictures of "people power" that succeeded elsewhere in the world and of *xiaodao xiaoxi* supplementing televised scenes depicting the unfolding situation "downtown,"[10] numerous individuals had the wherewithal to assess their priorities, to set aside their long-standing compliance habits, to link the authority of top leaders to their performances as well as to the traditional prerogatives of their offices, to construct a scenario which allowed for indecision on the part of the authorities, to discern that this hesitancy enhanced the probability of micro actions leading to macro outcomes, to sense that enough of their fellow citizens were engaging in similar reasoning to insure further the conversion of micro sentiments into corresponding macro responses, and then to participate in the proceedings by assessing where they might best fit in the collective endeavor.

It might be argued that while Tiananmen Square exemplifies the capacity of citizens to converge spontaneously as a collective force, it is hardly a reflection of relocated authority because the Chinese regime reasserted its dominance by a resort to force. Such an argument, however, falters in the face of two considerations. One is that despite the Chinese regime's crackdown, provincial and local Communist Party leaders throughout the country subsequently ignored directives from

---

[10] As the situation in Tiananmen Square reached a climax, *xiaodao xiaoxi* took a motorized form: "But the citizenry of Beijing were being kept alerted to troop movements through a group of hastily organized messengers known as the Flying Tigers, a motley collection of some several hundred private entrepreneurs and *liumang* [unemployed youths] who happened to own motorcycles and had deputized themselves to serve as the eyes and ears of the resistance movement." Orville Schell, *Mandate of Heaven: A New Generation of Entrepreneurs, Dissidents, Bohemians, and Technocrats Lays Claim to China's Future* (New York: Simon and Schuster, 1994), pp. 123–4

Beijing and pursued their own policies.[11] Secondly, spontaneous mass demonstrations did result in a relocation of authority in many other countries. The account in the above epigraph of the 1980 events that culminated in the acquisition of legitimacy by Solidarity in Poland serves as a good summarizing example of how micro spontaneity has preceded and fostered the macro coherence through which authority has undergone relocation.

If expanded analytic and emotional skills explain the spontaneous origins of new authority structures, it remains to account for how the skills get tapped and enable great numbers of people to coalesce into a potent political force. Such convergences are easy to comprehend when organizational channels or the mass media provide information on their scheduling and progress. But what about the many situations in recent years when the organizational networks and media were controlled by those who wished to prevent mass rallies and such rallies occurred nonetheless? How do hundreds of thousands of increasingly skillful people manage to concert their energies without the aid of an established organizational network or the assistance of extensive television or radio coverage?

Although tempting, it is not sufficient to respond to these questions by stressing that such convergences somehow "just happen." Obviously, systematic factors must be operative, factors that are less manifest than organizational cadres and the mass media but that nonetheless tap into the expanded skills of citizens in such a way as to guide, if not to coordinate, their actions. Three such factors, all of them independent of whether the mass media are controlled so as to provide people with distorted information (as was the case in Burma, China, the West Bank, and South Africa), can be identified. One of them involves the emotional skills of individuals, which operate as either supplements to or substitutes for analytic skills in the following way:

> the structures of the social world, especially as centered on the networks upholding property and authority, involve continuous monitoring by individuals of each other's group loyalties. Since the social world can involve quite a few lines of authority and sets of coalitions, the task of monitoring them can be extremely complex. How is this possible, given people's inherently limited cognitive capacities? The solution must be that negotiations are carried out implicitly, on a different level than the use of consciously manipulated verbal

[11] Nicholas D. Kristof, "In China, Too, Centrifugal Forces Are Growing Stronger," *New York Times*, August 26, 1990, sect. 4, p. 2.

symbols. I propose that the mechanism is *emotional* rather than cognitive. Individuals monitor others' attitudes toward social coalitions, and hence toward the degree of support for routines, by feeling the amount of confidence and enthusiasm there is toward certain leaders and activities, or the amount of fear of being attacked by a strong coalition, or the amount of contempt for a weak one. These emotional energies are transmitted by contagion among members of a group, in flows which operate very much like the set of negotiations which produce prices within a market.[12]

The other two factors that account for the remarkable timing whereby thousands of citizens converge under the adverse conditions of controlled and distorted mass media involve the energy of activists. Neither the analytic skills nor the emotional antennae of citizens is sufficient to initiate actions that get aggregated into collective pressures and outcomes. For this to happen, word of the aggregative processes must spread, and it is here where the activists in the population become agents of communication, either through uncoordinated but cumulative behavior or through *ad hoc*, informal organizational networks. The former type of activism is illustrated by the various forms of *xiaodao xiaoxi* that sustained communications through word of mouth that were no less central to the upheavals in Eastern Europe than they were to the developments in Tiananmen Square. In East Germany, for example, "Doctors called mechanics. Mechanics called construction workers. Construction workers called nurses. Nurses called doctors. Neighbors called neighbors. This is how the demonstrations came to life in Frankfurt, Paluen, Dresden, and, above all, Leipzig."[13]

Somewhere between word of mouth and the mass media lie the hastily formed, temporary, and rudimentary organizations of activists whose commitments lead them to create alternative channels of communications for distributing schedules, tasks, and ideas. An account of the events leading to the fall of the communist regime in Czechoslovakia provides a good insight into these pre-organizational dynamics. Faced with a "conservative official press" that prevented them getting "their word out to the working people," the students who began the translation of micro impulses into macro outcomes "overnight . . . created their own `mass media' on the streets":

[12] Randall Collins, "On the Micro Foundations of Macrosociology," *American Journal of Sociology*, vol. 86 (March 1981), p. 944 (italics in original).

[13] David Binder, "At Confessional East Berlin Congress, `An Absolute Break' with Stalinism," *New York Times*, December 18, 1989, p. A8.

> They covered the walls of the city's subway system, bus windows, escalator railings, shop windows, and street lamps with information on demonstrations and strikes and with posters saying: "Workers Join Us For Freedom!" "Students Against Violence Ask For Your Help!" and "Strike For Democracy." . . . These days virtually every public place in Prague is crowded with people reading notices, looking at pictures of the Friday night clashes and signing declarations . . . [14]

It is useful to stress that such accounts of spontaneous actions by citizens are offered as evidence not of a sudden lurch toward goodness on the part of humankind, but of relocated authority, of decentralizing tendencies having combined with newly refined skills of citizenship to produce a greater readiness to become involved in collective action. Let us be clear on this point. The thesis advanced here is not founded on an idealism which posits people as becoming more humane, intelligent, tolerant, and cooperative as a consequence of a more information-enriched environment. Nor does it spring from a naivety which presumes that more exposure to education and closer proximity through television to events unfolding in far-off places is encouraging individuals to be less selfish and more civic-minded. The point is, rather, that while the attitudes and priorities of publics may not differ from those held in the past, their skills in employing, articulating, directing, and implementing their attitudes and priorities have undergone a major transformation.[15]

Future scenarios

Although the evidence of expanded analytic skills fostering a greater capacity for collective action on a global scale is not conclusive, it is sufficient to pose the question of what such transformations might imply for politics along the Frontier. If it is the case, that is, that the world's adult population is ever more capable of relating to the course of events, does this mean that the decentralizing tendencies are likely to persist to the point where public order and governmental policy-making become increasingly fragile and chaotic? It might. Conceivably more upheaval lies ahead as people become increasingly accustomed to having their narrow self-interests served and their collective demands met. Or, pos-

---

[14] Esther B. Fein, "Students Ask Workers' Aid in Czech Rally," *New York Times*, November 24, 1989, p. A16.

[15] For an extensive case history that affirms this conclusion, see Susanne Lohmann, "The Dynamics of Informational Cascades: The Monday Demonstrations in Leipzig, East Germany, 1989–1991," *World Politics*, vol. 47 (October 1994), pp. 42–101.

sibly, a period of relative tranquillity may ensue as people become increasingly aware that the expansion of the Frontier enables them to engage in collective actions through which nonextremist accommodations can be fashioned.

Much of one's assessment of these contrasting scenarios depends on one's understanding of the values that are likely to accompany greater analytic and emotional skills. Such skills are, in themselves, neutral. They can foster a greater readiness to advance the well-being and dignity of groups, or they can heighten inclinations to serve greedy aims and promote the well-being of special interests. There is no necessary correlation between being more skillful and, thus, more altruistic or more selfish.

But if their expanded emotional skills enable individuals to sense more accurately whether altruism or self-interest predominates among their neighbors and in society at large, then one of these tendencies is likely to be in the ascendancy for long stretches of time as people reinforce each other's leanings. This means that the tendencies that have led subsystems throughout the world to press for greater autonomy within their more encompassing systems are likely to persist and even intensify into ever greater fragmentation in authority relations at all levels of governance. It seems doubtful, for example, that the decentralizing tendencies at work in the former Soviet empire will come to a halt if and when the nationalisms of that region achieve satisfaction. The skills which lead, say, Lithuanians to see value in their own autonomy may well lead to further fragmentation that pits various groups of Lithuanians against each other. As one observer of post-Ceausescu Romania commented about the absence of democratic experience in that country, "If anything, I worry about excessive pluralism. The peoples of Eastern Europe, after 40 years, are going to enjoy, even glory in, diversity for awhile."[16]

Yet, there may be one respect in which the greater analytic and emotional skills are not neutral. It is at least plausible that the more skillful people are in identifying their self-interests and relating them to the public arena, the greater will be their flexibility to appreciate when the tendencies toward decentralization and centralization become excessive and threatening. If this is so, if publics and their leaders are increasingly capable of reversing course, of perceiving that they collectively

---

[16] Stephen Szabo, quoted in Robert C. Toth, "Barren Trees Sported Pears, and Ceausescu Fell," *Los Angeles Times*, December 27, 1989, p. A12.

possess the competence to revise the priorities they attach to their system and subsystem loyalties, then the future is very likely to be episodic and turbulent, with a period of narrow self-interests being ascendant at one point in time, only to yield to the predominance of broad community interests at the next moment when the defects of the existing priorities become increasingly evident.

Traces of these cyclical fluctuations in which global tendencies toward centralization foster countertendencies toward decentralization, and vice versa, are readily discernible. The readiness of South Africans to follow the lead of Nelson Mandela and to reverse course at their moment of triumph by replacing their subsystemic goals with those of South Africa as a whole system is a classic instance of the skill revolution fostering, or at least permitting, reordered priorities. And similar traces of an emergent recognition that subsystem successes pose system-level problems have also surfaced in Poland, Germany, and Western Europe. The predominant trend may still be a decentralizing one – as occurred in Czechoslovakia – and it is surely reinforced by a worldwide momentum in the direction of free-market economies and their encouragement of individual enterprise; but signs of a new cycle can be cited by those who see a global need to focus on collective problems.

Furthermore, from a bifurcationist perspective the management of such cycles poses no great challenge. The bifurcated worlds of world politics are well suited to coping with the repercussions that follow as one stage of the cycle runs its course and gives way to the next: the structures of the state-centric world are amply capable of absorbing and redirecting the tendencies toward centralization and the need for collective approaches to the new interdependence issues, even as the structures of the multi-centric world can readily accommodate and channel the tendencies toward decentralization and the need for subgroup solutions to old independence issues.

In sum, the appearance may be one of chaos and turbulence, but the reality is likely to be one of an underlying set of structures sustained by increasingly skillful citizens eventually adapting to the dynamism of change. Doubtless excesses will occur in the form of stifling centralization and paralyzing decentralization, but as people become more competent, they cannot undo their new skills and revert to old habits. They may yield to repressive measures for a while, and they may selfishly champion their own self-interests for a while, but they cannot ignore what they have experienced or quell their newly accelerated propensities toward learning.

16   Leaders

Cape Town, May 9 – The power that had belonged to whites since they first settled on this cape 342 years ago passed today to a Parliament as diverse as any in the world, a cast of proud survivors who began their work by electing Nelson Mandela to be the first black president of South Africa . . .

Ninety minutes later he appeared on a high balcony at the old Cape Town City Hall, gazed across a delirious throng toward the bay where he spent more than a third of his adult life on an island prison, and spoke his presidential theme of inclusion.

"We place our vision of a new constitutional order for South Africa on the table not as conquerors, prescribing to the conquered . . . We speak as fellow citizens to heal the wounds of the past with the intent of constructing a new order based on justice for all."

news item[1]

As the previous chapter makes clear, the age of subgroupism is upon us. Everywhere – in the former Soviet empire, throughout Africa, and in Canada, to cite only the more obvious cases – ethnic, religious, linguistic, racial, nationality, and a host of other subsystems lodged in a more encompassing authority arrangement are finding their voice and successfully pressing for greater control over their own affairs. And where such pressures seem unlikely to overcome economic hardships and political persecutions, the Frontier is crowded with people relocating their subgroupism, leaving their homes and migrating to new ones.

Nor are these decentralizing trends merely transitional derivatives of profound global change. They are an integral part of the change and, as

---

[1] Bill Keller, "Mandela Is Named President, Closing the Era of Apartheid," *New York Times*, May 10, 1994, p. 1.

a result, the worldwide tendencies toward subgroupism are likely to persist for decades.[2] Unlike the 1950s and 1960s, when independence movements in the colonial world achieved statehood, the current surge of subgroupism is founded on a goal – greater autonomy – that may not be readily met by the accomplishment of a legal status and, thus, needs to be continuously serviced.[3] As global television widens its coverage of subgroup challenges to authority within the homeland, and as pervasive economic, political, and social dislocations swell the tides of human migration and the proliferation of diaspora – of "ethnic minority groups of migrant origins residing and acting in host countries but maintaining strong sentimental and material links with their countries of origin"[4] – the longer is the age of subgroupism likely to extend into the future. The decentralizing surge, in other words, is inherent in the emergent structures of world politics as each subgroup success feeds on itself and fosters tendencies toward further fragmentation.

Stated in still another way, two of the major dynamics at work in world politics today, the challenges to authority within states and the migrations from states, have their roots in deep psychological attachments to subgroups. People serve these attachments by staying put or by moving, but in either event they share the same special feelings toward the subgroup and the same inclination to suspect outsiders. Those who leave are no less likely than those who stay behind to carry a wide array of psychological baggage, deep-seated emotional ties to the homeland and enduring fears about its well-being. Their lives may end up in new physical settings, but their psychological landscape

---

[2] For the bases of the expectation that subgroupism will not be short-lived, see James N. Rosenau, *Turbulence in World Politics: A Theory of Change and Continuity* (Princeton: Princeton University Press, 1990), chap. 14.

[3] To be sure, in some cases, such as the Baltics, the aspiration to greater autonomy is equated with the achievement of statehood; but a preponderance of the tendencies toward subgroupism consist of pressure for self-realization and enlarged independence within the framework of existing states. Put differently, as the dynamics of decentralization led to the fragmentation of empires into states during earlier periods, so has the continued unfolding of these dynamics resulted in the transformation of coherent states into loosely-knit and fragile coalitions of subgroups. For an analysis that posits the various eras of subgroupism as "waves" of the same movement, see E.A. Tiryakian, "Modernization: Exhumetur in Pace (Rethinking Macrosociology in the 1990s)," *International Sociology*, vol. 6 (1991), pp. 166–70.

[4] The close link between human migrations and the proliferation of diaspora is developed in Gabriel Sheffer, "A New Field of Study: Modern Diasporas in International Politics," in G. Sheffer (ed.), *Modern Diasporas in International Politics* (New York: St. Martin's Press, 1986). See the same source (p. 3) for this definition of diaspora.

remains essentially the same composite of cultural premises, ancestral loyalties, and subgroup commitments.

For the individuals involved, of course, it makes a huge difference whether subgroupism occurs in a familiar or an unfamiliar setting, but from the perspective of politics along the Frontier the dynamics and problems are quite similar. Whether they are located within the homeland or spread globally as a diaspora, present-day subgroups commonly establish transnational links with governments or counterparts abroad who can supply needed resources or, at least, moral support. In turn, these links form networks that are part and parcel of a decentralized, bifurcated global structure in which the multi-centric world has emerged to rival, offset, or otherwise interact with the long-established state-centric world. Consequently, whether these worldwide tendencies toward decentralization lead to domestic upheavals, the establishment of new breakaway states, the acquisition of greater autonomy within historic states, the migration of large masses, or the proliferation of modern diasporas, the result is a restructuring of authority relationships and an intensified potential for local and regional conflicts capable of globally cascading along the fault lines of subgroupism.

While the turbulence model anticipates the actions of subgroups from the perspective of a bifurcated global structure and not in terms of the choices which subgroups face and make in the course of coping with challenges and pursuing their aspirations, here it is the latter perspective that serves as the analytic focus. Given the analysis of citizens and publics in the previous two chapters, the task is to assess the role of leaders in the processes whereby the tensions between centralizing and decentralizing tendencies are confronted, ignored, resolved, postponed, or otherwise managed. More specifically, the purpose is to explore leadership from a particular perspective: that of the special choices that have to be made at those moments when subgroups successfully achieve greater autonomy within their homelands. Successes of this sort can never be realized by diasporas – since some of their components have no intention of ever returning to the homeland – but the dilemmas posed by triumphant subgroupism offer quintessential insights into the problems leaders face as their fortunes fluctuate in a period of rapid change.[5]

---

[5] Although the contexts, tasks, adversaries, and challenges may be quite different for leaders of multinational corporations, voluntary associations, and other collectivities, the essential dilemmas inherent in triumphant subgroupism – achieving a workable balance between systemic and subsystemic needs and goals – involve choices comparable to those confronted by the leaders of any large-scale organization.

Triumphant subgroupism

Suppose you belong to an ethnic, religious, political, or any other sub-group that has suffered for years and decades, even centuries, at the hands of another group that controls the state. You and your family have been imprisoned, brutalized, and relocated. Your home has been burned, your talents neglected, your opportunities closed off. Yet, through all the adversity, and perhaps because of it, your sense of a common heritage remains intense and you never cease longing for a time when your shared sufferings can be relieved and the legitimacy of your group accepted. And further suppose that, suddenly and surprisingly, events take a sharp turn and your group acquires its freedom. The yoke is lifted. Your subgroupism is triumphant.

At this glorious moment and in the heady ones that follow, what do you do? Do you retreat within the subgroup to celebrate your identity? Do you turn on your oppressors and use your hard-won autonomy to exploit those who have ruled you? Or do you recognize that you and your adversaries are members of the same larger society and seek to work with them on behalf of common concerns?

Let us also suppose further that as the leader of a triumphant sub-group your skills have been honed by years of managing its survival, years in which your leadership has also linked you into a wide transna-tional network with a rich informational base and a keen grasp of global challenges. Given such a background, what do you do if your moment of triumph is followed quickly by an appreciation that large problems still loom, that triumphant subgroupism cannot undo a polluted environment, a bankrupt economy, or surging inflation? Do you con-tinue to emphasize the subgroup's separate identity and heed its swelling demands for the protection and advancement of its goals at the expense of the more encompassing system? Or do you begin to collab-orate with your former oppressors on the system-wide challenges to the environment and economy, trying all the while to get your followers to appreciate the need for moving beyond retribution and toward accommodation?

The record of four individuals – Vaclav Havel, Nelson Mandela, Andrei Sakharov, and Lech Walesa – facilitates addressing these ques-tions.[6] With the end of the Cold War, all four enjoyed triumphant sub-

---

[6] For an application of a turbulence model to the way five other national leaders of the current period confronted the waning years of the Cold War, see David F. Walsh, Paul J. Best, and Kul B. Rai, *Governing Through Turbulence: Leadership and Change in the Late Twentieth Century* (Westport, CT: Praeger, 1995).

groupism and were immediately compelled to confront these choices. And as the above epigraph eloquently indicates, all four chose to commit their talents and efforts in the service of the larger community over which their subgroup had triumphed. Is there a historic shift to be discerned in the actions of these four children of subgroup combat? Where the triumphant heroes of the past retained their leadership by championing their subsystemic victories, these four of the present have looked beyond their triumphs and sought to advance the needs and welfare of the larger systems that encompass their former adversaries. Whatever may be the success of their efforts, these modern heroes offer the basis for probing the choices which loom ever larger in a shrinking world that is marked by proliferating subgroup conflicts and by intensifying tensions between tendencies toward centralization and decentralization that are global in scope. And not only do their moments of triumph help identify the choices posed for anyone whose subgroup feelings run strong; they also suggest how decisions favoring the larger systems need not be counterproductive for their subgroups.

Much the same can be said from the perspective of the system that is host to the triumphant subgroupism. Suppose you are a member or leader of the dominant system that has just acknowledged the legitimacy and integrity of the victorious subgroup. At this sobering moment and in the difficult ones that follow, what do you do if the newly empowered subgroup demands more autonomy or otherwise takes actions that extend their triumph and lessen your coherence? Are you responsive to such demands or do you contest them? Do you see the demands as spreading to other subgroups and thereby threatening the integrity of your system, with the result that you are led to forego, perhaps unknowingly, the reasoning through which you enabled the subgroup to acquire legitimacy? Or do you adhere to that reasoning on the grounds that the integrity of your system is best preserved through acceptance of its inherent pluralism?

Again particular cases help clarify responses to such questions. The record of three recent individuals – F.W. de Klerk, Mikhail S. Gorbachev, and Wojciech Jaruzelski – who had to commit their talents and efforts to preserving their whole systems in the face of triumphant subgroupism are illustrative in this regard. The initial inclinations of all three men suggest another historic shift in which those with superior coercive capabilities seek other, nonviolent means to sustain systemic coherence. They too offer an opportunity to examine the clash between decentralizing and centralizing tendencies, thus allowing for further elaboration of what may be the most serious challenge that leaders face in the current era.

To organize the analysis around leaders who made key choices at the moment of subgroup triumph is not, however, to imply that these choices are merely the product of unique individuals who were able to grasp the need to expand their horizons and accommodate to their former adversaries. Leadership involves making such choices, but these micro actions can also be seen as a culminating stage of deep sociopolitical processes. Other individuals might have chosen differently and sought to trounce their former adversaries (as did leaders in Serbia and Afghanistan during the same period), but neither the accession to power of accommodating leaders nor their readiness to put triumphant subgroupism in the service of their more encompassing systems could have occurred without the operation of underlying macro dynamics.

There are, in short, sociological explanations of the courses followed when subgroups triumph. Simmel's notion of conflict serving to bind antagonists, for example, is surely relevant to the events that accompany triumphant subgroupism, and so are the various stages of collective behavior identified by Smelser, the functions of conflict proposed by Coser, and the nature of contracts specified by Durkheim – to mention only some of the more obvious contributions to the vast array of relevant literature.[7] Important and relevant as these sociological interpretations are, however, here the emphasis is confined to a narrow time frame, to that particular moment when all the deeper sources of collective action converge around the goals and decisions articulated by particular individuals. Such a focus neither denies nor negates functional approaches to conflict and collective behavior. Rather it springs from a concern with the pattern wherein redirections in the course of history occur suddenly and sharply, thereby emphasizing that sociological explanations must be supplemented by attention to the role of leadership and individual choices.

The legacies of triumph

In some deep sense, of course, subgroupism never triumphs. Large, system-wide problems always remain and victorious subgroups are never so free that they can ignore the stresses of the encompassing systems in which they are located or the dangers of splits within their

---

[7] Lewis Coser, *The Functions of Social Conflict* (New York: Free Press, 1956); Emil Durkheim, *The Division of Labor in Society* (New York: Free Press, 1947); George Simmel, *Conflict* (New York: Free Press, 1955); and Neil J. Smelser, *Theory of Collective Behavior* (New York: Free Press, 1963).

own ranks over how to manage their newly won autonomy. But history records moments when the sense of triumph runs strong, when the more enduring dilemmas seem puny in comparison to the rare short-run successes in which the oppressor retreats and enables (in the sense of not preventing) the subgroup to realize a goodly measure of the greater autonomy for which it has been striving. Since the present era is filled with such moments in every region of the world, the joys of triumphant subgroupism have lately become a recurrent feature of global politics. The world has long been accustomed to the struggles of outnumbered minorities and suppressed majorities and now it is witness to the unfamiliar delicacies of post-suppression adjustment, to an array of circumstances – what might be called the legacies of triumph – that can be obstacles to further momentum as the joys of victory subside and the realities of the new situation set in.

Uncertainty is one of the obvious legacies common to all such situations, irrespective of the circumstances that underlay the triumph and the kind of subgroup that prevailed. Triumphant subgroupism anticipates extensive changes, transformations that are far from trivial even as their contours are only barely visible at the moment of triumph. Such changes portend the attenuation of old habits of compliance and the establishment of new forms of governance, new foci of authority, and new consensus-building processes, all dynamics which are pervaded with so much uncertainty as to foster fear and impulses toward simple and unworkable solutions. The precedents of the past are of little value as the triumphant subgroup takes charge, confronting all concerned with degrees of uncertainty for which their recent memories offer no guidance.

More specifically, perhaps the most difficult legacies involve the lack of trust and community which prevail within both the newly triumphant subgroup and the larger system of which it is or has been a part. For triumph spawns losers as well as winners, and both the pains of losing and the joys of winning derive much of their strength from the cumulation of the grievances which sustained the struggle for and against subsystemic autonomy. The winners remember the jailings, the humiliations, the taunts, and the sleights of hand through which their issues were avoided and their status quo preserved, just as the losers recall the excessive demands, the subversive acts, and the deceitful claims through which their efforts to preserve systemic coherence were undermined. Neither side tends to recall the legitimate side of the position taken by the other and, most of all, at the moment of triumph neither is inclined to focus on their shared fate which is imposed by the historic circumstances and geographic proximity that gave rise to their conflict in the first place. Hence distrust is most intense and a sense of larger community is most fragile at the very time when trust and broad vision is needed.

In effect, therefore, the legacies of short-run triumphs can sow the seeds of long-run disasters. This is why the readiness of Havel, Mandela, Sakharov, and Walesa to work with their former oppressors without abandoning their own constituencies is so impressive. All four could have taken another tack at the moment of triumph. They could have confined their sights to subsystemic horizons and avoided any risk of losing the support of their adherents. They could have remained adamant in their opposition to those who previously presided over the larger system, refusing to acknowledge their perspectives or to accommodate the necessities of systemic coherence.

Cynics might argue that these heroes of subgroup combat had no choice – that Havel could not avoid the nearby presence of the Soviet Union, that Mandela could not disregard the large white minority in South Africa, that Sakharov could not dismiss his country's social malaise, and that Walesa could not wish away the dire circumstances of the Polish economy – but such an argument is easy in retrospect. At the moment of triumph these leaders did have a choice. They could have converted their victory into an inward-looking celebration rather than a sober, outward-oriented rededication to rebuilding the viability of the larger community. They could have yielded to the spirited voices within the ranks of their followers urging them not to compromise. That they did not do so, that they barely paused to savor the fruits of victory before moving on to larger concerns, testifies to the continuing possibility that imagination, decency, and common sense can prevail in troubled and turbulent times.

To be sure, today's heroes can be tomorrow's scapegoats. The most cynical among us might anticipate that triumphant leaders will eventually experience electoral defeat, jail, or other forms of oblivion, that in transferring their energies to the problems of a larger system they will irrevocably compromise the interests of their subgroup, or that they will prove incapable of stemming the tendencies toward decentralization – such as splits in the ranks of their followers – and will eventually succumb as the ultimate victims of their own triumphs. But even if such tendencies do evolve, the subsequent situations are bound to be constrained by the memories of their earlier heroism. In the meantime, during this period of uncertainty, their accomplishments highlight the virtue of exploring what the transformation of subsystemic triumphs into systemic renewal entails.

Most notably, it entails the redirection of subgroupism, the enlarging of perspectives so that the subgroup can be seen as viable in a larger context. To dwell on the fact that four diverse leaders – a playwright, a jailed revolutionary, a physicist, and a shipyard worker – lifted their sights to encompass wider horizons at the moment of their greatest triumph is not to downplay the obstacles inherent in decentralizing tendencies. Subgroupism is a state of mind, a deep psychological orientation toward the close at hand, toward the historically meaningful, toward the "we" who have long had to struggle against an ever-threatening "them." Such intense feelings are not easily ameliorated. They can survive isolation and they can withstand the counterpressures of a shrinking world in which proliferating networks of interdependence encourage new, transnational orientations and loyalties.[8] Hence subgroupism can be passed on for generations, thriving and felt just as deeply in the present era as it was in earlier decades or centuries. The fears and aspirations on which they are founded can, rightly or wrongly, foster suspicion toward those who see the need for compromise or who stress how the subgroup might suffer if it withholds support from collective efforts to address the environmental, economic, and social problems of the larger system. Even if former adversaries in the more encompassing society have been removed from power, coordination and cooperation with the larger system – placing long-term systemic needs ahead of short-term subsystemic goals – can readily be seen as undermining the very sources from which subgroupism derives its vitality and strength.

Precisely because it serves deep-seated emotional needs, in other words, subgroupism can at its very moment of triumph turn on, or at least away from, the larger community from which it has won a greater measure of autonomy and, in so doing, ignore and worsen the severe problems with which the larger community is confronted. How, then, can systemic renewal proceed? How can the transnationally minded heroes of subgroup combat sustain their leadership in the face of constituencies so imbued with their victory that they revel in their sub-

[8] For a compelling analysis of the fallacies of the "liberal" conception in which greater global interdependence is seen as breaking down and eventually terminating intense subgroup orientations, see Anthony D. Smith, *The Ethnic Revival* (Cambridge: Cambridge University Press, 1981).

groupism and resist efforts to recast their feelings in a systemic context? How can they transform the skills and discipline through which their followers triumphed into practices appropriate to the requirements of patience and conciliation in the post-triumph period? How might they persuade their followers that it is the better part of wisdom to bargain, even collaborate, with the adversaries over whom they triumphed, that it is unfair to hold the present generation of adversaries responsible for the excesses of earlier generations? How can they champion both the subsystem and the system, both the close-at-hand psychic needs and the distant socio-economic and political opportunities?

From subsystem triumph to system renewal

There are, obviously, no easy answers to these questions, and the effort to generate responses runs the risk of yielding to naive banalities. In addition, every situation encompasses different dynamics, so that what might advance systemic renewal in one situation could well retard it in another. Nonetheless, certain general propositions do seem worthy of exploration.

One concerns the broad strategy that guides the post-triumph conduct of the subgroup. At least six strategies, isolation, accommodation, communalism, autonomism, separatism, and irredentism, have been pursued in the past by subgroups in pluralistic communities.[9] None of these, however, seems relevant to triumphant subgroups in the present era. All six strategies involve measures for preserving and advancing the subgroup without concern for the renewal of the larger system of which it is a part and with respect to which its fate is now inextricably intertwined in an ever more interdependent, transnationalized world. None of the strategies provides guidance for addressing the deprivations of a stagnant economy or the intrusions of a polluted atmosphere. All of them presume that somehow the global economy and world politics are neutral constants that can neither enlarge nor constrain the subgroup's well-being. However, as the Lithuanians learned so poignantly, triumphant subgroupism today cannot ignore the cascades of issues, values, and threats that move quickly and pervasively on a global scale and that, thus, impose responsibilities and provide opportunities with which earlier subgroups did not have to be concerned. Only a strategy of systemic renewal, in which the subgroup's interests are not abandoned even as its horizons are lifted to

[9] A useful summary of these strategies can be found in *ibid.*, pp. 15–17.

encompass former adversaries, stands out as a viable long-run option under the turbulent conditions that mark the politics of the Frontier.

Whatever may be the components of such a strategy, clearly the quality of leadership, both within the triumphant subsystem and the system over which it has prevailed, is crucial to the convergence of former adversaries around actions which facilitate systemic renewal. But "quality of leadership" refers to more than the need for individuals with goodwill, dedication, vision, and toughness. Also needed are entrepreneurial leaders, people who can invent and broker new, innovative schemes for reconciling the diverse interests at stake subsequent to the moment of triumph. Such skills are vital because the tasks of systemic renewal amount to nothing less than institutional bargaining, to fashioning new arrangements for the resolution of conflicts among self-interested parties, each of which has the capacity to prevent, but none of which has the ability to impose, processes that can culminate in the system's renewal.[10]

Perhaps the prime key to inventive entrepreneurial leadership involves the redefinition of the problems, actors, and challenges that seemed salient throughout the period leading up to the subgroup's triumph. Both in servicing the demands of their constituencies and in moving the bargaining with former adversaries forward toward new institutional arrangements, the leaders need to break with habitual formulations and invent new ways of describing their aspirations and the obstacles that prevent the realization of goals. For the triumphant subgroup leaders this means that the systemic coherence necessary to renewal needs to be redefined in a way that it is seen as a set of opportunities for, rather than as threats to, the members of the subsystem. Such a redefinition requires dwelling on system-wide challenges and the necessity of treating former adversaries as partners needed to enhance the well-being and forward movement of the subgroup. Involved here is a reformulation of the "they" that blocks the progress of the "we." "They" becomes the stagnant economy or the polluted atmosphere rather than the repressive measures of the prior adversaries. "Progress" becomes a collective outcome and not just the subgroup's momentum toward immediate goals.

Redefining the structure of the post-triumph situation is not without risks, however. The more ideological members of the subgroup are

---

[10] For a discussion of the important role of entrepreneurial leaders in institutional bargaining, see Oran R. Young, "The Politics of International Regime Formation: Managing Natural Resources and the Environment," *International Organization*, vol. 43 (Summer 1989), p. 373.

likely to resist redefinitions which erode, or at least complicate, the simplified goals that have long motivated them and that are seen as the basis for their triumph. Such members are thus likely to become increasingly disenchanted with a leadership that develops new conceptions of the tasks ahead which includes former adversaries as partners in a more encompassing system. Indeed, the more that inventive subgroup leaders are in bargaining over new institutional arrangements, the more is the criticism of their ideological supporters likely to intensify. Contrariwise, the more subgroup leaders appear to cater to the shrill voices within their own membership, the more are the former adversaries likely to question the capacity of the subgroup to implement any agreements that are reached, thus further reducing the probability of successful negotiations over the terms of the new institutional arrangements.

Clearly, this twofold risk associated with innovative subgroup leadership involves delicacies and sensibilities on the part of the leaders that are difficult to sustain as the joys of triumph fade off into the realities of achieving system-wide coherence. How sensitive subgroup leaders should proceed under these circumstances will vary from one situation to another, with much depending on the strength of the ideological opposition and how the others at the bargaining table handle the challenges from their own ideological supporters. But a couple of guidelines seem applicable under any circumstance. Most importantly, the subgroup leaders have to cling both to the goals that underlay their triumph and to the redefined aspirations for the larger system. If either the ideologues among their supporters or those across the bargaining table seek to highlight the incompatibility of the two sets of goals, the subgroup leaders are well advised to endlessly demonstrate, patiently and eloquently, that such is not the case, that systemic coherence need not be a threat to the subsystem any more than subgroup autonomy is a threat to the system, that all concerned are parties to a nonzero-sum rather than a zero-sum game.

But suppose, it might be asked, this line of reasoning falls on deaf ears? Suppose the subgroup leaders are accused of betrayal by shrill voices among their supporters? And suppose there is some evidence that the shrill voices are widening their support base? Under these circumstances is it not mandatory to begin to back away from some of the more innovative proposals and give expression to one or another of the more shrill demands in order to retain the support of those who voice them? The answer to this last question is largely a function of how the subgroup leaders assess the competence of their membership. If the members are seen as lacking in analytic skills, as readily manipulable, as incapable of appreciating how a stagnant economy, a polluted environment, or the many other international challenges necessitate enlarged horizons and systemic coherence, then obviously the leaders are likely to back off from their entrepreneurial impulses and placate the more extreme elements within their ranks. If, on the other hand, the membership is seen as skillful and thus as capable of recognizing the benefits of new accommodations that do not undermine their sub-group's goals and unity, then the leaders' patience and eloquence on behalf of the redefined situation and nonzero-sum aspirations can be maintained with a reasonable expectation of continued and sufficient support from their followers.

Recent history testifies brilliantly to the fact that such sensibilities are not beyond the capacity of triumphant subgroup leaders. Even as Sakharov continued to demand that the Soviet Union move more decisively toward democratic institutions, so did he praise Gorbachev. Even as Havel insisted that Soviet troops be removed from Czechoslovakia, so did he call on the US Congress to provide aid to the Soviets. Even as Walesa held firm to the conditions for Solidarity's participation in the governance of Poland, so did he work with Jaruzelski toward the creation of new arrangements for governing the country.[11] And even as Mandela condemned the continuation of apartheid and the South African police as the instigators of riots among the Zulus, so did he speak of de Klerk and two other cabinet ministers as "serious" and "honest" men.[12] Each encountered some grumbling among their

---

[11] Upon his re-election as chairman of Solidarity, Walesa expressed his inclination to accord a higher priority to systemic than subsystemic concerns in this way: "To apply the idea today of a pure union means that today, now, we should declare a general strike. Can we do this? The conditions we have, all of them – price rises, unemployment and Communist bureaucrats in some places – it's all ready for a general strike. So then we uproot government. We need to be responsible. If we go in this direction, if we keep on demanding, we break down Poland. And then we are all out in the streets. Things will turn better, especially for those in touch with graveyards." Stephen Engelberg, "Walesa Again Chosen Chairman of Solidarity," *New York Times*, April 22, 1990, p. 10.

[12] Mandela's full observation here nicely illustrates how sensibilities toward both the sub-group's goals and those bargaining on behalf of the larger system can be sustained: "These three men to me are serious when they say they want a fundamental change in South Africa, and I deal with them on that basis. But I'm not misled by their honesty. They are honest, but I am concerned with harsh reality. And the harsh reality is that apartheid is still in place." Quoted in Anthony Lewis, "Mandela in the Storm," *New York Times*, April 3, 1990, p. A19. For a detailed account of the remarkable relationship between Mandela and de Klerk, see Allister Sparks, "The Secret Revolution," *The New Yorker*, April 11, 1994, pp. 56–78.

supporters and pressures to revert back to ideological purity, but none yielded in this regard and none was forced to relinquish their subgroup leaderships by the shrill voices seeking to constrain them. In the case of Sakharov, moreover, his death enshrined him as a visionary whose heroism served both fundamental human rights and the Soviet Union.

Triumphant subgroupism, in short, need not become narrow-minded groupism. Leaders and publics may well have the analytic skills and the emotional wherewithal to raise their sights and work toward systemic renewal.

The delicacy of the post-triumph bargaining situation raises the question of how leaders handle the temptation to engage in collusion with their counterparts across the table. Faced with shrill opposition within their own ranks, they might well be inclined to pursue the tactic of periodically asking their counterparts to make certain symbolic concessions which do not resolve the substantive issues but which give the appearance of their having held fast to their subgroup goals and allow them to claim success in the bargaining. Shrill oppositions may not be placated by symbolic gestures, but neither are they immune to signs of both firmness and progress. They can be diverted sufficiently to allow for the political time necessary to bargain through the substantive issues.

While any proposal involving collusion needs to be carefully phrased and cautiously advanced, there is much to commend it as a tactic. If both parties to the negotiations remain keenly aware of the need for systemic renewal and the large degree to which they are faced with a common set of economic and environmental threats, they cannot help but be cognizant of the fact that they are joined together in a common enterprise, that their status is as much one of current partners as of former adversaries, and that therefore their shared institution-building goals necessitate helping each other out with their respective shrill oppositions. Viewed in this way, actions that opponents might deride as collusion can be readily defended as the minimal cooperation needed to move the negotiations down the road to systemic renewal.

Conclusion

Whatever type of subgroup may be the focus of attention, it seems clear that the decentralization of authority inherent in the age of subgroupism confronts those authorized to act with some hard and delicate choices. At the same time it is equally plain that the direction these choices follow will be a major determinant of how world politics unfold in the years ahead. States continue to be important entities in world affairs, but they are by no means the only ones and the future course of global turbulence is as inextricably linked to how states cope with the challenges of subgroupism as to the way in which they manage the conflicts among each other.

17 Organizations

Something quite extraordinary has been occurring on the world scene over the past two decades, though it has escaped the view of all but a relative handful of close observers. A striking upsurge has taken place in organized voluntary activity, in the formation and increased activism of private, nonprofit, or nongovernmental, organizations in virtually every part of the world. In the developed countries of North America, Europe, and Asia; in the developing societies of Asia, Africa, and Latin America; and in the former Soviet bloc, people are forming associations, foundations, and other similar institutions to deliver human services, promote grassroots development, prevent environmental degradation, protect civil rights, and pursue a thousand other objectives . . . [A] veritable "associational revolution" now seems underway at the global level that may constitute as significant a social and political development of the latter twentieth century as the rise of the nation-state was of the latter nineteenth.

Lester M. Salamon[1]

The term "nongovernmental" has been resented by many organizations. It is indeed a manifestation of organizational apartheid – reminiscent of the "nonwhite" label so frequent in racist societies . . . the challenge is to discover the name . . . with which such bodies can identify. The problem may be insoluble, given the level of organizational apartheid practiced between organizations – even between NGOs. But if it is impossible to abandon the initials "NGO", perhaps it is possible to reframe their significance in a more positive light. One candidate might be "Necessary-to-Governance Organizations" . . . The corresponding reframing of "IGO" might then be "Insufficient-for-Governance Organizations" . . .

Anthony J.N. Judge[2]

[1] "The Global Associational Revolution: The Rise of the Third Sector on the World Scene," *Foreign Affairs* (July/August 1994), p. 109.
[2] "NGOs and Civil Society: Some Realities and Distortions," *Transnational Associations* (May/June 1995), p. 178.

Groups like Amnesty International, Worldwatch, Greenpeace, and Doctors Without Borders – plus Mobil, Mitsubishi, CNN, and various cultural associations – will be writing the script for world history at least as much as most of the governments that now monopolize voting in the UN.

Helena Cobban[3]

As previously emphasized and as cogently stated in the first of these epigraphs, recent decades have witnessed a staggering organizational explosion on a worldwide scale. The raw data descriptive of the proliferation of all types of organizations were noted in chapter 8, but here the purpose is to examine more closely the nature and implications of these trends. This is not as easy a task as it might seem at first glance. For not only is there a great variety of types of organization, but it is also the case that they have yet to be intensively explored. As one analyst puts it, " no one ... has undertaken a really systematic look at the NGO phenomenon – whether it is really historically 'different,' what particular confluence of agency and structure has caused this blossoming."[4] Indeed, as the second epigraph succinctly indicates, even the terminology used to describe the phenomenon is a source of considerable controversy.

Thus, while all the ramifications of the organizational explosion cannot possibly be traced in this chapter, there is much to be said for identifying some of its main dimensions, sources, and consequences as a means of stressing the large extent to which governance along the Frontier involves the organized world apart from the realm of governments. More accurately, our focus is wider than the intergovernmental organizations (IGOs) of the state-centric world and the major nongovernmental organizations (NGOs) of the multi-centric world that have subunits distributed across a number of countries and that are formally acknowledged by the UN. The latter are surely crucial dimensions of the global scene, as the UN Charter recognizes in articles 57, 63, and 71, but they are only part of the vast organizational networks through which governance unfolds. With the widening of the Frontier and the increasing porosity of the boundaries that separate local, national, and international life, even traditionally local organizations may be ensconced in one or another form of transnational relationship. Some of these relationships may have formalized dimensions through

---

[3] "From Empires to NGOs," *Christian Science Monitor*, September 14, 1995, p. 20.

[4] Ronnie D. Lipschutz, with Judith Mayer, *Global Civil Society and Global Environmental Governance: The Politics of Nature from Place to Planet* (Albany, State University of New York Press, 1996), p. 50.

Table 17.1. *Attributes of nongovernmental organizations: twelve continua*

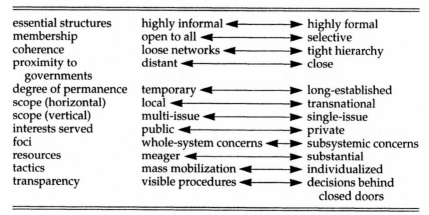

essential structures	highly informal ◄──────►	highly formal
membership	open to all ◄──────►	selective
coherence	loose networks ◄──────►	tight hierarchy
proximity to governments	distant ◄──────►	close
degree of permanence	temporary ◄──────►	long-established
scope (horizontal)	local ◄──────►	transnational
scope (vertical)	multi-issue ◄──────►	single-issue
interests served	public ◄──────►	private
foci	whole-system concerns ◄──►	subsystemic concerns
resources	meager ◄──────►	substantial
tactics	mass mobilization ◄──────►	individualized
transparency	visible procedures ◄──────►	decisions behind closed doors

regularized interactions, while others are essentially informal and *ad hoc*; but taken together they sum to a huge infrastructure, the multi-centric world, that is no less relevant to the politics of the Frontier than is the interstate system of sovereign states. To speak of the ever greater complexity of world affairs, in other words, is to refer to an organized complexity and not merely to a greater degree of interdependence and disarray.[5]

That the organizations presently active across the Frontier come in all sizes, shapes, and structures, and that their objectives, concerns, tactics, and resources are also marked by enormous variety, is suggested in table 17.1, which sets forth twelve of their attributes and the continua on which these can be located.[6] Some of the continua are mutually exclusive and some overlap, but taken together, they highlight the complexity of the organizational explosion and the difficulty of generalizing about its main features. Put differently, although the characteristics of many organizations cluster in one or the other column of table 17.1 – the nongovernmental organizations recognized by the UN, for example, tend to be formally organized, lacking in memberships, hier-

[5] Good analyses of the important differences between organized and unorganized complexity can be found in Todd R. La Porte (ed.), *Organized Social Complexity: Challenge to Politics and Policy* (Princeton: Princeton University Press, 1975).

[6] For another attempt to summarize the attributes of NGOs in tabular form, see Thomas G. Weiss and Leon Gordenker (eds.), *NGOs, the UN, and Global Governance* (Boulder, CO: Lynne Rienner, 1996), p. 42.

archical, long-established, close to governments, nondemocratic, and possessed of substantial resources – unfortunately there are numerous exceptions that render hazardous any categorization scheme; and the analytic task is further complicated by the fact that no continuum is simply dichotomous and thus considerable variability can occur between the extremes of each continuum.

How, then, to proceed? Given the absence of any systematic data on any of the continua, how to develop an analytic scheme that brings within its purview, say, the activities of Amnesty International, the Boy Scouts, the Coca-Cola Company, the Kentucky Department of Commerce, the Iroquois Federation, and the "third sector" that is "located somewhere between the public and the private sectors in institutional space [and that] belongs not to NGOs but rather to people's associations and membership organizations"?[7] In short, how to simplify the complexity so that its full range can be grasped?

Until such time as new data are gathered on the basis of an adequate analytic scheme,[8] perforce the answer to these questions involves reliance on interpretations of anecdotal data to highlight the substantial impact of organizations in the multi-centric world and thus to take note of how the attributes set forth in table 17.1 may underlie their conduct. In so doing a single label, NGOs, is used both to denote all the diverse nongovernmental organizations active in the multi-centric world and,

[7] Norman Uphoff, "Why NGOs Are Not a Third Sector: A Sectoral Analysis with Some Thoughts on Accountability, Sustainability, and Evaluation," in Michael Edwards and David Hulme (eds.), *Beyond the Magic Bullet: NGO Performance and Accountability in the Post-Cold War World* (West Hartford, CT: Kumarian, 1996), p. 23.

[8] What data do exist, and they are not insubstantial, have been generated by the Union of International Associations, which for more than three decades has published an annual compilation, the *Yearbook of International Organizations*, of established governmental and nongovernmental organizations active in the global arena. Indeed, the *Yearbook* has long been recognized by the UN as the authoritative source on IGOs and INGOs. Nevertheless, neither the official status nor the long experience of the Union is sufficient to reduce the conceptual and methodological problems inherent in mapping the organizational world to negligible proportions. The 1992/3 edition of the *Yearbook* has no fewer than thirty-two pages of appendices (all with two columns of fine print) that elaborate the definitions and classification rules used to generate, compile, and classify the thousands of diverse organizations it identifies. For a summary of the main outlines of the data presented in the 1992/3 edition of the *Yearbook* as well as for data on transnational corporations and a discussion of the methodological problems that attach to gathering materials on a variety of types of NGOs, see James N. Rosenau, "Organizational Proliferation in a Changing World," in Commission on Global Governance, *Issues in Global Governance* (London: Kluwer Law International, 1995), pp. 265–94.

following the lead of the second epigraph, to indicate they are all necessary-to-governance organizations.

The multi-centric system and the impact of NGOs

Not burdened by the inertia of a long history, and enlivened by a growing sense that counterparts in the world of states are beginning to heed as well as to hear their demands and aspirations, NGOs and other actors in the multi-centric world are experiencing a rapid growth in influence as well as a vast proliferation. Globalization, the skill revolution, and the advent of pervasive authority crises have all contributed to an explosive transformation of the private world that governments were created to serve and protect. The very same fragmegrative dynamics that mark failed states (e.g., in Somalia and the former Yugoslavia) and lead other states to engage in close collaboration (e.g., over the environment, human rights, and democratic institutions) have also absorbed the energies of NGOs and substantially expanded the roles they play in world affairs. Whatever one may think about the prospects for global order, one observer notes,

> conditions are ripe for non-state actors to play unprecedented roles in national and international security . . . While nation-building may require the presence of peacekeepers or civil police, these are fundamentally civilian, not military, operations. The opportunities for practical input from many kinds of individuals and non-governmental groups – from aid workers, human rights and election monitors, management trainers, constitution drafters, civil engineers, educators, accountants, medical professionals, refugee workers, etc. – are myriad.[9]

In addition to making such "practical inputs," moreover, the multi-centric world increasingly is giving direction to the course of events. Whatever may be the successes or failures of the UN and other multilateral endeavors, they are partly the consequence of the information, counsel, and pressures which NGOs contribute, directly as well as indirectly, to forming the global agenda and implementing the policies that emerge from the contested issues. A variety of groups – from environmentalists to indigenous peoples, from human rights activists to the dis-

---

[9] Edward C. Luck, "Security, Sovereignty, and the Growing Role of Non-State Actors," paper presented at a meeting of the Council on Foreign Relations project on "Sovereignty and a New World Politics: Defining New Roles, Strengthening New Actors," Washington, DC: (January 12, 1995), pp. 12, 19.

abled, from feminists to champions of children, to mention only a few of the many coalitions that have formed in recent years – have, as one observer puts it, "gone international," and collectively each has "developed distinct agendas at the global level, and in the form of nongovernmental organizations (NGOs) they are working with increasing sophistication to further these interests in international institutions." Indeed,

> NGOs have emerged as prime movers on a broad range of global issues, framing agendas, mobilizing constituencies toward targeted results, and monitoring compliance as a sort of new world police force. International regimes protecting human rights and the environment would arguably amount to nothing without initial and continuing NGO pressure, presaging a next wave of less developed but emerging norms that recognize other major nonnational interests and groupings. The corporate community is likewise asserting itself at the international level, often in counterpoint to the global public-interest community. The phenomenon even has its sub rosa parallel in the world of international criminal syndicates.[10]

Another analyst goes much further and argues that "the economic, informational and intellectual resources of NGOs have garnered them enough expertise and influence to assume authority in matters that, traditionally, have been solely within the purview of state administration and responsibility."[11] Put differently,

> what we face at this time is not just a *growth* of influence for NGOs, but a shift in the *balance* of influence as between NGOs and Nation State Governments (NSGs). The significance of NGOs becomes more apparent, as people find more and more suspect the claims of NSGs to absolute sovereignty. In a dozen ways, then, we are at a turning point in the historical evolution of State Power and Sovereignty: the spotlight is leaving the governments of totally Sovereign Nation States, and other actors are becoming visible on the global stage. In the long run . . . NSGs will be no more able to monopolise the political conduct of global affairs than OPEC can monopolise the world market for petroleum.[12]

---

[10] Peter J. Spiro, "New Global Communities: Nongovernmental Organizations in International Decision-Making Institutions," *The Washington Quarterly*, vol. 18 (Winter 1995), pp. 45–6.

[11] Ann Marie Clark, "Non-Governmental Organizations and Their Influence on International Society," *Journal of International Affairs*, vol. 48 (Winter 1995), p. 508.

[12] Stephen Toulmin, "The Role of NGOs in Global Affairs," unpublished paper, University of Southern California (October 1994), p. 8 (emphasis in the original).

While observers differ on the origins of NGO influence – with some arguing it began in 1865 with the founding of the International Committee of the Red Cross,[13] others suggesting that it started in 1961 with the founding of Amnesty International,[14] and with still others contending that "it was only [in 1975] with the Helsinki process that their role and influence in international affairs entered into the political spotlight in a significant way"[15] – few would quarrel with the proposition that they have become major players on the world stage. Indeed, the quantitative data descriptive of the proliferation of NGOs understate the extent to which they have become central features of world politics in the sense that their influence is likely to increase at an even greater rate than their number. Why? Because increasing numbers of NGOs are undergoing transformation from elite to mass organizations, with memberships that can be called on to lend concrete support to their leaders' efforts.[16] In addition, the Internet, the fax machine, and other products of the microelectronic revolution have made it easier for the various components of an NGO to communicate and concert their efforts. And the shift of the global agenda away from security matters and toward human rights, environmental, and economic issues has created many more points of access through which NGOs can bring pressure to bear on IGOs.[17]

The relevance of the new microelectronic channels of communication for the growth and expanding influence of NGOs can hardly be underestimated. Among other things, these channels serve to make information, technical knowledge, financial resources, and other forms of support accumulated by organizations in the industrialized world available to local groups in the developing world. It can readily be

[13] Toulmin, "The Role of NGOs in Global Affairs," p. 7.

[14] Spiro, "New Global Communities," p. 47.

[15] William Korey, "NGOs and the Helsinki Process," unpublished paper (no date), p. 1.

[16] Some analysts emphasize the distinction between elite and membership organizations by using different nomenclature to describe them: the "distinction is made between nongovernmental organizations (NGOs), which are intermediary organizations engaged in funding or offering other forms of support to communities and other organizations, and grassroots organizations (GROs), which are membership organizations of various kinds." Michael Edwards and David Hulme, "NGO Performance and Accountability," in Edwards and Hulme (eds.), *Beyond the Magic Bullet*, p. 15.

[17] For analyses of two avenues of access, see Dinah Shelton, "The Participation of Nongovernmental Organizations in International Judicial Proceedings," *American Journal of International Law*, vol. 88 (October 1994), pp. 611–42, and David Williams and Tom Young, "Governance, the World Bank and Liberal Theory," *Political Studies*, vol. 42 (1994), pp. 84–100.

argued that these channels are a major reason why hundreds of thousands of environmental NGOs in the developing countries alone have obtained the support necessary to get started and subsequently to flourish.[18] Perhaps even more important, the fax machine and Internet not only facilitate relationships between local and national or transnational organizations, but they also make it possible to build networks and alliances among like-minded organizations. So extensive have these networks of NGOs become, in fact, that they in turn have spawned new NGOs that define their role as that of serving as clearing-houses through which the networks can obtain information and advice. In order to prepare for the 1994 International Conference on Population and Development (ICPD) in Cairo, for example, more than 200 organizations in the United States concerned with human rights, religious, environmental, women's, health, and development issues formed the US Network for Cairo '94, which published a handbook detailing the history of the Cairo conference and the proposals to be considered[19] as well as convening "town meetings" in eleven different US cities "to engage the American public in the issues driving the IPCD."[20]

Further measures of the complexity that networks of NGOs infuse into world politics is readily evident in the following two summarizing accounts, the first focusing on human rights issues and the second on environmental issues:

> An international issue-network comprises a set of organizations, bound by shared values and by dense exchanges of information and services, working internationally on an issue. The diversities that make up the international human rights issue-network include parts of IGOs at both the international and regional levels, international NGOs on human rights, domestic NGOs on human rights, and private foundations. Other issue-networks will include a somewhat different array of actors, but international and domestic NGOs play a central role in all issue-networks.[21]

> All of these networks exist under the over-arching rubric of a general environmental ethic – what might be called an "operating system" –

[18] Bruce Rich, *Mortgaging the Earth: The World Bank, Environmental Impoverishment and the Crisis of Development* (Boston: Beacon Press, 1994), p. 284.

[19] Mark Valentine, *The Road to Cairo: A Handbook for the International Conference on Population and Development (ICPD)* (Bolinas, CA: Common Knowledge Press, n.d.).

[20] *Ibid.*, p. 44.

[21] Kathryn Sikkink, "Human Rights, Principled Issue-Networks, and Sovereignty in Latin America," *International Organization*, vol. 47 (Summer 1993), pp. 411–42.

although the specific form of relations through the network and structure of the actors at the ends and nodes of the network vary a great
deal. Some of these networks are quite deliberately contra-state, others
are oriented toward state reform; a few are both. Some networks
simply ignore the state altogether . . . Greenpeace is something of a
global network in itself, with both contra-state and state-reforming
tendencies; a number of observers even tend to view Greenpeace as a
purveyor of environmental "imperialism." The Asian Pacific People's
Environmental Network, based in Penang, Malaysia, includes both
urban and rural organizations, and operates at the international and
regional levels; the Climate Action Network, a loose transnational
coalition of environmental organizations, has branches in Asia, Africa,
North America, South America, Western Europe, Eastern Europe and
the Pacific . . . Even so-called indigenous peoples are creating such networks. These networks are organized around the protection of Nature,
they also address concepts of place, nationality, culture, species, and
issues.[22]

That NGOs have come to occupy central roles on the world stage
and that their activities can matter is plainly demonstrated by their
participation in the UN Conference on the Environment and
Development held in Rio de Janeiro in June 1992. Not only were more
than 4,000 individuals representing more than 1,400 NGOs formally
accredited to the conference, but the parallel Global Forum convened
down the street at the same time attracted some 25,000 other individuals from 167 countries. More importantly, the final documents of both
meetings reflected the significant pressure which NGOs can now bring
to bear on the course of events. Much the same pattern was evident at
the subsequent 1993 world conference on human rights and the 1994
Cairo conference on population. "At Cairo, in particular, a coalition of
NGOs and women's groups – above all, from developing countries,
which suffer most from the problems of family size – played a major
role in preventing the representatives of NSGs from making concessions to the Vatican, and other dominantly conservative and male religious groups, that tried to destroy the effectiveness of the Conference's
final documents."[23] In short, the notion that the world has bifurcated
into two worlds of world politics is never more brilliantly manifest
than when state representatives gather for summit meetings on major
issues: it is now commonplace that an NGO forum will also be con-

---

[22] Lipschutz, *Global Civil Society and Global Environmental Governance*, p. 59.
[23] Toulmin, "The Role of NGOs in Global Affairs," p. 12.

vened on the same issue in the same city, if not the same street or building.[24] In effect, this is one dimension of the bifurcated world that has
been institutionalized.[25]

Nor have NGOs always been limited to the role of lobbyists from the
outside. Worker and employer groups are formally represented in the
International Labor Organization (ILO) and business and labor
organizations hold comparable roles in the OECD. In addition, not only
have 978 NGOs been accorded consultative status in the UN's
Economic and Social Council (ECOSOC), but the leaders of other NGOs
have been included in national delegations and they have also participated in working groups that prepare for formal meetings. On occasion
NGOs have also taken over the delegations of small island states that
could not afford to send their own delegates to international meetings.
The Pacific island nation of Nauru, for example, lacked the resources to
send their own emissaries to the London Dumping Convention and
resolved the problem by "handing its seat to two American environmentalists."[26]

It is perhaps a measure of the successes recorded by multilateral
institutions and NGOs that increasingly concerns have been expressed
about the "democratic deficit," by which is meant the absence of procedures and institutions to hold the UN, its agencies, and NGOs
accountable for their actions. As more and more countries turn in democratic directions, and as values championing human rights spread and
become globalized, the gap between the conduct of IGOs and NGOs on
the one hand and their representativeness on the other becomes ever
more conspicuous. For many of the key issues on the global agenda at
any moment in time – questions such as who decides to address a
problem, who allocates resources for its amelioration, and who focuses
force or shame on the alleged culprits – have no immediate answer
because the relevant publics are not given a voice. The decisions are
made by officials, bureaucrats, and NGO leaderships who do not need
to answer to the constituencies whose interests they advance. Indeed,
NGOs "such as the World Wildlife Fund, World Resources Institute and

---

[24] An exception to the "same city" principle occurred with respect to the UN's Fourth
World Conference on Women held in Beijing in 1995. The host Chinese government,
apparently fearful of the unofficial voices that might be expressed against China's policies on compulsory abortion and sterilization (among other issues), forced the Forum
to convene at a site more than 30 kilometers outside Beijing.

[25] See Barbara Crossette, "Once a Sideshow, Private Organizations Star at U.N. Meetings,"
New York Times, March 12, 1995, p. 6.   [26] Spiro, "New Global Communities," p. 50.

Greenpeace more closely resemble multinational corporations, with annual budgets in excess of $100 million. They can be found in offices and projects around the world. Some even engage in 'friendly' mergers and takeovers (WWF and the Conservation Foundation, WRI and the US branch of the International Institute for Environment and Development)."[27]

Some observers go beyond decrying the democratic deficit and contend that NGOs have been coopted by counterparts in the state-centric world. In the case of China, for example, "an eminent Chinese historian in Beijing . . . smiled wryly and said, 'China has no NGOs, but only GONGOs – government-organized nongovernmental organizations.'"[28] Another critic argues that the cooptation is often more subtle, that NGOs represented at UN-sponsored conferences are,

> in terms of mind set, modes of thinking and methods of living . . . no different from the governments and multinational agencies which fund them. They use the same hotels, drive the same cars, drink the same wine together in the evening and commute together back and forth [to the meeting halls] . . . Yes, there are a few genuine and committed pro-people organizations and individuals but they are few and far between and their voices are not heard and often their thoughts are not allowed to be expressed. Above all, most NGOs are part of the problem and not a part of the solution.[29]

From a bifurcated perspective, however, the democratic deficit is perhaps less significant than the fact that actors in the multi-centric world serve as important checks on the states that dominate the state-centric world. As one analyst puts it, "If numbers are the benchmark of legitimacy, the NGO community easily passes the test. However imperfect the mechanisms of representation, environmentalist and human rights NGOs collectively speak for many times over the numbers represented by even medium-size states in the UN, and even narrowly defined NGOs would outrank the microstates."[30] Another observer makes the same point by stressing that

> Governments across much of the world are not at all sure how to handle non-government organizations (NGOs) – a growing force

---

[27] Lipschutz, *Global Civil Society and Global Environmental Governance*, p. 271, note 49.

[28] Quoted in Perry Link, "The Old Man's New China," *New York Review of Books*, June 9, 1994, p. 35, note 6.

[29] From a press conference statement offered by an "economist and social activist," Hiralal M. Desarda, at the UN Conference on Social Development, Copenhagen, e-mail message on Internet, March 11, 1995.   [30] Spiro, "New Global Communities," p. 52.

whose business is at least in part to make those in authority uncomfortable. On the one hand, governments see them as capable of taking a lot of work off them at little cost and recognize that NGOs are often better at achieving results on the ground than they are themselves. On the other, NGOs are not controllable. They keep saying things governments do not want to hear. What is more, damn it, they do so even though their funding sometimes comes from these same governments. For the bureaucrats, it can sometimes be all very unnerving.[31]

Still another analyst notes that the UN's problems twenty years ago were diagnosed as stemming from a "top to bottom" context, but that now "[s]teadily deepening ties between the UN and NGOs have given it a bottom – one bursting with energy, ideas and passion. But this new relationship between an institution created by states to serve states and NGOs, which are instead linking it directly to citizens, sometimes leaving out or cutting across the interests of national governments, is a new source of tension and perhaps resentment and a subliminal fear of losing control."[32]

To be sure, the NGO community is far from united around a common core of beliefs and is the site of conflict no less than of cooperation as different groups compete for scarce resources and access to publics and governments. In addition, there is an "inherent tension," a "continual struggle," between global networks and their local affiliates, "as the latter resist yielding up [their] particular identity to the former."[33] One analyst views the tensions within and among NGOs as such that the "manner in which different types of organization continue to disparage each other is a tragedy. Each kind of organization tends to think of itself as the only really useful organizational form. Other forms are considered as unfortunate obstacles or completely irrelevant."[34]

Stated differently, "the NGO community is not rational and uniform, but is an extremely diverse and sometimes fractious universe crisscrossed by contradictory forces. High levels of professionalism and contract-hungry and media-hungry amateurism coexist side by side, sometimes within the same organization."[35]

---

31 Derek Ingram, "NGOs Keep the Pressure Up on Bureaucrats," *Bangkok Post*, July 21, 1995, p. 5.

32 Jessica Matthews, "Citizens' Charge on the U.N.," *Washington Post*, November 20, 1995, p. A21.   33 Lipschutz, *Global Civil Society and Global Environmental Governance*, p. 000.

34 Judge, "NGOs and Civil Society: Some Realities and Distortions," p. 178.

35 Antonio Donini, "The Bureaucracy and the Free Spirits: Stagnation and Innovation in the Relationship Between the UN and NGOs," in Weiss and Gordenker (eds.), *NGOs, the UN, and Global Governance*, p. 97.

The convergence of the two worlds

Despite their differences and conflicts, the roles played by NGOs along the Frontier can hardly be underestimated. Viewed collectively as a multi-centric world, their interactions with the state-centric world are part and parcel of the rule systems that govern the course of events. As indicated, moreover, their contribution is essentially a positive one. Whenever IGOs or individual states are constructively innovative, adaptive, and forward-looking, it is likely that one or more NGOs were relevant to the adoption of the new policies. Indeed, it can even be said that actors in the multi-centric world are now deeply immersed in activities that amount to a partnership with counterparts in the public world of states, a partnership in which the efforts and well-being of states are preserved and enhanced by their reliance on NGOs and other non-governmental actors. In the words of one observer, "Non-state actors . . . are playing roles, meeting expectations, and filling gaps that national governments cannot fill on their own. So, rather than take the place of governments, non-state actors are helping them to do their jobs better in an increasingly complex and fragmented environment."[36]

Of course, the interactions between the multi-centric and state-centric worlds do not always approach partnership. In the case of multinational corporations the aspiration to protect and increase market shares often results in direct confrontations between states and the profit-oriented sector of the multi-centric world. Similarly, in public issue areas relations between the two worlds sometimes become acrimonious and, on occasion, even involve resort to violence (as the French did when ships flying the Greenpeace flag sailed into waters in the South Pacific where the French were testing nuclear devices). Whatever the direction of the relationship in particular situations, however, the level of interaction is high and continuous. A measure along these lines is provided by data on the extent to which organizations in each world cited other organizations when responding to queries about their activities posed by the 1992/3 *Yearbook of International Organizations*: all told, in 1992 4,878 intergovernmental organizations (IGOs) cited 10,968 nongovernmental organizations (NGOs) and 11,473 IGOs, whereas 27,190 NGOs mentioned 25,445 IGOs and 8,236 NGOs,[37] patterns that are suggestive of the

---

[36] Luck, "Security, Sovereignty, and the Growing Role of Non-State Actors," p. 26.
[37] Edited by the Union of International Organizations (Munich: K.G. Saur, 1992), p. 1671.

extent to which organizations, be they governmental or nongovernmental, interact and, in so doing, form the bases on which new structures are emerging out of the world's ever greater organizational
complexity.

In sum, as a study in the field of immigration found, NGO networks
are not simply pressure groups: " it is important to underscore that nongovernmental activism is not circumscribed to attempts to sway
governments";[38] rather, in a variety of ways such organizations also
seek to ameliorate directly the lives of those whose interests they represent before governments. In the words of one analyst, NGOs are transforming the state-centric system into "an egg-box containing the shells
of sovereignty; but alongside it a global community omelette is
cooking."[39]

Put less metaphorically, and as indicated in chapter 8, there are a
number of ways in which the convergence of the state-centric and multi-
centric worlds has become institutionalized, thus making it highly
probable that the bifurcation of global structures will persist for the foreseeable future as states remain predominant in the domains of diplomacy and security even as they share some of their authority with
transnational groups in the multi-centric world when the latter are well
organized, widely supported, normatively inspired, focused, endowed,
and powerful. Doubtless too, global complexity and organizational proliferation will continue to expand as the competition for resources, loyalties, and legitimacy persists in both the state-centric and multi-centric
worlds.

The challenge of the organizational explosion to governance in a turbulent world seems clear: the continuing proliferation of organizations
in both the state-centric and multi-centric worlds underlies a vast fragmentation of decision-making centers that is bound to make it more difficult to exercise control on behalf of new governance mechanisms. On
the other hand, whatever the shortcomings of the organizational explosion, it may well serve as a cushion to absorb the worst effects of rapid
and dynamic fragmegration. No mechanism is likely to achieve even a
modicum of success if it does not allow for the dynamics of organiza-

---

[38] Cathryn L. Thorup, *Redefining Governance in North America: The Impact of Cross-Border
Networks and Coalitions on Mexican Immigration into the United States* (Santa Monica:
Rand Corporation, 1993), p. 7.

[39] Ken Booth, "Security in Anarchy: Utopian Realism in Theory and Practice,"
International Affairs, vol. 67, (July 1991), p. 542.

tional proliferation and decentralization.[40] Put differently, the more elaborate, extensive, and decentralized the organizational networks are, the closer they are to the problems people face in their daily lives; and, equally important, the greater the complexity of the networks in which governments and NGOs along the Frontier are enmeshed, the less is the likelihood of any one or group of them introducing severe distortions into the course of events.

[40] For a discussion of this conclusion insofar as it pertains to the proliferation of states and IGOs in the state-centric world, see Giuseppe Schiavone, *International Organizations: A Dictionary and Directory* (London: Macmillan, 1983), pp. 1–12.

18   States

One can adopt a cosmopolitan approach and thus identify these cross-pressures as symptoms of the eventual demise of the state and the state-system and their replacement by some form of world government or "new Medievalism." Or alternatively, one can look at the changing reality of the closing years of the millennium through a non-Grotian approach and reach the conclusion that the state is in relatively good health, despite the growing challenges to its sovereignty.

Arie M. Kacowicz[1]

Like the shell of a lobster, the outer facade of the nation-state retains its general appearance and consistency, even as the societies which comprise each of them have been bombarded and saturated from outside to the point that they barely resemble the original contents. The lobster in the sea and the lobster on the plate are both lobsters, but the change in their circumstances is certainly qualitative. The same is true of states and their constituent societies amidst the political "warming" of the last generation . . . Their borders remain largely intact and their constitutions are in place, but the shells of these sovereign crustaceans have often proved too porous to prevent their contents from being cooked to someone else's taste.

Frederick S. Tipson[2]

We are all hostages to the state's impotence.

Izvestia[3]

[1] "Reinventing the Wheel: The Attacks on the State and Its Resilience," paper presented at the Annual Meeting of the International Studies Association, Chicago (February 22–25, 1995), p. 2.
[2] "Global Communications and the Sovereignty of States," paper presented at the Study Group on "Sovereignty, Non-State Actors and a New World Politics," Council on Foreign Relations, Washington, DC (April 27, 1995), p. 2.
[3] Quoted on National Public Radio following the end of the June 1995 hostage crisis in Budyonnovsk, Russia.

> From Haiti in the Western Hemisphere to the remnants of Yugoslavia
> in Europe, from Somalia, Sudan, and Liberia in Africa, to Cambodia in
> Southeast Asia, a disturbing new phenomenon is emerging: the failed
> nation-state, utterly incapable of sustaining itself as a member of the
> international community.
>
> Gerald B. Helman and Steven R. Ratner[4]

The proposition stressed in previous chapters, that a number of factors
underlie a slow but not insignificant erosion of the sovereignty, competence, coherence, and effectiveness of states at home and abroad, is
here subjected to closer analysis. Note needs to be taken of the subtle
ways in which states continue to be primary actors on the world stage
even as their control erodes with the widening of the Frontier. The
erosion is not a straight and steep downward slope. It consists, rather,
of erratic up and down movements that result in a barely perceptible
trend line in which their ability to realize policy goals appears to be
lessening. Put differently, at certain times in certain issue areas states
are very much in command of the course of events, but increasingly
their capacities to command have been subtly undermined as the turbulent dynamics of fragmegration reconfigure political, economic, and
cultural horizons. Hence the task in this chapter is not that of demonstrating that states are headed for oblivion; instead the goal is to elaborate nuance, to draw a balanced picture of how the roles they play are
shifting as their SOAs diminish and their proficiency in mobilizing
their publics is impaired.

Criteria of evaluation

Any assessment of the governing capacity of states in a rapidly changing world must perforce start on a cautionary note. Their performances
and attributes are not easily traced or measured. Interpretations of their
transformation must thus depend heavily on anecdotal evidence.
Equally important, the vast differences among states impel caution. Not
only does each state have its own unique history and circumstances,
and not only is there a huge variety of perspectives on which evaluations of states rest, but recent decades have been marked also by the
advent of many types of states and by the many ways in which they
have undergone alteration, thus enormously complicating the task of
deriving generalizations that are applicable to all states.

---

[4] "Saving Failed States," *Foreign Policy*, no. 89 (Winter 1992–3), p. 3.

One generalization is possible, however. All states exercise authority. The spheres within which they can do so may be diminishing, but they share a capacity to frame policies that seek to enhance their control over governance along the Frontier or, at least, prevent its further erosion. Thus it follows, to repeat, that the focus here is on their SOAs, how these may be shrinking, and how states are coping with the dynamics that are undermining the readiness of actors across the Frontier to comply with their policies.

Two criteria can be employed for making assessments along these lines. One focuses on the effectiveness of states.[5] Are they, or any given state, increasingly or decreasingly able to move toward their goals? Can they frame realistic objectives and maintain policies that enjoy public support, facilitate cooperation with other states, contest adversaries, or otherwise cope with the challenges of an ever more complex world? Is the complexity diminishing their capacity to engage in decisive and meaningful actions? Or are there reasons to believe that the diminution of their capacities is near an end?

The second criterion is a modification of the first. It narrows effectiveness to the politics of the Frontier. Given a focus on how states do or do not facilitate governance in a turbulent world, questions pertaining to their exercise of authority strictly within their own jurisdictions need not be probed. More accurately, only insofar as the impact of states on their own domestic scenes feeds back as a source of their conduct along the Frontier does their effectiveness within their own societies require assessment.[6] To what extent are states increasingly or decreasingly able to mobilize their publics on behalf of their international aspirations and obligations? Can they garner the internal support needed to recognize and accept a widening Frontier that lessens the scope of their sovereignty? Or can a state's sovereignty subtly erode before its officials and

---

[5] For a cogent discussion of how it is possible to probe systematically the effectiveness of any large collectivity, see Oran R. Young, "The Effectiveness of International Institutions: Hard Cases and Critical Variables," in James N. Rosenau and Ernst-Otto Czempiel (eds.), *Governance Without Government: Order and Change in World Politics* (Cambridge: Cambridge University Press, 1992), pp. 160–94.

[6] This is not to imply that the use of feedback from the domestic scene is only of peripheral concern to state leaders who preside over the conduct of foreign relations. On the contrary, even among the earliest states, "[t]here was a driving compulsion to establish state control within society, for that was the key that could unlock the doors to increased capabilities in the international arena." Joel S. Migdal, *Strong Societies and Weak States: State–Society Relations and State Capabilities in the Third World* (Princeton: Princeton University Press, 1988), p. 23.

publics become aware of the changes? Such questions, along with those ending the previous paragraph, underlie much of the analysis that follows.

To these assessment problems must be added the difficulties of fixing on an acceptable definition of what constitutes a "state" at this juncture in history. The problem lies not in the dearth of definitions, but in their plenitude. It is commonplace, for example, to identify anywhere from 5 to 145 separate definitions as useful for different purposes.[7]

The variability that marks efforts to define states serves as an important analytic guidepost. It suggests that it may be a grievous error to speak of "the state," that the concept has different meanings in different contexts,[8] and that therefore it is preferable to treat the state as one type of SOA among many that are evolving out of the dynamics of fragmegration. But how to differentiate SOAs presided over by states from other types? The answer is simple: since our focus is on states in a global context, they are defined as those collectivities accorded full voting rights in the UN General Assembly, with the vast differences among those encompassed by this general definition being treated as attributes of states that contribute to or detract from their effectiveness. This means that the analysis proceeds from a legal and diplomatic formulation not unlike the one adopted by the 1933 Montevideo Convention in which political units with four characteristics were defined as states: "(a) a permanent population, (b) a defined territory, (c) a government, and (d) a capacity to enter relations with other states" – characteristics that specify, in effect, SOAs and the people and space over which they are presumed to exercise control. Although this definition is not all-inclusive (it excludes Taiwan, for instance), it serves

---

[7] For the 145 definitions, see C. Titus, "A Nomenclature in Political Science," *American Political Science Review*, vol. 25 (1931), pp. 45–60. Other sources in which varied definitions are identified include seven uses of the concept in R.M. MacIver, *The Modern State* (Oxford: Oxford University Press, 1926), pp. 3–4; eighteen in G.L. Clark and M. Dear, *State Apparatus: Structures and Language of Legitimacy* (Boston: Allen and Unwin, 1984), p. 15; twelve in K.W. Deutsch, "State Functions and the Future of the State," *International Political Science Review*, vol. 7 (1986), pp. 209–22; six in the Marxist literature identified by R. Jessop, "Recent Theories of the Capitalist State," *Cambridge Journal of Econometrics*, vol. 1 (1977), pp. 353–73; and five in R. Benjamin and R.D. Duvall, "The Capitalist State in Context" unpublished paper, University of Minnesota, Minneapolis.

[8] As one analyst incisively observes, when those in the West "speak of a 'state,' a woman in Zimbabwe might think of the authority of a 'household.'" Christine Sylvester, "Reconstituting a Gender-Eclipsed Dialogue," in James N. Rosenau (ed.), *Global Voices: Dialogues in International Relations* (Boulder, CO: Westview Press, 1993), p. 39.

present purposes since the scope of all four attributes is, as will be seen, undergoing challenge in most states. That is, with current world politics marked by vast migrations, by boundary disputes, coalition governments, domestic restlessness, and limited foreign-policy capacities, the historic legal formulation used at the UN allows for a simple way of delineating states even as it also highlights some of the major dimensions along which they are differentiated and their effectiveness undermined. Moreover, this formal definition does not preclude analysis of new SOAs which are contesting for jurisdiction over spaces freed up by the widening of the Frontier.

Changes and continuities

While previous chapters point to a number of ways in which the roles played by citizens, publics, and NGOs have eroded state capacities, states still perform crucial functions whereby the collective needs of their peoples are enhanced, preserved, or otherwise met in the face of numerous challenges posed by an increasingly interdependent world. For better or worse, all states, the weak as well as the strong, the new as well as the old, share the aspiration of people for concerted policies that serve to protect their collective well-being and physical security. For better or worse, all of them provide a collective means for procuring resources and legitimacy from the world beyond their borders. For better or worse – and to greater or lesser degrees – all states possess jurisdiction over instruments of coercion and the right to use them.

Cast in terms of the politics of the Frontier, all states share at least four major preoccupations that consume much of the time of their top officials. All of them are preoccupied with issues surrounding their sovereignty, both as it is challenged by fragmenting forces at home and by globalizing forces at work abroad. Similarly, and relatedly, all states devote considerable energy to the preservation and enhancement of their authority over their increasingly articulate and analytically skillful citizens. No less common to all states is a preoccupation with the integrity of their borders and a felt need to police the human and nonhuman traffic that crosses them. Likewise, all states continuously work at steering their economies and societies along their historical paths.

Given the pervasiveness of these diverse activities, it should be clear that states are not about to walk off the world stage. Their sovereignty may be eroding, they may be changing in different ways at different rates, and their officials may be becoming custodians, "rather like museum guards,"[9] but few if any states remain static and most have demonstrated a capacity to adapt to a transforming world.[10] The capacities of their leaders are more circumscribed than in the past, but they still have substantial leeway to conduct their affairs. Thus, "[t]he question is not whether the state exists, is observable, and matters, but *to what extent* does a focus on the state explain those things we need to understand."[11] The thrust of this book is that such a focus is not sufficient, that shifting loci of authority highlight the need to be equally focused on how the dynamics of fragmegration are fostering new structures and processes through which the course of events unfolds.

The proliferation of states

An initial indicator of both the continuing legitimacy of states and the volatility that has come to mark their world is provided by their changing number. After a long period of state-making in which diverse independent political units such as cities and provinces that numbered around 500 in Europe in the year 1500 were aggregated and consolidated into 34 states by the end of the nineteenth century and 51 when the United Nations was founded, the number of states has increased dramatically since 1945. Membership in the UN has reached some 184 states today, an increase that not only reflects the break-up of colonial empires, but also gives eloquent voice to a worldwide set of values in which the state is posited as the most desired large-scale political organization.

Lately, moreover, these global values have been extended to the forms of government that states are expected to maintain. The surge in the number of states has been accompanied by a widespread preference for democratic forms of government, for authority structures based on the legitimately expressed will of peoples. Whether rigorous or generous criteria are used, the number of countries classified as democracies is

---

[9] The custodial metaphor is noted in Dennis Farney, "Even U.S. Politics Are Being Reshaped in a Global Economy," *Wall Street Journal*, October 28, 1992, p. 1.

[10] For an interesting assessment of the capacity of states to adapt to change, see Philip G. Cerny, *The Changing Architecture of Politics: Structure, Agency, and the Future of the State* (London: Sage Publications, 1990).

[11] Yale H. Ferguson and Richard W. Mansbach, "The Past as Prelude to the Future: Changing Loyalties in Global Politics," paper presented at the Annual Meeting of the International Studies Association, Acapulco, (March 23–27, 1993), p. 3 (italics in the original).

greater today than ever before and their number more than doubled between 1970 and 1990.[12]

The historic nation-states of Europe serve as the model for the world-wide readiness to attach highest priority to the state as the ultimate arbiter of internal disputes and thus to accord it the legitimacy to resolve conflicts through coercive means if need be. Notwithstanding the inequities and conflicts they sustained, Europe's nation-states came to be viewed as "natural" mechanisms for successfully organizing the well-being, security, and cooperation of people on a large scale. But the more appealing the European model became, the more did the connection between "nation" and "state" become ambiguous. The effectiveness of European states sprung in good part from the close correspondence between their state boundaries and their national cultures. For France, Britain, Germany, and the other countries of the continent, the nation and the state tended to be one and the same, a circumstance that enabled states to conduct themselves consistently with the aspiration of their national communities.

However, with the break up of colonial empires after World War II and the advent of dynamic technologies that shrunk social and geographic distances, the close links between states and nations tended to be overlooked and the rush to form new states became independent of their socio-economic foundations. What counted was the establishment of sovereign authority, irrespective of whether the authorities could draw on shared cultural and historical norms to obtain the compliance of those citizens and publics over which they exercised authority. The rush to independence was too powerful for attention to be paid to the question of whether the boundaries, resources, coherence, and sense of community appropriate to the operation of an effective state were available. Instead, states were quickly fashioned out of administrative territories previously created by the empires which, in turn, had been designed to serve the empire's needs rather than the well-being of the territories. As a consequence, in many instances the new states of the developing world were states only in a formal sense. They had sovereignty and recognition through admission to the United Nations, but many lacked a sufficient basis for effective governance. Indeed, sover-

---

[12] For the more rigorous criteria, see Larry Diamond, "The Globalization of Democracy," in R. Slater, B. Schutz, and S. Doerr (eds.), *Global Transformation and the Third World* (Boulder, CO: Lynne Rienner, 1993), pp. 31–69, while the more generous criteria are applied in Samuel P. Huntington, *The Third Wave: Democratization in the Late Twentieth Century* (Norman: University of Oklahoma Press, 1991).

eignty was their main resource. By claiming its protection, they preserved their independence in the absence of any other means of preventing the intrusion of the outside world. They were, in effect, legally independent but economically, politically, and socially dependent, an imbalance that led one observer to give them the label of "quasi-states."[13]

It follows that as the number of states has doubled and nearly doubled again since 1945, so has their variability. In 1990 the most populous state in the United Nations (China) had more than 1 billion people, while the smallest (St. Kitts-Nevis) had about 40,000 people, and such huge differences are paralleled along a number of other dimensions. Irrespective of size, in other words, the state continues to be regarded as the most desirable form of large-scale political organization. This was recently reaffirmed in the break-up of the Soviet Union, Yugoslavia, and Czechoslovakia. In each case subregions of these countries seized upon the fragmenting situations to press not for new forms of federal or supranational organization, but for statehood – for the creation of sovereign authority within long-standing ethnic boundaries. In some instances, such as Ossetia in Georgia or Chechnya in Russia, small enclaves within newly established states sought to carry the impulse toward independence further and agitated for their own statehood. In other instances, such as the Serbs in the former Yugoslavia, the notion of the state as the best and purest form of large-scale organization underwent severe distortion and fostered policies of "ethnic cleansing" designed to make state boundaries coterminous with the presence of a single ethnic group. In still other instances, such as the Kurds and Palestinians in the Middle East, the Quebecois in Canada, and the Basques in Spain, the predispositions toward state-making have not been immediately realized, but they are no less intense and may ultimately achieve fruition.

In short, there is no reason to presume that the proliferation of states has come to an end. Despite the shifting loci of authority and the numerous challenges that are rendering states increasingly fragile as effective large-scale organizations, the idea that they can serve as the ultimate providers of physical and psychic security continues to be appealing. At the same time, however,

---

[13] Robert H. Jackson, *Quasi-States: Sovereignty, International Relations and the Third World* (Cambridge: Cambridge University Press, 1990). For a similar analysis, see Caroline Thomas, *New States, Sovereignty and Intervention* (New York: St. Martin's Press, 1985).

the territorial basis of the political order, which is one of the pillars of the state system, is under attack in many places, while the incompatibility between the principle of established and recognized territorial frontiers and the principle espoused by the various brands of community-based political movements that have flourished beyond the Western world and on its doorstep (as in Yugoslavia), is becoming increasingly apparent. In fact, in all these societies, steadily weakening allegiance to the state has resulted in the proliferation of modes of political identification, subject to varying degrees of control, and the increased volatility of these modes, which has served to depreciate the state model into only one of many possible paradigms of public order.[14]

The state-centric world

One way to appreciate the changing role of states along the Frontier is to note those occasions when states act collectively in response to collective challenges from NGOs, corporations, and other actors in the multi-centric world. Direct confrontations do not occur often, as only rarely in either world are the actors so consensual as to put up a united front in their demands on those in the other world. The central pattern is rather one of cooperation among those actors in both worlds that have a common interest in ameliorating a problem. Most issues, in other words, touch upon only interested parties in each world and in these cases the representatives of states are usually open to, and even welcome, the input of counterparts in the multi-centric world. Thus it is, as already noted, that at the various UN-sponsored summit conferences on the environment, population, social issues, and women, states acknowledge the presence of NGOs, listen to their demands, seek out their advice, and otherwise accept the implications of a bifurcated world. However, at the human rights summit in Vienna and the social summit in Copenhagen, and perhaps on other such occasions, the state-centric world's representatives have balked at according access to their multi-centric counterparts when the time has come for formal deliberations and decisions. At such times they have barred their doors and refused to allow for the direct participation of NGOs, permitting them only to watch the proceedings on closed circuit TV. In short, states still cling to their authority and the exercise of their sovereign powers in direct confrontations involving the formalities of final decision-making.

[14] Bertrand Badie and Pierre Birnbaum, "Sociology of the State Revisited," *International Social Science Journal*, vol. 46 (June 1994), p. 163.

Some might interpret these closed deliberations at summit meetings as indicative of the continuing and unchanging competence of states. The ability to resist the protests of the multi-centric world and keep it at bay at these moments, it could be argued, speaks of the ultimate authority of states, the power they can exercise when push comes to shove. Such reasoning, however, ignores the many ways (noted below) in which the SOAs of states have shrunk, and it also overlooks the huge extent to which the multi-centric world shapes the agendas and issues that are addressed in the formal discussions that unfold behind the closed doors of the state-centric world. The outcomes of these deliberations may be formally adopted by the votes of states, but their substance is in many ways a product of the pressures from outside to which they have been subjected by diverse nongovernmental constituencies. An analogy to the United States is relevant here: while the two houses of its Congress do not allow nonmembers on their floors during formal sessions, it can hardly be said that their debates and the bills they adopt are independent of the enormous efforts of various lobbyists to shape the thrust and wording of the laws that pass. To understand governance in the United States, in other words, one needs to look beyond formal institutions and assess the stresses and strains at work in the larger community of which the institutions are an expression. Likewise, to grasp governance along the Frontier, one must appreciate the increasingly salient dynamics of the larger community to which states deem themselves responsible.

Fragmegration and the transformation of states

As stressed throughout previous chapters, the combination of internal and external dynamics at work in all societies generates simultaneous tendencies toward globalization and localization, toward more extensive integration across national boundaries and more pervasive fragmentation within national boundaries, toward a relocation of authority "outward" to transnational entities and "inward" to subnational groups. Viewed in this context, the probability seems high that the capabilities and sovereignty of all states will encounter new limits as the dynamics of fragmegration expand and deepen. By knowingly or otherwise accepting shifts of authority to transnational entities, in other words, states narrow the range of issues over which they can claim exclusive responsibility for their conduct, just as internal shifts of legitimacy to subnational groups reduce the extent to which they can mobilize support for actions designed to preserve their sovereignty. Stated differently, if it is premature to speak of a borderless world – as one observer does[15] – it is surely not inappropriate to stress that historic boundaries are in flux, that the forces which have made the nation-state the central focus of large-scale organization for centuries are no longer as "natural" as they once were.

This is not to say that states will be nudged aside as authority shifts in diverse directions. They may well have important roles to play as facilitators of the shifting flows of authority. It has been argued, for example, that

> the policies and practices of states in distributing power upwards to the international level and downwards to sub-national agencies are the sutures that will hold the system of governance together. Without such explicit policies to close gaps in governance and elaborate a division of labour in regulation, vital capacities for control will be lost. Authority may now be plural within and between states rather than nationally centralized, but to be effective it must be structured by an element of design into a relatively coherent architecture of institutions.[16]

The conclusion that the scope of state authority has narrowed is particularly applicable to the realm of territorial integrity. Whatever else may be said about the performance of states across the last three centuries, their provision of physical security against external threats has been largely successful. Even in this realm, however, recent years have witnessed a noticeable decline in the capacity of states to perform their historic task. Irrespective of how powerful a state may be, the advent of nuclear weapons has rendered it vulnerable to unacceptable destruction. In the succinct words of one observer,

> The individual in today's world . . . can no longer look to the nation as the main source of his security. For the nation is unable to protect him against invasion or assault from other nations. Nor is it able to guarantee the main conditions of his growth or to safeguard his values or institutions or culture or property. No matter how wide the oceans that surround the nation, no matter how bristling its defenses, its people have suddenly become vulnerable to shattering attack. The nation possesses retaliatory power, true, but even in the exercise of that power it engages in a form of self-assault, for power today has its effects

---

[15] Kenichi Ohmae, *The Borderless World: Power and Strategy in the Interlinked Economy* (New York: HarperCollins Publishers, 1990).

[16] Paul Hirst and Grahame Thompson, *Globalization in Question* (Oxford: Blackwell 1996), pp. 184–5.

against the delicate and precarious conditions that make existence possible. This is the central, overwhelming fact not just about national power but about national powerlessness in the twentieth century. The fully sovereign nation has become separated from its historic reason for being.[17]

Nor has the collapse of the Soviet Union and the end of the nuclear arms race between the two superpowers improved the capacity of states to provide their citizens with physical security against attack. For the proliferation of nuclear materials and the capacity to use them continues apace. Indeed, the likelihood of small states and actors in the multicentric world acquiring nuclear weapons continues to grow, thus further eroding – even emasculating – the idea of "national security" as a meaningful concept. Quite apart from nuclear weapons, moreover, "if the discourse of sovereignty is to retain its explanatory power it must also attempt to accommodate the emergence of liberation movements, guerrilla organizations, terrorist groups and mercenary forces, all of which threaten what was once believed to be a defining characteristic of the national state – its monopoly on the legitimate use of violence."[18]

For those states whose internal cohesiveness had long been highly dependent on domestic political and economic mobilization against external threats – what has been called the "national security state" (NSS) – the end of the Cold War was especially corrosive of the ability to exercise control over the Frontier. Not only did the globalization of national economies intensify interdependencies which, in turn, undermined traditional security strategies, but by making these strategies the organizing core of their military and economic policies, the NSSs made the well-being of their citizens subordinate to the well-being of the state. The Cold War was used to justify, for example, welfare policies, political campaigns, and educational goals, with the result that both officials and citizens of NSSs were dislocated by the end of the Cold War and the collapse of their reasons for being mobilized against potential enemies. This meant that they had to begin to look for new foci of their loyalties and enmities, a redirection that tended to foster domestic conflict and a delegitimization of the idea that the central purpose of the state is to maintain security against external threats. Significantly, in the United States and Russia this led to politicians and political parties routinely

[17] Norman Cousins, *The Pathology of Power* (New York: W.W. Norton, 1987), pp. 191–2.
[18] Joseph A, Camilleri and Jim Falk, *The End of Sovereignty? The Politics of a Shrinking and Fragmenting World* (Aldershot, England: Edward Elgar, 1992), p. 7.

committing themselves to campaigning against the state. American and Russian politics are marked by leaders trying to outdo each other as outsiders by depicting themselves as enemies of their governments and, in effect, running against Washington or Moscow. In Israel, parties and public accuse each other of betraying the nation, a rhetoric that contributes to political assassinations, the blowing up of government buildings, racial and ethnic attacks on minorities, and the evolution of a malaise over the loss of what were once fixed boundaries along the Frontier. In extreme instances citizens resort to the language of betrayal and take up arms against their neighbors. This happened in the former Yugoslavia, with the price being paid in massive destruction and death.

And added to the insecurities of citizens in former NSSs are those that are rooted in the dislocations of the global economy – in the threats to individual jobs and whole industries posed by production elsewhere in the world. It is hardly an accident, for example, that both American and Russian politics in 1996 surfaced presidential candidates who emphasized the need to build barriers around the Frontier in order to keep goods, illegal immigrants, and ideas from crossing through it.

As indicated in chapter 10, much the same can be said about the consequences of globalization for the ecological realm. The boundaries of states cannot ward off, contain, or otherwise prevent the intrusion of pollution and the many other environmental dangers presently threatening the world. The wind carries polluted air across boundaries, the currents carry polluted water onto foreign shores, and the ozone gap is no less oblivious of the borders of states. Accordingly, again there is no way that states can, on their own, exercise their sovereign rights to protect fully the well-being of their citizens.

Nor are the ramifications of globalization confined to the security and socio-economic realms. They are hardly less manifest in the realm of culture and communication. The role of the state in socializing its young, creating national heroes, memorializing national triumphs, and providing its citizens with the wherewithal for national coherence through shared educational, cultural, and historical experiences has also been noticeably diminished by the dynamics of fragmegration. Not only has the diffusion of identical consumer goods throughout the world reduced the uniqueness of cultural identities, but the diffusion of ideas in both words and pictures through new information technologies has been perhaps even more significant in breaking down the predominance of states as providers of the psychic ties on which national identities are founded.

To be sure, as evident in the entities that emerged out of the former Soviet Union and Yugoslavia, there are locales where nationalism is virulently active as a force for cohesion, but these situations are not so much expressive of the power of states to maintain cultural cohesiveness as they are of the fragmentation of state authority and the surge of ethnicity around narrowly defined subnational values. Furthermore, as has been vividly demonstrated by the Tamils' violent efforts to achieve autonomy in Sri Lanka and Chechnya's attempt to become independent of Russia, even the pockets of unrestrained ethnic fragmentation are the focus of global television and thereby become a feature of world culture as they demonstrate in yet another way the declining limits of state authority.

In short,

> the transnationalization of culture takes away one more fundamental task of the nation state. The scope of necessary standardized communication and standardized fundamental education has broadened dramatically. While the provision of educational services allowing people to communicate with each other has become more important than ever, these services no longer need to be supplied by nationally defined units.[19]

That new communication and information technologies are fostering the emergence of norms shared widely across national boundaries is readily discernible with respect to human rights and ecological concerns. The shared norms in these issue areas, along with the traces of a global culture noted above, serve as additional constraints upon the policy-making functions of states. Even states founded on authoritarian rule experience global pressures for recognition of human rights as clear-cut intrusions upon their sovereignty – if not by impelling them to adopt new humanitarian codes, then by inducing incremental changes that result in the releasing of some prisoners or constraining the tendency to imprison others. China and Burma are good cases in point. For all the frequent assertions of its sovereign rights with regard to the treatment of students involved in the upheaval at Tiananmen Square, the Chinese regime has released more than a few students from prison as a consequence of pressures from abroad. Likewise, despite harsh authoritarian rule and violent repression of student rallies, the Burmese regime appears to have been restrained by external pressures in limit-

---

[19] Michael Zurn, "The Challenge of Globalization and Individualization: A View from Europe," in Hans-Henrik Holm and Georg Sorensen (eds.), *Whose World Order? Uneven Globalization and the End of the Cold War* (Boulder, CO: Westview Press, 1995), p. 152.

ing its action to the house arrest and eventual release of the outspoken opposition leader, Daw Aung San Suu Kyi.

Authority crises

It is hardly surprising that the pressures inherent in fragmegration have given rise, in most states in every region of the world, to internal authority crises in which the legitimacy and governing powers of political leaders are being challenged, thwarted, or otherwise questioned by organized subgroups, social movements, issue publics, and individual citizens. For a wide range of reasons – from pervasive corruption among officials to persistent unemployment to unresolved socio-economic cleavages – governments are not the focus of widespread support on the part of their peoples. Instead subgroups are proliferating and loyalties are being directed toward them as people begin to doubt the worth of their national institutions. The prime consequence of these growing doubts is widespread cynicism toward politics and political institutions which, in turn, has contributed to the aforementioned replacement of traditional forms of legitimacy that entitled national governments to pursue whatever policies were deemed appropriate with performance criteria of legitimacy that are too demanding for most governments to meet.

Further intensified by the skill revolution through which citizens everywhere are becoming ever more adept at adjusting to the complexities of modern life, the proliferation of challenging subgroups seems bound to affect the loyalties on which states need to rely if they are to mobilize successfully support for their goals and policies. NSSs are not alone in this regard. As transnational and subnational actors become increasingly active and effective in all states, as they demonstrate a capacity to deal with problems that states have found intractable or beyond their competence, citizens will begin to look elsewhere than the national capital for assistance. Examples abound. In addition to the intense authority crises that are rendering the exercise of governmental authority highly problematic throughout the former Yugoslavia and Soviet Union, there are a number of present-day national systems beset with circumstances so dire that their continued existence can no longer be presumed. Zaire, for example, "doesn't really exist any more as a state entity,"[20] just as the central government in Burundi was expected

---

[20] A European diplomat quoted in Howard W. French, "Mobutu, Zaire's 'Guide,' Leads Nation Into Chaos," *New York Times*, June 10, 1995, p. 1.

to "disappear,"[21] observations that extend the contention in the fourth epigraph above that the "failed nation-state" has become a central feature of the global landscape.[22]

If failed nation-states are increasingly numerous, so are those that might be called "adrift nation-states" – that is, national systems that have long histories but have lost their moorings and are adrift in a globalized sea unable to find direction. Specific cases in diverse parts of the world can be readily noted. In India the Hindu–Muslim conflict takes ugly turns that may tear that venerable country once again into two parts or, perhaps worse, leave it foundering without legitimacy attaching to any governmental functions at the national level.[23] In France a society-wide malaise has deepened to the point where "a lot of French people don't know what it means to be French anymore,"[24] where the mood of pessimism is so widespread that "many Frenchmen have doubts about the capacity of their country to meet successfully the dangers, opportunities, and uncertainties which the future holds," as if "something is breaking apart, that society is decomposing," and that, indeed, "all the institutions built over the past 40 years are in crisis and are therefore incapable of responding."[25] In Italy the authority crisis persists in spite of national elections in which the parties and officials that sustained the long-standing system of corruption were trounced and followed by an effort to start over from scratch. In Russia, as already noted, the long-term absence of shared national values revealed by the collapse of communist ideology underlies a continuing deterioration that undermines authoritative institutions capable of fashioning a modicum of social order.[26] In China the same ideological failure,

---

[21] James C. McKinley, Jr., "Growing Ethnic Strife in Burundi Leads to Fears of New Civil War," *New York Times*, January 14, 1996, p. 1.

[22] For an analysis in which "the parastate emerges as the mutant offspring of an expiring failed state," see Misha Glenny, "The Age of the Parastate," *The New Yorker*, May 8, 1995, pp. 45–53. And for a compelling formulation of how the world should address the challenge of situations "where governments have crumbled and the most basic conditions for civilized life have disappeared," see Paul Johnson, "Colonialism's Back – and Not a Moment Too Soon," *New York Times Magazine*, April 18, 1993, pp. 22, 43–4.

[23] Edward A. Gargan, "Challenge to India's Leaders: Survived but Weakly," *New York Times*, February 27, 1993.

[24] Craig R. Whitney, "With Europe in Flux, No More Politics as Usual," *New York Times*, April 4, 1993, p. 3.

[25] Alan Riding, "France Questions Its Identity As It Sinks Into `Le Malaise,'" *New York Times*, December 23, 1990, pp. 1, 7.

[26] Present-day Russia is so lacking in shared underlying values that recently a widespread and intense debate surfaced over how the words of the national anthem should be

coupled with a booming coastal economy, has led provincial governments to ignore directives from the central government in Beijing and
confronted the latter with the troubling question of how to restore
commitments to a national society.[27] In Afghanistan, as in
Czechoslovakia and Yugoslavia, "the partitioning of the country into
three autonomous territories is becoming a fact of life."[28] In Greece
"more than half of the nation's taxes are never paid."[29] In Nicaragua "a
deepening quarrel between the President and the National Assembly
has plunged Nicaragua into a constitutional crisis, with leaders of each
branch of government citing rival constitutions and looking to competing Supreme Courts to support their claims."[30] In Algeria "the security
situation seems to be spinning out of control, raising the prospects of an
all-out guerrilla war involving big armed clashes across the country,
including the capital."[31] In Egypt the struggle of the secular government
to overcome the challenge of a well-organized movement of Islamic
fundamentalists is likely to persist for a long time, with the outcome
enough in doubt for the eventual "winner" to be hard pressed to re-
establish the authority needed for effective governance.[32] In Palestine,
"Arafat's fledgling government, and its police officers and courts, just
don't count. For [many Palestinians] a word from the powerful families
in their towns is still the only law they acknowledge."[33]

Nor is the United States immune from the dynamics of fragmegration. It has also suffered a decline in the capacity of its government to
mobilize widespread support for policies designed to reverse a growing

revised to reflect the country's post-communist circumstances. More than 4,000 citizens
submitted new wording, but thus far no proposal has engendered broad support. See
Fred Hiatt, "Those Russian Anthem Blues," *Washington Post*, March 9, 1993, p. 1. For
another way in which the absence of societal consensus is conspicuously evident, see
Fred Hiatt, "Regions Wrest Powers from Kremlin," *Washington Post*, May 25, 1993, p. A12.

[27] Gerald Segal, "Beijing's Fading Clout," *New York Times*, May 25, 1994, p. A15.

[28] Edward A. Gargan, "Afghanistan, Always Riven, Is Breaking Into Ethnic Parts," *New York Times*, January 17, 1993, p. 1.

[29] Marlise Simons, "Enforcing One of Life's Certainties Has Problems," *New York Times*, May 25, 1995, p. A4.

[30] Larry Rohter, "President and Legislature Dueling Nicaragua," *New York Times*, June 5, 1995, p. A7.

[31] Youssef M. Ibrahim, "As Islamic Violence Accelerates, Fears of a Showdown in Algeria," *New York Times*, February 22, 1995, p. 1.

[32] Youssef M. Ibrahim, "Muslems' Fury Falls on Egypt's Christians," *New York Times*, March 15, 1993, p. 1. A more general expression of concern can be found in Canon J. Ciarlo, "The Challenge of the Sects," *The* [Malta] *Times*, April 8, 1993.

[33] Amy Dockser Marcus, "Big Palestinian Clans Enjoy a Resurgence That May Hurt Arafat," *Wall Street Journal*, September 13, 1995, p. 1.

deficit and a number of long-standing and serious domestic problems. Cynicism toward politics is widespread and trust in all public institutions has declined discernibly.[34] Both major political parties are deeply divided, and even when one party controls both the legislative and executive branches, the stalemate of US governmental instruments persists. For a few weeks late in 1995, the stalemate twice resulted in a shut down of the national government. In foreign affairs too, deep cleavages in how Americans view the role of the United States in the world persisted during the Cold War and have since continued without let up.[35] While the United States may be the world's leading (and even its only major) power, it is hardly the superpower it was a couple of decades earlier, and in this changing role the processes of sovereignty's erosion are readily manifest.

It would be a mistake, however, to regard authority crises as confined to multi-ethnic systems. Relatively homogeneous societies are beset with the same dilemma, as has readily been evident in some European countries – most notably, Denmark, Britain, France, and Norway – over the issue of whether to form the European Community (EC) and its successor, the European Union (EU). And in Japan, the questions being raised are "of a kind Japan rarely asks about itself: whether the establishment has been so battered by a succession of scandals that it has finally lost the moral legitimacy to govern."[36]

In sum, what was once well-established and beyond question is now problematic and undergoing change. Everywhere the diminished competence of states to act decisively, combined with the processes of loyalty transformation, serve as a significant source of the authority crises that are presently at work in world politics. Clearly, the more such crises intensify, the more the capabilities of states decline and the more the loyalties of citizens become diffused.[37]

---

[34] Extensive data evidential of these patterns was presented in a five-part series by the *Washington Post*, January 28–February 1, 1996.

[35] For data plainly supporting this interpretation, see Ole R. Holsti and James N. Rosenau, "The Structure of Foreign Policy Beliefs Among American Opinion Leaders – After the Cold War," *Millennium*, vol. 22 (Summer 1993), pp. 235–78.

[36] David E. Sanger, "$50 Million Discovered in Raids On Arrested Japanese Politician," *New York Times*, March 10, 1993, p. 1.

[37] For other recent formulations which posit states as in varying degrees of decline, see Gurutz Jáuregui Bereciartu, *Decline of the Nation-State* (Reno: University of Nevada Press, 1994); Jean-Marie Guéhenno, *The End of the Nation-State* (Minneapolis: University of Minnesota Press, 1995); and Kenichi Ohmae, *The End of the Nation State: The Rise of Regional Economies* (New York: The Free Press, 1995).

Contrary perspectives

Although there are substantial indicators supporting the conclusion that the capacities, effectiveness, and sovereignty of states are undergoing considerable erosion, a nuanced evaluation necessitates elaboration on contrary perspectives held by many analysts – and summarized above in the first epigraph – who discount the indicators and focus on those aspects of states that point to continuing viability and clout. Mainly adherents of the realist or neorealist worldviews, they view states as infusing world affairs with vitality and as prime sources of the dynamics transforming world affairs. After all, they assert, it was the state-centric world that created international organizations, that developed the arrangements through which the nuclear revolution has been contained, that responded to the demands for decolonization in such a way as to produce the hierarchical arrangements that have enabled the industrial countries to dominate those in the developing world, and that framed the debate over the distribution of the world's resources – to mention only a few of the more obvious ways in which states have shaped and still shape the ongoing realities of world politics. To discern a decline in the capacity of states, this line of reasoning concludes, is to exaggerate, to engage in overly selective perception and thereby to run the risk of presuming that states are increasingly irrelevant as sources of action in global politics.

Some analysts go much further, not only explicitly rejecting the transformative patterns highlighted here, but contending instead that states are increasingly robust and far more capable than any other actors who cavort on the world stage.[38] This reasoning posits the state as so deeply ensconced in the routines and institutions of politics, both domestic and international, that the erosion of its capabilities and influence is unimaginable. The state has proven itself, the argument goes, by performing vital functions that serve the needs of people, which is why it has been around more than three hundred years. In its longevity, moreover, the state has overcome all kinds of challenges, many of which are far more severe than the globalization of national economies and the emergence of new types of collectivities. Indeed, there are all kinds of ways in which states may actually be accumulating greater capabilities

---

[38] See, for example, Ted Robert Gurr, "War, Revolution and the Growth of the Coercive State," in James A. Caporaso (ed.), *The Elusive State: International and Comparative Perspectives* (Newbury Park, CA: Sage Publications, 1989), pp. 49–68.

and, if so, the argument stresses, any trends that threaten to alter significantly the balance of bifurcated structures in favor of the multi-centric world are destined to founder because states retain the capacity to resist as well as stimulate changes that affect the basic framework of world politics. In sum, "the transformative literature has so far failed to provide a convincing or coherent account of the modern state itself. In particular, it tends to exaggerate the erosion of state power in the face of globalizing pressures and fails to recognize the enduring relevance of the modern state, both as an idea and as an institutional complex, in determining the direction of domestic and international politics."[39]

But a nuanced perspective on fragmegrative processes also requires appreciation of the large degree to which some perspectives, especially those of realists, are conceptually ill-equipped to cope with the dynamics of fragmegrative change. They are founded on the assumption of an underlying constancy in the nature of world affairs and, thus, continue to presume that states are the pre-eminent actors on the world stage and to make no allowance for the diminution of their authority. While governments founder and NGOs, social movements, and other types of collectivities become increasingly central, realists maintain their focus on states as rational actors that calculate their interests in terms of their relative power and as ever capable of resorting to force in the event their interests are thereby served.[40] They do not acknowledge the boundaries of many issue arenas are being narrowed by the dynamics of global change and thus they have yet to adjust their perspectives to allow for the widening Frontier where states are less authoritative. Indeed, realists are not averse to defending the absence of change mechanisms in their paradigm by pointing to the longevity of the interstate system and stressing that it would not have lasted nearly four centuries if it had been vulnerable to the transformational dynamics that seemed so salient at particular times.

[39] David Held, *Democracy and the Global Order: From the Modern State to Cosmopolitan Governance* (Stanford, CA: Stanford University Press, 1995), p. 26. For similar formulations in which the decline of state influence is regarded as erroneous, see Miles Kahler, "The Survival of the State in European International Relations," in Charles S. Maier (ed.), *Changing Boundaries of the Political: Essays on the Evolving Balance Between the State and Society, Public and Private in Europe* (Cambridge: Cambridge University Press, 1987), chap. 9, and Andrew Moravcik, "Why the European Community Strengthens the State: Domestic Politics and International Cooperation," paper presented at the Annual Meeting of the American Political Science Association, New York (September 1994).

[40] The classic statement of realism can be found in Hans J. Morgenthau, *Politics Among Nations* (New York: Alfred A. Knopf, any edition).

Some modification of this view of realism needs to be made with respect to neorealists. While hard-core realists focus on the likelihood of conflict and war, neorealists are more ready to acknowledge that states can define their interests in terms of economic as well as physical security, thereby enabling them to undertake cooperative policies and participate in the formation of international regimes devoted to maintaining order and stable arrangements in particular issue-areas.[41] The neorealist perspective does not systematically posit transformational dynamics that impel states to cooperate, but it does allow for change of this kind and, in so doing, it parts company with its realist predecessor. At the same time, changes of this sort are seen by neorealists as occurring within the context of an unchanging state system dominated by self-interested states. Neorealists are no more ready than realists to make conceptual allowances for the erosion and dispersion of state authority and the increasing relevance of other actors.[42]

While realist interpretations thus seem basically flawed, they do serve as cautionary notes. They remind us again that the argument for diminished state competence is subtle and depends on a lot of intangible processes for which solid indicators are not readily available. Perhaps even more important, the alternative perspectives warn us that the case for viewing the erosion of state capabilities ought not be overstated, that the criteria for viewing states as political units with permanent populations, defined territories, and governments capable of governing, and with the capability of entering into relations with other states, are highly abstract and allow for extensive diversity. The competing interpretations, in other words, give pause and reinforce our emphasis on the need to avoid treating states as constants. Viewed in terms of the full sweep of human history, states are relatively recent arrivals on the political scene, thus indicating that they are as susceptible to variability as any other social system.

Yet, even in the context of extreme analytic caution, the essential thrust of the foregoing discussion offers good reasons to focus on the vulnerabilities of states. Given the growing density of populations, the

---

[41] For cogent discussions of cooperation and regimes as theoretical foci in the study of IR, see Robert O. Keohane, *After Hegemony: Cooperation and Discord in the World Political Economy* (Princeton: Princeton University Press, 1984), and Stephen D. Krasner (ed.), *International Regimes* (Ithaca: Cornell University Press, 1983).

[42] A vigorous debate over the strengths and weaknesses of the neorealist paradigm can be found in Robert O. Keohane (ed.), *Neorealism and Its Critics* (New York: Columbia University Press, 1986).

expanding complexity of the organized segments of society, the global-ization of national economies, the relentless pressure of technological innovations, the challenge of subgroups intent upon achieving greater autonomy, the advent of the microelectronic revolution that has heightened the readiness of more analytically skillful citizens to question the legitimacy of governmental policies, and the endless array of other intractable problems which comprise the modern political agenda, it seems that world politics have cumulated to a severity of circumstances that lessens the capacity of all states to be decisive and effective. States may be marked by extensive variability in their capacity to cope with these circumstances, but none seem able to fully withstand the consequences of an ever more turbulent world. While they may not be about to exit from the political stage, and while some may even continue to occupy the center of the stage, all states seem likely to become increasingly ineffective as managers of their own affairs.

One useful way of differentiating among the degrees to which states are able to manage their affairs is to classify them as pre-modern, modern, or post-modern entities.[43] Those in the first category refer to states in the developing world that were created out of former colonial empires and that lack the resources to move effectively along the Frontier, while states in the third category are exemplified by those in the European Union that have adapted to the widening of the Frontier through cooperation and yielding some of their sovereignty to a more encompassing entity, thereby creating "transnational structures of political authority that lack a single head [and that have been called] 'international states.'"[44] The middle category encompasses the traditional Westphalian states that for several centuries successfully adapted to systemic pressures but that are now experiencing a diminution of their capacity to cope with myriad challenges that arise along the Frontier.[45]

---

[43] Georg Sorensen, "States Are Not Like Units: Types of States and Forms of Anarchy in the Present International System," paper presented at the Annual Meeting of the American Political Science Association, Chicago (September 1995).

[44] Alexander Wendt, "Collective Identity Formation and the International State," *American Political Science Review*, vol. 88 (June 1994), p. 392.

[45] A cogent analysis of how the capacities of this type of state are eroding can be found in Mark W. Zacher, "The Decaying Pillars of the Westphalian Temple: Implications for International Order and Governance," in Rosenau and Czempiel (eds.), *Governance Without Government*, pp. 58–101.

Implications for governance along the frontier

If it is reasonable to conclude that the authority, effectiveness, and sovereignty of states are under severe strain, the ramifications for global governance are enormous. Most notably, if global governance is conceived along the lines set forth in chapter 8 as all the structures and processes necessary to maintaining a modicum of public order and movement toward the realization of collective goals at every level of community throughout the world, the decline of states as foci and centers of authority suggests that the world is moving into a period of extensive disarray in which governance will be in short supply. For it is far from automatic that the vacuum resulting from the lessened authority of states will be quickly filled by other forms of political organization. At the very least it is likely that a long transition period will have to ensue while the necessary habits, orientations, and coherence cumulate to the point where the new organizations can be effective wielders of authority. Legitimacy and authority rest on deep-seated habits and these do not take shape overnight. They require repeated learning experiences which continually reinforce the inclination to comply with the directives of the new authorities. And if the transition period is marked as much by noxious as by satisfying experiences – as seems likely for all the reasons noted – the politics of the Frontier is likely to be makeshift and pervaded with tension for a long, long time.

19 Militaries

We are an army, not a Salvation Army.

US Secretary of Defense William J. Perry[1]

The army is *my* army. For me, it's the measuring stick of my life. It's my pride, my soul's pain, my labor and sweat. It's my entire life. It's my father, who defended Leningrad, and my brothers, officers of the armed forces. What is happening to all of it?

Lt. Col. Melis Bekbasynov, member of the Russian officer corps[2]

A curse on you all. Where are you taking the world?

Azerbaijani grandmother[3]

In our parents' day, [the army] could get away with [a compulsory draft]. People believed in suffering and sacrifice then. They believed they could do everything for the glory of the motherland and get no compensation for it. That's not a good argument for our generation.

news item[4]

Having indicated in previous chapters that globalizing dynamics have transformed the concept of security from a preoccupation with territorial protection to a concern for markets, trade, and economic well-being, and anticipating the central thrust of chapter 22 that traces a decreasing likelihood of interstate war, the purpose of this chapter is to identify

---

[1] Quoted in Bradley Graham, "Fund New Missions, Pentagon Pleads," *International Herald Tribune*, August 6–7, 1994, p. 2.

[2] *Los Angeles Times*, January 18, 1992, p. A8.

[3] Shouting at a helicopter loaded with military supplies, quoted in the *Los Angeles Times*, January 12, 1992, p. A8.

[4] Quoted in Rick Atkinson and Gary Lee, "Soviet Army Coming Apart at the Seams," *Washington Post*, November 18, 1990, p. A1.

what military tasks remain and what problems defense agencies will have to confront in order to perform their revised responsibilities. As suggested by the above epigraphs, offered from various perspectives on and within armed forces, militaries throughout the world have been rocked by enormous stresses and strains in the aftermath of the Cold War. These pose a compelling question as to how they will adapt to their altered circumstances: In a turbulent world of fragmenting polities, troubled economies, restless publics, refocused enmities, and vast international transformations, where do soldiers and military organizations fit?

Responding to this question in terms of the parametric transformations posited by the turbulence model, the task here is that of assessing whether signs of the skill revolution can be discerned in the behavior of enlisted men and officers, whether military organizations are undergoing crises of authority and turning to new forms of subgroupism, and whether the ever expanding complexity of a bifurcated world has altered the jobs armed forces are required to carry out. There is, in short, a powerful tension that needs to be examined, namely, the tension between the strong currents of turbulence and the rigorous commitment of militaries to disciplined command structures.

Two premises underlie the analysis. One is that despite all the changes at work within and among societies, military establishments are not likely to become extinct. With the space along the Frontier contested by ethnic factions, religious fundamentalists, drug dealers, crime syndicates, and a host of other actors, militaries are not likely to become extinct. On the contrary, they seem destined to have their assignments expanded as the Frontier becomes ever more complex and treacherous. Extensive interstate wars may be headed for obsolescence, as chapter 22 argues, but border skirmishes, proxy wars, domestic unrest, terrorism, and other physical threats to cherished values are still very much part of the political landscape. Thus, even as defense budgets have been trimmed and even as societal support has undergone change, publics and governments continue to regard their militaries as having important roles to perform. Few, if any, societies are likely to follow the example of Costa Rica and dismantle their armed forces.

The second premise provides a context for assessing the performance of traditional military roles in a turbulent world no longer dominated by superpower competition. The analysis rests on the presumption that no domain of human affairs has remained immune to the vast transformations of our time, that it is thus unimaginable that the huge changes at work on a global scale have not had enormous repercussions for military institutions and personnel everywhere. Put differently, as new constraints alter the viability of armed force as an instrument of public policy, so will changes occur in the role, morale, coherence, and effectiveness of armed forces. In short, presumably militaries have not managed to remain essentially constant – beacons of stability in a fragmenting, unstable world – so that their conduct is likely to be expressive of discernible and significant variation.

Armed forces in a turbulent world

It is not difficult to conclude that change is stirring upheaval within military institutions. Notwithstanding adherence to the canons of analytic caution, one cannot help but be impressed by the continuing stream of events indicative of how the transformation of all three parameters has introduced variability into the conduct of military personnel and the structure of military establishments. In the case of parametric changes stirred by the bifurcation of the macro parameter, the ensuing analysis briefly assesses these in terms of old roles being shed and new tasks being shouldered by armed forces, the constraints imposed by the emergence of global norms and vigorous transnational social movements, and the tendencies toward subgroupism within and across military ranks. The transformation of the macro–micro parameter is explored in terms of the impact of global authority crises upon the exercise of military discipline and the capacity of armed forces to maintain and replenish their ranks. The analysis of changes at the micro level probes how expanded analytic skills have affected the orientations of officers and enlisted personnel alike and how the need for sustaining the skill revolution has posed a delicate challenge to the command structure of military organizations.

Diminished roles and new tasks

One consequence of the centralizing and decentralizing tendencies that are reinforcing, offsetting, or otherwise sustaining the bifurcation of world affairs is that, paradoxically, armed forces are becoming more marginal even as their capabilities have become more relevant. That is, the weakening of nation-states, the proliferation of subnational organizations and groups in the multi-centric world, the shift of systemic agendas away from security and toward economic issues, the redirection of numerous adversarial relationships within regions and countries (as well as between former superpowers), and the contraction of military budgets – to mention only a few of the dynamics at work – has led societies to be less reliant upon and less respectful of their military institutions even as the very complexity that undermines their reliance leads them to seek out their militaries to perform new tasks – "what the Pentagon labels 'operations other than war'"[5] – that are also a consequence of greater complexity and extensive change.

This paradoxical pattern of lesser reliance and expanded tasks derives, in effect, from a variety of sources, ranging from the end of the Cold War to budgetary constraints to shifting norms which make the conduct of military operations less attractive. No longer are elites and publics inclined to view military actions as a solution to problems. Indeed, as will be seen in chapter 22, in some cases such actions are considered to be a major source of the difficulties with which people have to contend. High-tech weapons may allow for the quick defeat of a menacing enemy, but they are of no value in controlling the many enduring problems that continue to unfold away from the battlefield. It is no accident, therefore, that a number of wars have ground to a halt in recent years: as noted in chapter 22, each of these various situations had its own unique dynamics, but it seems clear that each also ran afoul of humankind's lessened tolerance for prolonged combat and its greater appreciation of the limits of military effectiveness. So viewed historically, there is less for armed forces to do – to protect, to threaten, to prepare for – and as a result their conventional roles have undergone attrition.[6]

On the other hand, the very same combination of budgetary constraints and shifting norms has given rise to a diversity of challenges which only the military, being well organized and still in command of substantial resources, seems competent to meet. As one NGO leader put it, "The military's logistics are best suited for addressing the problems we face in these humanitarian crises. Providing airport handlers, tanker trucks, pumping stations – they can do it much better than agencies who don't have the tools or the programmatic experience."[7] Troops of

---

[5] Graham, "Fund New Missions, Pentagon Pleads," p. 2.

[6] While the diminution of their roles has been largely, if reluctantly, accepted by most military establishments, it should be noted that occasionally defiance of such changes does occur. Cf. Calvin Sims, "Growls From Barracks Echo in Peru and Chile," *New York Times*, June 20, 1995, p. A8.

[7] Joelle Tanguay, Executive Director of the American office of Doctors Without Borders, quoted in Eric Schmitt, "Military's Growing Role in Relief Missions Prompts Concerns," *New York Times*, July 31, 1994, p. 3.

NATO, for example, were used to deliver emergency supplies to the people of the former Soviet Union. Similarly, the US military took on relief operations in southern Florida after Hurricane Andrew as well as the task of preparing shelters, sanitary facilities, and medical care for thousands of Haitians fleeing their country, a role that was widely viewed by defense officials as "a headache" but that was nonetheless accepted.[8] Subsequently, a similar request to take on a new leadership role in the war against drugs, made precisely because of its expertise in creating "a unified command authority," was rejected by the US military, and one of the reasons for the rejection suggests that the adaptation of service personnel to their diminished roles and new tasks is far from easy:

> Its reluctance now to take on a bigger role was described . . . as a consequence, in part, of the Persian Gulf War, which made some military officers scornful of mere anti-drug operations. But it was said to reflect also a Pentagon wariness about becoming too closely identified with the failure to make inroads against a potentially intractable problem.[9]

In addition to new roles in the fields of humanitarian assistance and drug control, militaries in various parts of the world are increasingly likely to be called upon to take on peace-keeping responsibilities. With the dynamics of bifurcation and shifting values toward international organizations thrusting the United Nations into the limelight as an instrument for coping with both intrastate and interstate conflicts,[10] more and more countries will be asked to contribute personnel to such missions. As of 1994, as many as seventy-four countries sent troops to one or another UN-sponsored peace-keeping operation. For those involved these new supranational tasks are likely, when combined with the growing incentives to honor subnational values, to confound further the increasingly complex question of the goals and purposes for which national military organizations are designed to serve (see below). Not only have militaries had to adjust to an obfuscation of their enemies, but the advent of assignment to UN commands has also beclouded the identity of their superiors.

---

[8] Melissa Healy, "U.S. Military Will Shelter Haitians at Base in Cuba," *Los Angeles Times*, November 26, 1991, p. A1.

[9] Douglas Jehl and Ronald J. Ostrow, "Pentagon Said to Reject Bigger Anti-Drug Role," *Los Angeles Times*, January 17, 1992, p. A12.

[10] Cf. James N. Rosenau, *The United Nations in a Turbulent World* (Boulder, CO: Lynne Rienner, 1992), chaps. 4–5.

Perhaps there is no better example of the dilemmas faced by military establishments than that of Israel, where

> After decades as the country's main unifying force – more than religion, certainly more than politics – the Israeli Army is slowly losing the enormous power it once had to shape this society. In the past, a shining army career was a sure ticket to later success as a civilian, and failure to serve usually meant a life of dead-end jobs and second-class status. While that can still be the case, the military is far from the ultimate social umpire that it once was. Peace treaties with some Arab countries, the absence of an imminent war threat, relative affluence, a greater emphasis on individual fulfillment and readiness to question venerable institutions – all have combined to alter Israelis' expectations of the military and undermine their once-unshakable conviction that it can do no wrong.[11]

Global norms and social movements

The spread of global norms and the greater coherence and effectiveness of social movements constitute additional constraints on the military stemming from the transformation of the macro parameter. More precisely, one norm, human rights, and several social movements, particularly the peace, women's, and environmental movements, have tended to narrow the freedom of action that armed forces have historically enjoyed. The efforts of the Organization of American States to hold members of the Haitian military accountable for their atrocities, the finding of Mexico's National Commission on Human Rights that a senior army general "bore the major responsibility" for the deaths of narcotics agents,[12] and court convictions of former East German border guards for explicitly violating the human rights of would-be escapees exemplify how a spreading preoccupation with performance criteria of leadership and a growing concern for the rights of individuals are subjecting military personnel to new forms of scrutiny and condemnation. It seems probable, too, that the increasing reluctance (noted below) of military officers to order their troops to fire on fellow citizens gathered for protests in town squares is, at least in part, a consequence of the emergence of human rights as a global norm.

In a like manner, the pressures generated by various social move-

---

[11] Clyde Haberman, "Israelis Deglamorize the Military," *New York Times*, May 31, 1995, p. A10. For an account of a similar process in another country, see Calvin Sims, "Argentina Demotes Its Once-Powerful Armed Forces," *New York Times*, November 24, 1994, p. A3.

[12] Tim Golden, "Mexican Panel Faults Army in Death of Drug Agents," *New York Times*, December 7, 1991, p. 3.

ments, all of them transnational in scope and global in appeal, have added to the limitations within which armed forces must operate. Just as the peace movement contributed to the diverse challenges to military authority discussed below, so has the worldwide preoccupation with the role of women encouraged many countries to open combat roles in their officer and enlisted ranks to females. Between the late 1960s and the early 1990s, for example, the proportion of women in NATO forces rose from 2 percent to 7.4 percent,[13] a pattern that has presumably been further reinforced by the exemplary performance of American women soldiers in the Persian Gulf War. At the same time it is also clear that the adjustment of military men to the arrival of female compatriots has not been easy. To note one of many instances that could be cited, the macro context in which military routines are sustained by the Corps of Cadets at Texas A&M University recently underwent change when some in its ranks were charged with mistreatment of its female members: for the first time an outside group was given the authority to examine the corps' policies and to suggest policy changes.[14]

Subgroupism

The opportunities afforded by the evolution of the multi-centric world and its incentives to seek subgroup coherence and privileges have not been lost on more than a few armed services. In effect, many appear to have broken a long tradition in which they operated as a tightly-knit elite acting quietly behind closed doors, pressing policies, pulling levers, stressing limits, or otherwise exercising influence. Historically, that is, the military has acted as an agent of the state, either protecting its civilian leaders from perceived adversaries or, in some instances, replacing them on behalf of perceived needs for order. With the transformation of the macro parameter, however, the military has moved from behind closed doors into the public arena, acting not as an agent of the state but as a claimant on its resources, much like the other subgroups that populate the multi-centric world. In Argentina, for example, "the military has become so poor and weak that it is leasing its property for commercial ventures, taking tourists around Patagonia in navy boats, renting airstrips for amateur car races, divesting unprofit-

---

[13] William Touhy, "Are Nations Set to Dodge the Draft?" *Los Angeles Times*, August 13, 1991, p. H4.

[14] Roberto Suro, "Female Cadets Charge Abuse on Campus," *New York Times*, October 7, 1991, p. A8.

able businesses, raising livestock and crops on army bases, and doing whatever else it takes to stay afloat."[15] Indeed, in China the People's Liberation Army (PLA) has entered the commercial world and become

> the country's largest business empire ... The PLA now runs more than 20,000 businesses ranging from telecommunications and transport to mining, hotels, restaurants, nightclubs and even massage parlours. Military-run enterprises reportedly generate revenue rivaling China's ... defence budget. The army recently took on the US-based financial giant Citicorp as a partner in its pharmaceutical business and has funneled huge sums into property development in Hong Kong and elsewhere.[16]

In short, where subgroupism within armed services used to refer to the cohesion of a governmental elite, now it also connotes the self-serving activities or plaintive demands of a besieged subgroup. Where the military could readily coopt other groups in the private sector, now they have to compete with them; and, in so doing, they have also come to emulate them. Notwithstanding the constraints of a long-standing commitment to organizational discipline, military leaders have been increasingly emboldened by the diminution of their funds, prestige, and tasks to seek redress through the rowdier methods of aggregation used by other actors in the multi-centric world. In Russia, for example, officers came together to concert their demands and issued a call for coverage by nationwide television and the formation of a "coordinating council" to represent their interests.[17] While some might dismiss the subgroupism of the military in the former Soviet Union as a special case resulting from a particularly sudden and unexpected set of events, it is equally plausible, given the bifurcation of global structures, that sub-

---

[15] Calvin Sims, "Argentine Military for Rent; Turns Swords Into Tin Cups," *New York Times*, January 29, 1996, p. 1. See also, Douglas Farah, "For Central American Armies, the New Battlefield is Business," *International Herald Tribune*, June 5, 1996, p. 1.

[16] Ruth Youngblood, "Conventional Ring to PLA Anniversary," *Eastern Express* (Hong Kong), August 2, 1994. See also Patrick E. Tyler, "China Military's Business Profits Being Put Back into Business, Not Arms," *New York Times*, May 14, 1994, p. A4. It is noteworthy, too, that the PLA's commercial successes have been closely watched and emulated by the Cuban military, which "is now involved in virtually every aspect of tourism in Cuba, including luxury hotels, hunting preserves, marinas, spas, bus tours, fishing excursions, a large taxicab fleet and airplane flights." Larry Rohter, "Cuba Finds the Army Rising as the Party Sinks," *New York Times*, June 8, 1995, p. A12.

[17] Serge Schmemann, "5,000 Angry Military Men Gather With Complaints in the Kremlin," *New York Times*, January 18, 1992, p. 4.

groupism among militaries elsewhere is likely to increase in proportion to their loss of status, support, and perquisites.[18]

One exception in this regard is the People's Army of Vietnam. It has extended its operations in the commercial world – having acquired 300 major state enterprises and entered into 49 joint ventures with foreign companies (including a Japanese candy firm) – but at the same time it has taken on the role of protecting Vietnam's internal coherence.

> At the recent Communist Party Congress, it strengthened its political clout and focused on a new mission, guarding against the "hostile forces" of Western influence unleashed by the country's newly liberated economy . . . In a time of fundamental change, Vietnam is counting on its military and security forces to maintain party control and to insure that the West, defeated in war, does not win over the country through economic and social change.[19]

The redefinition of interests

Turning now to the transformation of the micro parameter, there are numerous indicators of the skill revolution which are having an impact on armed forces. Perhaps the most noticeable involves the expansion of the skills with which both enlisted and officer personnel assess their own interests. Traditionally, military persons devoted little energy to pondering their personal interests. Rather, a deep-seated habit prevailed through which self-interests were equated with service and national interests. Now, however, there are signs that enhanced skills have led to a disaggregation of the concept of self-interest. If the concept of analytic skills is operationalized as a greater capacity to play out scenarios that locate where individuals fit in the processes of world politics,[20] it is not difficult to uncover widespread indicators of members of armed forces being preoccupied with their changing roles.[21] For the most part, this preoccupation takes the form of distress over the loss of support, tasks, and perquisites, and in turn the distress is most manifest

---

[18] For a case of intensive subgroupism on the part of a military unit in the United States, see John Lancaster, "Shrinking The National Guard To Fit the Times: In Mississippi, They're Fighting Mad About It," *Washington Post National Weekly Edition*, February 10–16, 1992, p. 33.

[19] Seth Mydans, "In Peacetime, Vietnam's Army Turns to Business Ventures," *New York Times*, July 21, 1996, p. 10.

[20] Cf. James N. Rosenau, *Turbulence in World Politics: A Theory of Change and Continuity* (Princeton: Princeton University Press, 1990), p. 336.

[21] See, for example, Eric Schmitt, "Reaching for the Stars in the New Military," *New York Times*, September 4, 1994, p. 5.

in a seemingly increasing readiness of servicemen and women to attach higher priority to their own welfare than to the military organizations or countries they serve. The plaintive lament of the Russian colonel quoted in the second epigraph is echoed not only in the words of many individuals in the military of the former Soviet Union;[22] comparable statements can be found in the expressions of counterparts in other countries that are scaling back their armed forces in the face of budget cuts and the end of Cold War rivalries. Consider, for example, the observation of Roger Spiller, a professor of military history at the US Army's Command and General Staff College: asked for a reading of the mood of the military after the Gulf War, he responded that "I think there's a good deal of anxiety. They'd have to be completely insensitive not to feel anxiety about the impending reductions in the Army. These are men and women acutely aware of their surroundings, which right now are rather hostile to their future plans."[23]

The growing preoccupation of military personnel with their own welfare is, of course, a violation of the traditional stereotype wherein the good soldier is supposed to accept unthinkingly whatever decisions their military and civilian superiors make with respect to their status and activity. This conception of military command structures lies at the very heart of combat readiness and effectiveness. Yet, nowhere can one find traces of it being voiced by either government officials and top-ranking officers. Some may be good soldiers in the sense that they are "remarkably philosophical" and "understand what is happening and the reasons for it,"[24] but few if any have publicly affirmed that the military is duty-bound to accede to the changes initiated by their political superiors. Indeed, it is a measure of how profoundly the military have been caught up in the parametric transformations at work in world politics that all concerned take for granted that military personnel are no longer silent and obedient with respect to their own welfare. In 1992, for example, the effort of Russian president Yeltsin to win over disgruntled officers by publicly offering them 120,000 apartments and 70,000 quarter-acre plots[25] would have seemed absurd, a form of public bar-

---

[22] For an analysis of the low morale and other problems of the post-Cold War Russian armed forces, see Benjamin S. Lambeth, "Russia's Wounded Military," *Foreign Affairs*, vol. 74 (March–April 1995), pp. 87–98.

[23] John M. Broder, "Cutbacks, Criticism Take Toll on Military's Morale," *Los Angeles Times*, January 16, 1992, p. A18.   [24] Roger Spiller, quoted in *ibid.*

[25] Elizabeth Shogren, "Officers Demand Unity for Ex-Soviet Military," *Los Angeles Times*, January 18, 1992, p. 1.

gaining entirely out of place in a military context. Today, however, such an offer seems more commonplace than anomalous, a cogent indicator of how military personnel are no longer treated as a constant in the political equation.

The most obvious trace of the skill revolution's impact is to be found in fragmenting countries, where the ethnic identification of military personnel is fostering the same kinds of divisions among them that divides their societies. The army in Algeria, for example, is considered to be "crossed by the same currents that cross Algerian society," with the top command "being dead set against the [Muslim] fundamentalists" even as this perspective changes "as you travel down the ranks."[26] Similarly, Ukraine's insistence that members of the armed forces stationed on its territory sign loyalty oaths bespeaks a recognition that enlisted personnel and officers are no longer dutiful, that they are inclined to analyze their situations, sort out their loyalties, and then to follow the course most appropriate to their personal commitments. And that is exactly what transpired. As one analyst put it, military units and many officers are "following their paychecks" to republican governments, with the result that "Soviet conscripts, more and more, are serving within the boundaries of their home republics in a process of homogenization."[27] Put even more poignantly, with the ethnic fragmentation of the Soviet military, "fathers are worrying about facing their soldier sons across a battlefield, if they end up serving different states. Officers are watching the unity of their troops give way to ethnic enmity."[28]

It would be a mistake, however, to view the disruptive consequences of the greater capacity of military personnel to extend their skills beyond the boundaries imposed by the canons of strict military discipline as confined to the enlisted ranks. The unity of top military leaders has also been splintered by the skill revolution. Or at least there are good indications that high-ranking officers are no more uniform in their underlying political attitudes than any other occupational elite, that the new license enjoyed by military personnel of all ranks to think analytically – to locate for themselves where military institutions fit in the panoply of societal dynamics – would appear to be as much a source of

[26] Youssef M. Ibrahim, "Algerians, Angry With the Past, Divide Over Their Future," *New York Times*, January 19, 1992, sect. 4, p. 3.

[27] Patrick E. Tyler, "U.S. Concerned That as the Union Breaks Up, So Does the Soviet Military," *New York Times*, December 10, 1991, p. A9.

[28] Carey Goldberg, "Colonel's Cry: `It's My Entire Life,'" *Los Angeles Times*, January 10, 1992, p. A8.

divergent perspectives as of widely shared consensuses among leaders of defense establishments. Even as many senior officers of the former Soviet Union, for example, gave expression to decentralizing tendencies and opted to give higher priority to their ethnic loyalties, so did others articulate centralizing values and press for the maintenance of the military as a single, united command structure. Likewise, just as some took a right-wing position favoring the use of strong-arm techniques to restore order, so did others resist the militant posture and voice support for democratic procedures.[29]

In short, the enhancement of skills among military personnel seems likely to undermine rather than reinforce traditional command structures. The roles played by top Soviet military leaders on both sides of the August 1991 coup and its subsequent failure, not to mention the reluctance of some Russian generals to follow orders in the war against Chechnya, are eloquent testimony in support of the presumption that military elites have not managed to avoid the divisive consequences of a transformed micro parameter.[30]

Technology and the expansion of analytic skills

Nor is the evidence of greater skills on the part of military personnel due only to the way in which turbulent conditions have heightened their self-interests. The increasingly technological nature of warfare has also contributed to their capacity to play out self-interested scenarios. High-tech weaponry cannot be operated by poorly educated and unskilled soldiers or sailors. Considerable advanced training is required to use modern weapons, thus necessitating that military institutions convert their recruits from physically able individuals to skilled technicians.[31] And once they do, once enlisted personnel are competent to use computers, complex targeting devices, intricate photographic equipment, and the other modern devices through which the instruments of war deliver their loads, the raw recruit is no longer an unthinking individual incapable of pondering cause and effect or discerning the diverse routes through which desired outcomes are produced. Rather, having

---

[29] Schmemann, "5,000 Angry Military Men Gather With Complaints in the Kremlin," p. 1.

[30] For a cogent discussion of these issues, see Brian D. Taylor, "Professionalism and Politicization in the Soviet and Russian Armed Forces," paper presented at the Annual Meeting of the American Political Science Association, Chicago (September 1995).

[31] For a cogent analysis of how new military technologies are revolutionizing "the way the world fights," see Oliver Morton, "The Information Advantage," *Economist*, June 10, 1995, pp. 5–20.

been tooled up in high-tech forms of warfare, he or she is possessed of new analytic capacities that can readily be extended into other, more political realms.[32]

A quintessential insight into the relevance of the skill revolution for military personnel is provided by the spate of TV advertisements in which the US armed forces stress the educational opportunities of military service. Designed to recruit volunteers, the advertisements concentrate on the subsequent, post-service uses to which technical skills acquired in the armed forces can be put, the underlying message being that one leaves the services a much more competent individual than one was before joining. The same insight is implicit in the complaints of former Soviet officers who were assigned young non-Russian-speaking draftees from Central Asia to operate complex, modern missile equipment.[33]

For closed and authoritarian societies like China the necessity of implementing a skill revolution poses a difficult challenge. On the one hand, the importance of high-tech weapons in the success of the US-led coalition against Iraq made clear to them that they would have to bring the skill revolution to their own armed forces if they wanted to be able to engage in modern warfare. At the same time it was equally clear that by pushing science, technology, and professionalism in their armed forces they would be risking the loss of ideological control, that the more sophisticated their fighting forces became, the less susceptible they would be to manipulation by the party. The 1989 pro-democracy protests in Tiananmen Square highlighted this dilemma and intensified the debate inasmuch as it was poorly educated troops from the countryside who fired on the demonstrators. Had the troops been recruited from urban centers, trained to operate modern weapons, or otherwise exposed to the skill revolution, some reasoned, they may well have refused to fire on the students. In effect, the potential transformation of the micro parameter has compelled Chinese authorities to face the question of whom they deem their enemies to be. As one diplomat put it, they have to decide whether the main threats are posed by the democracy movement and "peaceful evolution" or by foreign invasion:

> Are you going to have a million Soviet soldiers come streaming across the border? Are you going to engage in a high-tech war with Taiwan

---

[32] For a discussion of the transferability of computer and other technical skills acquired in the workplace, see Rosenau, *Turbulence in World Politics*, pp. 352–4.

[33] Goldberg, "Colonel's Cry: `It's My Entire Life,'" p. A8.

or the United States? Or are you going to face Tibetans and students? If you perceive your major strategic enemy being inside your own country, then your major concern is for political control.[34]

Furthermore, it can be readily argued that even this dichotomous choice may be short-lived. As the skill revolution spreads to the countryside through global television, satellite dishes, fax machines, and a host of other means, the political reliability of troops from rural areas may diminish accordingly.

For those many countries that are not so preoccupied with political control, the nature of modern warfare is tipping the balance ever more in the direction of sustaining the skill revolution in their armed forces. While 83 of the 140 countries with military forces employ some form of conscription, many are now reducing the number of conscripts and the length of their service in favor of recruiting volunteers and professionals.[35] This pattern is partly due to economic constraints that limit the funds available for large militaries, but it would also seem to be very much a consequence of the technical requirements of battlefield readiness.

The decline of discipline and the erosion of obedience

Given the refinement of skills at the micro level and the diminished roles, new tasks, global norms, subgroupism, and the many other dislocating constraints that have emerged at the macro level, it is hardly surprising that the transformation of the macro–micro parameter has had major consequences for armed forces everywhere. All of them appear to be undergoing an erosion of traditional discipline in the present turbulent era. The authority crises take several forms. A lesser form derives from the fact that no military establishment today can avoid the impact on command structures of its increasing reliance on technical expertise to operate its weaponry. The conventional lines of authority do not follow the distribution of expertise among the ranks. Often highly skilled technicians have to report to less knowledgeable superiors and, as a result, the former may be confronted with situations where they have to ignore their orders and inform their superiors they are wrong. Conversely, frequent may be the occasions when the superiors have no choice but to follow the lead of their more skilled subordinates.

A more obvious and consequential type of authority crisis occurs when

---

[34] David Holley, "China Debates How to Recruit Today's Army," *Los Angeles Times*, November 12, 1991, p. H1. [35] Touhy, "Are Nations Set to Dodge the Draft?" p. H4.

an elite officer corps defies constitutional principles and seizes power. While this classic case of military-inspired *coups d'état* need not detain us here – since it preceded the onset of turbulence and is the subject of a substantial literature – there is one turbulence-generated gap in the coup literature worthy of note: as will be seen, the classic case is likely to occur less and less often. The inhibitions against outright seizures are not so great as to rid world affairs of actual or failed coups, but the advent of parametric change does seem likely to give pause to military elites contemplating illegal takeovers and thus to reduce their frequency.

But we do need to examine the more complex and historically atypical forms of authority crisis fostered by the transformation of the macro–micro parameter. Perhaps the most conspicuous of these concerns the capacity of military organizations to maintain and replenish their ranks. Resistance to being drafted by new recruits and desertions by those serving appear to have become more commonplace in recent years. Although in some countries military service is viewed as a way to move out of humble origins (such as among peasants in China), the opposite pattern is more predominant. In most countries, and especially those at war, the proportion of young people who resist and evade being called into service appears to be growing. The figures may not alarm military planners, but the changes are apparently enough for service chiefs in many countries to recommend cutting back on drafts of conscripts and relying more heavily on volunteer personnel.[36] The pattern of draft resistance is also evident in a US Supreme Court decision to shut the door on thousands of asylum claims from young men trying to escape conscription by guerrilla or government forces in strife-torn countries of Central America and Asia.[37] In Germany, a sudden explosion of citizens registered as conscientious objectors occurred as the coalition against Iraq seemed increasingly likely to follow the military option, and a comparable pattern surfaced in Switzerland even though the Swiss make no provision for alternative service, thus compelling resisters to go to jail.[38] In South Africa, too, draft resistance intensified

---

[36] *Ibid.*, pp. H1, H4–5.

[37] Linda Greenhouse, "Supreme Court Limits Political Asylum," *New York Times*, January 23, 1992, p. A7.

[38] These patterns are cited in an unpublished 1991 paper by Lore Unt, "Draft Resistance in the Soviet Union," p. 2. It is noteworthy that emerging global norms relative to human rights have also made the military's problem of draft evasion more difficult: both the European Parliament and the UN Human Rights Commission passed resolutions in 1987 specifying that conscientious objection to military service is a universal human right (*ibid.*).

as the abolition of the law classifying every citizen according to race led white draftees to question compulsory conscription for whites when the law defining them as white no longer existed.[39] Similarly, when Serbia tried to strengthen its forces against Croatia by mobilizing its reservists, "thousands evaded the draft."[40] Likewise, in Japan, where the ranks of the Self-Defense Force are constitutionally limited to 300,000, the recruitment target has been difficult to meet despite pay increases, improved work conditions, and better barrack accommodations.[41] And even in Israel "today's conscripts are less motivated than their elders and less willing to volunteer for combat units . . . [T]he new Chief of Staff [said] he was concerned about an apparent rise in the number of young Israelis who consider military service 'inappropriate for them.' [The problem, he said,] is 'a preference for individualism over the collective in an age of liberalism.'"[42]

Nor, of course, were the superpowers immune to this form of authority crisis. Its presence was quite noticeable even at those times when they went to war against a clearly defined enemy. Indeed, the spectacle of widespread resistance to service during the US effort in Vietnam and the Soviet campaign in Afghanistan may well have contributed to comparable patterns elsewhere. And as the pattern of draft resistance reached massive proportions in the former Soviet Union in 1989-90 – from 871 in 1987 to 6,667 in 1989 and 135,000 in 1990[43] – so did evading service come to be "seen by young people as normative behaviour, which met with parental approval and found tacit understanding, if not endorsement from Konsomol officials and law enforcement authorities."[44] It has even been said that the Soviets could not even consider direct military participation in the coalition against Iraq because of massive resistance to the idea at home, just as it took less than a week for the same resistance to compel the Kremlin to abandon mobilizing reserves in the Russian republic to retake control of Azerbaijan from

[39] Christopher S. Wren, "Whites Defy Pretoria's 'White' Draft," *New York Times*, January 22, 1992, p. A3.

[40] Stephen Engelberg, "Yugoslavia's Breakup: Slovenia Is Secure, Croatia Is Uncertain," *New York Times*, January 16, 1992, p. A6.

[41] Louise do Rosario, "Attacked on All Fronts," *Far Eastern Economic Review*, March 7, 1991, pp. 26–7.   [42] Haberman, "Israelis Deglamorize the Military," p. A10.

[43] These figures were released by the Defense Ministry. Cf. Esther B. Fein, "Youths in Estonia Defying the Soviet Military Are Finding Eager Helpers," *New York Times*, April 5, 1990, p. A16.

[44] Natalie Gross, "Youth and the Army in the USSR in the 1980s," *Soviet Studies*, vol. 42 (July 1990), p. 483.

militants.[45] And when the Russians subsequently did undertake military operations, in Chechnya in 1994–5, the lack of commitment on the part of its soldiers was strikingly evident.[46]

As authority crises have hindered the recruitment of military personnel, so have they made it more difficult for defense establishments to maintain their force levels. The readiness of those in enlisted ranks to desert, once an unthinkable idea entertained by a few isolated individuals, has increased noticeably in many parts of the world. Most recruits, of course, complete their tours of duty, but the number who do not is no longer infinitesimal. This is especially so in the armed forces of multiethnic societies, where greater analytic skills and subgroupism nursed by ethnic loyalties have sometimes resulted in extensive defections. When civil war came to Yugoslavia, for example, its Serb-dominated armed forces experienced more than 1,000 desertions by Croats as well as a quarter of its Slovenian conscripts.[47] And not only did the Serbian army encounter substantial opposition in mobilizing its reservists, but "those who were inducted seemed to have little stomach for battle; Western correspondents have seen army reservists refusing to leave their armored personnel carriers to engage the enemy."[48] Similarly, in the former Soviet Union the effects of the authority crisis were cogently described as drawing the military inward in a process called "cocooning":

> They have sequestered themselves from the larger society and are concerned chiefly with hoarding food and supplies to survive the winter . . . Officers and enlisted men show loyalty only to their immediate superiors. They respond to their own chain of command. The guy immediately above you is the guy you trust and the guy to whom you report.[49]

It is perhaps noteworthy that tendencies toward disobedience within enlisted ranks are reinforced by the activities of more skillful citizens who pool their efforts on behalf of loved ones in the services. Anxious to protect their sons from the risks of warfare, for instance, parents have mobilized marches and other types of protests designed to exempt their

[45] Unt, "Draft Resistance in the Soviet Union", p. 19.

[46] David Hoffman, "Russia's Young Men Fleeing Draft in Droves," *Washington Post*, October 13, 1995, p. A1.

[47] Stephen Engelberg, "Yugoslav Army Trying To Correct Deficiencies," *New York Times*, July 15, 1991, p. A5.

[48] Stephen Engelberg, "Yugoslav Ethnic Hatreds Raise Fears of a War Without an End," *New York Times*, December 23, 1991, p. A8.

[49] Ilana Kass, quoted in John M. Broder and Jim Mann, "Military May be Tempted, Experts Say," *Los Angeles Times*, December 10, 1991, p. A11.

sons from commitments that could risk their lives. Such protests often get considerable publicity, especially if the marchers consist of mothers, and thus add further to the authority crises they are designed to resolve. As the level of fighting increased during the Yugoslavian civil war, for example, officials of the Croatian government "found encouragement in the mothers of army conscripts who traveled by bus from the country . . . to protest in Belgrade the continued fighting."[50] Likewise, the revelation in casualty figures that Montenegrins were paying a disproportionate price in lives led to large student rallies and, in one instance, to families of forty Montenegrin soldiers ordered to the front occupying the office of the Montenegrin president demanding the return of their sons.[51] Under special circumstances, moreover, the external incentives toward disobedience may originate with public officials. Authorities in the Baltic republics are a case in point: when the Soviets sought to draft Estonian, Latvian, and Lithuanian youth into the armed service, the fledgling Baltic governments refused to acknowledge the legitimacy of the draft order and helped young people to disobey it. The result was that less than 25 percent of the draftees in each republic actually showed up for duty and in Lithuania the figure was only 12.5 percent.[52]

In Western armies the authority crisis is less one of desertion and disobedience and more one of excessive caution (though conceivably it is a harbinger of things to come that a US soldier was recently court-martialed for refusing to put UN insignia on his uniform while serving in a peace-keeping operation[53]). Growing societal distaste for risking the lives of their soldiers in distant battles – that is, the continuing vitality of the "Vietnam syndrome" in the United States and elsewhere – has tended to undermine the readiness of those in field commands to take risks and order their troops into battle. As Gen. John M. Shalikashvili, the chairman of the US Joint Chiefs of Staff observed, "I'm concerned we do not start in our young leaders this notion that it's better to be hesitant and timid."[54]

The growing presence of what might be called the "loose cannon"

[50] John Tagliabue, "Serbia Promises Reply on Truce Plan," *New York Times*, August 31, 1991, p. 3.

[51] David Binder, "Montenegro Balks As Fighting Grows," *New York Times*, November 22, 1991, p. A4.

[52] Craig R. Whitney, "Moscow Is Sending Troops to Baltics to Enforce Draft," *New York Times*, January 8, 1991, p. A8.

[53] J. P. Barham, "Court-martial Ordered in U.N. Case," *Pacific Stars and Stripes*, October 21, 1995, p. 3.

[54] Eric Schmitt, "The Military's Getting Queasier About Death," *New York Times*, August 6, 1995, sect. 4, p. 5.

phenomenon is still another indicator of authority crises within the military. This refers to individuals or small groups who decide to take matters into their own hands, defy orders, and engage in acts that have wide consequences. If draft-resistance and desertion is, so to speak, the passive form of the erosion of obedience within armed services, loose cannon is the most active form. Of course, history is not lacking in accounts of loose cannon, but it is hardly surprising that its quantity, variety, and impact appear to be greater with the onset of global turbulence. The very complexity and interdependence of modern societies renders them more vulnerable to a small coterie of individuals who seek to prevent events from evolving in certain directions or who aspire to movement toward different goals. Terrorists are in some ways illustrative in this regard, but they stand out as deviants from societal discipline, whereas military loose cannon deviates from a discipline that does not allow entertaining the idea of individual initiatives. So it is a measure of authority in crisis that accounts of loose cannon seem to surface with increasing frequency. A few examples indicate the breadth of the phenomenon. It was "rogue local units acting without authority" that shelled the quintessentially medieval city of Dubrovnik in Croatia.[55] Similarly, momentum toward ending a four-year rebellion by an insurgent group in India, the United Liberation Front of Assam, was resisted and slowed down by several military commanders on the grounds that an earlier operation was blunted by the army's sudden withdrawal.[56] And even after peace was successfully negotiated in Angola, there remained a few loose cannons who could undo it: "Now thousands of idle young men without food remain near arms in the assembly points. Without guaranteed food, they will form banditry groups."[57] Even greater, of course, is a worldwide fear of loose cannon in the former Soviet Union which has access to stored nuclear weapons and which for any number of reasons may be impelled to use them.[58]

This is not to imply that loose cannon which breaks ranks ought necessarily to be judged harshly. One can readily imagine situations where their actions affirm one's own values and are thus worthy of applause.

---

[55] Stephen Engelberg, "Yugoslav Ethnic Hatreds Raise Fears of a War Without an End," p. A8.

[56] Sanjoy Hazarika, "India Reports Insurgents in Assam Agreed to End Their Four-Year Rebellion," *New York Times*, January 16, 1992, p. A6.

[57] Ramiro da Silva, quoted in *New York Times*, December 16, 1991, p. A9.

[58] Elaine Sciolino, "U.S. Report Warns of Risk in Spread of Nuclear Skills," *New York Times*, January 1, 1992, p. 1.

It was loose cannon in the national guard, for example, that initiated the process which led to the successful ouster of Georgia's authoritarian president, Zviad K. Gamsakhurdia.[59] Sometimes mutiny in the ranks of the military, in other words, might well be viewed as sacrifice and heroism. The point here is simply that loose cannons, whatever their desirability, reflect the breakdown of traditional lines of authority within armed forces and are thus an indicator of the turbulence to which militaries are presently exposed.

A final type of authority crisis worthy of noting is the central issue of domestic conflict in which armed forces are ordered to fire on their own people. The issue, of course, is as old as the use of organized coercion, but the historic pattern founded on strict military discipline is one in which militaries have obeyed the command to fire. While the prime function of armies has been to wage war against international enemies, the past is scarred with numerous occasions when the line between police and military functions was obfuscated and the weapons were turned inward and aimed at domestic enemies. And few, if any, are those historic moments when the orders to shoot on fellow citizens were defied. However, with the advent of turbulence in the parametric controls that sustain the conduct of public affairs, and perhaps especially with the weakening of states and the evolution of global norms that attach high value to human rights, there are solid indicators of a reluctance both to order attacks on fellow citizens and to comply with such orders. The 1989 collapse of the communist regimes in Eastern Europe is a conspicuous instance of this form of authority crisis. The collapse would not have occurred if the militaries in those countries had been ready to comply with orders to use force against their own peoples. The Ceausescu regime in Romania did issue such orders, but this exception affirms the central tendency. Leaders elsewhere in Eastern Europe, unlike Ceausescu, were aware of the authority crisis at work within their militaries, and they knew too that their publics would not tolerate such actions (as Ceausescu also found out at the expense of his life).

But, it might be asked, what about the recent roles played by the military in China and Burma? In both cases the army mowed down protesting citizens gathered in public squares and their political leaderships thereby managed to regain and retain political control. Are they not examples that stand out as indicators of the continued

---

[59] Serge Schmemann, "Stunned, Georgians Reckon the Cost of Independence," *New York Times*, January 10, 1992, p. A9.

effectiveness of strict military discipline? Yes, of course, they are, but again they seem more the exception than the rule (and even in China there were unconfirmed reports that more than 1,400 soldiers and 111 officers above the rank of battalion commander either fled the scene or defied the order to shoot in Tiananmen Square). Or at least there are enough instances of shifting values with respect to the avoidance of armed force against domestic publics to suggest that military personnel are beginning to set boundaries beyond which their disciplined responses in the command structure are no longer reliable. What has been said about the military in Yugoslavia might well be said about armed services in many other parts of the world: "most of the army real-izes they alone cannot hold Yugoslavia together at gunpoint. The army is only effective as a weapon when it is not used. They recognize that if the Yugoslav national army fires on the people, it loses all authority."[60]

Armed force and armed forces as agents of change

If the foregoing analysis is essentially correct and the world is destined to be ensconced in a long, if not permanent, period of turbulence, it seems likely that both armed force and armed forces will diminish as agents of change. The lessened utility of armed force can be anticipated because the world has become too complex to be managed through the exercise of coercive power, and the decreasing influence of armed forces can be expected because their command structures have been under-mined by the skill revolution and the worldwide crisis in authority. Given the constraints imposed by dense populations, shrinking budgets, war-weary publics, weakened governments, divided societies, and transnationalized borders, there are fewer and fewer degrees of freedom within which military power can be effective. High-tech weapons can strike targets with pin-point accuracy, but neither they nor conventional forces can be very effective when directed toward seg-ments of a bifurcated world marked by shifting loyalties, diverse ethnic groups, decentralized social structures, deep historic commitments, massive migrations, and interdependent economies. And if the body of personnel charged with exercising the armed force is itself conflicted, uncertain of its tasks, and aware of its limitations, the chances of effec-tive applications of coercive force are further diminished.

[60] Stephen Engelberg, "Yugoslavia: Healing Steps Are Modest," *New York Times*, May 11, 1991, p. A3.

The implications of this conclusion for military establishments are profound. They not only suggest that recourse to war across national boundaries is likely to be increasingly eschewed, but they also point to a counter-intuitive insight that negates a long-standing and widely shared core premise about the role armed forces play within their own societies: the premise is that the military, having control over the means of violent coercion, are the one institution that can bring order out of chaos and establish societal stability where none existed before. This premise is often voiced by observers fearful that too much societal disorder will lead the military to seize governing power, and it is also a premise that high-ranking officers in many parts of the world have articulated in the hope that their expression of the idea will be experienced as a threat that stabilizes situations bordering on chaos. In some cases, of course, military *coups d'état* have actually been undertaken on these grounds. As global turbulence mounts, however, the soundness of the premise becomes increasingly questionable. The skill revolution, authority crises, and bifurcated global structures – not to mention population explosions, dynamic technologies, and the globalization of national economies – have rendered societies too complex, resources too scarce, loyalties too diffuse, and military organizations too hesitant for the military-as-the-only-stable-institution scenario to retain its viability. As militaries in Argentina, Brazil, Burma, Chile, China, Haiti, the Philippines, and elsewhere have discovered, and as those in Algeria, Russia, and Serbia are presently finding, establishing and maintaining societal stability is no longer a simple matter even if military leaders are ready to resort to force and ruthlessly mow down their own people. For many of the reasons noted here, armed forces can no longer assume they have the competence to overcome the dynamics of internal turbulence and set their countries on a stable course; and, of course, the knowledge that this assumption is no longer tenable contributes to their hesitancy to act decisively, a predisposition which, in turn, further lessens their chances of success.

This counter-intuitive reasoning that ascribes a growing reluctance to military elites to initiate coups also applies to those situations where a military take-over is less a coup against society and more an action that immediately evokes wide support from diverse segments of society. If, for example, persistent economic disarray leads to extensive public backing for the military to restore order and productivity, as recently appeared to be the case in Venezuela and as many anticipate will occur in one or more countries of the former Soviet bloc, that backing is not likely to last long as the intractability of the problems reveals that a military regime is no more able to resolve them than was its civilian predecessor. Furthermore, a widespread public readiness to welcome a military take-over can be misleading: "When soldiers have moved to intervene, people's dissatisfaction with the civilians in power has generally turned out to be not so great after all."[61]

To be sure, most military establishments continue to be more hierarchical than other societal institutions. With few exceptions, the world is not witnessing an open season for the flouting of rank and the breakdown of command structures. On the other hand, traces of undermined discipline and expanded analytic skills fostering redefined self-interests, cocooning, and subgroupism are manifest in many countries. The multi-ethnic composition of some militaries has doubtless intensified the erosion of their conventional lines of authority, but even the most homogeneous military organization is faced with their hierarchies of rank being undermined by technical expertise and the highly trained personnel required to apply it.

Thus it seems crucial to view, say, the Russian military not as an exception, but as an extreme on a continuum, as indicative of a potential to which all armed services are susceptible during a period when established loyalties and organizational practices are everywhere subject to parametric transformations. Soldiers and officers are not exclusively habit-driven; they too are susceptible to learning and change as their skills expand and their opportunities narrow. And the changes they experience are as likely as not to mirror the transformations at work elsewhere in the world. Military establishments and their personnel may be distinguishable by the uniforms they wear and the weapons they shoulder, but otherwise their distinctive missions, roles, and services seem bound to become increasingly blurred as the dynamics of fragmegration widen the domestic-foreign Frontier.

[61] Tim Golden, "Democracy Isn't Always Enough to Repel Attempted Coups," *New York Times*, February 9, 1992, sect. 4, p. 3.

20 The United Nations

> It would be ridiculous if the first era of planetary interdependence were to find the world without a unitary framework of international relations. With all its imperfections, the United Nations is still the main incarnation of the global spirit. It alone seeks to present a vision of humankind in its organic unity. At no other time have so many people crossed frontiers and come into contact with people of other faiths and nationalities; the new accessibility is steadily eroding parochialism. In light of these slow but deep currents of human evolution, the idea of an international organization playing an assertive role in the pacification of this turbulent world may have to bide its time, but it will never disappear from view. History and the future are on its side.
>
> Abba Eban[1]

Assessed in the context of a bifurcated world, international organizations (IOs), and especially the United Nations (UN), serve as bridges across the frontier that separates states in the state-centric world and NGOs and other actors in the multi-centric world. As implied in the analysis of states in chapter 18 and the discussion of NGOs in chapter 17, however, IOs are bridges under considerable tension, often wavering dangerously in the turbulent changes that pull at their foundations on opposite shores. Despite their shaky existence, however, the traffic across them is heavy and continuous, suggesting that they are major features of the emergent landscape of world politics. Indeed, and to push the metaphor one step further, the course of events has become so reliant on the bridges provided by IOs that most of them have had to add lanes to cope with the expanding traffic of conflicts, agreements, goods, services, and ideas through which the interactions of the two worlds are sustained. Without such bridges, the treacherous waters of

[1] "The U.N. Idea Revisited," *Foreign Affairs*, vol. 74 (September/October 1995), p. 55.

global tensions would be far less traversable than is presently the case.[2] Without such bridges, the Frontier would be a rugged, incoherent political space inhospitable to efforts to traverse its pathways between domestic and foreign affairs.

Since a large and ever-growing literature on the strengths and weaknesses of IOs is available,[3] here the task is a modest one, namely, to assess how the UN contributes to the politics of the Frontier by serving as a primary institution that links the public and private worlds of global affairs. Full descriptions and analyses of the various agencies that comprise the vast UN system are not undertaken; rather the chapter seeks only to meet the challenge of grasping the organization's role as a facilitator between the two worlds, as a key actor in enabling states and nongovernmental actors to address their common problems, ameliorate their tensions, and otherwise cope with their bifurcated structures.

By focusing on the UN as a long-established, routinized organization responsive to its member states and as an adaptive organization sensitive to changing global circumstances and new constituencies, the tensions inherent in the UN's bridging role can be fruitfully analyzed. The task is not easy. As previously noted, present-day world affairs are pervaded with contradictions. With global interdependence and complexity becoming ever greater, issues do overlap, organizations do pursue conflicting policies, institutions do offset each other, changes do lead in opposite directions. More relevant to the present focus, some UN projects are utter failures and others are remarkable successes, just as on one day the UN Secretary-General can be rebuffed by a nationalist leader and on the next day a UN delegate speaks of the Security Council's policies as "sovereign."[4]

The essential argument of this chapter is that as a consequence of global bifurcation, the UN has become responsive to two masters, namely, the historic interstate system and the emergent multi-centric

---

[2] Given its new-found readiness to engage in humanitarian interventions and perform a variety of peace-keeping and peace-making functions, the bridging role played by the UN has also led to it being described as the world's "nightwatchman." Cf. Craig N. Murphy, *International Organization and Industrial Change: Global Governance since 1850* (New York: Oxford University Press, 1994), pp. 263–4.

[3] See, for example, the bibliography in Commission on Global Governance, *Our Global Neighborhood: The Report of the Commission on Global Governance* (New York: Oxford University Press, 1995), pp. 387–94.

[4] Roger Cohen, "Leader of Serbs Spurns a Meeting with Head of U.N.," *New York Times*, December 1, 1994, p. 1, and Barbara Crossette, "U.N. Plays Down Missed Sarajevo Meeting," *New York Times*, December 2, 1994, p. A15.

system. As noted, the needs and aspirations of these two systems are often in opposition, but it is also the case that in many situations their goals and activities are mutually reinforcing. Accordingly, many of the contradictions pervading world affairs today have become institutionalized in the UN and seem likely to endure for the foreseeable future. The argument concludes that the UN, by being responsive to both wings of the bifurcated global system, is at present the world's prime global mechanism for simultaneously maintaining historic patterns and absorbing profound changes. And it further concludes that the UN somehow manages the bifurcation sufficiently to persist and even (in some respects) to thrive.

To be sure, the UN's performances in the global system are often hindered and undermined by its responsiveness to the interstate system, but such limitations should not be allowed to detract from the notion that the organization moves concurrently in two worlds and that the contradictions inherent therein have been accepted as an integral part of the global landscape. Thus it seems unlikely that the UN will eventually yield to the dictates of one of these worlds. Rather, there are good reasons to anticipate that the circumstances of global bifurcation will persist and that the UN system will continue to balance the contradictory demands of states and peoples in such a way as to remain intact and adaptive rather than slowly collapsing into disarray and demise.

The UN as a facilitator

Given the premises of previous chapters – that the global system is undergoing profound transformations, that states are experiencing a diminution of their competence and sovereignty, and that powerful forces of globalization have become endemic to the course of events – it is hardly surprising that serving as a facilitator between the state- and multi-centric worlds has been added to the panoply of the UN's roles. Indeed, the facilitator role is itself comprised of multiple tasks and diverse activities. There are numerous ways in which the various agencies of the UN have evolved practices that deeply involve them in the domestic affairs of its member states and thus put them in direct contact with NGOs and publics as well as with national governments. This trend toward greater involvement in internal matters is plainly evident in the conduct of national elections (see chapter 13), and it has also been noted in the discussion of how the changing nature of sovereignty has allowed the Security Council to intrude into the human rights of Kurds and other minorities (chapter 11), in the advent of UN-sponsored conferences on major socio-economic and environmental issues that now occur with sufficient frequency to be institutionalized (chapter 17), in the emergence of global norms that give meaning to the notion of an "international community" with criteria of performance and standards of behavior to which governments are expected to conform (chapter 9), in the growing tendency to get the Security Council's seal of approval for major incursions into the domestic conflicts of failing states, and in the activities of the Economic and Social Council (ECOSOC), the World Health Organization (WHO), the Development Programme (UNDP), and other UN agencies that seek to facilitate development, reduce poverty, improve health, extend education, ameliorate the plight of refugees, and otherwise upgrade living conditions within societies.

To be sure, the charge to undertake many of these activities was written into the UN's Charter long before global structures underwent bifurcation. But more than a few of them are relatively recent and only in recent decades have those called for in the 1945 document become extensive commitments. If there ever was any doubt about whether the UN would come to occupy the role of facilitator, and thus become a transmission belt for interaction between the public and private worlds of global affairs, trends since the end of the Cold War make it clear that such doubts were misplaced. The UN may be formally responsible to the governments of the states that comprise its membership, but today it far exceeds those responsibilities and cuts a much larger swathe in global affairs than was anticipated at its founding.

The world of states and the interstate system

None of these developments could have occurred without corresponding changes on the part of states. The dwindling and end of the Cold War may have made it possible for the UN to expand its activities in the multi-centric world, but attitudinally states had to be ready for the expansion. They did not suddenly awake to a new day when the Berlin Wall came down and, in effect, say to themselves, "Now we can start fresh." Rather developments through the Cold War years had to foster slowly the formation of new attitudes toward multilateral cooperation, attitudes that acknowledged the world's growing interdependence and allowed for the possibility that problems in distant places could well become challenges close to home. Viewed in this way, it is hardly surprising that the end of the Cold War witnessed the readiness of states to enable the UN to expand the scope and direction of its activities. Many may have done so reluctantly and implicitly rather than enthusiastically and explicitly, but nonetheless their governments voted for the UN's enlarged responsibilities. Had their orientations been unchanged, had states emerged from the Cold War clinging to historic conceptions of sovereignty and with unaltered commitments to their narrowly defined national interests, the UN could not have become the major player and facilitator that it is today. By the latter years of the twentieth century, however, the historic orientations were no longer tenable. Social, economic, and political life within and between communities had become too complex and interdependent, too rife with turbulent change, for states and governments to retreat behind their territorial borders and confine their preoccupations, budgets, and military preparedness to the conventional issues that fell within these boundaries. Given the large degree to which major global parameters had undergone transformation, they had little choice but to become involved in the activities and well-being of distant peoples, and the UN proved to be a prime mechanism for moving in this direction.

Of course, viewed from the perspective of its formal structure, states still have the same prerogatives and they can still play the same roles in the UN as they did at its founding in 1945. They can still assert that their sovereignty entitles them to resist the UN's collective decisions; they can still withhold payment of dues and special assessments; they can still get the Secretary-General to yield to their dictates; they can still demand that NGOs be barred from their meetings; and the permanent members of the Security Council can still veto proposed resolutions. To a large extent, in other words, the UN's formal political culture continues to be a sovereignty-oriented, state-dominated culture driven by norms that place the needs of individual members ahead of the collective welfare.

But the recent past indicates that the informal culture and structures of the UN depart sufficiently from the traditional patterns to bring about the surge of diverse activities and programs noted above. The representatives of states may still give voice to sovereign prerogatives, but lately their practices are often at variance with their pronouncements and even the latter seem decreasingly laced with the stridency of sovereign rhetoric. Today the UN is so involved in intrastate conflicts, so much readier to undertake humanitarian interventions, that its peace-building, peace-making, and peace-keeping activities jumped from 10,000 troops from fewer than 50 countries engaged in 5 operations in 1987 to 72,000 troops from 74 countries committed to 18 operations in

1994. This explosion in the UN's roles is also evident in the fact that during the first forty-five years of its history the Security Council passed only six resolutions under Chapter VII in which "threats to the peace, breaches of the peace, acts of aggression were determined to exist," whereas it adopted thirty-three such resolutions between 1990 and 1992. Equally impressive, since the end of the Cold War a new consensus has evolved among both the permanent and nonpermanent members of the Security Council, resulting in the former rarely casting a veto and the entire membership unanimously adopting a preponderance of the resolutions it considers.

Perhaps no less relevant, the UN has moved well beyond the war–peace realm of human affairs. As indicated, it is now involved in a wide range of economic, social, political, and humanitarian activities. Especially indicative in this respect is the large extent to which the UN has become committed since 1989 to the promotion of democracy and human rights as well as peace and conflict resolution: as noted in chapter 13, evidence of an ever-expanding acceptance of its activities in the multi-centric world is provided by the UN's leadership in sending monitors to observe elections in a variety of countries in Latin America, Africa, and Eastern Europe. Nor have the UN's successes in the socio-economic and political realms been confined to the period since the end of the Cold War. Traces of the attitudinal development that culminated with a rapid expansion of UN activities after 1989 were also evident in prior decades. In the words of one observer,

> Among its accomplishments, the UN managed the transformation of colonies into countries, applied sanctions in South Africa and Rhodesia, stimulated economic recovery and monetary stability and extraordinary growth in the developing world through the International Monetary Fund and the World Bank, built global cooperation on weather monitoring and prediction, created the International Atomic Energy Agency to contain the nuclear game, wiped out smallpox, made international air travel and ocean shipping safe and possible, and allocated communication band widths to avoid global cacophony. By the fall of the Berlin Wall, the UN was less a peace keeper than a vital housekeeper for a more crowded, more inter-dependent world.[5]

Another way of explaining the orientational changes that underlie the expansion of UN activities is to view the organization's evolution and

---

[5] Jessica Matthews, "The U.N.'s Next 50 Years," *Washington Post*, January 17, 1995, p. A19.

its present condition bordering on system overload as part of a long-term process of international institutionalization. It is a process that includes the evolution of norms favoring multilateralism, the development of the habit of cooperation, the building of new formal governmental organizations and the expansion of old ones, an appreciation of the increasing porosity of the domestic-foreign Frontier, a growing recognition that genocidal and humanitarian issues anywhere are everyone's business, and a greater readiness to attach legitimacy to NGOs as key players on the global stage. These dimensions of the institutionalization process vary in the extent of their maturation, but traces of all of them are readily discernible in the present activities of UN agencies. The original purpose of the UN may have been to provide a league of states that would protect states' interests and make up for their deficiencies, but today the purpose has shifted, sometimes subtly and sometimes quite obviously, in the direction of institutionalized procedures to deal not only with the burgeoning transnational and global problems that cannot be managed through cooperation among states alone, but also with problems faced by peoples, by individuals whose needs and wants far exceed what they have. The opening reference in the UN Charter to "We the peoples" has become more than simply a ringing phrase; it now serves as a focus for action in the numerous UN agencies as well as for the periodic UN-sponsored conferences on diverse socio-economic and environmental problems. The transformation of the parameters posited by the turbulence model, in other words, is very much in evidence in the various facilitating roles the UN has taken on. Indeed, these changes go a long way toward explaining the declining use of the veto in the Security Council: the evolution of global norms relevant to international cooperation and the pressure of publics for their maintenance has made it increasingly difficult for any of the permanent members to take on the opprobrium that would result from negating the Council's will.[6]

This is not to say, of course, that the UN's accomplishments as a peace-keeper and housekeeper have been free of severe problems and setbacks. Quite to the contrary, its peace-keeping efforts foundered in Somalia and Bosnia, its readiness to implement stated goals and

---

[6] In opposing a 1996 extension of the UN mission in Haiti, for example, the Chinese were warned that their conduct "was unbecoming [for] a permanent [Security] Council member" and that they risked isolation in the Third World, with the result that they backed off their threat to veto the mission. Barbara Crosette, "U.N. Mission To Haiti Is Reprieved," *New York Times*, March 1, 1996, p. A8.

Security Council resolutions has lagged and amounted to what one observer calls "faint-hearted multilateralism,"[7] its bureaucracy has swollen and experienced waste and fraud, and the burdens of system overload in recent years have fostered more than a little despair about its future. And its attempts to rehabilitate failed societies and set them on a course to sustainable development have been compared to "walking on hot coals and broken glass at the same time."[8] Without ignoring or downplaying these numerous problems, however, the point here is that the UN has undergone enormous change since 1945 and its roles in *both* worlds of world politics are vastly different than might have been anticipated in 1945.

Nor is it to say that the attitudinal shifts that have sustained and accompanied the expansion of the UN's roles are free of controversy. For some analysts the UN remains the servant of the states that created it in 1945 and, as such, has expanded its activities. They stress that although the UN has become more central to the course of events than in the past, its expanded activities have been undertaken in response to Articles 7 and 99 of the UN Charter and to the wishes of its members as these have been expressed in resolutions adopted by the General Assembly or the Security Council and subsequently implemented by the Secretary-General or any of the more than fifty distinct agencies that make up the UN system. From this perspective states are seen as ever ready to curb or end the activities of UN officials deemed to have exceeded the authority granted them by the Security Council.

For observers who focus on the dynamic transformations of world politics, on the other hand, the very same expanded activities are interpreted as the exercise of independent autonomy by UN officials. They view the situations in which the UN becomes involved as so complex and urgent that the organization's representatives on the scene must perforce make quick decisions and initiate actions that cannot possibly be monitored by, or referred back to, the Security Council. In turn, such actions are seen as becoming precedents for future responses to a variety of situations. Consequently, from this perspective UN officials are considered to have a wide leeway that, for all practical purposes, is

---

[7] Thomas Risse-Kappen, "Faint-Hearted Multilateralism: The Re-Emergence of the United Nations in World Politics," paper presented at the Annual Meeting of the International Studies Association, Washington, DC (March 1994).

[8] Jonathan Moore, untitled manuscript (September 1994), chap. 2, p. 4, subsequently published as *The UN and Complex Emergencies: Rehabilitation in Third World Transitions* (Geneva, United Nations Research Institute for Social Development 1996).

often free of supervision and thus amounts to an independent, autonomous authority. In short, where the UN's culture in its early decades was founded on a perspective in which states were viewed as initiators, this premise has progressively been replaced by an orientation in which they are viewed as responders. As noted in chapter 11, this shift consisted of a transformation of a "convenience-of-the-state" mentality into a "states-are-obliged-to-go-along" propensity. Moreover, the latter attitude is regarded as so pervasive that states do not readily reverse or bring to a halt UN actions even though they continue to retain the formal right to do so.

Although this alteration in the UN's culture is subtle and often intangible, it is far from trivial. It refers to initial impulses, to acknowledging rather than challenging the legitimacy of proposed courses of action. Second thoughts may follow and result in a reversion to convenience-of-the-state tendencies, but such reversions seem to occur less and less frequently as the governments of member states appreciate more and more that they are confronted with needs and threats they cannot address on their own. Indeed, this appreciation goes a long way to accounting for why the UN has lately been overtaken by a gap between its commitments and its ability to fund them: being unable to address most global problems on their own, governments feel obliged to permit the UN to take on the new tasks even as their readiness to foot the bill or otherwise provide the necessary resources lags. In a similar manner this transformation of underlying attitudes toward the role of states in the UN helps to explain why the organization is now able to intrude into the domestic affairs of strife-riven and failing members in support of transitions to democratic institutions: states no longer object to such actions and, instead, see the need to go along with them because the consequences of not doing so may eventually add to their own burdens. In addition, this subtle but seismic attitudinal shift has been spurred by the world's growing conscience relative to the value of human life and rights.

Put somewhat more moderately, the seismic shift in the UN's culture is more an issue-area than a wholesale transformation. In the particular realms of human rights and democratic governance, that is, states have increasingly become attuned to the idea that what transpires within states is legitimately the business of all states. In effect, global culture now rests on a notion of concurrent jurisdictions wherein states still have primary responsibility for protecting human rights and maintaining basic democratic practices, but others – and especially the UN –

have the right to become involved, even to 'use force, if states do not fulfill their obligations in these areas.

Some might argue that this shift in the UN's cultural premises is temporary, more a matter of the world adjusting to the end of the Cold War that will soon be followed by a return to normal and the convenience-of-the state impulse. However, if the above estimate of the basis of the attitudinal change is correct, if it is due to a mushrooming of interdependence problems that governments alone cannot handle, then such a reversion to the earlier mentality is highly unlikely. Neither the problems nor the mushrooming of them seem destined to diminish, and thus the emergent states-are-obliged-to-go-along propensity is more likely to expand than to contract. It may well be that future generations will look back on this cultural transformation as a turning-point in humankind's slow progression toward problem-solving on a global scale. Call it a glaring contradiction or a logical evolution, but this may eventually seem like the period in which the anarchical interstate system underwent transformation into a semi-autonomous interstate system wherein its members are constrained from freely employing their sovereign rights. The UN has not – and probably will never – become a world government with authority over its members, but it does appear to have reached a point where states often seek its seal of approval for actions that were once regarded as their sovereign prerogatives. That a few countries occasionally deviate from this trend does not signify that the institutions of the anarchical state system remain fully intact.[9]

The world of NGOs and the multi-centric system

As the analysis developed in chapter 17 makes clear, NGOs in the multi-centric world have not only welcomed the attitudinal changes through which states have allowed the UN to expand its scope, but they have also actively promoted these developments. They can properly be regarded as major participants, along with states, in the building of the bridge that links the two worlds. Indeed, the more solid the bridge has become, and the more the traffic across it has increased, the more have NGOs been encouraged to press for access and influence in the UN's decision centers. As previously indicated, they have been especially

[9] For another, more extensive effort that suggests ways in which the institutions of anarchy are adjusting to the world's needs for collective action, see Barry Buzan, Charles Jones, and Richard Little, *The Logic of Anarchy: Neorealism to Structural Realism* (New York: Columbia University Press, 1994), sect. II.

central in the decisions to convene UN-sponsored conferences around particular themes and to monitor whether the commitments made by states at these summit meetings are carried out. By holding simultaneous parallel conferences in the same cities, NGOs have found a mechanism for keeping the pressure for change on states before, during, and after the global gatherings. Indeed, starting with the Rio Earth Summit in 1992, the mechanism has undergone institutionalization. That is, it is now a commonplace expectation that a parallel unofficial conference will convene at the same time and in the same city as the official UN-sponsored global conferences. Known as NGO fora, the parallel conferences have become, in effect, "an integral part of United Nations conferences. The unofficial organizations vary in size and importance, with some more radical and on the fringe than the rest. But many established groups are called on regularly to consult with national delegations. Some become part of official teams."[10]

That NGOs have succeeded in institutionalizing periodic global attention to particular problems is manifest in the fact that a parallel conference on the circumstances of women was convened in Beijing in 1995 and that this was the "Fourth World Conference on Women," the previous ones having been held in Mexico City (1975), Copenhagen (1980), and Nairobi (1985). But the Beijing conference also revealed that the bridge linking the state-centric and multi-centric worlds is not free of pot-holes, bumps, and other obstacles to the free flow of traffic. Some six months before the opening sessions, controversy broke out about who could attend and where the NGOs would convene. The disputes were not so much the result of UN deliberations as they were a consequence of holding the meetings in a country like China, where authoritarian controls are maintained over free speech, organizational activities, and the movement of people. The Chinese sought to structure the conference arrangements in such a way as to avoid the undermining of these controls. Not only did they suddenly announce, without prior consultation, that the NGO Forum would have to convene in a tourist area some thirty miles away from the main conference site, but they also limited the number of delegates to the NGO Forum to between 5,000 and 7,000 while at the same time successfully pressing the UN Secretariat to refuse the applications of some 500 unofficial organiza-

---

[10] Barbara Crossette, "Disputes Mar Parley on Women Set in China," *International Herald Tribune*, April 5, 1995, p. 5.

tions that sought to attend the NGO Forum. Included among the refused organizations were Taiwanese, Tibetan, lesbian, Asian women's rights, and human rights groups, as well as some Christian groups militantly opposed to abortion.

Conclusion

Yet, such instances of obstruction by a single state are increasingly anomalous. The trend-line is so fully in the opposite direction that it is difficult to imagine a cessation of the pattern of regularized parallel conferences on the world's major problems. It can even be argued that while the Chinese resisted the presence of certain groups whose orientations seemed too threatening, they did seek out the role of host country and they did accommodate to the presence of many groups whose policies were sharply at variance with their own. In so doing China acknowledged, even accorded legitimacy to, the UN's emergent role as a facilitator between the state-centric and multi-centric worlds.

In sum, it is reasonable to conclude that, notwithstanding those moments in history when the UN reverts to its traditional circumstances of being dominated (or paralyzed) by states claiming sovereignty and insisting on the pursuit of narrowly defined self-interests, the organization has become a main bridge across the gulf that separates the two worlds of world politics. The bridge provides NGOs access to the interstate world and states access to the multi-centric world, and across it flows the expertise, assistance, and funds that neither might otherwise be able to make available to the other. For all the reasons noted above, moreover, it is likely to be an expanding bridge, often adding lanes to accommodate increasing flows of traffic.

Consider, for example, the crowded flow of two-way traffic on the bridge when the UN undertakes a rehabilitation program in a country. At least six sets of actors are readily identifiable:

> (1) the host government, or other authority, in the recipient state which bears the primary responsibility for its own recovery, and to which external assistance programs must be closely connected; (2) the donor nations, which contribute to the UN programs, but also conduct separate bilateral aid programs based in diplomatic missions in the given country; (3) private voluntary, nongovernmental organizations (NGOs), both international and indigenous, which run humanitarian and development activities there . . . ; (4) UN operational agencies (technically called "UN Funds and Programmes"), such as the UN

Development Programme (UNDP), the UN High Commissioner for Refugees (UNHCR), the UN Children's Fund (UNICEF), and the World Food Programme (WFP); (5) more autonomous specialized agencies of the UN system, such as the Food and Agriculture Organization (FAO), the World Health Organization (WHO), and the International Labor Organization (ILO); and (6) other entities, including representatives of the UN Secretary General and Secretariat, the World Bank and International Monetary Fund (IMF) regional banks, and other regional arrangements.[11]

However, like any bridge that undergoes continuous repair to offset the heavy toll of daily traffic, harsh weather, and natural decay, the UN shows its age and is in need of constant renewal. Regrettably, this need has not been quickly or sufficiently met. Since its founding the organization has managed to adapt enough to remain viable, but the efforts at reform have been partial and spasmodic. The UN has adhered to the path of most large organizations and evolved entrenched habits, an overgrown bureaucracy, and more than a little waste, all of which call for renovation. Most notably perhaps, the UN's structures for participation and decision-making need to be overhauled to reflect better the present distribution of power and interests in the state-centric world, not to mention the emerging diversity and clout of NGOs in the multi-centric world. Similarly, the proliferation of agencies concerned with economic and social issues needs to be rationalized and better mechanisms developed for coordinating their congested flow across the bridge. And while recent years have witnessed improvement in peace-building and peace-keeping operations, there is still much that could be done to clarify lines of authority and otherwise reduce inefficiencies. The challenges of adaptation, in short, are ever present, and they must be the focus of constant attention if the UN is to cope with the mushrooming demands of an ever more complex and turbulent world.

There are more than a few signs that such a focus is becoming a worldwide preoccupation. From myriad conferences celebrating, or at least recognizing, the UN's first half-century to the reports of foundation study groups to the extensive recommendations of the Commission on Global Governance,[12] it seems clear that the desirability of UN reform and renewal has in itself become a global value. To be sure, the translation of aspirations into action is far from automatic; but despite the glaring contradictions that still pervade world affairs, there is some

---

[11] Moore, *The UN and Complex Emergencies*, p. 26.
[12] Commission on Global Governance, *Our Global Neighborhood*.

basis for concluding that they may eventually be brought within manageable limits. Together with a number of NGOs, the UN may well be regarded as an "embryonic public-service sector of a world community that does not yet exist."[13]

---

[13] Brian Urquhart, quoted in Matthews, "The U.N.'s Next 50 Years." Perhaps a measure of the extent to which the UN is still in an embryonic stage is the fact that it has "a total world-wide civil service staff of 51,484 serving the interests of 5.5 billion people in 184 countries, no more than the civil service in the state of Wyoming, population 545,000." (Moore, untitled manuscript, chap. 4, p. 4).

Part V
Conclusions

21 Democracy

Earlier we had order and no freedom. Now we have freedom and no
order. Is it not possible to have both?

Voter in 1996 Russian election[1]

We just want change, even boring change will be better.

Voter in 1996 Spanish election[2]

These frustrated expressions highlight the central theme of the chapters
that conclude this inquiry. They pose the challenge of whether a fragmegrative system can undergo change and sustain effective governance
that at least avoids collapse into widespread disorder and violence, if
not outright war, and that at most does so through widespread democratic practices. In the ensuing analysis the challenge is broken down into
three parts. This chapter looks at the prospects for democracy along the
Frontier, while the next probes the likelihood of interstate war and the
final chapter assesses the chances of effective governance evolving in
the new and widening overlap of domestic and foreign affairs.

On the quality of governance

In view of the criss-crossing currents of change that mark the politics of
the Frontier – the emergence of new SOAs, the competition for shifting
loyalties, and the fluctuation of identities – the question of whether
democratic practices and institutions can evolve along the Frontier

---

[1] Quoted in Michael Specter, "Ex-General's Voters Crucial to Yeltsin," *New York Times*,
June 22, 1996, p. 4.
[2] Quoted in Marlise Simons, "The Heirs of Franco Woo Spain's Centrist Voters," *New York
Times*, January 26, 1996, p. A3.

looms large. As expanding and contested political space that does not conform to established territorial boundaries, the Frontier has yet to develop extensive mechanisms for framing and implementing policies based on procedures that fairly represent the ever greater numbers of interests and people affected by the politics of the Frontier. What legislative institutions do exist, such as the European Parliament, are founded on the state system, with representatives being chosen on the basis of their country affiliations. Moreover, even if the European Parliament were to supersede the legislatures of its member countries, and even if other regions of the world were to develop comparable institutions, those encompassed by the Frontier would be woefully underrepresented and nondemocratic. How are the multinational corporations that occupy key command posts along the Frontier to be held accountable for their decisions? What mechanisms are available to insure that the decision-making processes of NGOs are transparent and open to inputs from people affected by them? How do new SOAs acquire legitimacy and the right to engage in governance? Where space along the Frontier is contested, what judicial bodies or adjudication procedures can be used to resolve the disputes authoritatively? How can the dynamics of globalization and fragmegration be brought under democratic control? In short, whatever the chances of effective governance along the Frontier, how can its quality begin to approach democratic ideals?

Answers to such questions are perforce elusive. Democracy as we know it within countries does not exist along the Frontier. More accurately, to the extent that the Frontier is marked by conventional democratic procedures, these are *ad hoc*, nonsystematic, irregular, and fragile. They lack the constituencies, scope, and support that are necessary to provide the diverse forces comprising the Frontier with adequate equity and voice. The Frontier is not chaotic; it does have some established patterns and others that are coming into being; and it also has pockets (such as externally monitored elections) wherein open democratic procedures are practiced; but at the same time neither the patterns nor the pockets are sufficient to suffuse the politics of the Frontier with accountability and responsibility.

Thus questions recur: How, then, to foster the authority and institutions that would bring greater degrees of democracy to governance in the Frontier's turbulent space? How to subject the decision-makers who impact upon the Frontier to a modicum of accountability and responsibility? How to insure the liberties of individuals who roam around, voluntarily or otherwise, the Frontier's spaces? And equally important, how to begin to answer these questions without appearing hopelessly naive, idealistic, or otherwise out of touch with the realities of politics along the Frontier?

The clearest response to these queries involves the necessity of not pondering them in the context of democratic notions appropriate to territorial polities. It is the very nature of the Frontier that territory is not a central organizing premise for actions and interactions. Hence, concepts of representation and accountability based on long-established territorial democracies in countries, provinces, or cities ought not serve as the basis for pondering the foregoing questions. For, in the absence of fixed boundaries along the Frontier, processes of representation and responsibility normally associated with democratic institutions are of limited relevance. Rather, imagination and flexibility are needed if the fragmegrative dynamics that sustain the politics of the Frontier are to be assessed in terms of their susceptibility to democratic control. What is needed is a capacity for discerning how the Frontier might evolve functional equivalents of the basic precepts of territorial democracy.

In a circuitous way, the very dynamics of fragmegration have embedded within them one major functional equivalent of democracy. By decentralizing SOAs in disparate and localized sites, fragmegration has greatly inhibited the coalescence of hierarchical and autocratic centers of powers. It is as if the politics of the Frontier, through having both integrative and fragmented components, mimics the global market with its shifting loci of limited decision-making authority and its subservience to macro tides of inflation, currency swings, and productivity breakthroughs.[3] Along the Frontier none of the SOAs can exercise extensive control over people and policies outside their own limited jurisdictions. To be sure, numerous SOAs, especially transnational corporations, are hierarchically organized and make decisions without concern for whether they disempower people or do ecological harm.[4] In 1992 it was estimated that the number of transnational corporations exceeded

---

[3] For an elaboration of the notion that world politics may mimic the global marketplace, see John Agnew and Stuart Corbridge, *Mastering Space: Hegemony, Territory and International Political Economy* (New York: Routledge, 1995), p. 207.

[4] The role of corporations as SOAs is essayed in Claire Cutler, Virginia Haufler, and Tony Porter, "Private Authority and International Regimes," paper to a workshop at the Annual Meeting of the International Studies Association, San Diego (April 1996), and David C. Korten, *When Corporations Rule the World* (West Hartford, CT: Kumarian Press, 1995).

35,000 and that, in turn, these had over 200,000 subsidiaries.[5] While these figures indicate that sizable areas of global life rest on a form of governance that lacks democratic accountability, they also suggest that the dispersal of authority along the Frontier is so widespread that severe violations of democratic values cannot be readily concentrated in hegemonic hands.

Equally important, as noted in chapter 17, there is no lack of pressures within the Frontier from NGOs and social movements for greater transparency and access on the part of hierarchical organizations, pressures that are in some respects functional equivalents of the various electoral, legislative, and journalistic checks that sustain a modicum of democracy in territorial polities. Indeed, SOAs in which NGOs are predominant face the danger of too much democracy, of multiple accountabilities – "'downward' to their partners, beneficiaries, staff, and supporters; and 'upward' to their trustees, donors, and host governments"[6] – that foster inefficiencies and indecisive policy-making. Put differently, just as markets are not democratic in their functioning, and just as they are insensitive to any damage they may do, so are they not systematic in any harm they cause – all of which can also be said about the fragmegrative dynamics that underlie the disaggregation of the Frontier and its new political spaces.

Although a stretch of the imagination is required to appreciate its functional equivalency, the widespread growth of the Internet, the World Wide Web, and the other electronic technologies that are shrinking the world offers considerable potential as a source of democracy. More accurately, by facilitating the continued proliferation of networks that know no boundaries, these technologies have introduced a horizontal dimension to the politics of the Frontier. They enable like-minded people in distant places to converge, share perspectives, protest abuses, provide information, and mobilize resources – dynamics that seem bound to constrain the vertical structures that sustain governments, corporations, and any other hierarchical organizations. As one observer put it, "Anyone with a modem is potentially a global pamphleteer,"[7]

---

[5] Robert Boyer and Daniel Drache, "Introduction," in R. Boyer and D. Drache (eds.), *States Against Markets: The Limits of Globalization* (London: Routledge, 1996), p. 7.

[6] Michael Edwards and David Hulme, "NGO Performance and Accountability," in M. Edwards and D. Hulme (eds.), *Beyond the Magic Bullet: NGO Performance and Accountability in the Post-Cold War World* (West Hartford, CT: Kumarian Press, 1996), p. 8.

[7] John Markoff, "If Medium Is the Message, the Message Is the Web," *New York Times*, November 20, 1995, p. A1.

while another admitted finding "electrons more fascinating than elections."[8] In other words, since these technologies have the potential "of bringing information directly into our homes any time we want it," they could render

> political institutions (*all institutions*) . . . far less important . . .
> Computers could displace schools, offices, newspapers, scheduled television and banks . . . Government's regulatory functions could weaken, or vanish. It's already a cinch on the Internet to get around the rules; censorship, telecommunications restrictions and patent laws are easily evaded.[9]

Nor can it be argued that this line of reasoning is misguided because the computer is available only to a relative small stratum of the world's population. To be sure, large numbers of people still do not have access to computer networks, but this circumstance seems likely to be dramatically altered as "[c]omputers keep getting faster, cheaper, and smaller."[10] Indeed, the decline in the cost of computer equipment is matched only by the acceleration of its power to process information: "The number of components that engineers could squeeze onto a microchip has doubled every year since 1959, [with the result that t]wenty years from now, a computer will do in 30 seconds what one of today's computers takes a year to do."[11] Accordingly, it is hardly surprising – to cite but two of myriad examples – that geographically remote Mongolia is now wired into the Internet[12] and that its use is spreading so rapidly in China that the Internet "can be accessed in 700 cities via local dial-up calls."[13]

In short, the multi-centric world of diverse nongovernmental actors is increasingly pervaded with checks and balances. These constraints are not formalized as they are in territorial polities, and they operate unevenly in the various segments of the multi-centric world, but more often than not they tend to inhibit unrestrained exercises of power and to subject unfair or criminal practices to the glare of publicity. In a few SOAs, such as the credit-rating agencies mentioned in chapter 8, the authority of the constraints is rooted in a reputation for even-handedness; in some SOAs, such as professional or epistemic communities, the

[8] James K. Glassman, "Brave New Cyberworld," *Washington Post*, August 29, 1995, p. A19.   [9] *Ibid.* (italics in the original).   [10] *Ibid.*   [11] *Ibid.*
[12] Elizabeth Corcoran, "How the 'Butter Fund' Spread the Internet to Mongolia," *Washington Post*, March 1, 1996, p. A1.
[13] "Internet Thrives in Nation Starved of Information," *Eastern Express* (Hong Kong), April 6, 1995, p. 9.

constraints derive from the dissemination of authoritative knowledge about problems and issues on the Frontier's agenda; in other SOAs, such as those active with respect to human rights, checks and balances are served through moral authority; in still other SOAs, such as cross-border coalitions among consumer activists or environmentalists, the capacity to restrain excesses stems from the kind of organizational work that suffuses demands and protests with a ring of authority; in many SOAs constraints arise out of coalitions of governmental and non-governmental actors that preside over issue regimes; occasionally, in issue-specific SOAs, social movements can initiate changes in the diplomatic chambers of the state-centric system by aggregating individuals to boycott the products of companies doing business with pariah states;[14] and so on through all the domains wherein governance of the Frontier occurs.

There is one SOA, however, where the pattern of constraints is nascent rather than currently active. The global market is unregulated and presently beyond the capacity of states to direct. Unwilling to protect their industries and labor forces, states allow the global market to prevail and it, in turn, unfolds by economic rules that amount to arbitrary rather than democratic governance. Considered from a long-run perspective, however, the global market is no less subject to fragmegrative dynamics than any other dimension of the emergent epoch. Most notably, if free trade agreements lead to excesses in which only the wealthy participate, other groups in societies may eventually become active along the Frontier and demand that the excesses be brought under control. The uprising of Mayan Indians in Chiapas and the 1996 presidential candidacy of Patrick Buchanan in the United States were both partly reactions to NAFTA and, as such, are illustrative of how the unregulated SOA known as the global economy subsumes nascent constraints capable of becoming major political forces. Whether the activation of these forces will expand the democratic dimensions of the Frontier is questionable. More accurately, democracy will be served if the upheavals like those in Chiapas result in greater autonomy for local

---

[14] Perhaps because the disinvestment campaign against apartheid in South Africa was so successful, this pattern appears to be recurring with greater frequency. Recently, for example, pressures have been successfully launched against companies to withdraw from Myanmar until its military rulers step down: "The Carlsberg and Heineken breweries both announced earlier this month they were ending business dealings there after pro-democracy groups called for a boycott of the companies' products." *New York Times,* July 19, 1996, p. A4.

populations, whereas it may well be set back if xenophobic politicians in industrial countries successfully persuade populations that their future lies in repressive measures designed to control the flow of goods and ideas.

Another way to formulate this problem of how to achieve democratic practices under conditions wherein state authority has been diffused is to focus on those dimensions of the diffusion that cannot be readily traced, those issues that have "leaked away ... gone nowhere, just evaporated."[15] That is, while it is possible to discern accountability in the upward diffusion of authority to supranational organizations such as the UN, the IMF, and NGOs like Greenpeace, and while the shift of responsibilities downward to provincial and local governments can also be easily appraised, it is perplexing to assess the shift of authority with respect to those economic, labor, and welfare matters from which states have retreated and been superseded by the anarchy of global markets. Assuming that the notion of continued economic growth keeping capricious markets in check is unsatisfactory – as continued growth is by no means assured – the question remains of what SOAs will evolve and "how much in the way of rules, supervision, and intervention [will they need] for the system's continued stability, equity, and prosperity ... What, in other words, is the sine qua non of political management for a capitalist market-oriented, credit-dependent economic system of production, trade, and investment?"[16] The answer to this important question is complex: "Just as experience and the record of history have clearly shown that society can tolerate a certain measure of violence and insecurity, that economies can carry on despite a certain degree of inflation in the value of money, a measure of financial instability, the answer to the question, 'How much anarchy is too much?' is by no means clear. To put the question another way, how much does it matter to the system, to the people living in and by it, that half of Africa and certain parts of Latin America and Asia remain sunk in political chaos, economic stagnation, and recurrent famine, endemic disease, and internecine warfare?"[17]

It follows that the diverse checks and balances embedded in different types of SOAs offer a mixed picture as far as being reliable instruments

[15] Susan Strange, "The Defective State," *Daedalus*, vol. 124 (Spring 1995), p. 56.

[16] *Ibid.*, p. 71.

[17] *Ibid.*, pp. 71–2. For a similar analysis that poses, in effect, this question, see Riccardo Petrella, "Globalization and Internationalization: The Dynamics of the Emerging World Order," in Boyer and Drache (eds.), *States Against Markets*, p. 81.

of democratic governance is concerned. There remain pockets, even large gaps, wherein democratic principles are systematically ignored, grossly violated, or paid only superficial lip service. Yet, the same sentence could be written about territorial polities regarded as democratic systems; they too are not lacking in distortions and assertions of democratic ideals that are not honored in practice. Besides, and to repeat, the test of whether democracy is evolving along the Frontier is not whether the institutions of representation and responsibility conform to those to be found in territorial polities; rather, the test lies in the degree to which *ad hoc* control mechanisms evolve to steer the politics of the Frontier in the direction of more checks on the excesses of power, more opportunities for interests to be heard and heeded, and more balanced constraints among the multiplicity of actors that seek to extend their command of issue areas. Viewed in this way, it seems reasonable to conclude that the more densely populated the Frontier becomes, thus promoting a greater sense of connectivity among widely separated peoples and groups, the more will its governance exhibit democratic tendencies.

Furthermore, it is likely that the more densely populated the Frontier becomes, the more will states be under pressure to "provide new vehicles for democratic expression at the national level that also provide national democratic access to supranational decision-making."[18] This is another way of saying that in addition to the control mechanisms that evolve within the Frontier, others exist (or are being nursed into being) through collaboration between state-centric and multi-centric actors. Consider such mechanisms as agencies of the UN collaborating with volunteer groups over issues of population growth, health, and environmental sustainability, governments that maintain foreign aid programs in the developing world working with local specialists to frame and administer program goals, representatives of the two worlds simultaneously holding adjacent summit meetings to consider progress in particular issue areas, provincial governments seeking to promote new trading partners abroad, or local communities engaging in exchanges with sister cities: all these (and doubtless many other) *ad hoc* mechanisms for superseding or by-passing domestic-foreign boundaries can quickly become institutionalized and thereby sustain SOAs that enlarge governance along the Frontier. To be sure, it has become

---

[18] Vivien A. Schmidt, "The New World Order, Incorporated: The Rise of Business and the Decline of the Nation-State," *Daedalus*, vol. 124 (Spring 1995), p. 77.

commonplace to conclude that "the current state of NGO . . . account-ability is unsatisfactory,"[19] but few would deny that the standards for assessing organizational performance have steadily risen and that what is judged to be unsatisfactory today would earlier have seemed like worthy goals on the road to more extensive democracy.

While some analysts treat this emergence of the Frontier's numerous, diverse, and collaborative SOAs, and the ways in which they may check and balance each other, as amounting to democracy in the sense that the result is an empowering of communities,[20] others envisage the politics of the Frontier as leading to "cosmopolitan democracy."[21] The latter argue that

> democracy can only be fully sustained in and through the agencies and organizations which form an element of and yet cut across the territo-rial boundaries of the nation-state. The possibility of democracy today must . . . be linked to an expanding framework of democratic states and agencies . . . [This framework is] "the cosmopolitan model of democ-racy," by which [is meant] a system of governance which arises from and is adapted to the diverse conditions and interconnections of differ-ent peoples and nations."[22]

Those who discern empowered communities and cosmopolitan forms of transnational governance recognize that these control mecha-nisms are still very far from mature institutions and that numerous obstacles must still be overcome if they are to become firmly embedded as features of the Frontier. Yet they perceive in the dynamics of fragmegration – in the overlapping of peoples, the shrinking of dis-tances, and the emergence of shared norms – hope that progress toward democratic forms of governance can be sustained.

Is the hope justified? Or are there reasons to fear that the bottom-line orientations of profit-making organizations and the self-serving tenden-cies of nonprofit actors are too extensive for the evolving structures of the Frontier to acquire the functional equivalents of democratic polities? Perhaps the only plausible answer is that "the jury is still out regarding the [liberalized new world order's] effects on global democracy and

---

[19] Michael Edwards and David Hulme, "Beyond the Magic Bullet? Lessons and Conclusions," in Edwards and Hulme (eds.), *Beyond the Magic Bullet*, p. 257.

[20] Agnew and Corbridge, *Mastering Space*, chap. 8.

[21] Daniele Archibugi and David Held (eds.), *Cosmopolitan Democracy: An Agenda for a New World Order* (Cambridge: Polity Press, 1995).

[22] David Held, "Democracy and the New International Order," in Archibugi and Held (eds.), *Cosmopolitan Democracy*, p. 106.

government generally"[23] and that thus both the hopes and the fears are warranted. So much change is at work that one can readily construct scenarios in which the politics of the Frontier become increasingly democratic, just as contrary scenarios are not far-fetched. Stated more positively, given a continuing skill revolution and proliferation of networks that link diverse and distant individuals, there is certainly no reason to abandon hope if one's concept of democracy allows for the growth of institutions unique to transnational rather than territorial political spaces.

[23] Schmidt, "The New World Order, Incorporated," p. 76.

22 War and peace

> Our points of view were very different; now they have converged around peace. No one here is interested in war anymore.
>
> Padrino Pilartes, guerrilla colonel in Angola[1]

A civilian is shot on a city street; a television cameraman, waiting at a dangerous crossroads to see somebody killed or mutilated, films the shooting; a soldier sent by the United Nations as a "peacekeeper" to a city officially called a "safe area" watches, unsure what to do and paralyzed by fear. The elements of this troubling collage are also elements of what some military analysts are now calling "postmodern" or "future" war. In their analysis, the wars between states and their armed forces that dominated history for several centuries . . . are now being replaced by a new kind of conflict, like that in Sarajevo, in which armies and peoples become indistinguishable. In such wars, states are replaced by militias or other informal – often tribal – groupings whose ability to use sophisticated weaponry is very limited.

> news item[2]

Most inquiries into the prospects for peace and war are locked into an underlying line of reasoning that can only lead to gloomy conclusions. Since the predisposition of individuals and groups toward conflict and violence ranges across the whole of human history, such reasoning asserts, the probability of these predispositions atrophying is nil. No matter that in the long run technologies transform practices, that societies evolve new perspectives, that institutions undergo huge changes, that generations break with their predecessors, that value orientations

---

[1] *New York Times*, December 16, 1991, p. A9.
[2] Roger Cohen, "In Sarajevo, Victims of a 'Postmodern' War," *New York Times*, May 21, 1995, pp. 1, 12.

shift direction, that individuals acquire new skills and have a capacity for learning – neither singly nor in combination are any of these dynamics conceived to make the slightest inroad into the violence-prone proclivities through which people have always conducted their lives.

Put differently, unlike any other realm of human affairs, the readiness to do battle over turf, status, and resources is widely treated as a constant rather than a variable. Histories of family structures, sexual practices, economic institutions, cultural premises, political organizations, and every other fundamental dimension of social systems are all pervaded with eras that come to an end and subsequent reversals of course. But histories of war are pervaded with continuity. Yes, transitions from the bow-and-arrow to the rifle to the tank to the airplane to the nuclear missile are seen to delineate evolutionary stages, but such periodizations are considered to confirm the central tendencies toward violent conflict resolutions, without any allowance made for possible breakpoints in which the impulses toward war undergo redirection and attenuation. It is as if the readiness to engage in organized violence is an innate trait over which only limited control can be exercised.

And the evidence supporting this underlying line of reasoning is overwhelming. From the earliest times down through the immediate present, voluminous outbreaks of war have been cited as proof positive that recourse to violence is an immutable characteristic of the human condition.

Such reasoning and the solid empirical data on which it rests has led analysts to search every aspect of the war-making process – from individual psyches to organizational requirements to societal demands – for clues as to how much of the variance each explains. And while they may differ on which aspects are the most powerful sources of war, all serious students of the subject avoid single-cause explanations and conclude that recourse to violence derives from a multiplicity of sources at diverse levels of aggregation that interact in such a way as to culminate in decisions to employ lethal weapons to attack, resist, or otherwise overcome adversaries.

The thrust of this chapter is that the advent of global turbulence, the bifurcation of world politics, the skill revolution, and the processes of fragmegration have had consequences that undermine the foregoing line of reasoning, that the propensities toward organized violence are no different than any other propensities, and that – as the epigraphs above implies – they are susceptible to redirection under appropriate circumstances. John Mueller's analogy to dueling and slavery – in which the disappearance of these well-established institutions which were once so deeply entrenched in human affairs is seen as indicative of the future of large-scale warfare – may seem far-fetched,[3] but it is founded on the sound premise that fundamental and seemingly immutable social processes are capable of undergoing profound change and even attenuation. The central question is not whether the analytic leap from dueling and slavery to war is faulty, but whether the conditions that sustain the propensities toward organized violence have undergone thoroughgoing transformation. My argument is that such a transformation is under way and well along to a set of conditions in which major wars are unlikely to mar the decades ahead.

Put differently, if one adopts an analytic approach that seeks to identify the obstacles that have to be overcome for war-making decisions to be made, rather than the more widespread practice of identifying the factors that propel national leaders to go to war, then the probabilities of hostilities breaking out in any situation take on a very different coloration. Viewed from an obstacles perspective, the probabilities seem very small indeed and, equally important, they appear likely to continue to decline as the obstacles (discussed below) become ever more resilient.

Interstate and other wars

Much depends, of course, on the kinds of wars to which reference is made. There is a widespread and understandable tendency in the literature on the subject to treat propensities toward violence as a generalized phenomenon, with the result that the concept of "war" is applied to a host of very different types of conflict. Viewed from the perspective of the combatants and their embattled publics, every war is a major war and each day it lasts is one day too long. On the other hand, approached from the perspective of changing systemic conditions, wars can vary considerably in their consequences for the structures of world affairs. Some types can lead to widespread casualties and destruction but be relatively minor in terms of their impact upon the established routines of international affairs, whereas other types can be vehicles of extensive structural transformations. Here it is the latter type that serves as the focus of analysis. Whatever may be the propensity toward organized violence inherent

[3] John Mueller, *Retreat from Doomsday: The Obsolescence of Major War* (New York: Basic Books, 1989). A similar perspective can be found in Paul Hirst and Grahame Thompson, *Globalization in Question* (Oxford: Blackwell, 1996), pp. 179–80.

in the human condition, it is argued that certain types of war – what are called "major" wars – are on the verge of extinction. More specifically, the argument identifies interstate wars as potential sources of structural transformation and it focuses only peripherally on the many other forms of conflict – e.g., internal wars, civil wars, guerrilla wars, and inner-city wars – that are often designated by the war label but that may not have global ramifications. As indicated by the second epigraph above, these various other types of war may well become more pervasive.[4]

One more differentiation needs to be drawn at the outset. Obviously, not every interstate war alters the underlying structures of world affairs. Periodic outbreaks of violent conflict between contiguous neighbors in regions of the developing world (say, between Honduras and Nicaragua or Libya and Chad) are not normally precipitants of global consequences. Only those wars in which one or more of the participating states are sufficiently militarized and strong to occupy, annex, or otherwise conquer another – and thus to introduce transformational dynamics into global structures – are here treated as "major" wars.

Several characteristics distinguish major interstate wars. First, they involve the mobilization of the entire society, a process which magnifies uncertainties, lowers living standards, highlights patriotism, emphasizes sacrifice, reduces tolerance for opposition groups, and otherwise undermines normal routines. Second, interstate wars start with attacks across national boundaries and, as such, their onset is unmistakable and the identity of the warring adversaries clearly established. The question of who was the original aggressor may be endlessly contested, but there is no ambiguity as to who are the enemies. Third, the goals, strategies, and conduct of interstate wars are readily discernible. Their armed forces are uniformed, organized hierarchically, and committed to battle plans that are not easily disguised. Total and explicit commitment, in short, are hallmarks of states that initiate major interstate wars and, for reasons elaborated below, these are characteristics that are especially vulnerable to the dynamics militating against the launching of such conflicts.

Four dynamics

To conclude that major interstate wars are passing into history is not, of course, to contend that such wars will never occur again. The ensuing

---

[4] Cf. Thomas L. Friedman, "Today's Threat to Peace Is the Guy Down the Street," *New York Times*, June 2, 1991, sect. 4, p. 3.

analysis is grounded in probabilistic premises. It seeks to anticipate central tendencies and not particular outcomes. As Iraq's attack on Kuwait illustrates, states still do war on each other and thus interstate conflicts may yet again collapse into violence. But the likelihood of such occurrences seems extremely low. At least four dynamics at work in world affairs are arrayed against recourse to military action in interstate relations. For a war to be launched each of these dynamics would somehow have to be quiescent, and the greater probability is that all of them will remain vigorously operative in the foreseeable future. All of them, moreover, are interactive and mutually reinforcing, thereby further intensifying and strengthening the improbability of a state unleashing its armed forces against another state with a view to occupation, annexation, or other forms of full conquest.

In addition, the improbability of major interstate war is augmented by the fact that each of the dynamics inhibiting its outbreak finds expression at every level of aggregation where the roots of war can take hold. Wars are undertaken by officials whose perceptions, calculations, and decisions are partly shaped by the policy-making procedures inherent in their polity's structures and by the aspirations embedded in their society's institutions which, in turn, are conditioned by the international context of their country's place in global affairs. At each of these levels – officials, policy-making procedures, political structures, societal institutions, and international contexts – all four of the dynamics noted below as paramount in world politics today operate to curb the processes that culminate in major interstate war.

Before elaborating on the four dynamics and their reinforcing interactions, it is useful to stress that the analysis does not rest on the potential of either nuclear weapons or hegemonic stability. Powerful as they are, nuclear weapons and the devastation they can precipitate are not the only deterrent to interstate wars. World politics has too many militarized and strong states that lack a nuclear armory to cite such weapons as the only reason why the readiness of states to war on each other may be atrophying. Likewise, important as the US military presence in East Asia is to the stability of the region, the ensuing analysis suggests that this arrangement is not the only factor inhibiting interstate war in that part of the world. Even if global politics was again to evolve a thoroughgoing hegemonic structure – and this seems highly unlikely in an ever more interdependent and complex world – the hegemon is likely to be so circumscribed as to resist the temptation to prevent challenges to its leadership by resorting to extensive military action. More accurately, only if it can mobilize the support of a broadly based coalition of the United Nations (as the United States did for a while over Iraq) is a major power likely to resort to the war alternative.

No, the argument developed here focuses on dynamics that have little to do with weapons technology or hegemonic controls. It proceeds, rather, from the ways in which the structures and processes underlying the (1) complexity, (2) weariness, (3) paralysis, and (4) emergent norms of societies late in the twentieth century reinforce each other to create conditions under which neither rational calculations nor distorted perceptions nor emotional needs nor public pressures are likely to converge around the alternative of going to war as a compelling course of action on the part of states with the means to wage triumphant military campaigns.

Complexity

For a host of reasons ranging from the impact of new communications technologies to the vast migrations of people, from the intensification of subgroup loyalties to the growing interdependence of public issues, societies in the present era have become such dense thickets of people, groups, organizations, and problems that the capacity of armies and navies to realize goals by attacking other states is undergoing continual decline. Powerful forces can still defeat less powerful enemies on the field of battle, but there is a growing awareness on the part of officials and publics throughout the world that military victory is not the equivalent of achieving desired postwar states of affairs, that the momentary psychic satisfactions which accompany military successes may well give way to economic costs and political difficulties that are much greater than would have otherwise been the case. As societies become increasingly dense and as the networks of relations that comprise global politics become increasingly thick and intricate, so do the chances of successful conquest seem increasingly tenebrous.

The complexity of life late in the twentieth century operates against launching major interstate wars in two important ways. One concerns all the domestic dynamics wherein societies have become burdened by internal conflicts, multiple loyalties, overlapping jurisdictions, and centrifugal tendencies, dynamics which make it increasingly difficult to undertake (and to decide to undertake) the full-scale mobilization that major interstate wars require. Yes, national loyalties are heightened by the threats and crises that mark the build-up to war, but few societies are any longer so coherent and consensual as to enable such build-ups to supersede the subnational loyalties, contrary perspectives, and political oppositions that stand in the way of an effective war-making commitment. It might be countered that these internal conflicts can be suppressed by ruthless leaders who use elite troops to launch a war, but even such leaders are likely to be increasingly aware that in so proceeding they are, at best, likely to generate a half-hearted mobilization which fails to provide what is needed for success on the battlefield and which thus can risk the loss of their domestic base.

Secondly, the ever-expanding complexity and dynamism of world politics seem likely to inhibit the initiation of major interstate wars in the sense that any potential "enemy" will loom as a vast set of intractable problems even if it is subdued. With conquest comes the need to occupy, or at least steer and control, the vanquished society. And the tasks inherent in postwar control are no longer simple. The very complexity of the defeated society, not to mention the web of international relationships in which it is embedded, renders monumental the aspiration to convert wartime goals into peacetime realities. Indeed, so complex have so many countries and regions become today that it is often a challenge to determine exactly who the "enemy" is and then, having somehow made that determination, to convince those who fall outside the definition that they are not targets of the military operations.

Still another way in which modern-day complexity constrains the war-making propensity of militarily competent states involves the globalization of national economies and the emergence of dynamics in the multi-centric world that can divert, subvert, or otherwise operate as barriers to successful wars. National economies, their trading patterns, production facilities, workforces, and currency flows, are not subject to the same degrees of governmental control as they once were. Many of the components states need for their war-making machines are produced abroad and the political as well as the financial costs of obtaining them can be exceedingly high, if not prohibitive. In addition, the moneys needed to pay for them are ever subject to interest rate and currency fluctuations in distant markets. No less relevant, a goodly proportion of the economic leaders and organizations whose support is crucial to the waging of major interstate wars are located in the multi-centric world and are as likely to be as responsive to its norms and procedures as they are to any state that lays claim to their loyalties. In the words of one inquiry, "state actions that damage individual and corporate gains from an international free market risk domestic resistance and refusal. The 'national' interest must now compete with the interests of the 'nationals.'"[5] In short, the globalization of national economies tends to render problematic how successfully governments can mobilize their resources to wage war; or, having won a war, how successfully they can direct and manage the society of their defeated adversary; or, if the war is lost, how successfully they can bring about a recovery of their economy.

It follows that the observation "wars do not pay" is more than an expression of a deeply held distaste for organized violence. Increasingly it is also an empirical statement, a description of unintended consequences and unwanted costs that those who contemplate going to war seem likely to find compelling, or at least not easily ignored even as their passions for doing battle mount. From the perspective of foreign offices, in other words, the world's ever greater interdependence has fostered ever more elaborate causal webs that make it ever more unlikely that outcomes can be controlled or problems solved through military means. To counter this reasoning with the assertion that Saddam Hussein was not deterred by the complexities of the international scene is to err grievously inasmuch as his experience with that complexity is now part of the history that others will ponder as they consider the prospects of launching a successful interstate war. It may be more than historical coincidence, for example, that within a year of the end of the Gulf War the government of Pakistan used force to prevent a march of its *own* "freedom fighters" from crossing into the Indian-controlled portion of Kashmir. "We've had three wars with India," the Pakistani prime minister observed; then, obviously sensitive to how little organized violence had accomplished in the past, he added, "We don't want to have a fourth war."[6]

Weariness

Closely related to – and in some ways an integral part of – the density and complexity of the current global scene is a pervasive weariness with respect to major interstate war. It is more than historical coincidence that six such wars came to an end in 1988 and, as noted below, that this pattern has continued to unfold in the ensuing several years. People, publics, and governments are tired of violence, of conflicts that collapse into the destruction of property, lives, and daily routines. Their sacrifice

---

[5] James M. Goldgeier and Michael McFaul, "A Tale of Two Worlds: Core and Periphery in the Post-Cold War Era," *International Organization*, vol. 46 (Spring 1992), p. 476.

[6] Edward A. Gargan, "12 Are Killed as Pakistani Police Fire on Kashmiris Marching Toward Border," *New York Times*, February 13, 1992, p. A3.

level on behalf of the remote goals of interstate wars appears to be undergoing a sustained erosion, undermining their commitment to the state and reinforcing their readiness to forego traditional criteria of compliance for criteria in which the performance of state leaders is subjected to close scrutiny.

Put differently, there are more than enough close-at-hand concerns and conflicts to occupy the energies of communities and their leaders and to undermine their readiness to do battle in distant wars on behalf of ambiguous symbols. Indeed, conceivably the increasing sense of fatigue which attaches to the idea of major interstate war may intensify the inclination to engage in local conflicts over concrete goals. Doubtless, for example, many of the very same young people in the outlying parts of the former Soviet Union who avoided military service that might have culminated in fighting for the integrity of sovereign boundaries in the Persian Gulf, or for any other international values in remote continents, are ready to be conscripted on behalf of their ethnic group's efforts to win greater autonomy.

It might be argued that war-weariness is only a temporary phenomenon, that a period of prolonged stability in which interstate conflicts do not culminate in organized violence will generate a greater willingness to accept the costs of war. People forget, and new generations have to learn hard lessons on their own, the argument continues, and thus today's weariness may yield to tomorrow's enthusiasm for pursuing abstract and distant values. Considered in the context of the complexity noted above and the paralysis and emergent norms stressed below, however, this line of reasoning breaks down. Any prolonged stability that may develop in the future is unlikely to be so free of constraints and burdens as to release energy for distant battle. However daily routines may be constituted in the years ahead, they will surely not be so easily maintained as to allow for militant energy expended on behalf of murky ventures abroad.

Recent history records, moreover, that war weariness is susceptible to conversion into political and constitutional prohibitions against military involvement. The fact that both German and Japanese politics became embroiled in the issue of providing military support for the thirty-two-nation coalition's efforts against Iraq serves as a quintessential example of how prolonged war weariness can take on a momentum of its own. To be sure, both countries had constitutional provisions imposed upon them that prohibited the build-up and use of their armed forces. But these constitutional barriers are trivial in comparison to the widespread political opposition that, in both Germany and Japan, prevented top political leaders from successfully pressing constitutional amendments which would have permitted military commitments to the Gulf War. These two cases are powerful evidence that aversion to war can become as much an ingrained habit on a society-wide scale as the predisposition to do battle.

Paralysis

No less relevant a constraint on the processes that build up to major interstate war is the pervasiveness of paralysis and stalemate among the world's governments. Due in large part to the intractable social and economic problems spawned by the world's deepening complexity and interdependence, national governments have become increasingly indecisive, often unable to address challenges, much less resolve them. Confronted with increasingly skilled citizenries and opposition groups, restrained by a lack of resources, fearful that any action will undo delicate equilibria, most of the world's governments are deeply divided over the proper policies to pursue at home and abroad. Thus, much more often than not, most governments are inclined to opt for inaction, for a form of paralysis that conveys the impression of activity even as the outcomes are nearly always the same. Again the resistance of the Germans and Japanese to revising the military clauses in their constitutions is illustrative. Clearly, these recent episodes reflect the dynamics of political inertia as well as those of war weariness.

Much of the pervasive and deep-seated tendency toward structural stalemate, of course, derives from the authority crises that have accompanied the onset of global turbulence, and these crises have, in turn, further complicated the capacity of states to mobilize their societies for major interstate wars. Indeed, a spiraling process can be said to be under way. The legitimacy of states is revealed to be slipping, all of which further emboldens individuals and groups to resist national policies, thereby reinforcing the tendency toward society-wide paralysis and stalemate. Under these conditions the build-up to launching an attack on other states seems likely to peter out early in the process, even if aggressive factions are somehow able to initiate it. Recall, for example, the discussion in chapter 19 of the widespread problem faced by military establishments in conscripting and keeping new personnel. Clearly, states cannot fight wars if the human resources necessary for fighting manage to avoid military service. As one astute observer put it, the consequence of public resistance to situations which may escalate into interstate war

422

is that the state *apparat* is likely to become isolated from the rest of the body politic, a severed head conducting its intercourse with other severed heads according to its own laws. War, in short, has once more been denationalized. It has become, as it was in the eighteenth century, an affair of states and no longer of peoples. The identification of the community with the state, brought to its highest point in the era of the two World Wars, can no longer be assumed as natural or, militarily speaking, necessary. No Third World War is likely to be fought by armies embodying the manpower of the Nation while the rest of the population work to keep them armed and fed.[7]

There is a paradox here. Those states that develop strong armed forces capable of waging major interstate wars tend to be the very same states whose high degree of complexity and dynamism paralyze or stalemate the war-making impulses of their governments. The inability of the Reagan Administration to launch overt military actions against Nicaragua, despite its obvious desire to do so, is illustrative in this regard. And so, of course, are the war-making efforts of the Soviets in Afghanistan and the United States in Vietnam.

Emergent norms

Finally, but no less relevant, the worldwide trend toward valuing human rights serves as a vital constraint on the war-proneness of states. To be sure, the dynamism of the human rights issue focuses on the mistreatment of individuals, but it is a short step from this micro value to its macro counterpart in which collective violence is conceived as an abuse of human dignity. The step is especially short today because of global television. Its capacity to depict the brutal horrors that attend the launching and fighting of wars has provided people everywhere with a wherewithal for revulsion that seems likely to foster ever greater sensitivities to the virtues of dignity and decency as well as to the preservation of human rights.

Stated more generally, there is a close connection between the breadth, depth, and successes of the peace movement in the 1980s and the concurrent evolution of human rights to the top of the global agenda. The sorts of people who join the peace movement may be quite different from those concerned about the treatment of individuals and minorities – the former being oriented toward the reformation of macro structures and the latter toward the well-being of micro actors – but the

[7] Michael Howard, "War and the Nation-State," *Daedalus*, vol. 108 (Fall 1979), p. 106 (italics in the original).

two share a concern for limiting states and their coercive powers. As a result, the global scope of the human rights issue has, in conjunction with the complexities, weariness, and paralysis of societies, become a central component of the dynamics rendering major interstate wars obsolete. Indeed, as suggested in earlier chapters and as indicated by the impact of television pictures of the plight of the Kurds in northern Iraq or of the tribal conflicts in Somalia and Rwanda, the evolution of global norms has expanded beyond a general affirmation of human rights to a specific set of justifications for humanitarian interventions across the Frontier and into the domestic affairs of states.

Furthermore, it is here, in the surge of commitment to the viability of individuals, that salience attaches to the way in which interstate wars begin. Whereas the onset of other types of wars is murky as the contestants attempt to blend into the underbrush or urban setting, often denying their commitment to force and disguising their military objectives, interstate wars begin with trumpets blaring as soldiers, ships, and planes move swiftly across borders. In the present context such events have a blatancy, a crudeness, that reaches deep into the wellsprings of distaste for violence out of which the human rights movement has evolved. With other types of war it is never clear who the combatants are and what is the extent of their commitment to destroying people and property, but in an interstate war it is obvious from the outset that the intent is to tear down, and this goal is so contrary to the emergent global perspective that it is likely to evoke responses that negate the very purposes served by launching the war in the first place. It is instructive, for example, to note the difference between the response of the American people to the North Korean invasion of South Korea and the Iraqi invasion of Kuwait on the one hand with their reactions to the war in Vietnam on the other. An event had to be contrived in the Gulf of Tonkin in order to mobilize their support for the Vietnam effort and this proved to be a poor substitute for a border crossing insofar as the public's commitment to the conflict was concerned. Such contrasts are expressive of a severe constraint that is unlikely to be ignored by those who would launch organized interstate invasions in this era of human dignity and global television.

An outbreak of peace

Subjecting the foregoing analysis to an empirical test is, of course, an impossible enterprise. Every day that interstate war does not break out

424

might seem like a successful test, but that is more a tautological than a convincing argument. The nonoccurrence of an outcome can hardly be offered as evidence that it is increasingly unlikely to occur in the future. But there is one set of empirical data that provides convincing support for the proposition that the likelihood of interstate war is on the wane, namely, the fact that in 1988, six wars came to an end within the space of a few months. This simultaneity puzzle has been extensively ana-lyzed elsewhere,[8] but a brief outline of what appears to be the most likely solution of the puzzle serves to uphold, if not to test, the pre-ceding identification of a war-decline trend line.

If there are turning-points in history that sharply reinforce the per-sistence of a trend line, normally they are discernible only years later when the elapse of time allows for retrospective inquiry. Occasionally a successful revolution or a technological innovation may be so clear in its implications for diminished conflict as to acquire immediate status as a major historical juncture, but usually the course of world affairs is too complex for such sharp delineations at the time of their occurrence. The twelfth to last year of the twentieth century, however, would seem to be an exception in this regard: a series of events in 1988, each explic-able by itself, cumulated to what some called a "peace epidemic" and what most seemed to agree constituted a historical juncture even before the year ended.[9] The similarity of the direction of these events, the simultaneity of their occurrence, and the diversity of their locales – serious steps to terminate six international wars initiated or completed within weeks of each other – suggest that 1988 may prove to be an unprecedented occasion in modern history when the balance between international cooperation and conflict shifted sharply in favor of the former, a singular moment when it could fairly be said that the world was being rewarded for having muddled through some four decades without a war among its great powers by having peace break out on a global scale.

It is precisely the simultaneity and singularity of these events that is so theoretically intriguing. One can readily cite unique circumstances

---

[8] James N. Rosenau, "Interdependence and the Simultaneity Puzzle: Notes on the Outbreak of Peace," in C.W. Kegley (ed.), *The Long Postwar Peace: Contending Explanations and Projections* (New York: HarperCollins, 1991), pp. 307–28.

[9] Richard J. Barnet, "Looking to a Post-Cold War World," *Los Angeles Times*, June 6, 1988, part II, p. 7; Editorial, "Stirrings of Peace," *New York Times*, July 31, 1988, p. 24; Stanley Hoffmann, "Lessons of a Peace Epidemic," *New York Times*, September 6, 1988, p. 27; and James M. Markham, "Some Wars Are Failing the Cost–Benefits Test," *New York Times*, August 15, 1988, sect. 4, p. 1.

that led to the Soviet withdrawal from Afghanistan, the accession to a cease-fire by Iraq and Iran, the truce and cease-fire in Nicaragua, the meeting of the parties to the war in Cambodia, the start of peace talks in Angola, and the agreement to end the thirteen-year-old war over the Western Sahara between Morocco and the Polisario Front guerrillas. But how to account for the fact that all six of these war-terminating processes began or culminated within relatively few weeks of each other? There is no obvious explanation for this simultaneity. The wars did not commence in the same time period; they were fought on four different continents; they were waged over different issues; they varied widely in their strategic circumstances; and they differed extensively in their intensity and scope.

Nor is the simultaneity limited to combat situations. If the analytic focus is expanded to include intense nonviolent-but-always-on-a-military-alert situations as well as those involving outright war, this period was also witness to four additional international conflicts, those between the United States and the Soviet Union, between the two Koreas, between Taiwan and mainland China, and between Greece and Turkey, in which the adversaries began to talk more directly and seriously with each other. Given their histories of deep-seated animosity, it is hardly less remarkable that these long-standing situations also underwent steps toward moderation in roughly the same time frame. So the question bears repeating: how to account for the simultaneity of so much effort at accommodation?

And if the concept of simultaneity is stretched somewhat to include the mid-1990s, and if the formulation is expanded to include intense and long-standing intrastate conflicts marked by deep-seated proclivities toward violence, the present era has also seen remarkable reversals of course in South Africa, Ireland, and between the Palestinians and Israel. The last two of these situations are still a long way from thoroughgoing amelioration, but all of them started down that road long before it seemed feasible that any movement was possible. Once again, in short, the initial question needs to be posed: how to account for the simultaneity in shifts toward accommodation?

The question is as puzzling as the reality is encouraging. It reminds us of how fully our theories of world affairs are oriented toward explaining the onset and persistence of conflict and how little they anticipate the outbreak and spread of cooperation. It confronts us with our own pessimism as we begin to appreciate that our understanding of the course of events is profoundly unidirectional, that it allow us to probe a conflict-ridden world but denies us the conceptual equipment with which to explore a more benign (if not a cooperation-pervaded) world. Yet, at the same time, the question also begins to alert us to the possibility that 1988 may have been witness to the first surfacing of the long-term processes of societal complexity, weariness, and paralysis accompanied by emergent human rights norms posited above as culminating in the increasing obsolescence of interstate war.

Some caveats

To be sure, caveats are in order. The outbreak of peace may be only a transitory development. As indicated by the violence that has racked Bosnia, the habits of conflict and the psychological and sociopolitical needs from which they spring may require many more than four decades to attenuate. So it is certainly possible that any or all of the war-ending situations and the several cases of domestic redirection will founder or prove illusory and return each situation to even greater levels of distrust and conflict. But this very likelihood makes the simultaneity of their 1988 reversals all the more extraordinary and provocative. Whatever may be their future course, and however intense the enmity inherent in these situations may yet become, history has recorded a brief moment in time when the improbable occurred, when global tendencies toward peaceful accommodation surfaced with unremitting clarity.

This is not to suggest, of course, that the outbreak of peace is universal. The years since 1988 have witnessed the Gulf War and continuing tensions in the Middle East. All in all, it has been estimated, some nineteen situations in 1988 ran counter to the mushrooming pattern of cooperation and were marked by the persistence of violent conflict.[10] Domestically, too, counter-trends can be cited, with the most notable perhaps being the reacquisition of control by power-based, authoritarian regimes in Burma, the former Yugoslavia, and parts of the former Soviet Union. Again, however, the very pervasiveness of violence makes the onset of ameliorative processes in ten major international situations all the more remarkable.

Still another caveat must be recorded. To derive encouragement from

---

[10] James Reston, "25 Wars Are Still Going On" *New York Times,* June 3, 1988, p. A31. This estimate includes the six wars treated here as moving away from violence and toward ameliorative resolutions. For another assessment that enumerated the existence of "36 full-scale conflicts, involving 40 nations and five million soldiers," see Markham, "Some Wars Are Failing the Cost–Benefits Test," sect. 4, p. 1.

Table 22.1. The simultaneity puzzle: summary of possible sources of ten conflict-terminating processes initiated or completed in 1988

	Iran–Iraq War	Afghanistan	Angola	Western Sahara	Cambodia	Nicaragua	Taiwan and mainland China	North and South Korea	Greece and Turkey	US–Soviet arms control
Coincidental simultaneity										
Idiographic factors	+[a]	–	–	–	–	–	+[b]	–	–	+[c]
Systemic simultaneity										
Fatigue factors	+	+	+	+	+	+	–	–	–	–
Obsolescence of force	+	+	+	+	+	–	–	–	–	–
Post-industrial factors	+	+	+	+	+	+	+	+	+	+
Lowering of superpower tensions	–	+	+	–	+	+	+	+	+	+
Contagion factors	+	+	+	+	+	+	+	+	+	–

Key:
+ Probably present as a source of the 1988 developments.
– Probably not relevant as a source of the 1988 developments.

Notes:
[a] The reference here is to the Ayatollah's failing health.
[b] The reference here is to the passing of Chiang Kai-shek's generation with the early 1988 death of his son as President of the Republic of China.
[c] The reference here is to the consolidation of Gorbachev's authority and to President Reagan's desire to secure a place in history as his administration came to an end.

the several signs of spreading cooperation is not to say, or even to imply, that the lot of people is improving. Poverty, famine, and disease continue unabated as global scourges, and the plight of many countries in the developing world evidences no indication of turning for the better. Political accommodation can result in economic gains if swords get turned into plowshares, but such a transformation is far from automatic. It may well be that with their swords sheathed people and communities will turn to nonproductive pursuits and economic rivalries. Our theories of long-term cooperation are too rudimentary to make reasonable estimates as to the likelihood that a more equitable distribution of wealth will became a hallmark of a more militarily benign world.

Yet, despite these caveats, 1988 remains a landmark. Even if subsequent events obfuscate its significance, it will long remain an intriguing theoretical challenge. Simultaneity across diverse political systems and international relationships is too rare a happening not to explore whether it is an indication of how the interdependence-induced dynamics of the Frontier may be altering the underpinnings of global life.

Types of simultaneity

Assuming that societal complexity, weariness, paralysis, and human rights norms underlay the 1988 outbreak of peace, two additional lines of inquiry might be pursued to come to terms with this remarkable simultaneity. One treats it as mere coincidence and the other presumes that it results from systemic dynamics which, interactively or otherwise, give rise to the same responses within the same time frame. Designated, respectively, as *coincidental* and *systemic* simultaneity, the former type is here judged as too improbable to be explored at length. A more extensive analysis of the latter type, on the other hand, facilitates a conclusion in which a combination of five systemic variables is considered to offer the basis for a cogent, multivariate solution of the simultaneity puzzle.

More specifically, as the summary in table 22.1 anticipates, the analysis assesses shifts in the values of none of the variables as alone sufficient for the onset of the ten conflict-terminating processes. Nor does it treat all of them as necessary to each situation. Considered as an interactive whole, however, the five sets of variables are suggestive of how it is possible for peace to break out on a global scale. Important idiographic factors may have been relevant in some of the cases (as noted in the footnotes of table 22.1), but the probability of ten major international conflicts all turning in cooperative directions within the same time

429

frame appears so remarkably low as to warrant exploring how common dynamics may have operated to initiate the processes of amelioration.

Contextual, causal, and system-wide variables

In order to resolve the simultaneity puzzle, it is important to distinguish among the values of three sets of variables: those that conduce to conflict-terminating processes by virtue of shifts in the systemic structures or contexts of conflict situations; those that foster these processes as a result of direct, causal stimuli to action; and those that precipitate stimuli to action on a system-wide or global scale. Henceforth these three sets shall be referred to, respectively, as *contextual, causal,* and *system-wide* variables.

In addition to the underlying dynamics fostering the obsolescence of interstate war, contextual variables involve those aspects of conflicts, their histories, structures, and resource distributions, that can undergo a shift in values such that the participants find themselves in new circumstances that enable them to ponder or seek an end to their hostilities. That is, if the values of key variables that underlie the onset and persistence of international conflict undergo change in directions that are conducive to the diminution of violence, the background conditions for the outbreak of peace will have been established. Being only a setting for action – rather than actions themselves – these contextual variables cannot in themselves trigger a reversal of course toward peace; but without their evolution as part of the setting within which conflicts are waged, there is little likelihood of peace overtures being offered or seized by the participants.

For conditions favorable to conflict-termination to be transformed into actual processes of tension reduction, contextual variables must be supplemented by causal variables. The latter consist of actions and interactions that alter opportunities and constraints and thereby influence perceptions and motives. Once such actions and interactions shift in directions conducive to the reduction of tensions and violence, they become causal in their impact. As such, as direct stimuli to action, they are different from those indirect contextual conditions which facilitate conflict-terminating responses.

But a further distinction must be drawn if simultaneous signs of peace in ten situations are to be explained. Some causal variables may be more situation-specific than systemic in their scope, with the result that their shifts in conflict-terminating directions may occur at various times and enable the global system to become more benign without giving rise to the circumstances of simultaneity. In the case of the 1988 peace outbreak, however, two system-wide variables can be identified as evolving values that may have fostered causal simultaneity, that is, two system-wide developments (represented by the bottom two rows of table 22.1) that impacted upon diverse situations at the same moment in time.

A fatigue factor

If wide public weariness can underlie an inclination to avoid the onset of war, so is pervasive fatigue even more relevant to the termination of wars. Either wars end through conquest and surrender or they grind to a halt and terminate with negotiated settlements. When the latter pattern occurs, it tends to result from a sense of fatigue on all sides bolstered by an appreciation that military victory is not possible. This fatigue factor is a contextual and not a causal variable in the sense that it does not determine when the turn toward peace will occur. Armies and publics can be exhausted for a long while before they abandon the goal of military triumph or otherwise decide that the descent into conflict is best reversed. Without the presence of considerable fatigue, such a turn is unlikely to occur, but the onset of fatigue does not necessarily predict when peace negotiations begin to loom as attractive and worthy of undertaking.

Since all the conflicts involved in the 1988 peace outbreak were of long duration,[11] it can readily be argued that each of them had persisted long enough to create the contextual conditions of fatigue – the sociopolitical breakdown of institutions and publics as well as military exhaustion on the battlefield – on which peace negotiations thrive. While this reasoning is tautological in the sense that, by definition, fatigue is operative in wars that do not end with an outright victory by one side, and while it is also faulty because it does not embrace any systemic processes that might explain why exhaustion should set in at exactly the same time in all the conflicts, it does call attention to one piece of the puzzle. The fact

---

[11] The situation in Nicaragua was the shortest of the conflicts (with US-assisted Contra raids having begun in 1981), followed by the Iran–Iraq War (1980), the Soviet invasion of Afghanistan (1979), the Vietnamese invasion of Cambodia (1978), the Portuguese departure from Angola (1975), and the onset of hostilities between the Polisario Front guerrillas and Morocco over the Western Sahara (1975). Three of the remaining four conflicts had their origins decades earlier with the onset of the Cold War in the late 1940s, while the start of Greek–Turkish tensions cannot be easily located at a fixed point in time.

431

that all of the conflicts had been in progress for years meant that the energy and capability levels of the combatants had moved from zeal and confidence toward doubt and hesitation, a mental condition that may have thus readied all concerned for accommodation when shifts in the values of other variables (noted below) altered the prevailing circumstances on which the conflicts had rested. To repeat, fatigue was surely not a sufficient condition for the simultaneity of the policy reversals, but it may well be regarded as one of several necessary conditions.

The obsolescence of force as a tool of statecraft

Another contextual variable – alluded to earlier – that facilitated decisions to seek an end to the long-standing conflicts may have been an emergent appreciation in national capitals that the costs of large-scale, prolonged military actions normally outweigh the gains and that world affairs have become so complex as to reduce the effectiveness of force as an instrument of foreign policy. Faced with a continuing depletion of their resources and a deepening erosion of public morale, aware of so many other situations in which the military conflicts dragged on at great cost to the opposing sides, and ever conscious that local conflicts run the risk of nuclear escalation, leaders in the six war-terminating situations had good reasons to conclude that they were banking on ineffective statecraft and that a reversal of course was in order. Force has proved useful as a deterrent; demonstrating its presence in navies and combat-ready troops may sometimes inhibit potential adversaries; and quick air strikes have been shown to produce desired outcomes; but modern history records that whenever a prolonged commitment to military action is undertaken, stalemate and exhaustion follow.

This is not to suggest that leaders in the six 1988 situations of interstate war independently, and within the same time frame, came to the identical conclusion that their efforts to realize their goals through organized force were founded on an obsolete instrument of statecraft. Rather, as with the fatigue variable, it can only be said that they shared a growing appreciation of how changes in the nature of global politics had undermined the utility of sustained military action and that this understanding also contributed to their readiness to accommodate to peace overtures when they arose.

Postindustrial variables

A third contextual dynamic that is global in its repercussions and that, as such, may have also facilitated the outbreak of peace is related to the aforementioned complexity factors that inhibit the onset of wars. It concerns the transformations inherent in the world's evolution from an industrial era based on manufacturing industries to a post-industrial order organized around information services. As stressed earlier, among the many ramifications of these transformations are the global tendencies toward decentralized authority and influence that postindustrialism has unleashed. While it is possible to exaggerate their consequences – the widening of the Frontier, through the weakening of states, the emergence of the global marketplace, the proliferation of transnational and subnational organizations, and increasingly skillful citizens – these tendencies are powerful enough to operate as contextual conditions of present-day conflict-terminating processes in the sense of facilitating a worldwide recognition that authority and legitimacy evoked on behalf of war efforts can be subject to review and revision, that publics can tire of long-standing conflicts, and that they can thus be effectively mobilized to undermine and oppose them.

The lowering of superpower tensions

In assessing the outbreak of peace in 1988 it is important to recall that while superpower tensions were beginning to moderate, the Cold War was still in progress and would not end for another year or two. Yet, the moderation of the superpower rivalry was sufficient to serve as a less general and more concrete source of the convergence of several peace processes. The fact that both the Soviet Union and the United States, each for their own reasons, began to appreciate that their arms race was counterproductive and moved toward accommodation in the military realm – a movement which, in turn, facilitated cooperation on a number of other issues and the fostering of a generalized atmosphere of global harmony – doubtless contributed to a momentum that spread to other interstate conflicts and provided a context for considering their termination. In other words, even as the two superpowers long served as exemplars of conflict behavior, so did their commanding positions enable them to assume a contrary role model in which their cooperative endeavors were deemed worthy of emulation.

In all probability, moreover, the weaknesses of the superpowers revealed by their efforts to accommodate to each other also operated as a contextual consideration. Once the Soviet Union exhibited the need to transfer resources away from the arms race, and once the United States sought to cope with its huge budget deficits by cutting back on defense spending, leaders in the various interstate wars may well have more acutely discerned the limits inherent in their own military commitments. With the superpowers moving into a period of accommodation, the leaders could reason, the opportunities for turning to one or either of them for help in the pursuit of their own wars were bound to diminish, thus casting their military calculations in a far different light than had been the case when they undertook to do battle.

Nor did the dynamics of lowered tension between the superpowers function only as contextual variables. There is substantial evidence that the "new thinking" of Mikhail Gorbachev led the Soviets to cut back on their support for allies in several of the wars, a policy change that occurred within the same time frame and manifestly operated as a causal variable (as did the concurrent change represented by the US Congress's refusal to provide continuing support for the Contras in Nicaragua). Indeed, it might be said that the outbreak of peace began with the Soviet indication of a readiness to withdraw troops from Afghanistan, a decision that reinforced the global atmosphere of accommodation even as it was also a concrete reversal of course that was quickly followed by a reduction in support for the Vietnamese in Cambodia, the Sandinistas in Nicaragua, and the Cubans in Angola.

Yet, it cannot be concluded that the lessening of superpower confrontations and the advent of new policies in the Kremlin are a sufficient as well as a necessary explanation of the outbreak of peace in 1988. It is doubtful whether any of the war-terminating processes would have begun if the superpowers had maintained their high levels of support for surrogates abroad, but the diminution of this support occurred in only four of the six war-terminating situations. As such they operated as causal dynamics that fell two short of being system-wide in scope. They account neither for the end of the Iran–Iraq War nor for the agreement to terminate the war in the Western Sahara. To be sure, by 1988 both the United States and the Soviet Union were pressing for a truce in the Iran–Iraq War, but this is hardly a sufficient explanation inasmuch as neither of the combatants had previously demonstrated a readiness to yield to outside pressures. It seems likely, rather, that the aforenoted dimensions of systemic context – the fatigue factor, the obsolescence of war, the advent of a postindustrial order, and the specter of superpower accommodation – combined to precipitate the onset of a peace process in those situations where the superpowers could not exercise leverage by withdrawing support from their surrogates. Such an interpretation helps to account for the shift of direction in the Greek–Turkish conflict as well as the Iran–Iraq War.

434

A contagion effect

Finally, there may have been one set of system-wide variables operative in all ten conflict situations that goes a long way toward infusing theoretical unity into the diverse considerations outlined above. It involves the communications technology inherent in the postindustrial order. The existence of a vast global network of electronic channels for the flow of information – computer hookups, television satellites, video cassettes, radio tapes, etc. – meant that mechanisms were available for direct links among the several conflict situations. Where word of developments in one part of the world once traveled in months and years via stagecoach and sailing ship, only seconds and minutes elapse before such information spreads in the postindustrial era. Thus can the politics of struggle and war in the Middle East have ramifications for comparable contests in Southeast Asia, Southern Africa, and Central America. Stated more generally, the microelectronic revolution has created the means for a rapid transformation of the global system's political environment, for quickly undermining a conflictful context and infusing it with an atmosphere in which accommodative actions seem plausible and acceptable.

Simultaneity, in short, is built into the current structure of world affairs. It is not a mysterious wind that, like a wildfire, cascades ideas and issues across continents and over legal and political barriers; rather, the cascades take concrete form in televised scenes, taped speeches, recorded deliberations, written appeals, and smuggled cassettes which leap from one national capital or revolutionary stronghold to another and, in so doing, foster the occurrence of similar events in diverse places within the same time frame.

Put somewhat differently, it is now possible to speak of a contagion factor, of specific emulative and learning processes in world affairs wherein public protests and policy decisions spread in traceable patterns across the full breadth of the global system. Indeed, it can be said that the system is now global precisely because a simultaneity of events can give rise to a shift in the tone of the global environment which then serves as the basis of political reality.

It follows that systemic simultaneity may have been at work in the 1988 outbreak of peace through the contagion factor. As a peace process was initiated in the six situations, so might each step in the negotiations of one situation have cascaded as reinforcing information for those who undertook conflict-terminating actions elsewhere.

435

A theoretical perspective reinforced?

To conclude that a number of variables underlay the converging events of 1988, all of them necessary but none alone sufficient as a basis for the simultaneity, is to highlight the density, complexity, and dynamism of the Frontier. It calls attention to the need for an understanding of world affairs which takes into account the extraordinary degrees of inter-dependence among the issues that crowd the global agenda and which allows for swift-moving developments that transform the issues into a coherent and structured web of relationships. If such a conception can be refined, then the simultaneity puzzle will no long seem puzzling. What once appeared to be separate situations marked by simultaneity will emerge, instead, as a singular process unfolding on a global scale. And conceivably this process has replaced the early postwar years of muddling through from crisis to crisis with a density, complexity, and dynamism that facilitates the cascading of cooperative inclinations from situation to situation.

Beyond rationality and nonrationality

In conclusion, it is useful to note two major concepts that do not figure in the foregoing analysis. One is that of democracy. Unlike the close correlation some analysts posit between the extent of democratic institu-tions and the reluctance of states to war on other states, thus anticipat-ing a decline in interstate wars because more and more states are turning to democratic forms of governance,[12] here this political variable is not considered central. This is not to render judgment on the pervasive finding that democratic countries do not war on each other. Nor is it to reject the calculation that because democratic countries are unlikely to war on each other, and because their ranks have grown since the collapse of the Russian empire, the likelihood of major interstate wars is further diminished. Rather, the democracy variable is not accorded conceptual prominence because there are indicators in these countries that their democratic commitments may be short-lived and give rise to stresses that lead them back toward authoritarian rule. If such reversions do occur, then the logic of this reasoning anticipates an increase in the like-lihood of major interstate wars, an expectation that runs counter to the foregoing analysis and thus seems improbable. Whether countries are

[12] Goldgeier and McFaul, "A Tale of Two Worlds," p. 486.

democratic or authoritarian, in other words, they still must confront the complexity, weariness, stalemate, and norms that pervade their societies and the international system, and these variables are regarded as sufficiently potent to inhibit any war-making propensities states may have. In effect, whatever its relevance for the quality of domestic life, the democracy variable is too susceptible to broad fluctuations to be treated as an ongoing source of the breakdown of war-making proclivities.

Second, and perhaps even more conspicuous, is the absence of any discussion here of rationality and nonrationality in the processes whereby boundary-crossing attacks are launched. While there can be little question as to the relevance of the perceptions, intelligence, and calculations on which officials rely to make decisions that may lead to the outbreak of interstate wars, and while there is certainly a rich and extensive literature that testifies to the importance of decisional variables, here the processes of rationality and/or nonrationality are conceived to unfold in the context of more encompassing dynamics. It is presumed that the rational or nonrational calculations of officials are bounded by whatever may be the ongoing social, political, and economic conditions in which they find themselves; consequently, if these conditions militate against the launching of wars, it is further assumed that no amount of either rationality or nonrationality is likely to produce contrary results. The complexity, weariness, paralysis, and global norms that underlie the present world order are the raw materials around which rational or nonrational reasoning must perforce be organized and, as such, they leave officials with little room for perceptions and interpretations that might lead them to unleash their armed forces against another state.

Is this to engage in the fallacies of structural determinism? Not at all. Recall that the underlying premises are probabilistic. They allow for grievous errors, for officials who are unimpressed by the conditions that bind them. Some may reason themselves into overt attacks on their enemies, but in probabilistic terms such outcomes seem increasingly implausible. The onset of turbulence may have heightened the chance of intense violence breaking out within states, but it also appears to have diminished the likelihood of escalated armed conflict among them.

Conclusion

It bears repeating that the concern of this chapter has been exclusively with the probabilities of interstate war, which is not to imply that the

437

future will be free of organized violence and marked by rosy sunsets into which humankind can walk confident that peace has been firmly established. To stress that extensive interstate wars are increasingly unlikely is not to argue that peace lies ahead. Even less is it to identify the roots of a peaceful global context. Other forms of war may well convulse the Frontier as the complexity and paralysis of states encourages subgroups to resort to coercive action on behalf of subgroup aspirations. All that can be said with conviction is that a particular form of organized violence is headed for oblivion, whatever bloodshed and destruction may be in the offing.

23 Exploring governance in a turbulent world

> The old is dying, the new is being born, and in the interregnum there are many morbid symptoms.
>
> Antonio Gramsci[1]

> So, is the coming of international government now logically unstoppable? Yes, but it will advance with much difficulty, because two of the three ingredients of the rise of the nation-state – identity and legitimacy – are still missing at the higher level. While the principle of non-interference in the affairs of nation-states may be weakening, the willingness of people to die to impose the world's standards is weakening, too.
>
> Nicholas Colchester[2]

The juxtaposition of these epigraphs serves as a good basis for concluding this book. The first summarizes the essential theme that change is pervasive, that something "new is being born," while the second suggests that effective governance along the Frontier may eventually emerge out of the "old." Yet, neither epigraph ignores the difficulties that must be confronted as the world moves out of one epoch and into another. Gramsci posits the transition as pervaded with morbid moments, while Colchester notes huge obstacles to the emergence of global governance.

Taken together, moreover, the two epigraphs highlight the frustrations inherent in exploring frontiers. For all the dimensions of a frontier that yield to the explorer's tools and become familiar terrain, in the

---

[1] Quoted in Stephen Gill, "Theorizing the Interregnum: The Double Movement and Global Politics in the 1990s," in Bjorn Hettne (ed.), *International Political Economy: Understanding Global Disorder* (London: Zed Books, 1995), p. 65.

[2] "Good-bye, Nation-State. Hello . . . What?" *New York Times*, July 17, 1994, sect. 4, p. 17.

process new dimensions are opened up that require further exploration. Just as the earth's last geographic frontiers began to be meaningfully charted, for example, so did humankind turn toward exploration of outer space. Frontiers, in short, are not finite; explorations of them are never concluded; their conquest only points to the need for further exploration.

So it is with the investigation undertaken here. Satisfying as it is to have explored the new political spaces opened up by the erosion of the boundaries between domestic and foreign affairs, in the end one is impelled to ask more questions that reveal how little of the Frontier has been surveyed and assessed. Having traversed new paths, uncovered new terrain, identified new tensions, probed new dimensions of cooperation, we have sought to map a new political frontier; but the result is at best an incomplete picture, one that has not even touched upon the nitty-gritty issues – such as Bosnia, the future of NATO, and the likely goals of an ever more powerful China – that are presently so preoccupying.

Toward further exploration

The unexplored questions are myriad. Some focus on how spreading capitalist practices are likely to affect the prospects for open and responsible SOAs coming to prevail in the politics of the Frontier. Others concern the likelihood of new institutions evolving as the new political spaces become increasingly familiar and accepted. Still others involve issues of equity and whether the politics of the Frontier are likely to confront and lessen the huge gaps that divide the rich from the poor. Indeed, if the reader shares the perception that huge changes and a widening Frontier mark world affairs in the present epoch, it will not be difficult to develop a sizable agenda of issues requiring further exploration. Hopefully the initial mapping of the terrain presented here will serve as a guide to those who have been provoked to carry on as explorers.

My own inclination as a frontiersman would be to start with a probe into the "morbid symptoms" of Gramsci's "interregnum" and the "logically unstoppable" processes of Colchester's trend-line with a view to clarifying what effective governance along the Frontier would entail. If these two observers are right and the "new" includes the "coming" of some form of global governance, how would we know when its institutions and practices were in place? How might they evolve?

It is not difficult to outline an answer to the first of these questions. Such governance would be recognizable by the presence of a modicum of stability and equity in all parts of the world and by the absence of the kind of authoritarian rule systems that foster pervasive intra- and inter-state violence. This tranquillity would not be a constant, as no system of governance can prevent moments of deterioration. Civil wars might break out in some countries and problems of equity might be ignored in various parts of the world, but for the most part such breakdowns would evoke responses from one or another of the disaggregated mechanisms of global governance designed to ameliorate the wars and address the inequities. And if the most immediately affected instruments of governance failed to take the initiative or were inadequate to the tasks of restoring order and a modicum of equity, then responsibility would shift to other levels of authority, to the more distant sites and institutions where disruptions of the prevailing order are seen as threats that must be countered. But whatever levels were engaged, we would know that global governance, whatever the degree to which it is founded on democratic practices, was operating effectively by virtue of the world's capacity to cope with its trouble spots.

If the question of recognizing the practices that amount to effective global governance is easily answered, the same cannot be said of the question of how these practices will evolve and alleviate the morbid symptoms. Such a query either staggers the imagination or encourages a resort to morose pessimism. Clearly, the obstacles are enormous – so much so that the analyst is bound to have a sense of naivety in even trying to suggest that, nonetheless, the obstacles may be subject to diminution or circumvention. Yet, if the previous twenty-two chapters are a reasonable first approximation of the various dimensions of politics along the Frontier as the millennium ends, there seems little choice but to risk the charge of excessive simplicity and undertake a response to the query of what the trajectory toward effective global governance will look like.

The new ontology: enduring or transitional?

The response can follow two different lines of reasoning, depending on whether the fragmegration that is expanding and transforming the Frontier is viewed as enduring or transitional and the morbid symptoms as permanent or temporary. A case for both conclusions can be made, one that posits the trajectory as moving toward a permanency of

441

ineffective governance and another that envisions slow but unerring movement toward increasingly effective control over the Frontier.

The argument for enduring fragmegration is the easiest to make. It rests on a logic in which the uncertainties and dynamics of the present period are seen as resistant to diminution and, thus, as likely to persist for the foreseeable future. Why? Because the parametric transformations are all in the direction of continuing commotion rather than stable patterns. They point to continued authority crises, to fragmenting tendencies that weakened states cannot reverse, to intense competition for scarce resources, markets, and status – all of which suggest a continued absence of effective governance mechanisms capable of eliminating the morbid symptoms of a world spiraling out of control. The symptoms are pervasive in all walks of life and at all levels of community. They extend from individuals whose identities have become obscure to communities that have lost their cohesiveness, from cynicism toward politics to ideologues who preach exclusion, from cultures that have been eroded by consumerism to political agendas that are comprised of intractable issues, from tribal genocide to terrorist bombs. In effect, the central tendency in the case of each parameter-turned-variable involves movement toward end-points that are inherently and profoundly pervaded with uncertainty and dynamism, with impulses to sustain change rather than settle for new equilibria, with a potential for restless dissatisfaction with governments and a continuing resistance to whatever structural arrangements may seem to prevail.

Since it is founded less on clear-cut indicators and more on traces of underlying dynamics that are not yet conspicuous, the case for viewing the interregnum and its morbid symptoms as transitional requires a more elaborate analysis. It begins with the presumption that the period between the end of one ontology and the evolution of a new one is bound to be disruptive as people cling to old ways of doing things in the face of new circumstances. A new common sense of the epoch and the habitual modes on which it rests do not automatically fall into place, such reasoning asserts. Time is needed for experimentation, for trial and error, for sorting out alternatives, for actors with different learning curves to arrive at the same plateau on which their new relationships can flourish. The attenuation of mental sets, the collapse of paradigms, and the abandonment of structural constraints is thus bound to be accompanied by morbid symptoms of decay before new orientations and structures are formed and become deeply rooted. History brilliantly affirms that it is easier to destroy institutions than it is to construct their replacements. Thus, a long transitional period will have to unfold before the foundations of a new ontology come fully into focus.

Equally important, the argument continues, the interregnum is bound to be transitional because, as indicated throughout the preceding chapters, one can identify a number of points at which a new set of rules and norms may evolve that facilitate effective governance along the Frontier. Yes, the morbid symptoms of commotion and tension at all levels of public affairs are distressing. And yes, the pervasive tendencies toward authority crises are debilitating and make it difficult to discern patterns and emergent structures. But, no, this is not the equivalent of the absence of governance or a disarray so pervasive as to suggest the persistence of morbid symptoms. Rather, traces of recurrent practices can be discerned that hint at the emergence of new orientations and structures which, while not always orderly, enable individual and collective actors to relate to each other, cooperate, conflict, or otherwise manage to move through time reasonably intact.[3]

In short, the world may not be spiraling out of control. The morbid symptoms have not rendered governance mechanisms along the Frontier patternless. Rather, the mechanisms are so closely and causally linked to each other as to be repetitive and recurrent, forming arrangements that are no less effective because they subsume uncertainties and contradictions.

The prospects for collective action

Several circumstances favoring concerted action along the Frontier can be added to the case for viewing the interregnum as a period of transition to more effective governance. First, support for such actions is widespread in the sense of a broad appreciation that situations anywhere are relevant to people everywhere. Providing the financial and material resources needed for collective action will doubtless continue to encounter resistance, and the details of each proposal for undertaking such an action will surely stir controversy, but opposition to the principle of shared efforts to address the world's trouble spots does not appear to be pervasive.

Second, given a growing readiness to resort to collective action, it may not matter if some of the United Nations' election-monitoring,

---

[3] For one account of shifting attitudes along these lines, see Dirk Johnson, "Amid Flags and Fireworks, New Meanings of Patriotism," *New York Times*, July 4, 1996, p. A1.

peace-keeping, or peace-enforcing missions fail. If the hypothesized cumulative shift to acceptance of multiple loyalties is correct, tolerance for situations in which UN efforts are thwarted is likely to grow even as loyalties remain anchored to collectivities at the local level. As responses in terms of multiple loyalties cumulate, people will begin to appreciate that they do not have to abandon their local or national commitments in order to be accepting of authority exercised at the global level.

Third, the foregoing analysis suggests that whatever agencies undertake collective actions, support for them has to be assembled out of ever more articulate and organized societal segments. With notions of territoriality deep in flux, the "collective" that engages in action can no longer consist exclusively of states. The nongovernmental and transnational sectors of global life need to be mobilized as well and, indeed, the mobilization efforts may well be initiated by them. With complexity mushrooming in every realm of activity, governance is no longer the preserve of governments, and thus new forms of collective action are likely to evolve. In the admittedly slanted words of one leader in the multi-centric world, the Chairman and CEO of the Coca-Cola Company,

> four prevailing forces – the preeminence of democratic capitalism, the desire for self-determination, the shift in influence from regulation to investment, and the success of institutions which meet the needs of people – reinforced by today's worldwide communications and dramatic television images, . . . all point to a fundamental shift in global power. To be candid, I believe this shift will lead to a future in which the institutions with the most influence by-and-large will be businesses.[4]

The adaptive capacities of business enterprises are still another reason offered for this "fundamental shift in global power": as one observer puts it, "'Going Global' has been far easier for firms than for governments, parliaments, trade unions or universities, which are not sufficiently flexible institutions ready to adapt easily or quickly to changing conditions. Without this strategic capability multinationals have found themselves as the only real global players at the global level."[5]

---

[4] Robert C. Goizeta, "The Challenges of Getting What You Wished For," remarks presented to the Arthur Page Society, Amelia Island, Florida, (September 21, 1992).

[5] Riccardo Petrella, "Globalization and Internationalization: The Dynamics of the Emerging World Order," in Robert Boyer and Daniel Drache (eds.), *States Against Markets: The Limits of Globalization* (London: Routledge, 1996), pp. 73–4.

Fourth, since fragmegrative processes leap across system levels, they do not lend themselves readily to moderation by individual governments. Policy-makers in a single center of authority who seek either to initiate or control the interaction of globalizing and localizing dynamics seem destined to flounder. Only through across-level coordination can they hope to give some direction to the course followed by fragmegrative cascades. It follows that as fragmegration expands and becomes increasingly central to the conduct of politics, so will the need for cooperation among diverse types of collectivities at various levels of aggregation.

Fifth, there are signs in some SOAs that a deeper understanding of the dynamics of change is evolving which may lead to new and creative endeavors to avert the more disastrous consequences of fragmegration. Intelligence officials in some governments, for example, are broadening their conceptions of security threats beyond traditional factors such as the massing of troops, weapons developments, and arms transfers. In these cases security concerns now include sensitivity to water table levels, infant mortality rates, high population growth and density, inflation rates, trade deficits, the absorption of young people into the labor market, the spread of deserts, and a host of other previously ignored factors that may be long-term predictors of famine, the collapse of governments, the spread of ethnic strife, and the onset of financial and political instability.[6] Presumably intelligence efforts along these lines can lead to collective actions which better anticipate and offset the morbid symptoms that have lately become familiar features of the world scene.

In sum, the processes of global adaptation may be accelerating. The future twists and turns of global history are likely to revolve around questions of how and by whom collective actions should be undertaken rather than whether they should be launched. Does this likelihood point to the evolution of new forms of governance along the Frontier in which the diffusion of information, goods, and services steadily fosters a worldwide culture that maximizes rational conduct on behalf of universalistic values? Probably. If the analysis advanced here is sound, then the future of collective security is not lacking in bright spots.

---

[6] Steven Greenhouse, "The Greening of US Diplomacy: Focus on Ecology," *New York Times*, October 9, 1995, p. A6.

The reformulation of identity and legitimacy

Finally, much of the response to what the trajectory toward effective global governance will look like depends on how the concepts of "identity" and "legitimacy" are formulated. The second epigraph posits the absence of these ingredients as the prime obstacles on the path to global governance. But it does so by implying that somehow supranational institutions must replace nation-states as the focus of identity and legitimacy. Such an image, however, may be too conventional, as if nation-states and supranational institutions pose choices involving a zero-sum game in which people can only direct their loyalties toward one or the other. It ignores the many transformations traced in the previous chapters – trends toward the globalization of economies, the evolution of widely shared norms on human rights and environmental challenges, the erosion of sovereignty, the diminution of the competencies of states, the advent of the Internet and other means of communicating around and across national borders – that suggest the long-standing processes of identity and legitimacy formation may no longer operate and are being replaced by the emergence of a capacity for multiple loyalties. The dynamics of change may well lead people to look beyond concrete territorially based units and, instead, view themselves as participants in the concrete issue-based processes that criss-cross the Frontier. That is, considered in the context of the ramifications of pervasive globalization and the continued obliteration of domestic-foreign boundaries, the long-term may witness a shift in which people slowly expand their state-oriented definition of self-interest to include the notion that their interests are also well served through adherence to procedures and standards that are transnational, even global, in scope.

To be sure, despite the circumstances that favor a slow and erratic evolution of new conceptions of identity and legitimacy, the preceding chapters also highlight a number of turbulent factors that can inhibit, impede, obstruct, or otherwise prevent movement in this direction. The pervasive tendencies toward subgroup identities and competition, the failure of some UN peace-making activities, the genocidal conflict in Bosnia, the inclination of some states to cling to outworn conceptions of sovereignty, the turn of numerous individuals toward self-centered forms of citizenship, and the policies of governments that favor the rich and ignore the poor are among the many dynamics that seem bound to hinder progress toward outcomes the epigraph describes as "logically unstoppable." Certainly it is the case that for every example of redefined

446

identities one can cite counter-illustrations of reinvigorated identities. And for every instance where authority and legitimacy has undergone a shift or diminution, one can readily point to situations where long-standing sources of authority and legitimacy have been reinforced by the course of events.

But it is not difficult to argue that the instances of identity and legitimacy shifts are mounting and may eventually outnumber those in which traditional attachments prevail. Intensified nationalism and persistent ethnic wars capture headlines, but the more pervasive dynamics are those that span, transgress, or otherwise undermine long-standing boundaries. Nor are the boundary-eroding dynamics confined to transnational corporations, NGOs, and international organizations. They can also originate at the same local levels where boundaries are heightened. Communities that pass ordinances favoring the environment and opposing local interests are no less commonplace than those that shortsightedly opt to protect immediate interests. In short, the burden of the preceding chapters is that we cannot be sure where the politics of the Frontier will lead humankind, and in this uncertainty lies the possibility that they will lead, unstoppably, to some form of global governance.

Of course, huge questions remain. Given a continuation of the turbulence generated by parametric transformations, how long might it take for new identities to evolve and for the disaggregated patterns tending toward order and equity to become so deeply rooted that they overwhelm those that foster intergroup conflict and poverty? And if the former ultimately yield a saner and more just world, how will signs of progress in this direction be manifest so that policies intended to support and hasten the processes of effective global governance can be pursued?

While the question of the time required for the appropriate identities and governance practices to spread across the dispersed and diverse systems of rule is presently unanswerable – there being so many imponderables – it does seem possible to suggest developments that will be indicative of movement in this direction. In the first place, it seems clear that such movement will occur in small increments and that observers must thus look for tell-tale signs in isolated events that, when viewed in a larger context, form salutary patterns. Looked at from a decadal perspective, for example, a slow, erratic, and almost imperceptible decline in people's sense of territoriality and a correspondingly sporadic movement toward the removal of inequities would be suggestive of a trend toward the establishment of conditions in which effective

447

governance along the Frontier could take root. Second, it seems reasonable to anticipate that some of the movement in this direction will surface in unexpected places – in the interstices of societies where new identities can evolve along with new attitudes toward citizenship and community – as distinct from such obvious realms as economic statistics, governmental policies, and flag-waving ceremonies. Third, if it makes sense to presume that humankind has long been ensconced on a learning curve and is capable of inching to higher locations on the curve, then our analytic sensitivities should be alert to widespread catastrophes – be they initiated by nature or people – and the possibility that they might foster doubt about traditional identities and promote learning which is open to new sources of legitimacy. Fourth, assuming that successive generations will define and react to their circumstances in very different ways, our analytic antennae must be alert to unfamiliar attitudinal and behavioral patterns that, however absurd they may seem to a passing generation, are expressive of underlying tendencies toward the degrees of accommodation that are requisite to effective global governance.

Lastly, and as already implied, it would be a mistake to assess progress along the Frontier in terms of the conventional understandings of how identities are expressed, how governments function, and how public order and societal equity is realized. In a turbulent world where large-scale structures are in flux, authority relations in transition, and citizens ever more skillful, it is quite possible that the formation of new identities, the tasks of governance, and the maintenance of decent communities will be achieved through mechanisms that are not presently known or imagined. For it is the central lesson of the preceding chapters that the dynamics of change do not adhere to long-established patterns and that anomalous deviations from the norm can eventually become entrenched as new patterns. Put in this way, the turbulence that seems destined to stir world affairs for the foreseeable future is to be welcomed. It offers the hope that humankind can eventually alter course and settle into forms of mutual adjustment through which governance can flourish effectively and bring a measure of tranquillity to the politics of the Frontier.

The future of governance

If this conclusion seems naive, it can be clarified by an acknowledgment that the author, perhaps like the reader, feels that the book should end on a positive note, that there ought to be more to this account of a disaggregated and fragmenting global system of governance. It is an unfinished story, one's need for closure asserts. It needs a conclusion, a drawing together of the "big picture," a sweeping assessment which offers some hope that somehow the world can muddle through and evolve techniques of cooperation that will bridge its multitude of disaggregated parts and achieve a measure of coherence which enable future generations to live in peace, achieve sustainable development, and maintain a modicum of creative order. You need to assess the overall balance, one's training cries out, and show how the various emergent centers of power form a multipolar system of states that will manage to cope with the challenges of war within and among its members. Yes, that's it, depict the overall system as polyarchic and indicate how such an arrangement can generate multilateral institutions of control that effectively address the huge issues which clutter the global agenda. Or, perhaps better, indicate how a hegemon will emerge out of the disaggregation and have enough clout to foster both progress and stability. At the very least, one's analytic impulses demand, suggest how worldwide tendencies toward disaggregation and localization may be offset by no less powerful tendencies toward aggregation and globalization.

Yet, compelling as these alternatives may be, they do not quell a sense that it is only a short step from polyarchy to Pollyanna and that one's commitment to responsible analysis is best served by proceeding with caution. The world is on a path-dependent course, to be sure, and some of its present outlines can be discerned if allowance is made for nuance and ambiguity. Still, in this time of continuing and profound transformations, too much remains murky to project much beyond the immediate present and have confidence in long-term trajectories. All one can conclude with conviction is that in the decades ahead the paths to governance will lead in many directions, some emerging into sunlit clearings and others descending into dense jungles.

Epilogue

Social scientists are not alone in recognizing the breakdown of long-standing boundaries. Their analyses of the sources and consequences of these transformative developments are necessarily wide-ranging and elaborate, but the voice of the poet offers a succinct way of summarizing the deep and enduring implications of the changes. Hence it is appropriate to conclude this volume with the wisdom of a contemporary Polish poetess, Wislawa Szymborska.

PSALM

Oh, the leaky boundaries of man-made states!
How many clouds float past them with impunity;
how much desert sand shifts from one land to another;
how many mountain pebbles tumble onto foreign soil
in provocative hops!

Need I mention every single bird that flies in the face
    of frontiers
or alight on the roadblock at the border?
A humble robin – still, its tail resides abroad
while its beak stays home. If that weren't enough, it won't
    stop bobbing!

Among innumerable insects, I'll single out only the ant
between the border guard's left and right boots
blithely ignoring the questions "Where from?" and
    "Where to?"

Oh, to register in detail, at a glance, the chaos
prevailing on every continent!
Isn't that a privet on the far bank
smuggling its hundred-thousandth leaf across the river?
And who but the octopus, with impudent long arms,
would disrupt the sacred bounds of territorial waters?

And how can we talk of order overall
when the very placement of the stars
leaves us doubting just what shines for whom?

Not to speak of the fog's reprehensible drifting!
And dust blowing all over the steppes
as if they hadn't been partitioned!
And the voices coasting on obliging airwaves,
that conspiratorial squeaking, those indecipherable mutters!

Only what is human can truly be foreign
The rest is mixed vegetation, subversive moles, and wind.

Index

absolute gains, 42–3
activists, as agents of communication, 307–8
actors, proliferation of, 67–8
adaptive systems, 155n, 445
Adler, Emanuel, 49n
Afghanistan, 232, 316, 357, 434
Africa, 112, 177, 326, 409
Agnew, John, 3n, 405n
AIDS, 20, 22, 72, 115, 177
Albania, 303n
Albert, Mathias, 6n
Algeria, 300, 357, 374, 385
alienation, 114, 175, 294n
Alker, Hayward R., 5n
Allcock, John B., 110n
Alonzo, William, 282n
altruistic citizenship, 290–2, 309
Amato, Dennis J., 257n
Amnesty International, 117, 167, 230–1, 327, 332
anarchy, 9, 42, 151–2
  of interstate system, 48, 64
Anderson, Benedict, 129, 129n
Andreas, Peter, 169n
Angola, 265, 382, 426, 431n, 434
anomalies, 15–17, 18, 21, 25–7
apartheid, 171, 323
apathetic citizenship, 293–5
Appadurai, Arjun, 4n
Apple, R. W., Jr., 294n
Arafat, Yasser, 357
Archibugi, Daniele, 23n
Argentina, 300, 370–2, 385
Aristotle, 218
armed forces, as agents of change, 384–6
  recruitment of, 377, 378–80
Armenia, 300

Aronson, Jonathan, 235n
Ascherson, Neal, 303n
Ashley, Richard K., 6n
Asia, 163–4, 326, 378, 409
Asian Pacific People's Environmental Network, 334
Atkinson, Rick, 364n
Atlas, James, 37n
authority, 5, 6, 9, 10, 19, 20, 28, 113, 220, 363
  challenges to, 312, 325
  relocation of, 27–8, 29, 39, 43–4, 50, 61–4, 83, 153–6, 195–6, 243, 245, 286, 302–3, 306, 308, 313, 324, 350–1
  sources of, 61–2
  spontaneous, 302–8
  structures of, 8, 42, 140, 141, 142, 151
authority crises, 43, 62–4, 67, 68, 115, 116, 202, 235, 244, 251, 275, 280, 282, 286, 292, 296, 299, 355–8, 366, 442
  and disasters, 203
  and elections, 264
  and the military, 365, 377–84
  persistence of, 281
  and sovereignty, 223
  and war, 422–3
Azerbaijan, 379

Badie, Bertrand, 349n
Baker, Russell, 24n
balance of power, 36–7
Baldwin, David A., 32n, 161n
Balkans, 131
Baltic republics, 381
Bangladesh, 62
Barber, Benjamin R., 38n, 128n, 289n
Barham, J. P., 381n
Barnet, Richard J., 425n

452

insufficiency of, 27–9
  juxtaposed, 47–52
Woutat, Donald, 289n
Wren, Christopher S., 379n
Wriston, Walter B., 137n, 219n

xenophobic reactions, 84, 414

Yankelovich, Daniel, 281n
Yeltsin, Boris, 373
Young, Oran R., 147n, 160n, 321n
Young, Tom, 332n

Youngblood, Ruth, 371n
Yugoslavia, 29, 62, 101, 126, 137, 179, 230,
  246, 248, 300, 330, 348, 349, 353, 354,
  355, 357, 380, 381, 427
  military in, 384

Zacher, Mark W., 58, 160n, 362n
Zaire, 225, 355
Zak, Marilyn Anne, 255n
Zapatistas, 50
Zen Buddhism, 97
Zurn, Michael, 99n, 354n

CAMBRIDGE STUDIES IN INTERNATIONAL RELATIONS